The Word Has Been Abroad

The Word has been abroad, is back, with a tanned look
From its subsistence in the stiffening-mire.

Geoffrey Hill, *Annunciations*

The Word Has Been Abroad

A Guide Through Balthasar's Aesthetics

Aidan Nichols OP

THE CATHOLIC UNIVERSITY OF AMERICA PRESS

Published in Great Britain by T&T Clark Ltd,
59 George Street, Edinburgh EH2 2LQ, Scotland

This edition published under license from T&T Clark Ltd by
The Catholic University of America Press
620 Michigan Ave, N.E.
Washington, D.C. 20064

The lines from *Annunciations* by Geoffrey Hill are reprinted by permission from
Collected Poems (Penguin 1985) and *New and Collected Poems 1952–1992*
(Houghton Mifflin Co, Boston and New York 1994).

First published 1998

ISBN 0–8132–0924–2 (HB)
ISBN 0–8132–0925–0 (PB)

Typeset by Waverley Typesetters, Galashiels
Printed and bound in Great Britain by Biddles Ltd, Guildford

Contents

Preface

The light of revelation shines in a clearing in the forest of the world. Faced with the thickets of the seven volumes of Balthasar's *Herrlichkeit*, 'The Glory of the Lord', even the reader with the best will in the world can lose his or her way. Balthasar stakes out the position by reference to so many of his sources and predecessors – not only the biblical and patristic authors, and the mediaevals, but ancient philosophers, modern metaphysicians and a whole host of poets, mystics and thinkers in between – that the ground seems impossible to cover.

This analytic exposition of Balthasar's text is intended to allow the reader to find his or her way through. And the goal is to discover the heart of theological aesthetics – the transfigured, blood-stained features of Jesus Christ where the glory of God streams forth as the beauty of the love that will save the world.

But the splendour of the sacrificial divine Goodness is also deed and truth. In two subsequent studies, therefore, I shall consider Balthasar's theological dramatics and his theological logic, as well as the 'epilogue' to the trilogy as a whole, and end with a critical evaluation of this most impressive of all twentieth-century Catholic theologies.

I am most grateful to Professor Geoffrey Hill for graciously permitting phrases from his poetic work to serve as titles for these studies, and to Stratford Caldecott for suggesting as cover image for the present volume David Jones' *Vexilla Regis*, the original of which is in Kettle's Yard, Cambridge. The Word's foreign travel into the realm of flesh on earth leaves behind the mighty tree of salvation, redemptively overshadowing (to left and right) the tree of fragile natural goodness and the tree of ambivalent power. Only thus can nature and culture, multiply symbolised in Jones' picture, find fulfilment and peace.

Blackfriars
Cambridge
Memorial day of St Hugh of Lincoln, 1996

*To the Brethren of the
Fraternité S. Vincent Ferrier,
Chémeré-le-Roi,
in whose kind company
this 'Guide' was written*

An Introduction to Balthasar

Hans Urs von Balthasar was born on 12 August 1905 at Lucerne, the most Catholic city of a pre-secular Switzerland. His was a long-established patrician family, though on his mother's side, his roots were Hungarian.[1] Indeed, the Austro-Hungarian imperial family, in decorous flight from Vienna, put up at the Pension Felsberg, run by his grandmother, baroness Margit Apor, in the summer of 1918. His immediate family were linked to the Catholic Church in a variety of ways: his father, Oskar, an architect of church buildings among others; his mother, Gabrielle, an office-bearer in the Swiss League of Catholic Women, whose foundations and early history she chronicled; his sister, Renée, for many years superior-general of a Franciscan order of nuns. One of his Hungarian relations was a bishop who would die of injuries inflicted by the invading Red Army in 1944.[2]

Balthasar's childhood and youth were dominated by an obsession with music. His first book, published in Germany in 1925, when he was twenty, would be called – with characteristic ambitiousness – *The Development of the Musical Idea. Attempt at a Synthesis of Music.*[3] The influence of Benedictine monks whose abbey school at Engelberg – in another of the four 'forest-cantons', the *Waldstätter* of central Switzerland – offered a fine musical education, was paramount here. Before finishing his secondary education, however, Balthasar was moved by his parents – for reasons which have never been made clear – to a Jesuit college in the Austrian Vorarlberg, which adjoins the eastern border of Switzerland. The decision was all the stranger in that the peace negotiations of St

---

1 P. Henrici, S.J., 'Hans Urs von Balthasar: A Sketch of His Life', in D. L. Schindler (ed.), *Hans Urs von Balthasar. His Life and Work* (San Francisco 1991), pp. 7–44; numerous details of his forebears, including Joseph Anton von Balthasar (1692–1763), Jesuit missionary among the Indians of California; Josef Anton Felix (1737–1810) and Joseph Anton (1761–1810), founders of, respectively, the city and cantonal libraries at Lucerne; Ludwig Felix (1825–47) who fell fighting for the liberty of the Catholic cantons in the Sonderbund war, in E. Guerriero, *Hans Urs von Balthasar* (Cinisello Balsamo, Milan 1991), pp. 11–19.

2 For Vilmos Apor of Györ, see J. Közi Horvath, *Leben und Sterben von Bischof Apor* (Munich 1985²).

3 *Die Entwicklung der musikalischen Idee. Versuch einer Synthese der Musik* (Braunschweig 1925).

Germain had not yet taken place: the Danubian monarchy, Austria-Hungary, was still in the death throes of its final dissolution. This experience of parental *Diktat* was evidently unwelcome, because, without his parents' consent and before the equivalent of the British 'sixth form' years were over, he removed himself from school and matriculated in the faculty of *Germanistik*, German studies, a mixture of literature and philosophy, in the University of Zürich.

From one point of view Balthasar never abandoned that faculty. I do not mean that, of course, in a physical sense: indeed, as was not unusual when pursuing higher studies in the universities of German-speaking Europe in the late nineteenth and early twentieth centuries, he was peripatetic already as a student. In the process of acquiring his doctorate he took courses in Berlin (where he studied as a sideline both Indian thought and, through the priest-philosopher Romano Guardini, Kierkegaard) and at Vienna (where he discovered Plotinus). His own mature theology would attempt to identify the elements of truth in both Existentialism, represented here by Kierkegaard, and Neo-Platonism, summed up in Plotinus, while at the same time identifying over against these the specifying features of a distinctively Christian metaphysics. It may also be relevant to mention here, *vis-à-vis* the topic of Hindu philosophy, that Balthasar's version of Christian apologetics attempts to show how the Christian gospel, and the characteristic thinking it generates, can find space within itself for the authentic spiritual aspiration represented by each of the great world religions while also showing up the errors on which their enterprise founders. This is the idea of Christian revelation (and the thinking that accompanies it) as a 'totality than which no greater can be thought'. Also worth noting, in the context of Balthasar's perambulations as a young man *im deutschen Sprachraum* is the influence upon him of Rudolf Allers, a fellow-citizen and erstwhile pupil of Freud in the Vienna of the 1920s, a convert to Catholicism whose journey from Freudian reductionism, where the self is not much more than a bundle of instinctual drives, to a Christian psychotherapy where primacy is given to interpersonal love as the proper medium of human existence, was assisted by his studies of mediaeval philosophy and theology.

To return, then, to my statement that in one sense Balthasar never left the German faculty at Zürich. This is in an extended or metaphorical sense true, for he continued to regard the marriage of philosophy and literature as the best possible preparation for theological existence. Or, to put the same point in another way, the offspring of that marriage provides theology with its most serviceable handmaiden. That Balthasar was already, even as a young layman engaged in purely academic work, thinking in religious and theological terms, is clear both from his life-story and from the massive and (it has to be said) not entirely digestible text which his studies produced.[4] In the year when he submitted his thesis, 1929, he entered the Bavarian Province of the Society of Jesus; ironically, his university was situated in the most radical

---

4 *Geschichte des eschatologischen Problems in der modernen deutschen Literatur* (Zürich 1930).

Protestant of all Swiss cities, where opposition to any relaxing of the 'articles of exception', forbidding the activity of the Jesuits, was at its most vociferous.[5] And furthermore, the thesis he handed in was itself a form of tacit or implicit theology. Its subject was modern German literature, examined from the viewpoint of its attitude, explicit or implicit, to the 'Last Things' – the final or eternal destiny of the human soul. Much of the material of this thesis would find its way into the first of his major works, *The Apocalypse of the German Soul*, a massive tripartite study of the eschatological bearings of the work of numerous major German philosophers, dramatists and poets of the late eighteenth, nineteenth and early twentieth centuries.[6] Despite wandering at times from his brief in chapters on the vitalist philosopher Henri Bergson, an important figure, in more-than-Germanic perspective, in the overcoming of the rationalist element in nineteenth-century thought, and on the Russian novelist Dostoevsky, whom he treats as a Christian counterpart to Nietzsche, Balthasar more or less succeeds here in his self-appointed task. Taking German philosophers from Lessing to Heidegger and German poets from Goethe to Rilke to be the most penetrating intelligences at work in the unfolding of European culture in their periods, he tries to show that they divide ultimately into two principal attempted solutions of the riddle that is existence, what he calls the 'Promethean' and the 'Dionysian' solutions, after respectively, the Greek hero, Prometheus, and the Greek god, Dionysus. *Prometheus* for Balthasar is the symbol of man's attempt to raise himself by his own bootstraps to the level of the gods. The human 'I' exalts itself in self-affirmation, seizing fire from heaven – not only emancipating itself from inherited constraints, whether biological or historical, but aiming at the total mastery of existence. The Promethean outlook is manifested in the writers of the Enlightenment, and in such Idealist philosophers as Hegel with his project of reaching absolute knowledge, where the human mind coincides with the divine mind in realising that everything is, and has happened, just as it ought to have if infinite spirit is to become self-aware in man. *Dionysus* for Balthasar is a symbol of a more tragic attempt to resolve the puzzle of existence. Dionysian man resembles Promethean man in the unboundedness of his aspirations but his interest lies more in escaping the limitations of existence, rather than in dominating them. Faced with transience and mortality, he leaves reason behind in a flight towards the unnameable heights of whatever lies behind everyday existence. But characteristically this movement of mystical exaltation is followed by a falling back, disenchanted, into a sense of the absurdity of everything. The Dionysian temper is reflected in such artistic and philosophical movements as Expressionism and Existentialism.

5 Such laws, in the context of a less dispersed system of authority in the post-Revolutionary Swiss Confederation, had been framed in the aftermath of the mid-nineteenth century religious war, lost by the principal Catholic cantons (which included Lucerne). Thus C. Gilliard, *Histoire de la Suisse* (Paris 1987⁹), pp. 120–121.

6 *Apokalypse der deutschen Seele. Studien zu einer Lehre von letzten Haltungen* I. *Der deutsche Idealismus* (Salzburg 1937); II *Im Zeichen Nietzsches* (Salzburg 1939); III *Die Vergöttlichung des Todes* (Salzburg 1939).

The upshot is that only fitfully and in fragments do this vast range of writers and thinkers, spanning two centuries of enormous conceptual creativity, come close to the truth. The truth being that humans find their destiny only in self-transcendence, in transcending themselves towards the reality that is always greater than everything they can be, think or imagine, namely, God. We could in fact describe the *Apocalypse of the German Soul* as a testing of the dogmatic affirmation of the First Vatican Council that human beings, through the light of human reason, can develop a sense of God as not only the author but the goal of nature and history. It was Balthasar's conviction, evidently, that attaining a just doctrine of transcendence – seeing humans as called to transcend themselves towards an absolutely or unconditionally transcendent reality – is, without Christian revelation, no easy matter. Significantly, Balthasar ends this work with a study of his older Swiss contemporary, the great Protestant Neo-Orthodox dogmatician Karl Barth.

Apocalypse of the German Soul is the expanded, published form of Balthasar's *History of the Eschatological Problem in German Literature* and as such it gives us an insight into the making of his thought at a crucial and formative, if immature, stage. But by the time *Apocalypse* was given to the public in the years 1937 to 1939, Balthasar had completed his Jesuit training in the Jesuit studentates of Pullach, near Munich and Fourvières, near Lyons, and on the basis of this combined Franco-German tuition, had received ordination as a priest in November 1936, at the hands of the aristocratic German prelate, already celebrated for his resistance to the ethos of the Third Reich, Cardinal Michael von Faulhaber whose ancient see of Freising had been combined a century previously with the Wittelsbach court-bishopric of Munich to form the primatial church of Bavaria.

Balthasar did not have very much that was favourable to say about the Neo-Scholastic manuals in use in the Jesuit study houses of France and Germany in the 1930s. While of course not dismissing all their themes as misplaced, or treating all of their theological judgments as wrong or shallow, he spoke harshly of the arid, desert-like quality of the theological landscape in which he was made to wander. He wrote later:

> My entire period of study in the Society was a grim struggle with the dreariness of theology, with what men had made out of the glory of revelation.[7]

To understand the acerbity of this remark, I must look ahead briefly to Balthasar's mature work, the great trilogy which consists in, first, a theological aesthetics, secondly, a theological dramatics and thirdly, a theological logic. It may not have escaped the reader's notice that Balthasar's strictures on Jesuit theology in the 1930s were fundamentally stylistic in character. The large-scale rejection of a theological culture simply on the ground that its textbooks were poorly written may seem dilettantish or frankly bizarre. But not to one whose theological logic

---

7 H. U. von Balthasar, 'Einleitung', in A. von Speyr, *Erde und Himmel, Ein Tagebuch. Zweiter Teil*, II: *Die Zeit der grossen Diktate* (Einsiedeln 1975), p. 195.

would not be finished until he had completed a theological aesthetics and dramatics. The revelation which Christian theology set itself to study was the disclosure of a beauty beyond all worldly beauty in the supreme artwork of Jesus Christ; in it the transcendent beauty – in biblical language, the *glory* – of the ever-greater God came to expression. How could a theology genuinely attuned to its own subject-matter be ugly? Similarly, the salvation history which Christian theology set out to represent, and into whose ambit, as players in an ongoing *déroulement* of the plot, it invited its readers to enter, was a drama in which God set forth his own philanthropy, his own goodness to men, in the midst of a conflictual and agonistic world. How could a theology really faithful to its own subject-matter be lacking in dramatic power and tension? And because the truth which theological logic sets out is the truth of the gloriously beautiful God in his incarnate Word, the truth of the dramatically philanthropic God in that play whose director is the Holy Spirit, could a theology which was unprepossessing and dull be adequately true, even given the qualifications we have to enter when faced with the notion of the adequate conceptualisation of a revelation of the living God who exceeds all our categories? Although my way of expressing here Balthasar's grounds for disliking Jesuit Neo-Scholasticism as he experienced is indebted to his later work, it would not, I think, be difficult to show that these most basic intuitions about divine beauty, divine goodness, divine truth, and the mark these qualities should leave on theology itself, were already in his possession from the earliest years of his priesthood. They show themselves above all in the choice of topic and manner of treatment which typify the series of short books on patristics and Christian literature which he wrote in the wake of *Apocalypse of the German Soul*, and the manner in which he praised his earliest theological hero, Karl Barth.

Before embarking on a description of those books I must pause, however, to record a qualification that has to be set against any notion that Balthasar could find nothing good to say about his Jesuit mentors. There were in fact two that he lionised, one at Munich whom he came to know at Pullach, the other at Lyons whom he learned from while at Fourvières. The first was the Polono-German fundamental theologian Erich Przywara whose chief influence on Balthasar was to show him the amazing theological possibilities present in that key doctrine of Christian Scholasticism, the *analogia entis* or 'analogy of being'.[8] Przywara and Balthasar share an attitude towards the *analogia entis* doctrine which makes that teaching not (as is often the case) a commonplace of metaphysics, but a specifically religious doctrine of enormous spiritual power. Essentially they turn the analogy of being idea into a doctrine of participation, of a sharing in the divine life which, intimately present in the constitution of the human creature, presses that creature to go beyond itself in the direction of God. That there is an analogy between our being and God's should not make us seek to domesticate God but, on the contrary, lead us to recognise an invitation – inscribed in the very nature

---

8 'Einleitung', in L. Zimmy (ed.), *Erich Przywara. Sein Schrifttum* (Einsiedeln 1963), pp. 5–18.

of our being – to enter his mystery. The more man is permitted to live his life from out of this divinely impelled movement, the more he will realise that God is the ever-greater Lord. The more intimately he shares the divine life, the firmer his grasp of the divine transcendence as infinitely above him. Przywara's highly theological commentary on the 'spiritual exercises' of the Jesuit Society made Balthasar appreciate their true depth. Indeed, it might not be too misleading to say that what Przywara, and Balthasar after him, hoped to do was combine the mind of St Thomas with the heart of St Augustine, all in the spirit of St Ignatius Loyola, that burning obedience – at once interior and missionary – to the Word of God.

Balthasar's other hero was Henri de Lubac – later, after various vicissitudes, to be like himself, a cardinal of the Roman church. De Lubac, on whom Balthasar, in the last decade of the latter's life, would write an entire, if concise, book,[9] inspired him not only by his encyclopaedic grasp of the Catholic tradition of commenting on Scripture, his love of the Fathers, and his willingness to grapple with alien metaphysics, from Buddhism to the French socialist Proudhon, in the service of faith but also by the sheer range of his enterprise. Both men, in a sense, were capable of creating, and did create, at least in bookish form, a Christian culture of a comprehensive kind all on their own.

During his student days a number of Balthasar's books on the Fathers and on the literary art of twentieth-century Catholicism were happily gestating. This is true of his substantial essays on the seventh-century Greek Father St Maximus the Confessor, and his fourth-century predecessor St Gregory of Nyssa, both of which appeared during the Second World War, as well as his slighter study of the ante-Nicene writer Origen of Alexandria – which, published in Austria in 1938, only achieved its definitive form in a French version in 1957.[10] At the same time, stimulated both by de Lubac and Pryzwara, no mean students of Augustine, he was compiling two anthologies of texts from the North African doctor, for which purpose he read through the entire corpus of Augustine in class, with earplugs in to block out the sound of lectures.[11] Balthasar was lucky enough to be living in France at the time of a major Catholic literary renaissance there, and this bore fruit in his books on the novelist Georges Bernanos, *Le chrétien Bernanos,* as well as his translations

----

9 H. U. von Balthasar, *Henri de Lubac. Sein organisches Lebenswerk* (Einsiedeln 1976).

10 *Kosmische Liturgie. Höhe und Krise des griechischen Weltbilds bei Maximus Confessor* (Freiburg 1941); to this should be added: *Die Gnostische Centurien des Maximus Confessor* (Freiburg 1941); his Nyssa essay is: *Présence et pensée. Essai sur la philosophie religieuse de Grégoire de Nysse* (Paris 1942); note also in this connexion *Gregor von Nyssa, der versiegelte Quell. Auslegung des Hohen Liedes* (Salzburg 1939); on Origen, there is: *Origenes, Geist und Feuer. Ein Aufbau aus seinen Werken* (Salzburg 1938), an anthology produced in the course of writing 'Le Mystère d'Origène', *Recherches de Science Religieuse* 26 (1936), pp. 513–552, 27 (1937), pp. 38–64, which itself was later reconstructed as: *Parole et mystère chez Origène* (Paris 1957).

11 *Aurelius Augustinus, Ueber die Psalmen* (Leipzig 1936); *Aurelius Augustinus. Das Antlitz der Kirche* (Einsiedeln-Cologne 1942).

of the poet and dramatist Paul Claudel.[12] I do not list these books merely for the sake of being comprehensive. The decision to write them had a wider significance. What that was is in one sense specific to each study.

The Maximus book presented Christ as the key to the cosmos, tying together in his own person all the pathways of creation and redemption. The Nyssa book set forth for the first time the related themes of desire, *erōs*, and charity, *agapē*, presenting the stream of *erōs*, which is never exhausted by any object in this world, as the concrete form of man's openness to transcendence, on which divine grace, then, can set to work, turning desire into self-giving. The Origen book is a modern restatement of the idea of the spiritual sense of Scripture, a sense more important than the literal in being not more foundational – for the literal is always that – but higher, more open to the full dimensions of God's self-revelation. The study of Bernanos presents major themes of sin and forgiveness, confession and judgment. Claudel was sought out for his ideas on the nature of poetic knowledge and the need for sympathy – connaturality – between the knower and the object known. *Connaissance*, 'knowledge', in its highest reaches, is *co-naissance*, 'co-birth', familial intimacy. But more widely, these books represent an appeal to broaden, deepen and above all humanise the Scholastic tradition, going back behind it to the Fathers with their mystical warmth and rhetorical power, and going ahead of it (or to the side of it) by appeal to literary artists who could put Christian experience, the wider sense of the faith, into compelling, unforgettable form.

At the time when this stream of what we could call his ancillary works – for the great trilogy of the aesthetics, dramatics and logic, is surely his master-work – began flowing, Balthasar was living neither in France, however, nor in Bavaria but in his native Switzerland, at Basle. That city on the Rhine, the border between the French- and German-speaking worlds, a Protestant city with a Catholic hinterland, soon gave him what he saw as the finest opportunity and the worst crisis of his life. But first I must explain what he was doing there in the first place. I said that in canton Zürich Jesuits were not allowed at all; but in fact throughout the Swiss Confederation Jesuits were inhibited by the constitution from running schools or parishes. The Swiss Jesuits, who until 1947 had no separate organisation of their own were, if not simple, unlettered men then certainly forced by circumstance to restrict themselves to pastoral work of a low-profile, and even marginal, kind. There was, however, one type of institution which the anti-clerical laws of the 1840s had not envisaged because it did not then exist, and that was the student chaplaincy. Given that Balthasar had already written more books than all the other Swiss Jesuits put together, his superiors decided that – unless he wished to go to Rome, to teach at the Gregorian University – this was the place for him. Balthasar threw himself into the work with his

12 *Bernanos* (Cologne-Olten 1954). I cite the title of the French version, *Le chrétien Bernanos* (Paris 1956). The Claudel translations are: *Paul Claudel. Fünf grosse Oden* (Freiburg 1939); *Paul Claudel. Der seidene Schuh* (Salzburg 1939); *Paul Claudel. Maria Verkündigung* (Lucerne 1946); and others taken up into: *Paul Claudel. Gesammelte Werke, I. Gedichte* (Einsiedeln 1963), and *Paul Claudel. Corona Benignitatis Anni Dei* (Einsiedeln 1964).

customary energy, founding a system of parallel lectures for Catholic students so comprehensive that it was almost a parallel university, giving Ignatian retreats and editing throughout the War a collection of anthologies, called the 'European Series' intended to help save Europe's cultural heritage in the face of National Socialism and capitalistic philistinism.

I call Basle the city of Balthasar's opportunity and crisis, because it was, on the one hand, the home of the two people – the dogmatician Karl Barth and the mystic Adrienne von Speyr – who more than any others were to determine the direction of his work; and, on the other, the occasion of his traumatic break with the Jesuits. His dispensation from vows and consequent acceptance of the status of a secular priest was, in the climate of the time, a perfectly adequate explanation for his cold-shouldering by Church authority. Even today the Roman Curia looks somewhat askance at exclaustrated Religious, even though they may continue to be worthy priests.

Balthasar's admiration for Barth, which was reciprocated, is expressed in his book *The Theology of Karl Barth*,[13] which began life as a series of lectures on Barth given in Barth's presence: a daunting undertaking when one considers that Pope Pius XII called Barth the greatest Christian thinker since Aquinas. In the opening section of his study of Barth, Balthasar waxes lyrical in his praise of Barth's manner of practising theology. He calls Barth's work 'beautiful' on the grounds that it combines 'passion' with 'objectivity'. Barth's theology is objective in the sense of being thoroughly immersed in its object, God as revealed to the world in Christ. But the effect of this objectivity is that the theologian himself becomes involved in, and fascinated by, what he studies, and that at the deepest level: hence passion. The combination, Balthasar remarks drily, is not that common in contemporary Catholic theology.

To Balthasar's eyes, Barth shows us a true understanding of what theology should be. The 'principle' of theology is nothing other than the content of revelation itself. But this revealed content cannot be separated from revelation perceived as the *action* of God. It is not primarily the communication of truths, but God himself, very Truth, revealing himself in all his sovereign freedom. Consequently, theology must be a con-templative exploration of God's self-gift. In theology's case, we cannot dispose of the principles of our discipline, in the way that we can with profane studies. Furthermore, it is not just that, in Barth, revelation's content provides theology with its foundational principles. The *style* of Barth's theology expresses the immensity of this revealed content, the extraordinary greatness of the dramatic event of revelation.

Balthasar made no secret of the fact that, while he wished Barth's manner of theologising to inspire Catholic theology, he also wanted to convert Barth to Catholicism. Nor was this by any means an unrealistic aspiration though it was of course unrealised. Balthasar, who had a great

13 *Karl Barth. Darstellung und Deutung seiner Theologie* (Olten-Cologne 1951); E.t. *The Theology of Karl Barth* (New York 1971; San Francisco 1992²). For the consonances between the two theologies, see J. Thomson, 'Barth and Balthasar. An Ecumenical Dialogue', in B. McGregor, O.P., and T. Norris (eds), *The Beauty of Christ. An Introduction to the Theology of Hans Urs von Balthasar* (Edinburgh 1994), pp. 171–192.

reputation in Basle as a convert-maker, had more success with Adrienne von Speyr, a medical doctor, though herself a woman in chronically poor health, who through her two marriages was intimately connected to the academic echelons of the upper bourgeoisie of the city: a perfect Jesuit catch. Balthasar himself considered that von Speyr's rôle in his life had exceeded anyone else's, and in case posterity was in any doubt wrote in later life a study of their common work, *Unser Auftrag*, 'Our Mission', explicitly intended to prevent any prising apart of his theology from her mystically generated contemplative reading of the Scriptures.[14] Certainly von Speyr provided several of the main themes of Balthasar's theology of the atonement, as well as of his mariology, ecclesiology and eschatology, not to mention his understanding of the specific mission in the Church of such (canonised or uncanonised) women mystics as Thérèse of Lisieux and Elisabeth of Dijon, on whom he wrote substantial studies.[15] Though one might suspect a degree of chivalrous overstatement in Balthasar's references to von Speyr (he was deeply angered by what be regarded as the dismissive way her mystical experience was being treated, despite the full satisfaction she had given Jesuit professors, both German and French, deputed to examine her credentials and 'mission'), he described the task of spiritual director to a mystic as essentially an auxiliary one. Speyrian insights received at Balthasar's hands fuller articulation and suitable positioning within the corpus of Christian doctrine, gaining enhanced power to illuminate the biblical revelation in the process. And so, by a seeming paradox, a content drawn in significant part from Adrienne's experience could be placed within a theological structure inspired by that relentless critic of the Christian mystics, Karl Barth. As the doyen of 'post-critical' theology in the United States, the Lutheran George Lindbeck, has written, a discernible 'family resemblance' links the theologies of Balthasar and Barth. Both are wary of transposing biblical revelation into categories alien to itself, seeking rather to describe the world in terms that are scripturally rooted; the appeal of both to the Bible is, nonetheless, not lacking in intellectual power for they find there a sophisticated coherence, treating Scripture as a narrationally (Barth) or dramatically (Balthasar) as well as typologically unified whole.[16]

In 1945 after a retreat in the second-order Dominican monastery of Estavayer, in canton Neuchâtel, Balthasar founded with von Speyr a secular institute or society of consecrated life for lay people living in the world as also for diocesan priests. The Community of St John became more widely known three years later when Balthasar produced a theology for secular institutes, the first book to be published by the Johannes Verlag, a publishing house established with the help of a friend at Einsiedeln, halfway between Lucerne and Zürich, and named after the Gospel writer, St John, who predominates in both von Speyr's work and his own.[17] Neither the local bishop nor the Jesuit superiors supported the

---

14 *Unser Auftrag. Bericht und Entwurf* (Einsiedeln 1984).
15 *Schwestern im Geist. Thérèse von Lisieux und Elisabeth von Dijon* (Einsiedeln 1970).
16 Lindbeck, 'Scripture, Consensus and Community', in R. J. Neuhaus (ed.), *Biblical Interpretation in Crisis: The Ratzinger Conference on Bible and Church* (Grand Rapids, Mich. 1989), pp. 74–101.
17 *Der Laie und der Ordenstand* (Einsiedeln 1948; Freiburg 1949²).

venture, and the Society made it clear, after an interview with its Belgian Father General J. B. Janssens, that Balthasar must choose between the Jesuits on the one hand and his collaborator and spiritual children on the other. Balthasar made known his decision in a short printed statement sent to friends:

> I took this step, for both sides a very grave one, after a long testing of the certainty I had reached through prayer that I was being called by God to certain definite tasks in the Church. The Society felt it could not release me to give these tasks my undivided commitment. . . . So, for me, the step taken means an application of Christian obedience to God, who at any time has the right to call a man not only out of his physical home or his marriage, but also from his chosen spiritual home in a religious order, so that he can use him for his purposes within the Church. Any resulting advantages or disadvantages in the secular sphere were not under discussion and not taken into account.[18]

And for his Jesuit confrères he explained, with references to St Thomas and the seventeenth-century Spanish Jesuit theologian John de Lugo that, in cases where obedience to the Order and a prayerful evaluation of the demands of obedience to God's will conflict, a resolution is not to be found 'absolutely and in every case in obedience to the Order'. Shortly before his death, Balthasar asked the present Jesuit General, Fr Peter Kolvenbach, to receive him back into the Society, but this negotiation foundered over, once more, the question of the Community of St John. Kolvenbach attempted to sweeten the pill by obtaining for Balthasar as cardinal the Roman titular church of Sant' Ignazio, one of the glories of the Jesuit Baroque, but this proposal also met with canonical difficulties. At first Balthasar's secularisation laid a heavy burden on him. Without funding – it was several years before a bishop would incardinate him into a diocese – he had to give lectures here, there and everywhere to earn his keep. The Roman Congregation for Seminaries and Universities (as it then was) inhibited him from accepting at least one offer of a chair from a Catholic theology faculty, that of Tübingen. In any case this was not what he wanted, and the time which might have been given to seminars and academic organisation was bestowed instead on spiritual direction and – above all for our purposes – his remaining books, and notably the trilogy, consisting in fact of fourteen books, six on theological aesthetics, five on theological dramatics and three on theological logic with which his name will henceforth be identified wherever Catholic theology is seriously studied.

The key to the trilogy is found in the Scholastic notion of transcendental determinations of being, qualities so pervasive throughout reality that they crop up in all the categories of particular being, and so may be said to 'transcend' such categorial distinctions as those differentiating substance and accident, quality and mode. It is the existence of these

---

18 Cited in, Henrici, 'Hans Urs von Balthasar', in Schindler (ed.), *Hans Urs von Balthasar*, p. 21.

transcendental determinations – of which the most relevant to Balthasar
are *verum*, the true, *pulchrum*, the beautiful, and *bonum*, the good, which
allows the analogy of being, the various intensities of reality as
manifested in the varying activity of beings at all levels, from amoeba to
angel, to be pressed into service by patristic and mediaeval theology for
speaking about God. For that which can be ascribed to being itself must
surely have some validity in discourse about the ultimate Source of
being, God.

There is a correspondence, an analogy, as well as a staggering
disproportion – we remember how for Przywara both comparability and
incomparability increase as we move closer to God – between worldly
beauty and divine glory. There is a correspondence, an analogy, as well
as a staggering disproportion between finite freedom and the infinite
freedom of God. There is a correspondence, an analogy, as well as a
staggering disproportion between the structure of created truth and the
structure of divine truth. If the God of glory wished to show his beauty to
the world in his incarnate Image he must at once take up forms within
the world and shatter them so as to express the Glory beyond beauty. If
the philanthropic God wished to show his goodness to the world in the
protagonist of the saving drama that is the Lamb slain and victorious he
must at once take up the dynamic pattern of human freedom and burst it
from within so as to express the sovereign Love beyond all goodness. If
the God of truth wished to make known his primordial truth to the world
– himself as the *prima veritas*, the 'First Truth' as St Thomas and St
Catherine call him – then he must use, and in using take beyond their
limits, laws of human thought and language so as to convey a revelation
of truth beyond the heart of man in the incarnation of the Logos and the
outpouring of the Holy Spirit.

I draw this introduction to a close by a brief evocation of Balthasar's
last years and end. The ending of the Council, and the ensuing post-
conciliar crisis, coincided with the decline and death of Adrienne von
Speyr in 1967. It was surely no coincidence that Balthasar's honouring
and exploitation by Church authority began almost immediately after-
wards. Separated from Adrienne, with whom Catholic officialdom has
only in the last few years begun to come to terms, and his intellectual
stature increasingly self-evident, he was exactly the kind of anti-liberal
but reforming theologian, neo-patristic in his sympathies, with whom
the Roman see in the later years of Paul VI's pontificate and that of John
Paul II, liked to do business. It did no harm that his book on *The Office of
Peter and the Structure of the Church* is theologically the profoundest book
on the papacy ever written.[19] Not that Balthasar angled for church office
or honours. On the contrary he shunned the proferred cardinalate, and
only accepted, in view of a later conclave, and at the pope's urgent
request, in an Ignatian spirit of obedience to the Roman pontiff, as well as
with a subsidiary hope that the honour might vindicate Adrienne. He
died at Basle, with the *Johannesgemeinschaft*, on 26 June 1988, three days

---

19 *Der anti-römische Affekt. Wie lässt sich das Papsttum in der Gesamtkirche integrieren?*
    (Freiburg 1974); E.t. *The Office of Peter and the Structure of the Church* (San Francisco
    1989).

before his investiture as cardinal. A fellow German-speaking cardinal, Joseph Ratzinger, said in his panegyric:

> In a sense, his intuition was confirmed by the call to the next life which reached him on the eve of receiving that honour. He was able to stay entirely himself. But what the pope wanted to express by this gesture of recognition and even of respect remains justified: not in some isolated and private fashion but in virtue of his ministerial responsibility the Church tells us that he is an exact master of the faith, a guide towards the sources of living waters – a witness of the Word from whom we learn Christ, from whom we can learn life. 'For me, to live is Christ': this phrase . . . from the Letter to the Philippians sums up in a final way his whole journey.[20]

20 J. Ratzinger, 'Ein Mann der Kirche für die Welt', in K. Lehmann and W. Kasper (eds), *Hans Urs von Balthasar. Gestalt und Werk* (Cologne 1989), pp. 353–354.

1

⚜

The Fate of Beauty

Why aesthetics?

Balthasar's theological aesthetics opens in its first volume with a promise
that here we shall find – probably to our surprise – a theology that is
practised in the light of *beauty*. Owing to the interconnexion of the true,
the good and the beautiful (so Balthasar explains in his preface), neglect
of the third member of this trio can only be gravely damaging to the
flourishing of the other two. Yet precisely that is what has transpired.

In the early pages of *Herrlichkeit*, Balthasar offers a lament over the
departure of beauty as a transcendental determination of being – a
quality, somehow, of all that exists – from the sensibility of the contemporary West. The world of antiquity refused to understand itself without
beauty; even the nineteenth century still 'held on with passionate frenzy
to the fleeing garments of beauty' – a reference to Goethe's *Faust* where
Faust himself is left with Helena's evanescent robe as her body leaves this
world. But we in the twentieth century have downgraded beauty to a
mere appearance, an adjunct to be at best quality-controlled, at worst
exploited; and we despise reverence for beauty as a relic of an outworn
bourgeois past. Even religion, he writes, turns its back on beauty – the
reference may be to the advent of modernist functionalism in church
design and 'decoration' in contemporary Catholicism – and as a punish-
ing result becomes to a degree incomprehensible to human beings. What
to the ancients was a world penetrated by divine light had already
degenerated for the Victorians, and their continental counterparts, into
something of a land of dreams. But now, in the contemporary period, all
that remains is matter – and a matter which, in its brute facticity or
'thereness' has taken on the character of what Balthasar calls, thinking
probably of Sartre's novel *La Nausée*, 'an indigestible symbol of fear and
anguish' – an experience of materiality all too evocative of existence when
unilluminated by the mystery of being, with its truth, goodness and
beauty. It is, then, in sharpest contrast to this picture, that Balthasar
promises to provide for his readers (after, as he chronicles, long years
of neglect) a theology written by the light of beauty, the 'third transcendental' of developed Scholastic metaphysics.

In a world without beauty, the good loses its attractiveness and what
Balthasar terms its 'self-evidence', that is, its intrinsic authority, owing to

1

precisely this sundering from its fellow transcendental. And if that can happen to ethics, then what on earth will happen to Being itself – to that which declares itself in the good, the beautiful and the true? What remains when the radiance of Being is no longer perceived is just a 'lump of existence', without any inherent pattern or integral value, to be jerked into some simulacrum of life only by the string-pulling of the human puppeteer; or in another metaphor for what Balthasar intends here, to take on colour and vitality only through the projection, as onto a screen, of images humanly devised.

In order to commend the approach of beauty to (it may be) rationalistically minded readers – and this certainly includes many modern theologians – Balthasar prefaces an initial statement of the aims and native subject-matter of a theological aesthetics by pointing up the peculiar ontological importance of the 'primal phenomenon' of the beautiful at large. In what is lovely: 'We are confronted simultaneously with both the figure and that which shines forth from the figure, making it into a worthy, a love-worthy thing.'[1] And in this description of the 'primal phenomenon' Balthasar finds the same structure, or, better, the same combination of structure-with-inner-power as also holds good in such utterly basic realities of our daily experience as body and soul; the communication of our interiority to others (and even to ourselves); and language itself which is at once a rule-governed activity and yet the sheerest freedom. All of these are examples of spirit incarnate, and earthly beauty is their paradigm.

Balthasar is keenly aware of how easily an incarnational attitude to living – and even an incarnational faith in the 'Flesh that rises to eternal life' (namely, the Word incarnate's risen humanity) can collapse into either a dualism of matter and spirit as only incidentally related or a mere materialism where spirit is but an epiphenomenon of matter. Endeavouring to give due weight to both spirit and matter in their unity-in-difference, and drawing on the first volume of his theological logic, Balthasar writes:

> The freedom of the spirit that is at home in itself . . . is simultaneous with the 'keyboard' which it has appropriated and which allows the spirit self-expression. Such simultaneity is possible because it is the spirit's native condition always to have gone outside itself in order to be with another.[2]

From plant through animal to man, there is a deepening both of interiority and of the freedom of a creature to express itself in a 'play of forms'. Yet the thought that, by virtue of being bodily, man is *already* communicated (we do not choose whether to appear in the world or not!) reminds Balthasar that man cannot be the archetype of Being or spirit, but only – in more lowly, though still significant fashion – their image. And anticipating, at the level of natural theology, the conclusion of *Herrlichkeit*, Balthasar moves swiftly forward to the claim that:

---

1 H. U. von Balthasar, *The Glory of the Lord. A Theological Aesthetics* (E.t. Edinburgh and San Francisco 1982–89). Cited subsequently as *GL*, and here at I, p. 20.
2 *GL* I, p. 21.

As a totality of spirit and body, man must make himself into God's mirror and seek to attain to that transcendence and radiance that must be found in the world's substance if it is indeed God's image and likeness – his word and gesture, action and drama.[3]

But the soteriological implications of this are not yet Balthasar's subject. At the moment he is exploiting this seam of conceptual ore for the sake of a fundamental anthropology. Man's being, as it comes forth from its Creator, is form, and as such is both spirit and freedom.

Despite the intrinsic difficulty of Balthasar's language for those reared in an Anglo-Saxon culture no longer attuned to metaphysics, it is possible to see how strenuously he tries to define the aesthetic here as a co-ordinate, not a competitor, of the ethical. Just as for Origen – to take an ancient example – the moral meaning of revelation is not found alongside its mystical significance but within it (as the urgency with which the light of revelation strikes the heart), so for Schiller – to take a modern – the ethical enables beauty to unfold its full richness as a transcendental attribute of Being. Only the form which stands within the spiritual space of the ethical can truly claim the name of beauty. A person with a life-form (we note how rapidly Balthasar can move from a sacred text to an artwork to a human life, but this is not surprising if what he is speaking of is truly a *transcendental*, which precisely transcends the categories of objects that there are) is worthy of the beauty of Being; one who lacks such a *figural* existence 'decays to expressionlessness and sterility' like the dry wood of the Gospels. Alas, in our cultural epoch, it is no longer second nature to us to 'work from the whole to the parts'. We are better at dealing with the quantitative and the fragmentary, our minds are less apt for the perception of wholeness.

The historical development, or degeneration, of culture is highly relevant to how we experience. In some ages, beauty seems ubiquitous, so abundant are the forms produced. In others, the disfigurement and even denial of form turns the world nihilistically into a seeming void. For Balthasar, this is not just of interest to historians of art, or, more widely, to students of human *mentalités*. There turns on it (doubtless, not exclusively) nothing less than our readiness to be evangelised at all. To find our way to that single Image which the primal Maker of images has shaped for us – Jesus Christ, and in him our own humanity as God's likeness – is either more difficult or less in dependence on the relative inaccessibility or accessibility of this starting point.

Balthasar does not despair of the task of reChristianisation. He does, however, insist that in our time this task is going to fall to a select few – an 'elect', a term not a million miles removed from an *élite*, though he hints that in salvation history things were ever thus. 'Only the few who (as often before) bear the weight of the whole on their shoulders will receive eyes to behold the primal form of man-in-existence . . .'[4] And Balthasar predicts that their courage in 'embracing this primal form' will illuminate once more not only the beautiful but also the true and the good.

3 *GL* I, p. 22.
4 *GL* I, p. 26.

Not that Balthasar is wholly opposed to any and every kind of analytical approach. He admits that form is determined by many antecedent conditions. Yet this in no way prevents its indissolubility: the conditions are not an *explanation* of form. Considered as a unique totality it cannot, by definition, be rendered in their terms alone. And just as the rôle of various antecedent materials (one might think in man's case of his evolutionary prehistory, or the unconscious life of the human subject) does not account for form, so neither is form incapable of actively 'informing' (as we say) materials that subsequently accrue. In Balthasar's preferred example: the life-form which is marriage can extend its influence through all the dimensions of life – down to its biological roots and up to the heights of grace. Suddenly, all fruitfulness and freedom are found in the form of marriage itself – as one of Balthasar's favourite imaginative writers, the early twentieth-century French poet and dramatist Paul Claudel suggested in his *Fifth Ode*.

And coming at last to his central, theological, concerns, Balthasar affirms that being a form is, *par excellence, what a Christian is*. Justification and sanctification guarantee a spiritual form that 'will thrive as the greatest of beauties'. In Catholic piety, the faithful love their saints because 'the image of the saints' lives is so love-worthy and engaging'. In the redeemed, the archetype of Christ is set to work on the image of ordinary existence, for its transfiguration, by that almighty Creator Spirit who has no need to destroy the natural so as to attain his more-than-natural goal.

And this brings Balthasar to the source of which the saints are merely the effects. The 'supreme object' in his theological aesthetics will be 'the form of divine revelation in salvation-history, leading to Christ and deriving from him'.[5] This object will not be approached, however, in splendid isolation from the natural objects of aesthetics found in creation and culture. Balthasar can say with T. S. Eliot: 'O Greater Light, we praise thee for the less.'[6] Or in his own words:

> The same Christian centuries which masterfully knew how to read the natural world's language of forms were the very same ones which possessed eyes trained, first, to perceive the formal quality of revelation by the aid of grace and its illumination and second (and only then!) to interpret revelation.[7]

The incarnation 'perfects the whole ontology and aesthetics of created Being', using it at a hitherto unheard of depth as a language and means of expression for the Uncreated Reality.

Balthasar's aim, then, will not be in the first place the correction of a deficient philosophical ontology, an account of being impoverished because it has lost sight of beauty. Much less will it be the restoration (much needed though this is) of a metaphysical sensibility to the criticism and the practice of art – the kind of thing attempted in England until his

5 *GL* I, p. 29.
6 T. S. Eliot, 'Choruses from The Rock', X, in *Collected Poems, 1909–1962* (London 1963), p. 183.
7 *GL* I, p. 29.

premature death by the deliberately anti-modern theoretician of art Peter Fuller. Rather, as a traditional theologian whose sense of the aims of theology is governed by the Fathers, the mediaevals and the best of the divines and spiritual writers of the early modern and modern periods, Balthasar's enterprise centres on the confrontation of beauty with revelation in the context of dogmatic theology. It is at a renewal of dogmatics, made possible by a recovery of the lost transcendental, beauty, and its theological correlate, glory, that he aims, a renewal of dogmatics which will be at the same time, as we shall see, a transformation of fundamental theology or apologetics – of, that is, the way we approach the revelatory action whose content it is the business of dogmatics to explore. Very properly, he warns that we shall come at this centre only slowly. Although the first volume of the theological aesthetics will give us an initial glimpse of it, by presenting us with the formal structure both of the act of faith and of the event of revelation in Jesus Christ, not till we reach the last volume of the aesthetics, on the New Testament's definitive disclosure of the content of God's glory, shall we have reached the heart of the matter.

In a first sketch of his aesthetic Christology, Balthasar deftly indicates some of the themes he will expand, with help from a host of writers, in the volumes that follow. Let us enumerate some of the most important. First, in bearing witness to God as a man, Jesus is what he expresses (God himself) but not whom he expresses (the Father): an apparent paradox which Balthasar calls the fountainhead of a distinctively Christian aesthetics. Secondly, to perceive Jesus as the Word incarnate, the very image of the Father, familiarity with his life-form is needful: this Balthasar identifies with St John's *menein*, an 'abiding' with and in Christ. Thirdly, just as a viewer must step back from a painting to 'take it in', so the disciples could only discern the true content of Jesus' life and teaching with the benefit of hindsight, in a retrospective remembering of what had been seen, their original *conversio ad phantasmata* – 'turning to the images'. Fourthly, what is seen thereby, with the assistance of the Holy Spirit, is the *proportions* proper to the mystery of Christ: the interior relation of divine and human, of invisible and visible. And to this belong other proportions and relationships: with the Old Testament, the promise, of which the New is the fulfilment, and with the created world as a whole. Fifthly, the disciples gave their testimony to the original form, Jesus Christ, not only in oral ways but also in written ones. And the canonical expression – form – of the New Testament reproduces what they perceived of the form of revelation in him. Thus Scripture is the 'likeness' of the original image. It follows that truly fruitful biblical studies (fruitful that is, for ecclesial faith and practice) must always start from the single form found in the multiplicity of texts and theologies in the New Testament, and also return to it. Sixthly, the effect of seeing the divine form in Christ is that the disciples are enraptured, transported, and indeed only form can have this effect. Mission takes its rise from such contemplation.

But if the contours of Balthasar's theological aesthetics are beginning to emerge, how historically justified is his enterprise? Is there any precedent in tradition for such a Christology of beauty – even in the large sense which he gives that word? Has Balthasar not been guilty of slipping too easily from the natural to the supernatural, without reference to that searing divine judgment which revelation makes on all things human?

Balthasar admits that in aesthetics the world *does* tend to glorify itself – more so than in metaphysics or ethics. Where this happens, revelation unmasks it, and theology, as befitting its place as the handmaid of revelation, should obediently reflect this judgment. But Balthasar also stoutly defends his proposed aesthetics of the theological against the charge of presumption and imprudence. To begin with, divine judgment of this world does not always mean condemnation of it! Such judgment may well be, rather, 'a saving act of taking up and transfiguring what is human'. But also, there is a real continuity between the action of the Creator and that of the Redeemer, and, that being so, we must not assume that the main rôle of grace in aesthetics is to 'demolish the bridge between natural and supernatural beauty'. The Greek word for grace, *charis*, means also the attractiveness of the beautiful, and, Balthasar finds that more than a coincidence. In artistic formation spirit can submit to a 'higher shaping hand' without losing its autonomy, while in artistic inspiration, enthusiasm – *en-thousiasmos*, the 'spirit that contains the god' – may find itself obliged to obey a higher command.

It is fair enough to warn against the *unchecked* application of categories borrowed from this-worldly beauty to the unique glory of God's self-disclosure. By such transgressions of thought theological aesthetics degenerate into 'aesthetic theology': a term which many would regard as synonymous with Balthasar's undertaking in *Herrlichkeit* but which he reserves for rogue versions of his project. Still, 'a dangerous road remains a road': *abusus non tollit usum*.

These persuasive sweetmeats dropped into our lap, Balthasar evidently feels secure enough in moving on to an account of the divine art – *God's* aesthetic 'formings' to which man contributes only when he refrains from resisting the Potter's hand. (Balthasar alludes here to Catholic orthodoxy's understanding of the relative rôles of grace and free will in the origination of our salvation). Despite all dissimilarity between created natural form and uncreated supernatural formation, there is also analogy.

> Admittedly, the divine principle of form must in some ways stand in sharp contrast to the beauty of this world. This contrast notwithstanding, however, if God's will to give form really aims at man as God truly wants to shape him – aims, that is, at the perfecting of that work begun by God's 'hands' in the Garden of Eden – then it appears impossible to deny that there exists an analogy between God's work of formation and the shaping forces of nature and of man as they generate and give birth.[8]

And this 'art' is seen in the life-forms of God's chosen instruments in the history of the covenants, both Old and New. From the patriarchs and

8 *GL* I, p. 36.

Moses, through the judges and prophets up to the Baptist, still the arc ascends until it reaches Mary, the Lord's handmaid in whom:

> the feminine and bridal plasticity of the Daughter of Zion is totally recapitulated and who presents to us the highest paradigm of what is meant by the 'art of God' and by 'well-structured sanctity': in each of these cases we confront life in the Holy Spirit, hidden life which is inconspicuous, and yet *so* conspicuous that its situations, scenes and encounters receive a sharp, unmistakable profile and exert an archetypal power over the whole history of faith.[9]

The traditional antecedents for such an aesthetics of revelation are threefold. First, there is the theology of creation: the aesthetic values found within the creation must be ascribed 'in a more eminent mode' to the Source of creation, God himself. Secondly, there is the theology of creation's mending and exaltation (soteriology) and its final perfecting (eschatology). As God's supreme handiwork, the redemption and the consummation of the world must surely mirror, and indeed surpass, the beautiful artistry of its original making. Thirdly, there is the theology of the resurrection, when the glorious form of created being prepared in God's eternal plan is first poured out on earth through the Easter victory of Jesus.

All three presuppositions left their mark on not only the content of the theology of the Fathers (in particular) but on its very style. A beautiful subject-matter requires beautiful handling. Balthasar repudiates the suggestion that all of this is owed to that too convenient all-purpose theological scapegoat 'Hellenism'. The contemplative aspect of patristic theology from Origen to Maximus, from Hilary to Leo, is not the invasion of the Christian religion by an alien philosophical presence. Rather is it 'the flashing anticipation of eschatological illumination, the presaging vision of transparent glory in the form of the Servant . . .'[10] – the afterglow, in other words, of Jesus' transfiguration. The importance of that transfiguration theme for the art of the icon is well known, and one might have thought that icon theology would be Balthasar's next patristic port-of-call in establishing the credentials of theological aesthetics. But despite his ringing affirmation of the evangelical authenticity of patristic theology, Balthasar shows himself surprisingly cool on the subject of the iconodule theology of the later Fathers. He treats Byzantine iconoclasm as a valuable corrective, and sees the iconophobe arguments of the theologian-emperor Constantine as a useful warning against 'allowing the Image of himself that God made to appear in the world – the Image that is his Son – to be extended without critical distance whatever into other images . . .'[11] a distinctly anodyne presentation of Constantine's actual religious policy! What prompts Balthasar's sympathy for the image-breakers here is his concern that the Church should show vigilance in distinguishing, both in theory and in practice, the transcendental beauty of revelation from its natural counterpart.

9 Ibid.
10 *GL* I, p. 39.
11 *GL* I, p. 41.

So far we have heard a good deal about the Fathers, but much less about Scripture. Balthasar's claim that Scripture too underwrites a theological aesthetics turns (in his 'Introduction' at least) on the Wisdom literature – that 'contemplative *caesura*', as he terms it, between Israel and the Church. The self-contemplation of the divine Wisdom in these inspired writings throws an aesthetic light on the past – on the historical and prophetic books of the Old Testament, and on the future – on the New Testament to come. (Balthasar will mention here Paul, John and Hebrews in particular as manifesting a transfiguring or contemplative stance towards the life, death and resurrection of Jesus Christ.) And so, in reading these texts:

> we are witnessing the radiant drawing out into consciousness of the aesthetic dimension which is inherent in this unique dramatic action, a dimension which is the proper object of a theological aesthetics.[12]

As the application of literary criticism to the Bible has shown in its identification of a variety of inner-Scriptural genres, the Spirit of God has placed numerous forms of human expression at the service of his poetics. Yet that poetics remains *his* – and thus the methods of modern biblical study must remain ultimately subordinate to a more holistic appreciation of God's 'style'.

Contestants and supporters

The rest of Balthasar's Introduction deals with some *op*ponents, and prophetic *pro*ponents, of a theological aesthetics in the early modern and modern periods. Or, to change the image from a debating chamber to a law court, Balthasar marshals various witnesses for the prosecution and the defence. The first, unmistakably for the prosecution, is Luther – whose soteriology, as *Mysterium Paschale* will show with great force, Balthasar takes absolutely *au sérieux*. For Luther was opposed not only to the use of philosophical rationality as a source for principles of understanding in theology. More fundamentally, his objection was to any aesthetic harmonisation of humanity and divinity – of which the conceptual elegance of reason is just one example. As Balthasar presents Luther's viewpoint:

> Every form which man tries to impose on revelation in order to achieve an overview that makes comprehension possible – for this is presupposed in beauty – every such form must disintegrate in the face of the 'contradiction', the concealment of everything divine under its opposite, the concealment, that is, of all proportions and analogies between God and man in dialectic.[13]

One might have thought that Balthasar would strenuously resist such a root-and-branch attack on theological aesthetics. But, as with the iconoclasts of the eighth and ninth centuries, he treats the sixteenth-

12 *GL* I, p. 43.
13 *GL* I, p. 48.

century German Reformer as a useful – nay, necessary – warning signal to careless steersmen. The question for Balthasar is not the justice of Luther's intuition but what we are to make of it. Shall we treat it (with, he believes, the overwhelming majority of later Protestants) as a 'cold methodological protest', which sunders the dialectic of the divine mystery and its human embodiment from the divine love which engendered it in the first place, and makes of it merely a negation. Or, alternatively, and following in the steps of the twelfth-century Augustinian canon Richard of St Victor, shall we understand it in terms of

> the exuberant outpouring of the Gospel's nuptial love, a love which, in the 'blessed despair' of a wholly self-surrendering faith, places all human skill and art at the disposal of the one divine Art.[14]

Balthasar's account of how Protestantism eliminated aesthetics from theology – until that is, the time of his own contemporaries Karl Barth and the lesser known Gerhard Nebel, on whom more anon, is subtle. There is more than one way to skin a cat: removing aesthetics from religion *might* mean an onslaught on all expressive forms in favour of a purely interior faith; or again it *could* produce a dialectical system, such as those of Böhme, Schelling and Hegel, where God is held to exteriorise himself into his opposite – *das Nichtige*, nothingness – in order to reconcile all contradictions in himself. And Balthasar is not slow to point out that, contradictorily, the pure faith of the former claims to entertain an *image* of redemption in its totality, while the system of the latter generates an *aesthetic overview* of the whole. Thus *pulchrum*, cast out unceremoniously through the front door returns unnoticed by the rear exit.

Kierkegaard believed he had finally exorcised the demon of the aesthetic. For him, the internal tensions of the aesthetic domain can only be resolved by passing onto the ethical sphere, just as in turn, the inner problematic of the ethical can find its solution only in the religious – that is, the christological. That the chasm thus created between Christic *agapē* and human *erōs* robs people of all joy in the aesthetic is a price Kierkegaard is ready to pay. Balthasar, however, holds that Kierkegaard is, *malgré lui*, akin to the Hegel he execrated: both take the human spirit as their starting point and adopt accordingly an anti-dogmatic stance. Their intellectual progeny is diverse, but alike in impotence to restore aesthetics to theology. The descendants of Kierkegaard treat the Christian reality as entirely inward, a question of existential decision. They finish with Bultmann, for whom revelation has neither an imagery nor a form. The descendants of Hegel, the speculators on history, end up with 'biblical scientism', a solvent of any and every possible perceptible revelatory form.

The fate of Protestant divinity were sore indeed had it not been for Barth. Balthasar finds it more than coincidence that Barth on the one hand overcame the *damnosa hereditas* of Hegel and Kierkegaard by using their strengths to supply for their weaknesses, and on the other hand, in his theology of God, restored the attribute of beauty to the Deity. With Hegel

14 Ibid.

and against Kierkegaard, Barth realised that dogmatics must have a norm and a form; with Kierkegaard and against Hegel, he also appreciated that the content of this form must be a relationship of personal faith between man and God through the Mediator of our redemption. By contemplating the divine story told in Scripture, Barth comes to emphasise God's glory for which, he thinks, beauty is a necessary auxiliary concept. Referring over the heads of the Reformers to the mediaevals and Fathers, Barth hymns God's unique beauty as arousing pleasure, creating desire, rewarding with delight. Barth attaches God's glory to his perfect form as the Holy Trinity, the reconciliation of identity and non-identity, of movement and peace, but he sees the fullest exhibition of divine beauty in the incarnation. In the unity of the humiliation and exaltation of the incarnate Son, God displays his proper comeliness; his splendour radiates from the Crucified. Balthasar praises Barth for his courage not only in going behind the Reformation (since the Reformers could offer no guidance in this realm), but also in accepting the consequences for his personal theology: Barth retrenched his 'actualism', his *staccato* rendition of God's self-disclosure as isolated acts, in order to 'make room alongside it for the concept of authentic objective form'.

But where Protestant theological aesthetics are concerned the palm must go, so Balthasar believes, to the much less familiar figure of Gerhard Nebel whose *Das Ereignis des Schönen*, 'The Event of the Beautiful' appeared in 1953. If Luther over-looked the fact that glory is a feature of the past and present dispensations of Old and New Testaments, and not just a characteristic of the Age to Come, Lutheran Pietism, and later, Idealism, brought back the theme of the beautiful with a vengeance in the notion of the *inner* splendour of Christian souls. With Nebel, however, we have a true Protestant theological aesthetics for the first time. Nebel opposed to a 'static' analogy of being what he termed an 'analogy of event': the God of grace eventualising, putting in an appearance, within the happening which is beauty.

> The *daimōn* of the beautiful [Nebel wrote] must be brought into relation with the triune God. It must be given its place within the Bible. We cannot spare ourselves such an integration by appealing to the ready-made argument that theology and philosophy are simply different, that God belongs to theology, and that Being belongs to philosophy since it may be attained by the efforts of our thought. . . . If we are in earnest, we will see that the truth is one, just as God is one and Adam is one.[15]

Nature's beauty, and art's, disclose for Nebel the wholeness of God's creative work (for in art man 'witnesses to creation's well-wrought structure'). Beauty is that in his creatures which justifies God's self-acclaim. As creation in its wholesome integrity, the beautiful was always meant to be the locus of the covenant relationship established between YHWH and Adam. Consistent with his view that the beautiful is not a state but an event, Nebel regards it as, in Balthasar's words, 'the

15 G. Nebel, *Das Ereignis des Schönen* (Stüttgart 1953), p. 148.

revelation of the paradisal and eschatological possibilities present in the midst of a sinful world'. But if there is an analogy between the 'event of the beautiful' and the 'event of Christ', then a criterion for establishing the authenticity of Christian aesthetics at once suggests itself: *Is the event of the beautiful truly a pointer to the event of Christ?* If so, then beauty is the

> blazing forth of the primal, protological and eschatological splendour of creation even in this age of death, in which redeemed man is admitted to participation in God's act of praising himself in his creation.[16]

Balthasar lauds Nebel's work for theological and biblical seriousness, but it also betrays, he thinks, its Protestant origins in its underlying concept of revelation, incarnation and church. For Nebel, beauty belongs exclusively to the created side of the gulf between creation and Creator. Nowhere does he speak of Christ's image-character, or of the trinitarian aspect of revelation, and he has no time for the marian dimension in Christian sensibility. Unlike the great Fathers, he fails to recognise that it is the 'art of God' in creation, redemption and consummation which is the transcendent archetype of all beauty in nature and culture.

We cannot, says Balthasar, rest happy with these exclusions and failures of perception. To do so would be to acquiesce in the elimination of contemplation from the act of faith, the sundering of seeing from hearing, the denial that faith includes the beginning of glory (*semen gloriae, inchoatio visionis*), and the 'relegation' of the Christian to the old *aiōn* that is now passing away.

But if, since Luther, Protestantism has dealt harshly with theological aesthetics, it cannot be said that Catholicism has always given it a secure home. In Western thought, ever since philosophy and theology, nature and grace, were nicely distinguished, there has been the danger that the congruence of each pair might be overlooked. Gazing back over the history of Latin theology, Balthasar finds his sympathies to lie with those thinkers – Anselm, Aquinas – who espoused a unified or integrated philosophical-cum-theological method, by contrast with those who, from the time of Descartes onwards, felt obliged to take their cue from the growing separation of philosophy and theology inevitable once the epistemological ideal of the natural sciences became the lodestar of the former. Those who clung to the ancient unity of theology and philosophy – such as Pascal, for whom the 'irreconcilable contradictions of [man's] being are transcended by the all-embracing cosmic law of the God-man Christ, who brings everything into unity' – were increasingly the minority. And Balthasar shows how by the mid-nineteenth century all such attempts to hold on to or re-create the ancient harmony of natural and supernatural thinking had collapsed. If only the divines of the nineteenth-century Catholic revival in Germany, Austria, Belgium had followed the example of Leibniz, in seeking precisely a harmony of the two disciplines, rather than, with Hegel (and behind Hegel, Spinoza)

16 *GL* I, p. 68.

their ultimate identity, all would – or might – have been well. As it was they tried to prove too much. Thus, in the Catholic Tübingen school the attempt to show that all the great idealistic systems of modern philosophy depend on a covert theology led quasi-inevitably to the conviction, much in evidence across the linguistic border at Louvain, that all authentic metaphysics derive, through tradition, from a revelation to Adam. If this position, which effectively denied all truly natural knowledge of God suffered condemnation at the First Vatican Council, the same was true of its counter-image, Hermesianism, which turned not philosophy into theology but theology into philosophy, holding that, if faith generates rational understanding this is because in the last analysis it forms part of reason's own structure. Here it is not philosophical wisdom that undergoes shipwreck but the freedom of God to disclose more of himself and his ways than the mind of man can fathom.

At the same time, the predominant school in German philosophy at large – Hegelianism – was itself disintegrating, with the Left Hegelians as dialectical materialists on the one side, and the Right Hegelians, as Lutheran theocrats on the other. Balthasar finds it significant that, at this moment of the internal collapse of the unity of Christian thought (at least when considered by an inhabitant of *deutsche Sprachraum*), Catholic theology began to accept its own parcelling out into various specialisations. Actually, the differentiation of speculative and positive theology (the most important of those specialisations from Balthasar's present standpoint) is a late sixteenth-century (rather than early nineteenth-century) phenomenon, but he may be right to see the pace of specialisation as accelerated by the loss of a philosophy that could be married with theology as a whole. Certainly, only in the modern (as distinct from 'early modern') period do we find historical science equipped with presuppositions, methods and, above all, the self-confidence to sit as judge and jury over the truth-claims of Christian revelation as a whole.

And this is Balthasar's chief concern: too much has been conceded by fundamental theology to historical theology, taking that latter term to include the study of the origins of Christian faith by literary-historical criticism. The deeper understanding of the Scriptures, of dogma, of Christian ethics, is always revelation-dependent, and grasped by what Augustine called *intellectus*, and Origen *pneuma* – namely, the spiritual intelligence at work in faith. To be sure, Christian revelation is displayed in history. It cannot, consequently, be divorced from historical facts. But this does not mean that Christianity can properly be 'subsumed under the historical sciences', still less that its authentic content can be extracted (for the first time?) by 'exact scientific method'. Balthasar shows how this historicising tendency has affected various aspects of Catholic theology – conservative as much as progressive. Fundamental theologians are keen to prove the historical wellfoundedness of Christian revelation and of the Catholic Church's claim to be its rightful interpreter. Dogmatic theologians wait to hear from exegetes what the correct historical meaning of this or that text of the Bible may be – and spend the rest of their time writing the history of dogma. Moral theologians too are less interested than once they were in the philosophical elements of their discipline, which they reconceive as the 'historical encounter [of moral agents] with the Word of God in an ever-changing historical situation'.

There could scarcely be a sharper contrast with, say, Thomas' account of how theology may be termed 'scientific'.

> Theology's exceptional position is seen by him [Aquinas] to be founded on its participation through grace – directly in the personal act of faith but mediately by virtue of the authentic pattern of faith presented by the Church – in the intuitive saving knowledge of God himself and of the Church Triumphant. Only in this dimension is the vision of the distinctively theological 'form' and its specific beauty possible.[17]

While eschewing any programmatic hostility to historical studies (on the contrary, Balthasar says how much they can give theology), the Swiss dogmatician concurs with the French theologian of exegesis François Dreyfus in the judgment that, if the tendency towards an 'exaggerated scientism of the *littera*' is allowed full rein, it will lead to a state of affairs where only a new caste of doctors of the law – the scientific exegetes – have access to the Word of God.[18] In sharpest contrast, Balthasar holds that all the really great theologians have been dilettantes, amateurs, enthusiasts – think of the rhapsodic, confessional style of the principal Church Fathers. But what of such cooler, conceptual articulations of the Christian mystery as the definitions of the ecumenical Councils or the careful distinctions of the high Scholastics? The former – from the Synods – are *guidelines* for theology, and the latter – from the Schools – were at the service of theological forms or schemes which carry telltale signs of the *infused* (and not merely acquired) understanding enjoyed by their makers.

> The work of Aquinas, and also that of Anselm, Bonaventure, and Albert the Great, radiates the beauty of a human power of shaping and structuring which has been supernaturally in-formed in this manner. It makes no difference whether or not they are expressly speaking of the aesthetic moment as they methodologically order and elucidate their material. . . . They would not enjoy such a shaping power nor, therefore, such an overpowering historical influence, if their talents had not themselves been transformed through and through by the Spirit's shaping power: if, that is to say, these theologians were not in a Christian sense ecstatics, had not been caught up and drawn into the unity of enthusiasm and holiness.[19]

In all genuine theology, one expects to find the supernatural disposition to judge rightly of Christian truth, and even the personal touch of the Holy Spirit in the gift of understanding at work within the laboriously acquired 'science' of the student. This is not to deny the value of detailed work in the specialised research of scholars – not least because the same

---

17 *GL* I, pp. 75–76.
18 See my 'François Dreyfus on Scripture Read in Tradition', in *Scribe of the Kingdom. Essays on Theology and Culture* (London 1994), I, p. 33.
19 *GL* I, p. 78.

process should be visible there too, and must be if their learning is to bear fruit in the Church. Their results will not be theologically relevant unless they are amenable to the proper form of theological thinking, not in the sense of incorporation within one theological system but in that of docility to the animating spirit – the *erōs*, Balthasar calls it – of theological, rather than, simply human, enquiry.

Balthasar now turns, however, to a rather different question, though one which still falls, certainly, under the rubric of 'introduction' to his subject. There has sometimes been a concern with the artistry of the Bible or the aesthetic potential of Catholicism which seems at first sight identical with his own project, but which he would sharply distinguish from it. In his own preferred terminology, an 'aesthetic theology' is not yet a 'theological aesthetics', and it is the latter alone that he seeks. Balthasar's objections to the more limited objective of such aesthetic exegesis or apologetics is twofold: first, the beautiful, *pulchrum*, is here removed from its original position as a total reading of Being (a transcendental), and reduced to a separate object with a (limited) science all its own. And secondly, this partly coincides with, and partly reflects, the abandonment of the attempt to see the biblical revelation within the total form of a theology that *includes* philosophy. The main push towards the making of an aesthetic theology, as Balthasar sees it, came from the side of German Idealism. For, on the one hand, in a period when, over against the rationalism of the French Enlightenment, the human value of a traditionally transmitted popular culture was in process of being rediscovered, Christianity was too rich a resource to abandon. If it could not be presented as truth, it could at least be salvaged as beauty. And on the other hand, for those who continued to find the Protestant gospel believable in its own terms, and wished to commend it to others, some imaginative refurbishment seemed necessary for a religion too often reduced to (literally) bare essentials by the more zealous disciples of Luther, Calvin and Zwingli.

Balthasar has no objection in principle, of course, to the bringing together of a theory of beauty and Christian revelation: the question is, How is it to be done? In effect he creates the category of 'aesthetic theology' for attempts in this direction which, though well-meaning, are not quite correctly conceived. Thus in J. G. Herder, there is a misconstrual of the relationship between theological beauty and the beauty of the world: the particular miracles of Scripture are but the universal miracle of existence made image. The Spirit's bestowal at Pentecost is only the manifestation of what man should and could be. Speaking of Herder's Spinozist-sounding treatise *Gott*, one of his last writings, Balthasar comments that

> Herder's ambiguities in this work are but one expression of the great amphiboly between pantheism and Christianity that pervades the whole age, from Fichte and Schelling to Hegel: the fluid identification of the natural and the supernatural which both 'humanized' Christianity and failed to hear its true message.[20]

20 *GL* I, p. 90.

And he proposes, harshly enough, that, in comparison with such aesthetic harmonies as these, the 'trenchant antitheses' of not only Schiller and Kierkegaard but even Karl Marx would do the Church less harm. Again, in René de Chateaubriand – whose *Génie du Christianisme* arose, like Herder's enterprise, from the desire to answer Voltairean scepticism – an aesthetic apologetics using a criterion of this-worldly beauty, human and cultural, is applied not only to the *effects* of Christianity (which is legitimate) but to Christianity's *essence* as well.

> In his [Chateaubriand's] work, the world of revelation does not bring with itself its own criterion and its own beauty, a criterion and beauty *by which* man, the world, and culture could measure themselves. The point of reference lies, at best, in the harmony *between* nature and supernature, but for the most part it is to be found *in* nature, in its own satisfaction and development.[21]

At the same time, however, even these projects provide Balthasar with some valuable contributory themes. Examples from Herder would be the notion of the imagistic texture of Scripture as a series of poetic worlds, and the idea that, as made to the image and likeness of God, man can see, in his own imagehood, both himself and his divine origin. Also congenial to Balthasar is Herder's notion that, to be interpreted aright, the images of Scripture must be interpreted in the Spirit: only so can they be transparent to *der Bildende*, the Maker of images – God himself at work by way of union with man. Again, Balthasar mentions with apparent commendation Herder's conviction that a 'philosophy of beholding', defined in terms of the interplay of signs and their significance, is more important, taps more fully the deep springs of our being, than does conceptual demonstration. Herder's idea of divine revelation as a throwing open – but only in the form of an unveiling by signs – appeals to the Swiss theologian, as does his habit of speaking of Christ as the expressive image of the Godhead in and through all the ways his humanity communicated itself, right up to his resurrection. In a sense for which his continued bodiliness is essential, Christ's life is the highest form of religious 'sculpture'. Lastly, Herder always thinks of Greek culture within the world of the ancient Near East as a whole, and in so doing avoids that programmatic contrasting of the Christian and the Hellenic which, in Balthasar's eyes, has vitiated much modern theology.

In Chateaubriand, despite the latter's fervent Catholicism, Balthasar finds less to his purpose, though it can hardly be strange to his method to 'approach Christianity where it has become incarnate in culture', so long as this is done by one who has grasped 'the fact of Christianity from the very depths and fulness of his being as subject, with a heart that longs to believe, to hope and to love' – Balthasar's summary of Chateaubriand's fundamental approach.[22]

At the beginning and mid-point of Germanophone Romanticism, a movement which is both contemporary with, and intricately related

21 *GL* I, p. 94.
22 *GL* I, p. 91.

to, German Idealism, Balthasar finds figures who exemplify the
strengths, rather than the weaknesses, of 'aesthetic theology'. Balthasar
can hardly award higher praise than in saying of Jakob Georg Hamann
that he

> was alone in seeing that the real problem was how to construct a
> theory of beauty . . . in such a way that, in it, the total aspiration of
> worldly and pagan beauty is fulfilled while all glory is at the same
> time given to God in Jesus Christ.[23]

Though Hamann presents the beautiful, in optimistic fashion, as the
world's primordial being, he also recognises that nature – and especially
human nature – is alienated from its origin, such that the glory is concealed. A major theme not only of Balthasar's theological aesthetics but of
his Christology and triadology at large is first heard when we read of how
Hamann treats the Word of God, witnessed to in Scripture, as a new
revelation of God's glory in its seeming opposite. One of his major
presuppositions is contained in the recollection that, for Hamann, not
only Judaism but also paganism are providentially ordered towards the
Word, who fulfils both by his disclosure of the 'primal splendour of the
love of a God who humiliates himself'.[24] Glory as *kenosis*: the formula does
justice both to the eighteenth-century philosopher and to the twentieth-
century theologian. Hamann celebrates the folly of the God who as
Creator penetrated into nothingness and as Redeemer became man, to be
exalted on the gibbet of Golgotha. What in *Zwey Scherflein* ('Two Mites'),
Hamann had called the 'aesthetic obedience of the Cross' brings us to
the inner heart of all reality: the bridal union of the Word made flesh
with his fallen and dismembered body of his Bride, humankind, who in
his dying he at last takes home again to himself. If only Hamann had
been understood the story of the relation between theology and beauty,
Christianity and culture, would have been, so Balthasar believed, a great
deal happier.

What Hamann represents, as a Lutheran, at the opening of the
Romantic era, the little-known Swiss religious thinker Alois Gügler
presents in Catholic form at its high noon. Since Gügler was born in
Balthasar's own city, Lucerne, there may be some local pride at work in
the description of his writing as the inspired perfecting of Romantic
aesthetic theology. Though conscious of the characteristically Romantic
and Idealist temptations to which Gügler was prone, Balthasar evidently
regards the massive five-volume study *Die heilige Kunst* as worthy of a
much fuller theological investigation than he could find space for in
Herrlichkeit.[25]

For Gügler the (general) divine self-revelation in creation, once grasped
at depth, discloses the supernatural orientation of the world and
humanity. The art of all peoples shows some glimmerings of awareness of

23 *GL* I, p. 80.
24 *GL* I, p. 82.
25 The only study, written before the posthumous publication of the final volume of
    Gügler's work, is biographical rather than theological in focus: and this is J. L.
    Schiffmann, *Lebensgeschichte Alois Güglers* (Augsburg 1833).

this mystery, but only the Hebrews testified in an adequate way to this primal experience. Only they managed not to misuse the image-making faculty which mediates between the 'holy night' (an expression taken from the poet Novalis) of the inner world of mystery and the 'day-world' of the senses. They persevered in the sanctuary of an 'adoring silence' before the God whom no man can image. By contrast, the Greeks fragmented the divine 'Rock' into the many faces of mythology – itself a medium suited well enough to communicating *worldly* beauty, but not divine. Mythology is 'the pervasive falling away from pure infinity and the thoroughgoing deification of nature and of man'.[26] Nonetheless, sparks from the true Source can occasionally pass through the myths of the pagans. The attraction of this basic conception for Balthasar can easily be discerned in his encomium of it.

> The advantages of such a conception are, first of all, the 'redeemability' of all that is outside the Bible as it is taken into the reality of revelation in Christ [though in point of fact, his summary of Gügler's thought has yet to mention the incarnation]; second, the consequent applicability (albeit with caution) of the universal phenomena of life, nature and history to our interpretation of revelation properly so called; and third, the avoidance of an isolationist historical 'positivism' of Biblical revelation in favour of a view of the relationship to God that sees it as already having been established in the very essence of all created reason and nature, even though its presence and reality have somehow been 'buried alive'.[27]

For Gügler, Hebrew history manifests the truth of all history, while Christianity is the fulfilment of all religions. All the principal stages of human history, from the childhood of man, through his adolescence to his less than perfectly integrated maturity are brought to expression in the history to which the Hebrew Bible bears witness; while in Jesus Christ the gap between what is and what ought to be is bridged, in such a way that both nature and history are fulfilled. This outline of Gügler's overall conceptual scheme enables Balthasar to explain what his *Luzerner* forebear meant by art in general, by the 'holy art' of Scripture in particular, and by the interpretation of that unique art which is exegesis.

By a synthesis of Romantic and Idealist motifs, Gügler defines art as the expression (into *form*) of the interior feeling of infiniteness which derives from the complete dependence of a finite 'I' on the infinite 'I', thus leading to an exteriorisation of the experience of God through the affections. Gügler speaks of this in a musical metaphor as the tuning (*Stimmung*) of God and man. 'Man has been attuned by God's breath to reflect and express the attunedness (*Gestimmtheit*) of matter and spirit, nature and God.'[28] The goal of revelation is precisely this attunement of man's heart to God, the Bride to the Lamb, as the Father draws us to

---

26 A. Gügler, *Die heilige Kunst* I (Landshut 1814), p. 143, cited at *GL* I, p. 96.
27 *GL* I, p. 97.
28 *GL* I, p. 100.

him through the Son, Jesus Christ, while the Holy Spirit in our hearts is the attunement itself.[29]

And this explains what the 'holy art' of the Bible must be. Hebrew aesthetics will not take worldly beauty as the measure of divine revelation. On the contrary, it will subordinate its symbols to the hidden Source which the religious art of the pagans has largely lost. Then in the New Testament what is given with the Old comes to its fulfilment, for an art that embodies infinity and spiritual wholeness necessarily reaches perfection when *God himself* is incarnate, embodied, in this world. However, Balthasar draws attention to an ambiguity here in Gügler's thought. Because the relation of promise and fulfilment in Christ appears to be the interpretation by a Word deriving from without of a light breaking forth from within, Gügler deflects attention from the visibility of Jesus Christ to his luminous presence in souls and to the significance of his *verbal* elucidation (*Erklären* – the pun on terms for 'light' or 'clarity' is the same in Latin and German) of the ancient covenant to the Jews.

From this it follows that exegesis – the due interpretation of *die heilige Kunst* of Scripture – will necessarily have a specific character. In Balthasar's words: exegesis (for Gügler) is

> the progressive returning of everything history has formed back to the original Light . . . and the interpretation of it by reference to this origin. Such exegesis is possible only from the perspective of a total overview of salvation-history and of all God's revelation . . . , an overview too of Christ's totality . . . and above all, of a living interior contemplation of the divine life . . [30]

It is not difficult to divine in Gügler's requirements that exegesis be contemplative, and that it attempts to draw out the central themes of Scripture in the light of revelation's totality (and notably the interrelation of Old and New Covenants), an early premonition of Balthasar's own view.

And yet Balthasar does not exonerate Gügler from his wider criticisms of Romantic theology at large, and notably from a tendency to a monistic identification of light and eye, object and subject, truth and knowledge, as well as to the equating of spirit with the supernatural, so that the former's distinction from nature becomes identical with the latter's provision of grace and revelation. Gügler's deep intention was to trace analogies here: his central 'model' of art should have carried instructions as to how it was being set to use, with sameness and difference, in various realms of the real. Unfortunately, the categories of Romantic thinking could not provide him with the understanding of analogical method he needed. We have here a clue, dropped by Balthasar, of how his own theological aesthetics will not turn its back on the achievements of Scholastic – and especially *Thomistic* – divinity. Thus Balthasar is not sorry – despite the desiccation to which Neo-Scholasticism was prone – that the Thomist

29 Cf. A. Gügler, *Die heilige Kunst* II (Lucerne 1817), p. 197.
30 *GL* I, pp. 101–102.

revival, assisted none too unwillingly by the authority of the papacy, should have brought the Romantic theology, and its 'aesthetic and religious monism', to the ground.

For what he terms 'the basic intuitions of the common Tradition' were perfectly capable of expression in Thomist form, so long as (and this qualification is extremely important to him) the Thomism in question 'sought to grow beyond strict scholastic requirements and develop a universal perspective'.[31] In fact, his only example of how an aesthetic theology might be so refined and corrected as to become an authentic theological aesthetics comes from the pen of a Thomist Ultramontane, albeit one of an unusual sort: Matthias Joseph Scheeben.

Balthasar's criticism of Scheeben – whose theological journey follows a remarkably straight course from the early *Natur und Gnade* of 1861 to the uncompleted *Dogmatik* of the 1870s and 1880s – is not that he is a Thomist but that a theological aesthetics inspired by Thomism (I have called it elsewhere 'that extraordinary thing, a lyrical Scholasticism'[32] should, first, have defined itself so thoroughly by the pursuit of a separation (not just distinction) of nature and grace and secondly, and not un-connected with this, a 'certain ahistoricity' in his theological plan of things, entailing a failure to take in the more negative aspects of the world – sin and suffering – with full comprehension. In context it was an intelligible and perhaps even a necessary counter-reaction that Scheeben should so have turned around the characteristic impulse of Romanticism to identify God's first gift, creation, with his second gift, grace. In his insistence that grace is in no sense merely a modal supplement to nature, Scheeben snaps the links that could suggest a smooth passage from the second to the first. Grace is not merely a new dignity for man, but a new substance, a new being, pulling him free from the limitations of nature. In Balthasar's graphic – indeed startling – illustration:

> God's revelation of himself, according to Scheeben, means the transporting of man from his own immanent and finite sphere into the divine, transcendental, and infinite sphere, an experience such as is portrayed, for instance, by the well-known Renaissance wood-cut which shows a man piercing the sphere of the world with his head and gaping with astonishment at the mysteries beyond the world.[33]

If this will not do, no more will Scheeben's failure to focus more clearly on the darkness of a fallen world. Just because his departure point is the world of grace, worldly existence and its ruptured condition enter his optic only obliquely. One consequence especially baleful in Balthasar's eyes is the failure to 'understand the "beauty" of the Cross without the abysmal darkness into which the Crucified plunges'.[34] The bridal union of

---

31 *GL* I, p. 104.
32 A. Nichols, O.P., 'Homage to Scheeben', in idem., *Scribe of the Kingdom. Essays on Theology and Culture* I (London 1994), p. 213.
33 *GL* I, p. 106.
34 *GL* I, p. 117.

humanity with God, if its biblical basis is to be taken *au sérieux*, has as its background the harlotry of Zion.

And yet these defects leave the central achievement of Scheeben's theological aesthetics intact. The glories of grace, being as these are the glories of God himself, are infinitely more sublime than any natural beauty. As the preface to *Herrlichkeiten der göttlichen Gnade* has it,

> The *beauty* . . . of the Catholic faith lies precisely in the fact that, in the mysteries of grace, it displays before us an immeasurably exalted *elevation* of our nature.[35]

By the punning connexion of 'sublimity' (*Erhabenheit*) and 'elevation' (*Erhebung*), Scheeben wishes to bring out the way the beauty relevant to theology is ultimately God's own substantial beauty, poured out onto creatures. In the present life, such grace-beauty is believed on, not seen, and yet by what Scheeben terms a 'transposition of our eye' to God's own viewpoint we begin to contemplate now what we shall enjoy for ever in heaven. God's plan for the world is what the *Dogmatik* calls a 'work of creative universal architectonics',[36] but Christian wonder is directed above all to the transfiguration of the creature through grace as found, first of all, in Christ, and then, through the God-man, in the 'sponsal' being of Mary.

As Scheeben's powers mature, the dualistic impression left by his early work begins to fade, for more and more is he absorbed by the interpenetration of the orders of nature and grace. Balthasar, if not exactly lost for words, nevertheless considers the mature Scheeben's work the last word of all previous theology in its character as an expression of '*erōs*' – the attractive pull of the divine glory. And in a fine précis, he sets forth Scheeben's vision of faith in terms of three moments: the Trinity as a mystery of self-giving fruitfulness; the hypostatic union of divinity and humanity in the person of Christ who thus can mediate the trinitarian self-communication to a creation made to receive it; and Mary's bridal motherhood as the epitome of a world that the grace of Christ has prepared for itself. What is breathtaking in Scheeben's thought is the way this trio of interrelated doctrinal themes is made to yield the criterion for a rethinking of every aspect of ecclesial and Christian reality, and not for these alone but for a reconceptualisation of the nature of the world and the formal structures of being. God's plan for the world is marian: it is for the 'glorification' of nature in its 'servanthood'.

> The uniqueness of Scheeben's conception lies in the fact that the vision of faith allows him to grasp certain fundamental laws of Being in such a vital manner that he is then able to illumine faith's mystery from the standpoint of ontology.[37]

---

35 M. J. Scheeben, *Herrlichkeiten der göttlichen Gnade* (Freiburg 1862), p. 1.
36 Idem., *Handbuch der katholischen Dogmatik* III (Freiburg 1887), section 268.
37 *GL* I, p. 110.

In particular the philosophical concepts of matter and form, applied by Scheeben to the duo of nature and grace, undergo a transfiguration at his hands when re-conceived in the light of the bride–bridegroom relationship of the world and God's grace in Christ and Mary. Nature is the 'womb of matter' without which the shaping power of grace has nothing to render fruitful. Scheeben sets this principle to work at all the analogically related levels of the real. Thus the human will too, spiritual though it be, is natural material to be in-formed by grace. Grace *begets* in the will. When we think of grace so acting on the will as to inspire the affections and indeed its entire interior disposition we should do so by using the analogy of a *fructifying seed*, rather than the notions either of (merely) moral influence or (sheerly) physical impulsion. Only a 'conceptive', feminine attitude to grace can enable the will to proceed in a 'partitive', generative fashion to gracious decision-making. The same approach characterises Scheeben's account of the foundation of all revelation-dependent thinking and acting – the act of faith itself. Just as in ordinary living there is such a thing as 'natural faith', whose logic issues from the esteem we accord to the 'dignity' of the person speaking, and our desire to 'model' ourselves on this person in trust, so in specifically Christian, supernatural faith, the light of grace, containing within itself a judgment of the trustworthiness of the divine speaker, couples with the pre-existing relation between the reason of the would-be believing subject and the object with which revelation history has presented him or her. The light of faith constitutes, then, as Balthasar approvingly cites Scheeben on this point, the 'seed and impulse, or the running start, . . . the paving of the way, and initiation' of the assent of faith itself.[38] All of this will be highly pertinent to Balthasar's own 'aesthetic' presentation of these same topics.

Nor does the exemplary force of Scheeben's theology for Balthasar restrict itself to the area of fundamental theology. It penetrates into dogmatics proper as well. Unhappy with the Scholastic formula of Christ's humanity as the 'conjoined instrument' of the Logos, he used the marital analogy to speak rather of the in-formation of Christ's humanity by the Word of God, leading to the 'reciprocal information of two forms', one human, the other divine. And this same *wechselseitige Ineinandersetzung zweier Formen* is nothing other than the 'co-inherence' (*perichōrēsis*) of divine and human in Christ once proclaimed by the Greek Fathers and now rethought in terms of a Christian ontology. While, then, Christ's human nature has a supernatural foundation, his total person can be described as, in a profound sense, wholly natural – 'in the sense that in this union all nature's organic, moral, and matrimonial relationships find their highest form and fulfilment and indeed their ultimate ground'.[39] At this point, Balthasar fears, some Protestant readers may feel that Scheeben has closed the gap between nature and supernature only *too* successfully!

In this unique person, Jesus Christ, God and God's creation are nuptially united. His Calvary sacrifice, and its acceptance in the resurrection,

---

38 M. J. Scheeben, *Handbuch der katholischen Dogmatik* I (Freiburg 1873), section 38, quoted in *GL* I, p. 113.
39 Ibid. II (Freiburg 1878–80), section 223, cited at *GL* I, p. 114.

means the outpouring of the whole glory of God onto the substance of the creature whose surrender in self-oblation the Father wills not as destruction but as a making room for the fire of the divine Love. It is in the closing paragraphs of his account of Scheeben's thought that Balthasar for the first time introduces the punning sense of *Herrlichkeit* as not only 'glory' but 'lordliness' (from the German *Herr*, 'Lord') which the English translators of his theological aesthetics will incorporate into their title 'The Glory *of the Lord*'.[40]

40 *GL* I, p. 116.

2

❧❀❧

The Subjective Evidence

Balthasar is now in a position to set forth the 'task and structure' of his proposed work. So as not to anticipate too presumptuously the conclusions of the search he will make into the tradition's resources, Balthasar proposes to limit himself at this stage to a relatively simple and straightforward description of terms.

Splendour in form

Even on a 'layman's' version of aesthetics, two elements would enter into an account of the beautiful – the form of some object, and the splendour with which it strikes a beholder. And while those two elements indeed recur in every major aesthetic theory received from the past, Balthasar intends to name them, with Thomas Aquinas, *species* (or *forma*) for the first and *lumen* (or *splendor*) for the second. These will be his key words in an initial statement of the aims and shape of a theological aesthetics.

Not that there is anything simplistic about the way Balthasar approaches the first of these crucial concepts, that of *form*. It would hardly be too much to say that his entire general ontology is summoned to his aid. Considerations drawn from the psychology of perception or the aesthetics of harmonious proportion go some way towards explaining the attraction of beautiful form. But full justice cannot be done to it without a metaphysic which itself draws on a 'comprehensive doctrine of Being'.

> The form as it appears to us is beautiful only because the delight that it arouses in us is founded upon the fact that, in it, the truth and goodness of the depths of reality itself are manifested and bestowed, and this manifestation and bestowal reveal themselves to us as being something infinitely and inexhaustibly valuable and fascinating.[1]

Form, as Balthasar presents it, cannot be understood without invoking a dialectic of reality and appearance. It is no shimmering, evanescent

1 *GL* I, p. 118.

23

phenomenon but the 'real presence of the depths, of the whole of reality'. And yet it cannot be understood without appreciating its sign character – the way it points beyond itself. Form is, as he puts it , a 'real pointing beyond itself into the depths'.

Now notoriously, in different phases of Western culture poets and artists have privileged either the profound intelligibility of form – that is a typical viewpoint or presupposition of classical or neo-classical culture; or the wider, less objectifiable setting and backcloth of discrete, comprehensible forms, an attitude characteristic of Romanticism and its historical foreshadowings and residue. But Balthasar refuses to decide between a classical and a Romantic approach to his subject. To a classical mindset superlatives are reserved for perfect form, which form contains all the profundity one might ever wish for; to the Romantic, by contrast, what is truly wonderful is the boundless, the infinite, where an essentially limited form transcends itself in the direction of depths it may signify but can never exhaustively express. To Balthasar, this is but a question of emphasis. 'Both aspects are inseparable from one another, and together they constitute the fundamental configuration of Being.'[2] To explain this seeming paradox, Balthasar has recourse to the remaining term of his indispensable twosome, *splendour*. The radiance of form is the tell-tale mark of form's revelation of depth, yet, thus beckoned, the enchanted observer will never manage to enter those depths if at the same time he proposes to leave form behind as something superficial.

Balthasar admits that this concatenation of terms and concepts cannot be applied as it stands, in some straightforwardly univocal fashion, to the unique divine Object of all Christian thought. Christians are not pantheists. The living God of the Scriptures and the Church's preaching is not to be understood as merely a 'ground', a Ground of being, which makes its appearance, ineluctably, in all phenomena. And yet neither are Christians deists. The activity of that God in creating, reconciling and redeeming, really *is* his epiphany, his self-manifestation to the world. Balthasar gains confidence that the key terms of aesthetics can be applied in some fashion – analogously, then – to the God of revelation when he considers the Christmas Preface of the Roman rite, indebted as this is to the theological doctrine of the fifth-century Roman pope, Leo the Great.

> In the wonder of the Incarnation
> your eternal Word has brought to the eyes of faith
> a new and radiant vision of your glory.
> In him we see our God made visible
> and so are caught up in love of the God we cannot see.[3]

Here Balthasar finds in embryo the two sorts of 'evidence' – subjective evidence and objective evidence – which divine revelation yields up to us when it is studied in the perspective of theological aesthetics. For, first, the mind's eye is struck by a new and hitherto unknown radiance

---

2 *GL* I, p. 119. For their contrast, see T. E. Hulme, 'Romanticism and Classicism', in H. Read (ed.), *Speculations* (London 1968).

3 'Preface of Christmas, I', *The Roman Missal* (Alcester and Dublin 1975), p. 406.

(subjective evidence) which enables the person to contemplate (objective evidence) an object which is actually divine but is mediated by – in the broadest sense – a sign or sacrament of itself: in fact, an ordered constellation of signs, a sacramental economy. And furthermore, this vision – at once subjectively and objectively enabled – sparks off in the beholder a passionate movement of loving desire for the Infinite now made present through visible form.

Basing himself at this early juncture on the Latin text of the Nativity Preface just quoted, Balthasar emphasises that, as in the Judaeo-Christian tradition as a whole, not only seeing is involved but also hearing and believing, both of which could be counterposed to seeing – though in Balthasar's theology they are not. For Balthasar, believing in the theological sense – that is, faith – is *itself a kind of seeing*. It is the establishment of a communion of reciprocal knowledge between God and myself, in Jesus Christ and his Church, on God's initiative – all this without prejudice to the future eschatological mode of such knowledge as full vision when I shall know even as now I am known. Furthermore, Balthasar regards language, the verbal content of hearing, as itself a product of what is seen, and a testimony to it. Although the Preface of Christmas speaks of what is seen in the incarnation as the *Word* made flesh, and inasmuch as the fleshliness of that Word points to a divine mystery treats seeing as an initiation (only) into believing, that great text of the Liturgy of the Theophany does not emphasise in fact the differentiation of these various aspects – hearing and believing as well as seeing, but stresses the global act of perception – in German *Wahrnehmung* (literally, a taking to oneself what is true) – which includes both hearing and seeing, believing and appropriating as one's own.

But, for this to be possible – for the Father's glory to be perceived in the visible sacrament of the Son – a 'light' of a new kind must begin to shine on the percipient's horizon. The 'light of faith' is a familiar phrase in classical Western theology for the provision of fresh epistemic resources in supernatural believing: mind is illuminated, just as will is rectified, so that in the revealed object the believer may find the Revealer himself. What is distinctive of Balthasar's presentation is that the new light does not simply enable believers truly to see the form by illumining their gaze at the innermost point of their personal subjectivity. It is not just that the grace of faith enlightens the mind, as moved by the will and enables it to see in such signs as, for instance, the New Testament miracles, the fulfilment of prophecy and the moral perfection of Jesus the activity of the self-revealing God, thus turning a religion which natural reason could judge capable of being believed (having what the Neo-Scholastics called *credibilitas*, credibility) into a religion which is actually believed on the authority of the God who can neither deceive nor be deceived (enjoying what the Neo-Scholastics called *credenditas*, the property of being believed through a divine supplementation of human motives). For Balthasar, by contrast with this picture, taken for granted as it was in the predominant Catholic apologetics, both popular and scholarly, of the early twentieth century, the light of faith also breaks forth from *within the revelatory form itself*. In Balthasar's version, then, light enters the picture not just through a merely mental event, albeit one in which the Sun of all spirits begins to shine more powerfully on a human intelligence. Rather, does what is seen – the humanity of Jesus, as personalised in the Logos – itself give out radiance, the radiance God has communicated to it in its splendid being as the real sign of his own infinite Essence. What God offers man is, consequently: 'offered in such a way that man can see it, understand it, make it his own, and live from it in keeping with his human nature'.[4]

Without this philanthropic economy, whereby God adjusts the mystery of his self-manifestation to human capacity, the Preface's claim that the one who sees the Word made flesh is caught up by love (*amor*) of what is Unseen could not be sustained. For this movement of loving desire is *erōs* not *agapē*, *amor* not *caritas*. To be sure, the authors of the Preface presuppose that invisible gracious love of God for man which lies behind the entire scenario of the saving revelation, but what they actually say concerns what Balthasar calls 'the event whereby man is transported because of having seen the *Deus invisibilis* in a human way'. What God has shown generates in human beings a mighty drive, a profound propulsion, towards the reality now thrown open to them. This movement towards God involves the collaboration of, on the one hand, human *erōs* (despite all the resistances and hesitations caused by sin), and on the other, the Holy Spirit of God who lends that human and all-too-human desiring, thirsting, longing, his own divine enthusiasm and inspiration. Balthasar was passionately convinced of the thoroughly evangelical character of the employment of this language of *erōs* – jealous and zealous, consuming and ecstatic, a love which takes God out of himself into the world and stimulates in creatures a similar love for him. Its principal champion in Christian tradition, Denys the Areopagite, was, he believes, far more biblicist than Neo-Platonic.[5] It is indeed vital to Balthasar's project in *Herrlichkeit* that, in his own words:

> all of this quenches and more than fulfils the human longing for love and beauty, a longing which, previous to and outside the sphere of revelation, exhausted itself in impotent and distorted sketches of such a desperately needed and yet unimaginable fulfilment.[6]

And yet over against idealisms of all sorts, Balthasar insists that *Christian* enthusiasm is to be defined not in terms of the rapturous flights of which subjectivity is capable, but *vis-à-vis* a soberly conceived (Thomistic-type) realism of being. Only because the actual being with which Christians are presented through grace and faith is so wonderful are such enthusiastic reactions justified. The union of splendour with solid reality reaches its clearest expression in the disciples' experience of the risen body of Christ – in, then, transfigured biology. At the same time, in this divine art even sin and hell are included – not merely, as Augustine thought, so as to provide an aesthetic counterpoint to glory but (in a way yet to be explained by Balthasar though already hinted at) as integral

---

4 *GL* I, p. 121.
5 Much use is made at this juncture in *Herrlichkeit* of a justly famous passage on the divine *erōs* in Denys' *The Divine Names* IV. 13 (cited at *GL* I, p. 122).
6 *GL* I, p. 123.

features in the depiction of the self-humbling divine Love, which is what glory, on the Swiss theologian's reading of Scripture in Tradition, turns out to be.

Continuous reference to the form and manner of God's appearance in salvation history, as witnessed to by Scripture, is indispensable for Balthasar if the beauty of the divine nature is to be spoken of in a truly *Christian* theology. God's style is an indispensable clue, in other words, to his nature: the two are always to be related, even though they can never be equated. For the mystery of the divine Essence lives beyond the form of God's appearing, even though that Essence cannot be more nearly approached except by deeper penetration of God's historical epiphany. This dialectical statement can also be rendered, as Balthasar points out, in the time-honoured language of 'negative' and 'positive' theology which achieved Christianisation at the hands of his friend Denys. As with the sixteenth-century Spanish explorer of the divine darkness, St John of the Cross: soaring off into the heights of the *via eminentiae*, through the clouds of the *via negativa*, is only possible if one maintains constant contact with ground control, in the *via positiva*. Or, using another internal contrast in patristic divinity, that between *theologia*, an account of God in himself, and *oikonomia*, God in his self-manifestation in history: the *Anschaulichkeit*, or 'vivid discernability', of God's revealed form, must at all times be borne in mind in any account of his intrinsic mystery.

Apologetics and dogmatics

What it all comes down to, then, is a bipartite theology. Considered as apologetics or fundamental (sometimes called 'foundational') theology, a theological aesthetics will propound a theory of vision. Just as Kant used the term *Ästhetik* for his doctrine of perception via the senses, so here a Balthasarian aesthetic will treat of the perception of the revealed form of God's self-disclosure. Considered as dogmatic theology, a theological aesthetics will organise the materials of Christian doctrine around two themes: the incarnation of the divine Glory and the consequent raising up of humanity to share in its radiance. (There is here a certain family resemblance with the themes of early mediaeval monastic theology, especially among the Cistercians.) And to those who may gib at an intellectual enterprise which, from the very manner of its establishment, precludes scholarly detachment, Balthasar retorts that in theology there are no 'bare facts' to be thus dispassionately considered.

> For the object with which we are concerned [in all theology] is man's participation in God which, from God's perspective, is actualized as 'revelation' (culminating in Christ's Godmanhood) and which, from man's perspective, is actualized as 'faith' (culminating in participation in Christ's Godmanhood).[7]

This lapidary formulation carries within it a plea for change in the disposition of the theological treatises which make up Catholic divinity.

7 *GL* I, p. 125.

Because the theories of vision and rapture, of faith and salvation, are ultimately inseparable, so must be the fundamental and dogmatic theologies of which they are the aesthetic transcript. To Balthasar's mind, apologetics is incipient dogmatics, and dogmatics is matured apologetics. At the risk, then, of confounding the respective rôles of reason and faith in the reception of divine revelation, he will underscore the difference made to reason by its encounter with revealed form. Though there is, he accepts, such a thing as the *preambula fidei*, which he defines as an appropriate pointing up, in multiple ways, of the form of divine revelation (and here, no doubt, the philosophy of religion, and historical study of the evidences of special revelation, would come into play), it is a path where the *ambulans*, the walker, is already affected by the divine light – affecting him not only subjectively, from within, but objectively, from without, from the object which it is his intention to investigate as he looks at the truth-claims the Christian revelation makes.

> The facts of revelation are perceived initially in the light of grace, and faith grows in such a way that it allows the self-evidence of these facts – an evidence that itself was 'enrapturing' from the outset – to continue to unfold according to its own laws and principles.[8]

Apologetics bears all future dogmatic theology within it on its own mission of presenting, and rendering credible, to the unbeliever the 'image' of divine revelation. For this reason, the dual format of Book I of *Herrlichkeit* – on whose substantive task Balthasar will now embark – is misleading. Dividing the book – which is an initial statement of the theological aesthetics at large – into two sections which deal with respectively its subjective and objective aspects is to separate what should remain together. The subjective evidence for God's self-revelation in Christ is found, firstly, in the act of faith and its conditions of possibility, both noetic and ontological – that is, what we need to *know* before we can believe ('noetic') and what we need to *be* before we can believe ('ontological'). That same 'subjective evidence' is found, in the second place, in Christian experience, itself the normal fruit of the act of faith thus made possible. But – and this is the innovatory part of Balthasar's analysis at least insofar as modern theology is concerned – the subjective evidence in question cannot really be properly described in abstraction from the objective evidence for God's self-revelation in Christ. And *that* is found in *the compellingness of the form of revelation itself,* centred as it is on Jesus as the God-man, mediated by the New Testament Scriptures and by the Church with her sacraments and dogma, and 'attested', as Balthasar puts it, by a threefold witness. The 'witnesses' to the climactic revelation in Christ (with which, in the next Chapter, I shall end this investigation of the all-important opening volume of *Herrlichkeit*) are: the absolute Source of all being, including divine being – the Father; world history – as found in that elect representative of the nations, Old Testament Israel; and the cosmos – embodied in what biblical thought calls the 'powers' or the angels.

8 *GL* I, p. 126.

On Balthasar's account of the subject-object relationship (laid out most fully in the first volume of the theological logic), there will always be something factitious though also pedagogically justifiable about the separate description of the two. To his mind, the subject only comes to itself through the object, while the object only possesses its full signifi- cance on its entering the sphere of the subject. And what holds good of the subject-object relation at large, does not cease to be the case in this unique instance of the greeting of subject and object which is man's perception of the divine Glory in Jesus Christ. Given, moreover, that the 'subjective evidence' is as closely bound up with apologetics as the 'objective evidence' is with dogmatics, we can see why Balthasar goes out of his way to warn his readers that the greater unity of fundamental and dogmatic theology – greater in significance, that is, than is the meaning of their distinction – will hold his attention at all times.

Faith's light, faith's experience

So much said, he can now begin his exposition of the 'subjective evidence' which divine revelation has left behind itself in history – the interrelated phenomena of the light of faith and the experience of faith, as these strike and typify, respectively, a multitude of human subjects, those human beings, namely, whom we call 'Christian believers'.

He opens by pointing out something at once sublimely obvious and yet easily overlooked. We owe the peculiar importance of the concept of faith, as a way of speaking of Christian existence as a whole to what Balthasar terms those 'two great theologies which conclude the New Testament corpus' – he means the teaching of St Paul and St John. The Scriptures come to such a convergent and resounding climax on this point that for subsequent tradition 'to be a Christian and to be a believer are simply synonymous'. So important does the concept of faith come to be at the end of Scripture that its entire course can be interpreted in its light. And so the history of God's dealings with his people comes to be seen as the story of an unfolding *revelation*, to which faith is the appropriate response. I single out from all the subtle, nuanced and frequently complex things Balthasar has to say about faith as the subjective correlate of revelation, in the theologically aesthetic perspective of the perception of God's glory, three points which are pivotal for his account.

My first point to be underlined here is one already touched on, namely Balthasar's quasi-identification of believing and knowing. Like such early Alexandrian theologians as Clement, his theological *beau idéal* is the Christian gnostic. For such a one, the faith first received kerygmatically, that is, in the form of an authoritative gospel preached and heard, and in this sense exterior to the self and heteronomous, for it calls into question all the internal norms for truth, goodness and beauty the individual has so far made his own, becomes contemplatively appropriated as the believer is ever more perspicuously enlightened, the Logos uniting him interiorly to himself – something imaged by Origen in his *Commentary on John* in the figure of the beloved disciple resting intimately on the breast of Jesus. Thanks to the grace of faith, working through baptismal illumina- tion – *phōtismos*, a favoured term of the Greek church for Christian illumination – the believer comes to grasp what the historic revelation has always aimed at portraying. As Balthasar writes:

> To say that for the gnostic the earthly veil enveloping revelation has become transparent means . . . that in the letter he sees the Spirit, in the Old Testament he sees the New Testament, and in the latter the promised eternity; in Jesus' humanity he sees his divinity, and in the Son, through the Spirit, he sees the Father.[9]

Where Balthasar is more careful than the Alexandrians is in his determination never to allow such contemplative appropriation of the kerygma for one moment to be defined *over against* faith. What is involved is nothing other than the 'turning of faith to its own interior authenticity', and he connects this with Paul's insistence in his Corinthian correspondence that faith, like hope and love will endure in the face-to-face vision of God. It belongs to the messianic era, which we inhabit, that we have *knowledge of salvation*, something expressed in Pauline terms as a science and wisdom derived from the Spirit of God, and the indwelling Christ, and in John in the language of the signs of Jesus, which prompt in the disciple a vision of the glory of Christ, and of the Father's glory in Christ. 'We believe *and we know* that you are the Holy One of God' (John 6:69). Balthasar takes St Anselm to task, therefore, for what he regards as the merely partial or unilateral character of his celebrated definition of Christian reflection as 'faith seeking understanding'. The New Testament does not present faith, he claims, as searching and tentative but rather as solid and all-encompassing. Yes, in one sense the believer *is* a *quaerens*, a 'seeker', because in Balthasar's formulation faith 'interiorly strives away from the believer on into the light of God and into the evidence found in God alone', but no, such a one is not *merely quaerens*, he is also and already, *inveniens*, a 'finder', because the knowledge now given from the start in faith itself is, as Balthasar puts it, 'a knowledge which needs no further instruction so long as it remains faithful to the principle which enlightens it' – one of several theological claims in which the Swiss theologian influenced Pope John Paul II in the latter's emphasis on the strictly unnecessary nature of such subsidiary instruments of soteriological analysis as, for instance, sociological or psychological theory about human welfare and fulfilment. The authority which legitimises the act of faith as an action genuinely compatible with man's dignity as a rational agent is not only a supernatural authority, as Neo-Scholasticism was content to say, but the authority of, more specifically, the divine Glory, and this Glory bathes every aspect of the Word which is its expression in the light of divine Reason.

> God's Logos is the identity of God's free Word and of God's Reason; and, if the believer cannot at times penetrate the inner reasonableness of the free Word, nevertheless, from the sole fact that it is God speaking, he knows directly that his Word is Reason itself.[10]

9 *GL* I, p. 137.
10 *GL* I, p. 140.

A revelation of glory, Balthasar writes, 'needs no justification but itself'.

The second point to emphasise is the way Balthasar attempts to unify the entire previous history of fundamental theology, while at the same time avoiding both the Scylla of what has been called 'robotic apologetics', whereby demonstration is offered in terms of philosophical and historical argument which would *coerce* assent to the claims of Jesus as a divine legate or spokesman though not yet as Son of God and Saviour; and the Charybdis of treating faith illuministically, as the mere operation of a religious a priori, which simply finds in the data of religion whatever it is in the evolutionary development of the human spirit that it needs to encounter there. Of these two kinds of justification of Christian belief the first is typical of the officially approved apologetics of the anti-Modernist reaction in the turn-of-the-century Catholic Church, while the second is the hallmark of Catholic Modernism itself (as also of Liberal Protestantism which deeply affected the exegetical style of the Catholic Modernists, though not their ecclesiology) and constitutes the ever-present danger to which Transcendental Idealism, as represented by the disciples of Karl Rahner, is exposed. If the second is doctrinally unacceptable, the first, to Balthasar's taste, is theologically unpalatable. And yet, as he explains, each is a distorted presentation of one of two authentically traditional and in fact complementary kinds of apologetic – two sorts of initial, approach to the mystery of Christ.

The revelatory form of Christianity, what Newman in the *Essay on Development*, termed its 'Idea', may be read in two ways. First, it may be interpreted in terms of the 'historical signs and the manifestations of an acting God', signs and manifestations which, in their intrinsic credibility and their convergence (what Balthasar calls their 'reciprocal support') constitute persuasive appeals to human reason. Secondly the revealed form may be approached as the self-attesting of God's eternal truth which, as the inwardness of absolute Being, is itself the proper, if ultimate, object of the striving of the human spirit towards the real. Once revealed in the trinitarian disclosure of Jesus Christ – for absolute Being, as will emerge from the completed whole of the theological logic – is essentially absolute Love and hence the Holy Trinity, this eternal reality of God is fallen upon by the spiritual subject (ourselves) with a glad cry.

What Balthasar does is to marry these characteristic approaches of, on the one hand, Baroque Neo-Scholasticism and, on the other, Alexandrian and Augustinian theology, with the result that the deficiencies of each are made good by the advantages of the other. This happy union is achieved by the rethinking both of an apologetics of ostensive sign, the first approach, and that of interior light, the second approach, by reference to the fundamental categories of a theological aesthetics. As he writes:

The beautiful is above all a *form*, and the light does not fall on this form from above and from outside, rather it breaks forth from the form's interior. *Species* and *lumen*, in beauty are one, if the *species* truly merits that name (which does not designate any form whatever, but pleasing radiant form). Visible form not only 'points' to an invisible, unfathomable mystery; form is the apparition of this mystery, and reveals it while, naturally, at the same time protecting and veiling it. Both natural and artistic form has an exterior which appears and an interior depth, both of which, however, are not separable in the form itself. The content does not lie behind the form but within it. Whoever is not capable of seeing and reading the form will, by the same token, fail to perceive the content. Whoever is not illumined by the form will see no light in the content either.[11]

The 'form' in that passage is of course that of Jesus Christ seen as the organising mid-point of the entire constellation of apologetically persuasive biblical signs in both Old and New Covenants.

The third and final pillar supporting Balthasar's exposition of the 'subjective evidence' which faith brings to the exploration of revelation, concerns the notion of Christian experience, which not many years before his publication of *Herrlichkeit* I had been something of a conceptual *persona non grata* in Catholic theology, owing to its association with, on the one hand, Lutheran and Reformed ideas of assurance and election, and on the other, the attempt of Modernism to drag magisterial doctrine before the bar of 'religious experience', its claims or demands. Really, until the epoch-making *L'Expérience chrétienne* of the abbé Jean Mouroux was published in 1952 (and this is, incidentally, a book to which Balthasar refers gratefully on a number of occasions) the consensus of Catholic theological opinion tended to regard Christian experience as a synonym for mystical experience, and so to treat it as a resource only for ascetical and mystical theology and hagiology. A faith which is essentially *ex auditu*, coming from hearing, could, it was thought, scarcely appeal to experience in the construing of its own central dogmata. Balthasar, while holding mysticism not only in honour but also as fruitful for theology as a whole (with Adrienne von Speyr at his elbow he could hardly have done otherwise), is obliged by his recasting of both dogmatic theology and fundamental theology as a theological aesthetics for which perceptual acts are indispensable, to re-evaluate in a more positive light the significance of Christian experience for the entire spectrum of theological treatises and topics. Indeed, the two issues I have already isolated as of special interest in this first half of the opening volume of the aesthetics – the light of faith as internal to the revelatory form and the unity of faith and knowledge – already point in this direction. If it is by obedient surrender to the radiant light of the revelatory form that the subject can share in the wisdom of the self-revealing God, then, in matters of theology, the 'more obediently one thinks' (as Balthasar puts it) 'the more accurately he will see'. Thinking is only Christian if the form of revelation impresses itself on human subjects in their whole existence – which must include their intellectual life. If, again, faith is to grasp itself in knowledge, its act must be so deeply rooted in the person, and the person so obedient to the divine light, that such faith, as the seed of glory, becomes the norm of his or her entire being. 'This is why', Balthasar writes,

the deepening and revitalisation of the person which occurs within the act of faith (as a living act which includes love and hope) has

11 *GL* I, p. 151.

been described by Thomas, along with the whole tradition, as the unfolding of the Spirit of God in the spirit of man. The 'gifts of the Holy Spirit', bestowed seminally by grace, lead the believer to an ever deeper awareness and experience both of the presence within him of God's being and of the depth of the divine truth, goodness and beauty in the mystery of God.[12]

And yet in introducing here the word 'experience', Balthasar takes every precaution to guard against the possibility of its abuse, and notably its possible hijacking by those who would degrade the authority of Scripture and Church Tradition. By presenting Christian experience as a derived participation in what he calls 'archetypal' biblical experience – the biblically testified experience of God by Israel and then Jesus Christ, as of Christ as the God-man, by the Mother of Christ and the apostolic eye-witnesses – Balthasar creates for it a deliberately subordinate place beneath Scripture. At the same time, by describing distinctively ecclesial experience in terms of four structuring factors – not only the Pauline, which he defines in terms of the irruption of charismatic and visionary graces productive of mission, and the Johannine which concerns both contemplative love and the onward march of the Church to the heavenly Jerusalem, but also a Petrine structuring factor which through preaching and sacraments hierarchically incorporates the apostolic eye-witness into the succeeding Church, and a marian defining element which makes Mother Church (like the original virgin-mother) essentially bodily and visible, her sacraments and institutions the occasion for the spiritual experiencing of Christ and of God, Balthasar gives ecclesial experience, likewise, a crucial inward orientation to the *sensus fidei*, to the total, hierarchically ordered Church's feeling for revelation as transmitted in tradition.

> . . . The Church, basing herself first and last on the experience of the Lord's Mother in the flesh, who was the Believer pure and simple, can teach her children the Word of God and communicate to them from the heart of her motherly and bridal experience not only its meaning but its taste, its smell, and its whole incarnational concreteness . . . As an individual I can respond correctly [to the Word of God] only within the context of this unified and total answer: and this total answer is all-embracing and feminine, and, for this reason, it is especially adapted to the sensory realm.[13]

---

12 *GL* I, p. 166.
13 *GL* I, pp. 421–422.

3

❧❧❧

The Objective Evidence

Revelation in form

It might be thought entirely obvious that, if one is to have a religious world-view at all then some kind of objective revelatory form – some self-presentation of the divine in terms drawn from the world – is a necessity. And yet, as Balthasar points out, in principle a religious vision or system *could* dispense with objective revelatory form altogether. If for instance with *advaita* (non-dual) Hinduism, one considered that ultimately God and self are identical and only apparently separated by veils of illusion which account for the human experience of error, guilt and finitude, then the need for objective revelatory form disappears. In point of fact, the call for an objective mediation of the divine Spirit, the requirement that revelation be concrete, though it may strike non-Christian or post-Christian readers as quite reasonable (whether they think such a form de facto available to perception or not), depends on presuppositions found within the body of the Church's dogmata; and notably three which Balthasar now spells out. They are: creation, incarnation and Trinity.

The presuppositions of form
First, creation. A world which has been brought into existence gratuitously, as the act of an infinitely free subjectivity, namely God, is not a world where the human religious subject could ever be regarded as self-identical with the divine. Moreover, because of God's transcendence of the world, and so of man, even were God to communicate purely interiorly with the human soul he could not dispense with some kind of spiritual form in which to communicate himself. A totally unmediated self-revelation of God to man is therefore unthinkable. Not that there is any need to think in terms of a purely interior contact between God and man anyway, for as the Creator, God has provided a general revelation of his glory in the creation – however much what Scripture says of him in this context, as, for instance, Paul in Romans, emphasises the far greater dissimilarity between God and creatures. The glory of God is already seen, in general terms, in the form of the world.

Secondly, the incarnation is precisely the pouring out of God's glory into the form of the world in one of its principal embodiments, humankind. *A* form is thus taken up so that God may transfigure the whole of creation. This self-revelation of God in Christ is not a mere prolongation or intensification of the revelation given with the creation. The personal substance of the Father in his Word is now lavished on the world. And yet, because the creation was from the beginning oriented towards its own supernatural elevation, and because too the incarnation, taken in the fulness of its unfolding, from the annunciation, through the resurrection to the parousia, entails the bringing together of everything in heaven and *on earth* under one divine–human Head, it follows that the self-manifestation of God in Jesus Christ brings the form of the world to its perfection, and in that way uncovers the fulness of its significance for the first time.

Thirdly, the Trinity: the form of the revelation in Christ is perceived as the unsurpassable perfecting of the form of the world only when it comes to be seen, by the eyes of faith, as the appearing of the triune God. What appears in Christ is, for Balthasar, the 'becoming visible and experience-able' of the divine Triunity.[1] The glorious, transcendent quality which comes through in the figure of Jesus is not, as Balthasar puts it, the manifestation of a formless divine Infinite, but the 'appearance of an infinitely determined super-form'. The Trinity, as the ultimate source of Being, is infinite, yes, but not infinite in the negative Hellenic sense of *to apeiron*, that which has no boundaries and is therefore formless. God's infinitude takes the form of the circling intercommunication of Father, Son and Spirit, the expression of which in the creation leads to the indefinite profusion of finite forms we find in the world. Of course what distinguishes the form of Jesus Christ from all other forms is that here, thanks to the hypostatic union, we are not dealing simply with *an image* produced by the trinitarian super-form in impressing itself on created being. For here in the God-man both *image* and the *archetype of the image* are available in *one single being*. The image does not stand over against the archetype, as with all other forms, but is of interest – that is, *Jesus' humanity* is of interest – only inasmuch as in this image (and nowhere else) *God* really portrays himself in the fulness of his inter-personal, yet absolute being – making this form, Jesus Christ, what Balthasar calls

> the crowning recapitulation of everything in heaven and on earth [and hence] the form of all forms and the measure of all measures, just as for this reason it is the glory of all glories in creation as well.[2]

As the revelation of the free, creating and self-incarnating triune God, then, revelation *necessarily* has an 'objective form'.

Before going on to speak of Jesus Christ as the centre or midpoint of this form (and this is where Balthasar will make it most explicit that he is engaged in a Catholic version of Barth's Christocentrising revolution of theology in the *Church Dogmatics*), a number of broader – and not

---

1 *GL* I, p. 432.
2 Ibid.

only profound but also sometimes difficult – points remain to be made more widely on the topic of the Christological character of revelatory form at large.

The Christological character of form

To begin with, under the rubric of the form 'as fact' Balthasar reminds us of the conclusions he has already reached, with the help of the philosophical concepts outlined in the first volume of his theological logic, on the way Jesus Christ originally strikes us with his revelatory claim. Here he recontextualises those conclusions by reference to the incarnationalist and ultimately trinitarian presuppositions which, whether they are adverted to or not, are the source of the insistence that revelation must have objective form, and give such insistence whatever validity it possesses. Like any wonderful aesthetic form, Jesus is both the sparkling radiance of being, a light, and the imagistic representation of being's non-apparent depth, a sign. This truth of theological aesthetics in its apologetic mood – that is, in its concern with *subjective evidence* – can now be re-expressed in dogmatic terms – that is, in terms of the *objective* revelatory *form*. The 'image and expression of God' is the 'indivisible God-man: man, insofar as God radiates from him; God insofar as he appears in the man Jesus'.[3] Balthasar offers an extended meditation on the opening text of the Letter to the Hebrews with its contrast of the 'manifold and fragmentary ways in which God spoke of old to the fathers through the prophets', and the fashion in which in these last days God has spoken to us by a son who is the 'heir of all things', 'reflecting the glory of God' and 'bearing the very stamp of his nature' (1:2–3). Since he not only possesses historical facticity, as the human Jesus, linked to his forefathers by the biological and cultural continuum, but is at the same time God's mighty Word, sustaining all creation, the Son can inherit both the words of the Old Testament and what the Greek Fathers called the *logoi* of creatures – the intelligibility bestowed on them with their concrete natures by the Creator and which Balthasar prefers to term the 'individual words of Being'. Creatures are such words of the Being that flows from God only because of the divine generativity or outgoingness whereby the Father from all eternity produced his essential Word, and similarly, they are a glorious manifestation of God in the creation only because the Word and Son is everlastingly the 'radiant splendour of [the Father's] glory' and the 'im-pression and ex-pression' of the Father's reality as God – Balthasar's paraphrase of a metaphor of sealing which deliberately accentuates the iconographic or at any rate aesthetic quality of the Hebrews formulation. And drawing on the conclusions of his study of St Maximus, *Kosmische Liturgie*, Jesus Christ could not be the 'point of intersection of all partial words of history and of all individual words of Being if he were merely either the "factual" man Jesus or the supra-historical, all-sustaining Logos'.[4]

Taken in conjunction with the language of *doxa*, glory, in the opening affirmation of the letter, Hebrews, then, ascribes to Jesus Christ both

3 *GL* I, p. 437.
4 *GL* I, p. 435.

flowing radiance and impressed form, the two complementing each other in giving expression to the primal Beauty, a primal Beauty which is identical with the man Jesus, who descends simultaneously from the prophets and fathers and from *the* Father whose Son he is. For Balthasar the revelatory form is endangered whenever the unity of structure whereby the glory of God is seen in the face of Christ is tampered with, whether (as sometimes in Athanasius and Thomas Aquinas) by treating the humanity assumed as simply the 'conjoined instrument' of the Logos, or, Platonically or idealistically, by regarding the corporeality of Christ as at best a starting point for spiritual reflection, at worst a concealment which must be laid aside. Picking up a concern of Karl Rahner's in the early volume of his theological *Schriften*, Balthasar underlines the indispensability of the humanity of Christ even for the beatific vision.

> The glory of God is nowhere, not for a single instant, separated from the Lamb, nor is the light of the Trinity divorced from the light of Christ, the Incarnate Son, in whom alone the cosmos is recapitulated and elevated to the rank of the bridal City.[5]

Kierkegaard, taking up a theme of Luther's Christology, had regarded the Son who was made not only man but 'sin' as being, in the humanity which was his in a fallen and guilty world, someone hidden *sub contrario* – beneath their own contrary. That entailed the 'crucifixion' of the senses of those who would have liked to perceive the glory of God in Jesus Christ in an appealing way. But Balthasar takes just the opposite view. True, the sin of the world obliges God's expressive image to adopt a particular modality – going down into the darkness of the passion, the death and Hades itself. But so far from abolishing the revelatory character of the sensuous image, the cross and its consequences *intensify* it, so that it becomes the *supreme* self-expression, to human perception, of God's eternal life. Anticipating not only the last chapters of the theological aesthetics but also the theological dramatics and its important extended footnote *Mysterium Paschale*, Balthasar finds in the final intensification of the form in the atoning sacrifice of Jesus Christ the reason why surprise at the more seemingly improbable of the Church's doctrines, such as the eucharistic presence and the resurrection of the flesh, is out of place. All of this is, as he puts it: 'already included in the self-commitment of God who with divine freedom, but also with divine consistency, has fashioned for himself in his creation a body through which to reveal his glory'.[6]

This is not to say, however, that the revelation of God in Jesus Christ is something blindingly obvious. After all, not only in a Protestant setting Luther, but also in a Catholic one, the familiar and profound devotional lyric ascribed to St Thomas – the *Adoro te* – says of Calvary and the Eucharist, respectively: 'on the cross thy godhead made no sign to men/ here thy very manhood steals from human ken' (in Hopkins' translation).

---

5 *GL* I, pp. 438–439; cf. K. Rahner, S.J., 'The Eternal Significance of the Humanity of Jesus for our Relationship with God', *Theological Investigations* I (E.t. London 1967), pp. 35–46.
6 *GL* I, p. 441.

This is a revelation, certainly, but a revelation in hiddenness: nor is this concession anything to be wondered at, given the general ontology Balthasar regaled his readers with in the opening volume of his theological logic. For there we read that, though Being indeed appears, the worldly forms whose imagistic surfaces invite us to interpret the beings that are the words of Being, do not, for that very reason, make Being perfectly plain. Being appears in beings, and concretely, in the forms which we can read off from images in the world around us, but that is precisely to say that Being does not present itself to us in an immediate way. Furthermore, the mediated self-presentation of Being is never done in such a manner that we can suck out from it Being's exhaustive content. Part of the fascination of form lies in its pointing us towards depths that do not appear. What all this boils down to, therefore, is that in the very moment of its unveiling, its disclosure, Being also conceals itself. Its self-revelation, just because it is the revelation of an inexpressible plenitude, necessarily comes over to us as a veiling, an enclosure. And if then there is some analogy between the revelation of Being in form, and the revelation of the glory of the Father in Jesus Christ, we are already prepared for Balthasar's confession that Christian revelation is not only an all-illuminating fact but also, and equally, a revelation in hiddenness. 'Truly, you are a hidden God, O God of Israel' (Isa. 45:13).

In *Herrlichkeit*, three reasons are adduced by way of explanation of this cry of wonder from the Hebrew Bible. Only the first has so far been touched on – namely, that the revelation of God is a revelation in being. Balthasar takes the opportunity to deepen the analogy of disclosure and concealment in, respectively, revelation and the beauty found in nature and art. An artist will conceal himself in his work as well as reveal himself. Desiring to manifest the world as he has understood it, 'his' world or perspective on the world, *Weltanschauung*, he makes himself of little prominence. Of course with God, every possible world that he may make will point to its author; and yet this thought is counterbalanced by another, that the distance in God between Creator and work is infinite. At this juncture we need an analogy with *natural* beauty in order to dispel any Deistic misunderstanding of the model of visual art: the world is not the canvas of a divine Rembrandt or the fugue of a divine Bach, a letter from God which once despatched becomes detached from him. Here it is better to think, rather, of the relation between the forms of nature, *natura naturata*, and the self-expressing life-principle, *natura naturans*, at work in those forms in a *necessary*, *internal* and *living* way. And showing his debt to the dramatists, philosophers and poets of the age of Romanticism and Idealism in Germany, Balthasar remarks that 'we are initiated into these mysteries [of cosmic forms] because we ourselves are spirit in nature, and because all the expressive laws of the macrocosm are at work in ourselves'.[7] In the steps of Goethe's morphology of nature, Balthasar maintains that nature is most fully grasped, not with the combination of observation and quantification of the exact sciences, but by expressly including the dimension of mystery within the act of observing. In such a reading of form the fragment points to the whole.

7 *GL* I, p. 444.

And this brings Balthasar to an important corollary of the claim that revelation is necessarily revelation in hiddenness for the simple reason that it is a revelation in being. All knowledge, and not just the knowledge of salvation, begins with a kind of 'natural faith'. For the early apologist, Theophilus of Antioch, all human conduct depends on a certain trusting faith both in nature and in Providence. Similarly, against Eunomius, the Cappadocian Fathers argued that even the tiniest creature can be grasped only through its utterances, so hidden is even creaturely *ousia*. The conclusion is, in Balthasar's words, that 'a "supernatural" piety, ordered to God's historical revelation, cannot be such unless it is mediated by a "natural" piety, which at this level presupposes and includes a "piety of nature" and a "piety of Being"'.[8] The critical history of metaphysics in volumes 4 and 5 of the theological aesthetics will bring this out.

But we still have to consider the second and third reasons why revelation is necessarily as much concealment as it is disclosure. The second is that revelation takes place in the Word, the free divine Word, which as such cannot be captured within the net of the created order. As Balthasar puts it: 'Creaturely beings, thrown into existence, reveal themselves in obedience to a natural necessity; but God creates freely.'[9] From which he draws the conclusion that while the contingency, the non-necessity, of the world has the positive effect of revealing God as the world's free Creator, for nothing comes from nothing, by that self-same fact the world's contingency conceals God more dramatically than it reveals him, since at no point can we make any firm deduction about the final meaning of his unique Essence. What, then, one might object, becomes of the claim with which Balthasar opened the entire second part of *Herrlichkeit* I, with the help of Hebrews, that the form of creation is at all times radiant with God's glory? His reply, along the lines of his earlier attempt to render the teaching of the First Vatican Council on the divine knowability more palatable to Karl Barth, is that

> We will never be able to determine exactly the extent to which this splendour, given with creation itself, coincides objectively with what Christian theology calls 'supernatural revelation', which, at least for Adam, was not yet a specifically distinct revelation given in the form of words. A distinction is possible only from the standpoint of intention and in this sense the first word was directed to man as a creature that had come forth from God, and the second word addresses him personally as a child of God's grace and calls him home to the heart of God.[10]

Because, then, no creaturely form as such transcribes in straightforward fashion the meaning of God's sovereignly *free* Word, a revelation which takes place in that Word must always be to some degree riddling. The revelatory Form will not so much leap to the eye as require strenuous discernment. And because the Word in which it comes to be as form is *sovereignly* free, the human percipient will not be able to follow the

8 *GL* I, p. 447.
9 *GL* I, p. 448.
10 *GL* I, p. 449.

archetype in the image without the willingness to practise obedience. The concept of obedience, drawn from Paul and Ignatius Loyola,[11] is crucial to Balthasar's theology in various of its sectors – not least here where, as he writes:

> before [infinite Freedom] created reason must persevere in an attitude of primary obedience that is beyond all demands, longings, enterprises. This is the manner in which God's Word really touches the creature at the most intimate point of its self-transcending being[12]

– what Paul calls the 'obedience of faith' (Rom. 1:5).

The third and last reason why the revelatory form will necessarily be a form that hides as well as discloses is that it is a revelation *in the human*. If *man* is to become the language of God then the unique will have to appear in the ordinary, the super-significant in the insignificant. By and large, supernatural revelation, the revelation of grace in Old and New Testaments, is not so much the establishment of a new form in the world as it is a new manner of God's presence in the form of the world. In the Adamic state, Balthasar speculates, God's speaking of this message – that man is now called to be the child of the Father – would have come purely through a *locutio interna*: God's presence through grace would have resounded unmistakably in the voices of nature and of the heart. It is owing to the deafness of fallen humanity that the *locutio Dei* becomes a *locutio externa*, a word spoken from outside, for the Old Covenant in law and prophecy, for the New in the incarnate Word and its prolongation as the Word found in the Church. There is then a *penitential* aspect to a revelation made through audible and visible human signs. That is so even though those signs are the outward expression of the interior inspiration of prophets and apostles and notwithstanding too the fact that by means of them God can lead human history, despite its self-inflicted chaos, to an even more wonderful fulfilment than that offered to Adam – by way of the glory that emanates from the sign of the cross.

God's revelation takes place in man by in the first instance *judging* man. But that for Balthasar has not only a negative charge; it has a positive one as well. In judgment, God both manifests his sublime transcendence over against all that is worldly and at the same time makes known his immanence within the human which he sets out to fulfil by *redirecting humanity to himself*. In conformity with the usual Balthasarian principle that, in divine matters, comparability and incomparability with the world develop in direct proportion to each other: the more God makes known his justice in the saints of Israel (the more, that is, he reveals himself), the more colossally unlike them he shows himself to be (and so the more he hides his face). As Balthasar puts it:

> The whole ascending period of God's revelation in Israel is also the time of an ever greater concealment of God, in spite of the ever greater evidence pointing to a revelation which is truly unique and different from all other religions.

11 See 'Introduction to Balthasar', above, for the Ignatian dimension.
12 *GL* I, p. 451.

And, illustrating this claim from the post-exilic period:

> The return which appears to fulfil the promises is everything but fulfilment, and, while interiorly the Holy Spirit is bringing the canon of the Scriptures to maturity, externally the kingdom is disintegrating even before Christ's coming, so that Yahweh's faithful ones can understand themselves only as the 'remnant' which survives what spiritually has already fallen into decay.

The conclusion is that

> while he is quite comprehensible in his revelation and even demands the understanding of faith, the God of Israel proves himself in history to be ever more incomprehensible and, as such, he exhibits himself ever more truly as who he is. And only the most living kind of faith, sustained by revelation, is capable of knowing him in precisely this form of revelation as the true and living God.[13]

This is the pattern which is brought to perfection by the simultaneously consummate revelation-and-concealment of God in the man Jesus. Even without referring as yet to the passion of Christ, the incarnation of the Word – his embodiment as flesh – means the most extreme manifestness of God, for now God is explained to man not chiefly through words or instruction, but through his own being and life. In other words, he interprets himself to man by no other medium than himself. And yet at the same time, the entry of the Godhead into its human creation is the most complete concealing imaginable. In language drawn, surely, from Kierkegaard's treatise on *The Difference Between a Genius and an Apostle*, Balthasar speaks of the Flesh-taking as the 'translation of God's absolutely unique, absolute and infinite Being into the ever more dissimilar, almost arbitrary and hopelessly relativised reality of one individual man in the crowd'.[14] The hiddenness of this individual lost in history would not be so scandalous as an expression of the Word if it were meant to represent the silence of the Word, God's sheer concealment from all that is not God. But no, this hiddenness is to be the speech in which God eloquently makes known in a definitive manner what he himself is really like.

For Balthasar none of this is intelligible unless we approach the figure of Christ in a way determined by one ecclesial doctrine – that of the Trinity – and one philosophical doctrine – that of God as, in the fifteenth-century cardinal theologian Nicholas of Cusa's phrase, the *Non-Aliud*, the 'Not Other', which is the positive aspect of his Being as the 'wholly Other', the non-competitiveness implied in his unconditional transcendence. Readers of the Gospels will soon discover that Jesus was in simultaneous fashion extraordinarily humble and amazingly self-certain, that he was incredibly unassuming yet overwhelmingly exigent in his demands, lamblike in meekness yet leonine in angry zeal. For Balthasar these tensions may

13 *GL* I, p. 456.
14 *GL* I, p. 457.

reveal polar aspects of Christ's humanity, but they can be understood, and above all, *resolved*, only when considered as functions of the trinitarian dimensions of his being. 'Although only the Son of God is man, his humanity necessarily becomes the expression of the total triune essence of God; only thus can he be the manifestness of absolute Being.'[15] But because the Holy Trinity, as the concrete form of absolute Being, is not in competition with any of the forms internal to its own creation, God in Christ can reveal himself as both God and man – not alternatingly but simultaneously .

These complications of the dialectic of revelation and concealment in the sensory form of the incarnation are intensified, yet also cut through and simplified, by the passion and death of the incarnate one. For now we have to discover in the deformity of Christ, his *Ungestalt* – the 'he had no comeliness that we might desire him' of the Suffering Servant (Isa. 53:2) – a mystery of *Uebergestalt*, of transcendental form. His being made sin for us (2 Cor. 5:21) is, in a key statement of Baltharian theology, 'understandable only as a function of the glory of love'. Thus precisely in the cross and the descent into darkness we have before us pure glory; the concealment now becomes a function of its opposite, the revelation. Just as an art redolent of the precarious and fragmentary character of earthly beauty can move us to tears because it awakens in us a kind of eschatological hope, a hope aroused by the promise of splendour it seems to contain, so the form of the Redeemer takes the ways of being of a fallen world onto itself so as by redemptive suffering to give them new and unheard of value. Here, despite all that has been said so far about the hiddenness which hangs about the revelatory form, the dialectic of revelation and concealment is basically resolved in favour of revelation, for the hiddenness is now not the non-appearing depth of the being revealed, but the overwhelmingness of its totally open disclosure.

> God's incomprehensibility is now no longer a mere deficiency in knowledge but the positive manner in which God determines the knowledge of faith: this is the overpowering and overwhelming inconceivability of the fact that God has loved us so much that he surrendered his only Son for us, the fact that the God of plenitude has poured himself out, not only into creation, but emptied himself into the modalities of an existence determined by sin, corrupted by death and alienated from God. This [alone] is the concealment that appears in his self-revelation.[16]

Jesus Christ himself as centre of the form

Which seems a good point at which to move onto Christ as the centre or mid-point of the revelatory form. Here Balthasar discusses such themes as the plausibility of the Christ-form, its measure and quality, power and uniqueness, and how its rejection or misapprehension can be explained theologically. Essentially, this section of the theological

15 *GL* I, p. 458.
16 *GL* I, p. 461.

aesthetics is Balthasar's engagement with other, conflicting Christologies; it contains some of his sharpest writing in this otherwise serene if passionate work, and notably his most acerbic remarks about the contemporary critical study of the Gospels.

For Balthasar Christ is the centre of the form of revelation: that is, he alone makes the total form of supernatural revelation coherent and comprehensible. The plausibility of Christianity stands or falls with Jesus Christ. To support such an edifice the foundation must be indestructibly solid: it cannot deal in mere probabilities, or in subjective evidence alone. Despite the richness of his doctrine of the subjective evidence for revelation, here Balthasar is firm. The subjective conditions for the possibility of seeing an object for what it is must not be allowed to intrude on the description of that object's intrinsic authority – in Balthasar's terms the constitution of its 'objective evidence'. Even the scholastic axiom that 'whatever is received is received according to the mode of the receiver' is to be brushed aside in this context along with those of its modern variants which would have it that the object in question requires a categorical or existential prior understanding, some idea or some felt human need to which it can correspond. For, in a most important programmatic statement:

> if Christ is what he claims to be, then he cannot be so dependent on subjective conditions as to be hindered by them from making himself wholly understandable to man nor, contrariwise, can man, without his grace, supply the sufficient conditions of receiving him with full understanding.[17]

Here hermeneutics, whether cultural or philosophical, are sent packing, on the grounds that One who is both God and man cannot but draw what is universally valid in human life and thought to himself. Balthasar's aesthetic Christology will consist in bringing out the form and content of Christ's revelation as the New Testament presents it. In the last analysis, Christ is the all-important form because he is the all-sufficient content, the only Son of the Father. The aim will be, first, to show the interior rightness and intrinsic power of this form – as we might ascribe that to a sovereign work of art or a mathematical formula of extraordinary precision as well as beauty, and secondly, to point up its power to transform all existence by its light. Balthasar's essential objection to much modern Gospel study is that by, for instance, bracketing the trinitarian dimension of the unfolding form of the Redeemer, or its issue in the bodily resurrection, or by decomposing that form into, on the one hand, a Jesus of history and, on the other, a Christ of faith, it renders the rest of the New Testament – beyond the Gospels – unintelligible. As he remarks, each element is 'plausible only within the wholeness of the image'.[18]

And here, so as not to anticipate excessively the fuller christological exposition of the final volume of *Herrlichkeit*, I shall simply sketch some of the aspects of the Christ-form which Balthasar regards as foundational.

17 *GL* I, p. 465.
18 *GL* I, p. 467.

Under 'measure and form', for instance, he deals with the perfect con-cordance between Christ's mission and his existence, something which is, he shows, not merely a Johannine theologoumenon but a given of the Synoptic tradition for which Jesus identified his existence with his divine mandate – which explains why without hesitation he could throw that existence onto the weighing-scales of history. Moreover, as the identity between the divine demand and the human fulfilment he is *the* measure, the norm of right relations, first with God and then, since God wills it so, with neighbour: thus the Pauline identification of Jesus as the 'righteousness of God' is but the re-expression of the Synoptic testimony of how he claimed for himself an authoritative power, manifest accord-ing to his hearers in his words, and sovereignly communicated to his followers. Punning on the German words for 'to tune' and 'to be in tune' as well as for a 'pitch' of music or of mood, and hence in the latter case, for 'disposition', as well as 'harmony' and 'concordance' – here Balthasar's study of the Swiss Romantic theologian Gügler has stood him in good stead, he draws the theologically aesthetic conclusion that, by trans-ference into the kingdom of the Word's marvellous light 'we already participate in the sphere where things are fundamentally right and attuned and where, therefore, if we so will it, things can be similarly right for us as well'. And, reverting to the language of measure, while address-ing the issue of Jesus and his community, he writes:

> With the appearance of Christ, the Church is already posited: that is to say, his appearance is the measure which God applies to the world, the measure God has already communicated to the world, bestowed on the world, as a measure of grace and not of judgment, as a freely conferred measure which no one can arrogate to himself but which is given in such a way that anyone so desiring can take it to himself.[19]

According to Balthasar anyone with an 'eye for quality' can see the difference in *this* phenomenon as it unfolds. He notes, with Pascal, how the evidential power of this form does no violence to personal freedom and decision: since love is its content, it cannot impose but only testify to its own authenticity – this is where Balthasar locates the Marcan messianic secret and the Johannine hidden glory. He records the inner harmony of the form: no mistake in its construction or proportions is discernible.

> The interrelatedness of the different aspects is such that, while each aspect, taken in isolation, could be considered questionable, none-theless the balance that dominates the whole does not allow the definitive elimination of any one aspect.[20]

This *interdependence of aspects* of the Four Gospels as, in their convergent totality, they left the hands of their final redactors, though frequently denied by historical-critical exegesis, accounts for the fascination of the

19 *GL* I, p. 478.
20 *GL* I, p. 486.

Christ-form not only to ecclesial contemplation but also to academic exegesis itself which – Balthasar cunningly remarks – cannot turn away from its object even as it fiercely disputes it.

The complexity of this form does not, however, overthrow its *unity*, though Christ's particular kind of unity requires a 'glance that traces a course back into the very mystery of God', since he is both himself and another – the divine being. In the mystery of divine freedom, as in that of art, a supreme freedom can coincide with a perfect obedience or necessity. An aria by Mozart could hardly be other than it is, yet it has all of Schiller's definition of beauty as *erscheinende Freiheit*, 'freedom appearing'.

Balthasar links such 'necessary freedom' to what he terms the effort-lessness of Jesus' self-representation, his simplicity. It is a simplicity sought for by all the religions of Asia but never found by them since – disastrously – they seek it in technique as well as – fatally – aiming at God through bypassing man. In contrast, Christ's simplicity is a lived sharing in the divine simplicity, from a centre (Balthasar is referring to the hypostatic union) where the duality of God and man is bridged and God's Word has become indistinguishable from its human expression.

All of this makes the form of Christ both inherently powerful and unique. We sometimes note of a great work of art its power to touch and even alter the lives of those who come into contact with it. Such power, *dunamis*, Paul ascribes to Christ not only in his resurrection but also – already – in his cross. Taken by itself, the image of Christ would remain merely two-dimensional. Only the power which the New Testament goes on to identify as 'Holy Spirit' gives that image plasticity and vitality so that it can form, transform, the lives of believers. Even if it is only in the Spirit of the resurrection and Pentecost that Jesus becomes Lord, as the Spirit bestows on form and on the gospel an interior vitality – the intrinsic power these need if they are to impress themselves (whether on the individual disciple in justification or on the apostolic preaching itself), nonetheless this same Spirit *proceeds from Christ*. He is the dynamism which Christ radiates. Included in the objective evidence for revelatory form is, therefore, the existence of the Christian saints, for their enthu-siasm – and here Balthasar distances himself from Ronald Knox's pejorative use of that term in the history of spirituality – constitutes a *precise* response to the precision of the image of Jesus drawn by the Spirit.

But this form is not only powerful. It is also unique. Jesus escapes classification by any typology known to comparative religion, religious phenomenology or cultural anthropology. He differs from other religious founders who proposed to reveal a way by declaring himself to be *the* way, identifying himself with the 'myth' of the sacrificed but fructifying grain which he preaches. Whereas they underwent experiences of conversion, enlightenment, rapture, his teaching is identified with his entire existence. He achieves no divine apotheosis through the successful crowning of a human drama, but the drama of his human dissolution becomes the revelation of divine love. In contrast to the other schemes of salvation on offer, he neither negates the being of the world for the sake of divine being nor restores some divine primordial principle of worldly being now obscured; instead he negates the decadent mode of the world's existence in its alienation from God, lifting it up through the exercise of his sacrificial charity – thus simultaneously recognising *both* the foundational goodness of created being *and* its radical need of redemption. In disclosing the mystery of the Trinity, and its indissoluble yet unconfused union with humanity in his own person, he also solves the central problem of religious metaphysics, that problem of the One and the Many which has defeated all other religions, constrained as they are to remain midway between the One and the Many, as with Islam, or to abolish the Many for the sake of One, as in Asiatic mysticism, or to incorporate the One into the Many as in polytheism and pantheism. At the same time, the Christ-form is not unique in such a fashion that it appears as a bolt from the blue, unrelated to all about it. On the contrary, it is related, through the Old Testament, to the treasury of natural religious forms found in human experience, related, then, to an overall order of which, however, it does not itself form part. Its uniqueness is all the more striking for being set within a general historical determinateness, and as Balthasar points out:

> By fulfilling in himself Israel's message of promise, Christ at the same time makes historical contact, through Israel, with mankind's religious forms, and in this way, too, he fulfils not only Israel's expectation but the longing of all peoples.[21]

His form relates to itself 'as the ultimate centre the comparative uniqueness of all other forms and images of the world', whatever their source.

By now enough has been said to indicate how the misapprehension – the mistaking – of this form is feasible. As Balthasar puts it; 'A whole symphony cannot be recorded on a tape that is too short.' The 'shortness' may lie in our not making sufficient space for God's almightiness, the range of his possibilities. It may lie in a premature decision not to attend to certain of the Christ-form's interdependent parts (for Balthasar, heresy *is* the 'selective disjoining of parts'). Or it may lie in erecting a screen which foreshortens the image cast by the divine Glory, owing to some prior methodological, conceptual or historic-religious commitment, or any combination thereof. And behind all of these things there lies the mystery of iniquity, the 'darkness which does not see, recognise or receive the Light'. The tone of the preacher, never wholly silent in Balthasar's theology, returns with peculiar vigour at the close of his account of the objective revelatory form when he delineates, in conclusion, the figure of the apostate.

> Through and through he remains branded by the image he rejects: with terrible power this image leaves its imprint on his whole existence, which blazes brilliantly in the fire of denial. Wherever the fugitive may turn his glance he is met by the 'eyes like flames of fire', he hears the 'voice like the roar of mighty waters', he feels the 'sharp two-edged sword from his mouth', and he hides in vain from the 'face like the sun blazing with full strength'. (Apoc. 1:14ff.)[22]

21 *GL* I, p. 498.
22 *GL* I, pp. 524–525.

Mediation of the form

In what way, then, is this supreme form 'mediated' to us, and how is it 'attested'? As to *mediation*, Balthasar's answer to that question is, by Scripture, in the Church – a rather commonplace response, one might think, before noticing the originality with which he presents it. The 'body' of Christ which is Scripture (an archaic, Alexandrian way of speaking, no longer practised in Catholic theology but which Balthasar would revive), like the 'body' of Christ which is the Church (a never abandoned locution) are like that body of his taken from blessed Mary and, in its transfigured, paschal condition self-identically given us in the Holy Eucharist: in their different modes each is the single Christ-form as communicated to the world. Here we shall find one of Balthasar's most extended discussions of the Bible, and exegetical method – seen, however, in connexion with the Mass and the mystery of the Church.

Mediation in Scripture
For Balthasar the grace of revelation is potent enough to animate the response to revelation as well. And so 'in the very form in which it addresses man, the Word of God already wants to include the form of man's answer to God'.[23] From this all-important principle, various consequences flow. First, in the theological realm, only faith secures rationality – that is, the objective, rounded knowledge of what is revelationally given, and so only believing exegesis is 'scientific'. Secondly, if we apply Balthasar's axiom to the single most knotty problem raised by biblical scholarship for the Church's faith, the question of the real traits of the 'Jesus of history', we shall conclude that while only Easter faith can read aright the 'form' that began to appear in the letters of history in Jesus' earthly career, this in no way implies the 'retrojection' onto the historic ministry of alien *credenda*, for: 'the outlines of Jesus' earthly form could not have been filled out and completed in any way other than in the fully realised form of the Christ of faith'.[24] Here as elsewhere we see what the Christ-form is by what it does, and one crucial thing it does is to shape that response which is the New Testament. To suppose that the final version of the gospel tradition, or of the New Testament itself (and therefore the Bible as a whole), obscures the real Jesus is woefully to underestimate the shaping power of his form.

The biblical canon (and Balthasar joins modern 'canon critics' in North America when he emphasises the significance of canonicity) is (considered as a literary structure) hard, objective, exclusive. And this tells us that, though the faith of the Church, in that faith's biblical expression, results from a process of receiving the self-revealing Word, this is 'no modernistic subjectivity'.

> The Church's *memoria*, reflecting on which she creates Scripture and brings it forth from herself, is not in the end a subjective memory but a memory that hearkens back to the objective interpretation of the whole of revelation by the risen spiritual Christ ...

23 *GL* I, p. 538.
24 *GL* I, p. 539.

Scripture is not a self-reflection on the part of the Church, but a faith that goes back interiorly and a tradition that goes back exteriorly. It is the testimony about something that dwells within the Church but is not the Church herself.

In a comparison with the rôle of the Virgin in that primordial receiving of the Word that was the annunciation:

Mary's faith does not generate the form of Jesus; rather, this form is given as a gift to her faith. Nor does the Church's faith generate the form of Scripture; rather, the Holy Spirit uses the Church's formative energies in order to give full shape within her to the image of faith that has been bestowed on the Church.[25]

For Balthasar, Scripture is both wonderful and disappointing – but chiefly wonderful. As Christ's own self-interpretation by his personal Spirit working on the liberty of the faithful, Scripture is sublime, 'an expression of Christ's fulness and glory'. Yet in this very office, the Bible draws attention to the humility of his *hiddenly* glorious form by its literary lowliness – and Balthasar looks for a partial explanation of the duality of (limited) letter and (unlimited) spirit or meaning in Scripture to his own theological ontology of form as offered in the earlier pages of *Herrlichkeit* I. The key to the letter–spirit duality is Christ, whose bodily form manifests God while also concealing him. And yet in the case of the incarnate One and his mediated form, the Bible, this dialectic of manifestation and concealment presses towards showing, not hiding. Unlike other 'bodies': 'the body of Scripture is . . . a garment that has an inherent tendency to assume the brightness and transparency of Jesus' clothing on Tabor'.[26] This literature, however inadequate it may be to the total mystery of salvation is, after all, uniquely a work of grace.

Balthasar insists on the multi-dimensionality of Scripture: the variety of perspectives on the Christ-form allowed by the different writers – the New Testament's 'stereoscopy' – is imperilled if we insist on crediting only what critical scholars can regard as the most primitive level of the historically accumulated deposit. The testimony, from whatever source, really belongs to revelation itself. On the other hand, and here Balthasar praises the redaction critics who have drawn attention to the distinctiveness of each evangelist, the discovery of variety saves us from supposing that Scripture is itself revelation: what is attested essentially transcends the testimony given it. And *pace* those who seek only the *ipsissima verba Jesu*, what is precisely contemporary with him, Balthasar remarks:

Although Christ could, and in fact had to, institute the sacraments without mediation, Scripture could be completed only at the end of the apostolic age: this is so because the portrait of Christ first had to be meditated upon by believers since many of its features could

25 *GL* I, p. 540.
26 *GL* I, p. 541.

come to light only through this meditation and since not only *Christus caput*, but also *totus Christus, caput et membra* belongs to the total objective image of God's revelation for the world and in the world.[27]

The image of Christ is not fully visible, in other words, without the shaping deed by which he poured his life into the communion of the Church.

And this helps Balthasar to answer the question, is the Church *below* Scripture or *above* it?

> As Bride and Body of Christ, the Church cannot possibly have above herself any superior 'court' other than her Bridegroom and, in him, the triune God ... In order to know Christ, the Church must but question her own Spirit, which is the common Spirit of Christ and of the Church.[28]

So Scripture, then, is definitely subordinate to the Church? By no means, for she:

> does not possess this her Lord other than as her incarnate Saviour and blood-Bridegroom. Therefore, an essential part of her self-consciousness as the bride who has been redeemed and washed in blood is her awareness of the event of salvation-history, which through the centuries can remain fresh and present for her only through its objectivation as Scripture.[29]

If in the sense just explained Scripture is the normative image of revelation for the Church, this is not through a biblicism which would regard the form of the biblical Word as identical with that of revelation itself. We are talking not about straightforward *identity* but a due *proportion* between the two – and that all-important 'proportion' is available to view only theologically, not by way of philological, literary or even historical method. The biblical canon serves the Holy Spirit as a vehicle for his actualising the 'total historical form of the revelation of salvation', but the Spirit puts the canon to use by, first, transforming the Old Testament christologically through its unification with the New, and second, transposing the literal sense (of the New Testament as well as the Old) into that spiritual sense which is the Christ-event as lifegiving *for me*. There is nothing objectionable, Balthasar writes, about Bultmann's existential interpretation of Scripture in terms of this *pro me* principle – so long as we add that the 'me' in question is the Christian who is such 'only in the Church and through the Church, . . . only in faith and in anticipation of the eschaton'.[30] That for Balthasar is the lesson taught by Henri de Lubac's investigations into patristic and

27 *GL* I, p. 543.
28 *GL* I, p. 545.
29 *GL* I, pp. 545–546.
30 *GL* I, pp. 548–549.

mediaeval exegesis, in *Histoire et Esprit* (his Origen book) and *Exégèse médiévale*.[31]

The idea that the New Testament fulfils the Old is a commonplace. For Balthasar it is an inadequate commonplace, since what is involved in the distinction between those Covenants is a 'radically new re-creation of all meaning through the death of God's Logos'. Just for that reason, a 'philological theology' will never do justice to Scripture in its entirety. Here the Fathers and the mediaevals have the upper hand.

> The older contemplators of Scripture possessed the art of seeing the total form within individual forms and of bringing it to light from within them. But this naturally presupposes an understanding of totality that is spiritual and not literary and philological; that one accomplishes in the obedience of faith the decisive step from word to spirit, from earthly form to resurrected form; and that, in so doing, one . . . keeps one's eyes set on that universal concrete reality which is Christ himself universalised in the Holy Spirit and witnessed to by Scripture.[32]

The variety of ways in which such interpretation can be accomplished is one pointer to the fact that 'the canonical validity of Scripture, *pace* Protestantism, does not exclude, but rather includes an ecclesial teaching authority'.[33]

After Newman, the customary fashion in which to express the relation between Scripture and teaching authority would surely be by saying that the latter exists so as to judge putative developments in the understanding of the former. Balthasar concurs, even to the point of embracing that metaphor of organic development which, after Newman, was seen as central to the 'theory'. Yet he shares with much twentieth-century Eastern Orthodox theology a wariness of overenthusiastic appeal to 'development' of a kind that might reduce to pygmy status the understanding of the gospel by apostles and prophets.

> We cannot say that the first Christians understood [the canonical image of revelation] only fragmentarily and that successive generations attained to a more complete understanding and an increasingly better grasp of it. Rather, for eyes that have been illumined by faith, the image in its totality is simple and visible at a glance, . . . and the super-abundant fulness is not a threat but rather the description of this simplicity.[34]

Time will bring no major shifting of the centre of gravity, no seismic disruption of the proportions of this scriptural image, and since 'ecclesial vitality' in the reinterpretation of the Bible carries, consequently, its own dangers (for not all of individuals' bright ideas are good ideas), the 'light'

31 H. de Lubac, *Histoire et Esprit. L'intelligence de l'Ecriture d'après Origène* (Paris 1950); *Exégèse médiévale. Les quatre sens de l'Ecriture* (Paris 1959–64, four volumes).
32 *GL* I, p. 550.
33 *GL* I, p. 552.
34 *GL* I, p. 552.

of the canonical form of Scripture is shed inerrantly over the entire Church (believing people together with magisterium), allowing us to test later developments against the original form.

And here as everywhere in revelation, Christ is the centre. It is because Scripture is not its own centre that the many inner-biblical theologies can coexist without detriment to its coherence, and the even more numerous extra-biblical theologies come to be, in the service of ecclesial thought, without jeopardising its originality.

> This is possible only because the fulness of the Bible crystallises concentrically around a human and divine centre, a centre which is indeed expressed in Scripture and everywhere flooded by its light, but which essentially transcends Scripture and rests within itself as a sovereign reality. This centre which transcends Scripture, both as image and as force, has the power to organise the millennial history of thought and to effect within this history an *évolution homogène*.[35]

The principal task of the magisterium, accordingly, is not so much to generate new theological forms (though Balthasar does not altogether exclude this – since 'many problems of form will arise at the practical, organisational and psychological levels') as it is to protect the primal form against distortion in one or more of its aspects. It is perfectly suitable, for Balthasar, that the magisterium's pronouncements should be found in the thematic jumble of Denzinger's *Enchiridion* – for the magisterium does not intend to produce an overall form of its own.

These remarks, however, are not intended to exalt theology at the expense of the teaching office: no more than the magisterium is theology to substitute a form for that which is found in revelation. A theologian should strive for 'beauty of form' but precisely as service of the Church and homage of her Lord, not (in other words) as an 'improvement' on the revelation dominically given. So long as the theologian is faithful to these marching orders, Balthasar is happy for him (or her) to aim at privilegeing various qualities in theological style – system, it may be, or conceptual clarity, or again depth of intuition or simply practical usefulness to the magisterium. These properties remain, on the Balthasarian view of things, ancillary rather than essential. They cannot compete with the more primordial attributes of holiness, contemplativity and thinking with the Church, for the mind of the saint, of the praying person and of the total Church in her supra-personal transcendence of the individual is the epistemic goal at which the theologian aims.

Mediation in the Church of the Saints

It is in the form of the Church that the biblical form (like that of the sacraments) must be fulfilled. So by a natural progression of thought Balthasar now considers the ecclesial mystery as another mediation of the revelatory form. If, in the Johannine passion narrative, the Church,

---

35 *GL* I, p. 554. The reference is to the classic Neo-Scholastic study of the idea of development, F. Marín-Sola, O.P., *L'Evolution homogène du dogme chrétien* (Fribourg 1924).

founded on baptism and Eucharist, flows from the side of Christ, that is because her form of being is altogether dependent on him.

> Whatever the Church may possess by way of 'personality' and 'nature' she has from Christ, whose 'fulness' she is because he has first poured his own fulness into her, so that the Church is nothing other than Christ's own fulness. . . .[36]

Here the analogy between husband and wife on the one hand, Christ and Church on the other, breaks down – for the Church does not possess the kind of autonomy of form that would enable her to be Christ's *alter ego*, his *Gegenüber* or *vis-à-vis*. And Balthasar applies that notion not simply to the inner life-principle of the Church – for it is *Christ*'s Spirit that is the Church's 'soul' – but even to her external offices and ministries. Their *raison d'être* consists exclusively in so building up the Church that the Christ-form is fully implanted in the ecclesial body. And though this be a task never finished till the eschaton, it shows that the Church's public servants are not aiming to create something ecclesiastical but to reproduce something Christological, and so divine.

> The Church is not Christ, but she can claim for herself and for the world no other figure than the figure of Christ, which leaves its stamp in her and shapes her through and through as the soul shapes the body. In this, the element of structure, which emerges as the institutional element in the Church, is at the service of the highest possible similarity to the archetype itself.[37]

Since we are talking about the *mediation* of Christ's form, the form of the Church will have to be transparent not only to her Lord but also to the world; she will have to be as universal as the world, and so larger than her historical origins just as God is 'larger' than the Jesus of history. But is there not a danger that in so emphasising, even for the best of missionary reasons, the necessity for thought and action of a universal structure as wide as rationality itself, Balthasar will effectively abolish both Church and Christ, since these are ineluctably concrete, and so particular? This is the challenge of the Enlightenment, best known from its Protestant version in the work of Gotthold Ephraim Lessing, critic and dramatist, who asked how truths of fact could ever carry the burden of being universal truths for reason – though Balthasar prefers to refer to it in its Catholic guise, in the *Aufklärung* cleric Ignaz Heinrich von Wessenberg, whose simplified liturgies and Catechism threatened to subsume supernatural revelation under the most general form of God-man relationship, and so annul its distinctive character. Balthasar replies that no mediating interpretation of the faith to the world is legitimate that does not at all points respect the integrity of the revelatory form.

> It is solely in this image and form that the 'concept' of God and of man becomes truly concrete for us; the idea becomes radiant only in

36 *GL* I, p. 558.
37 *GL* I, pp. 559–560.

the *conversio ad phantasma*, it is in this turning to the image which is Christ (and, with him, the Church).[38]

If anyone is sceptical about the likelihood that the Christ-form ever really becomes impressed in the Church-form, Balthasar's answer is a ready one: What of our Lady and the Saints? The high place which (according to Balthasar) Mariology should enjoy in theological aesthetics derives from its demonstration of the 'transferability' of the Christ-form to the Church:

> Mary's form, as faithful image, reveals Christ's form as sole arche-type both in its specificity and in its divine creative, forming power. Nor is Mary's form isolated from that of all other Christians, since she is precisely the model of our 'being formed in the likeness of Christ' (Rom. 8:29; Phil. 3:10, 11). Hence, the image of her interior reality stands before the eyes of Christians and should stand before their eyes whenever the conditions for their becoming conformed to Christ are being considered.[39]

Mary's 'watchful waiting' appears glorious only to the eyes of faith – and in this it reproduces the *chiaroscuro*, shadow and light, of the form of Christ itself. Virginal obedience produces nuptial fruitfulness, in the image of the Jesus who was obedient to death for our salvation. All the saints, for Balthasar, stand under this same law. By contrast with the Church of saints, both Paul and Peter weep over the failures of the Church of office, the 'institutional Church' – Paul for the deficiencies of others, Peter for his own. Balthasar will not allow that such failings – and hence obfuscations of ecclesial form – are inevitable; by the grace of God the New Testament pattern of apostolic authority – humiliation precisely in elevation – is available to all holders of office, and allows the institution to become what it ought:

> a means for the preservation and the intensification of the relation-ship between the Head and the members, a channel (corresponding to God's Incarnation) through which the Head may work in the members in a living manner, that is to say, in a mode that is mediated through living persons and which yet remains pure, unmuddied and unobstructed by sinners.[40]

Mediation in the sacraments

But Scripture and Church society are unthinkable for a Catholic without *sacrament* – and above all the eucharistic cultus. The Mass takes its form from the pasch of the Lord, the death and resurrection which do not merely figure in his life, but 'figure' his life, marking it with their form.

38 *GL* I, p. 561.
39 *GL* I, p. 563.
40 *GL* I, p. 569.

This cult is a meditation in retrospect on the event which in the first place constitutes the Church, the outpouring of the bodily-spiritual reality of Jesus as Son of the Father, his release from the confinement of his earthly individuality into the social reality of the Church, which arises only from Jesus' outpouring of self.[41]

But, as the conciliar tradition of the Catholic Church insists, this cult is no mere memory, no bare commemoration. 'The Beloved who died for us becomes alive and present for us in the midst of our remembering (*in meam commemorationem*)'.[42] The real presence – the encounter of Christ and the Church in the eucharistic conversion and communion – comes first; yet Christ is present not least in order to energise the community which 'as it realises him by remembering him, also realises itself'.[43]

It is when Balthasar moves on to consider the sextet of sacraments which accompany the Holy Eucharist that he lays down the crucial principle of his sacramental theology, germane as it proves to 'mediating the form'. 'The fundamental figure of grace is Jesus Christ himself, and all sacramental forms are grounded in his form in a most concrete sense.'[44] The statement has a cutting-edge, directed against alternative accounts, as is made plain when Balthasar goes on:

All sacraments (and in this they are like the Eucharist) are a saving act that God performs in Christ Jesus for the ecclesial believer. They are distinguished from one another by the manner of this saving action, which is not primarily specified by man's universal socio-logical situations and the contexts in which the believer finds himself, but by the ways in which Christ has brought us his salvation, which are the ways of his life in human form.[45]

Naturally, were the sacraments simply signs in which the social animal, man, responds to the sacred, they would be complete 'non-starters' if what we are looking for is mediations of the form of revelation in Jesus Christ. In each sacrament, the christological form infused into the human form is determinative. How readily does the Paul of Romans use the theologically aesthetic language of 'likeness', for instance, for our baptismal conformation to Christ's death and resurrection! Aspects of a sacrament's symbolic content may be universally intelligible (and so susceptible to illuminating interpretation by anthropologists), but this is not the crucial thing, it is only a pointer to Christ's 'corporeal and spiritual gesture', a gesture the believer can grasp not simply because of the pointer but thanks to 'Christ's unique symbolic power as God and man'.[46] Unusually, it is neither of the two principal sacraments, Eucharist and baptism, but penance which Balthasar regards as the paradigm for a

41 *GL* I, p. 572.
42 *GL* I, p. 573.
43 Ibid.
44 *GL* I, p. 576.
45 *GL* I, p. 576.
46 *GL* I, p. 579.

general theology of sacramental form – and this for the indispensable rôle played therein by the conscious participation of the penitent believer, for whom no one can stand proxy, and nothing subsequent supply, if the sinner's 'conversion' is lacking. During his ministry, when sinners met Christ they met 'the offended God and the offended neighbour all in one'; with his very existence, therefore, penance had 'already received its full sacramental form',[47] though naturally the aspect of the ministerial absolver had still to be added. But:

> the Gospel image is not obscured by the fact that absolution is given through Christ's delegate, who is empowered to bestow it in the name of the offended God and of the offended community of saints. This delegate concretises in a sacramental manner both the forgiving God and the forgiving Church, and it is necessary that the form of his image represent both these things in unity.[48]

So more important to Balthasar than either the hylemorphic analysis of the sacraments (as matter-and-form) or their treatment as *instruments* of Christ (another very popular way to proceed in theological tradition) is their *figural* character.

> The 'matter' that is to be formed is man himself in his concrete situation: as a person who is to enter into God's Kingdom, as a person who is to be washed, nourished, anointed, as a human sinner to whom the great absolution of the Cross must ever anew be applied and who is to undertake the decision of Christian maturity, Christian matrimony, ecclesial ministry, as a person who stands before the gates of eternity. In this person a process of formation is at work whose form is Christ himself.[49]

Mediation in dogma and doing

And after Scripture and the Church of the Scriptures, the Eucharist and the other sacraments, Balthasar now rounds off his remarks of the 'mediation of the form' by asking after the *form of faith itself*. This can hardly be because he is unaware that Bible, Church and liturgy presuppose faith. His concern is, rather, that one key feature of believing peculiarly distinctive of the *Catholic* understanding of Christian faith – namely, its emphasis on dogmatic propositions, well-honed and clear-cut – should not be regarded as alien to 'ecclesial aesthetics'. Especially interesting in Balthasar's account is the way he stresses the 'fiducial' element in faith – faith as trust – which many would consider at the antipodes from a theology of faith as doctrine. For him, faith is essentially absolute trust in the God who has given us his Son to be his self-communication, his Word. But the apostolic proclamation in its summons to just such trust is, on Balthasar's understanding, 'already dogma' in that

47 *GL* I, p. 581.
48 *GL* I, p. 581.
49 *GL* I, p. 583.

it 'demands of a special faith in God that it make the decision to become a special faith in God's self-revelation and self-surrender to man in Jesus Christ'[50] – and the only possible justification for such a demand is the *homoousion*, '*the* dogma', the assertion that Jesus is the unique divine Son. All the propositional complexity of Church dogmatics follows – so Balthasar affirms with startling simplicity – from this.

> This dogma, which expresses the fundamental form of Christian faith, can and must be variously secured and formulated in the course of the Church's reflection on faith, as it is prompted by erroneous historical interpretations and attacks: this buttressing and development must be carried out in the interests of the dogma itself (christologically), of its presuppositions in the image of God (doctrine of the Trinity), and of its consequences (ecclesiologically). Around the dogma there develops 'dogmatics', which is to say the numerous affirmations that explain, defend, and illustrate the dogmatic centre ever more adequately.

Put in more theologically aesthetic terms: everything is admissable by way of dogmatisation so long as it clarifies the 'interior form of revelation in its proportions and articulations'.[51]

And if in this way dogma is inextricably bound up with the Christ-form, that form also moulds (or should) the main modes of the Church's activity, beginning with preaching – defined by Balthasar as not so much the 'ministry *of* the Word' as ministry *to* the Word. The task of theology here is to help make preaching transparent to a Christoform revelation, and to help the preacher avoid a 'schematic account of Christianity of his own devising'.[52] Ecclesial discipline, ecclesial obedience, only make evangelical sense in terms of the realisation of the Christ-form, and the same is true of the life of the counsels lived by Religious and members of 'Secular Institutes'. And as to theology (when Balthasar considers it for its own sake and not simply as an adjunct to preaching), a Christian aesthetics can be lyrical in appreciating that science. For, as the example of Origen shows, despite all human limitations (here Balthasar adverts to one of his first loves among the early ecclesiastical writers), theology really can attain to its own proper form as

> a figure drawn up by God himself and it can, therefore, pass back and forth from the realm of pure logical exactness into an experience which radiates from the archetype – an experience which leads to contemplation and can become truly mystical: this fact confirms rather than questions its character as form.[53]

And Balthasar anticipates his conclusions in the second and third volumes of *The Glory of the Lord* when he adds

50 *GL* I, pp. 590–591.
51 *GL* I, p. 591, translation slightly amended.
52 *GL* I, p. 597.
53 *GL* I, p. 601.

The convergence of the aesthetic and the mystical in the great mystical theologies ... is striking and can only be explained by affirming that what in God is formless and ineffable is offered as a super-form which fascinates and transports man, eliciting from man and claiming for itself the answer of man's shaping powers.[54]

That Scripture and the Church have now been shown (Balthasar at least is satisfied) to be a divine work as well as a human one, means that they can also be considered as conjoined to the form of Christ (the principal form in theological aesthetics) so as to compose one total form – and this will be pertinent to Balthasar when he goes on, as he now does, to consider the form's 'attestation'.

Attestation to the form

This is the question of the form's 'witnesses' whom Balthasar has already identified as, first, the Source of all being; secondly, world history, and third, the cosmos – his version of the multiple attestation ascribed to the authority of Jesus in the Fourth Gospel, where the Son receives testimony from the Father; from the past history of revelation; and from his works, expressive of the cosmic power the Son receives, as well as from the Holy Spirit whom John links to the sacramental signs of water and blood, baptism and Eucharist.

The witness of the Father
Of these attestations, that of the *Father* – the absolute Source of all being, whether created or divine – is clearly the most important. The one invisible God appears in his Christophany not simply in the way that creatures do (Balthasar had described this in the first, anticipatory volume of the theological logic) – entering visibility yet remaining concealed in their ground – but appearing and not appearing in 'such a way that this polarity reveals itself to us as a personal relationship [the Father–Son relationship] within God's very nature'.[55] That the non-apparent Father *does* witness to the authoritative form of his Son, Jesus Christ, is plain to anyone who really grasps that form's authenticity. As with a great work of art (Balthasar cites Mantegna for painting, Mozart for music), *full* accrediting can only be done from *within*.

Whoever is able to read the form will at the same time understand the witness which the Father interiorly gives to the Son. Whoever is able to hear the Son as Logos of the Father – as the witness to himself which the Father exhibits to the world – that person will also be listening to the interior dialogue between Father and Son wherein the Father utters his entire divinity, his power, and his love to the Son. The Father accredits the Son's words and works as stemming from himself, the Father; by so doing he also accredits the Son's form

---

54 *GL* I, pp. 601–602.
55 *GL* I, p. 609.

of humiliation and obedience as an authentic expression of the divine nature.[56]

The Johannine statements that Jesus both does and does not bear witness to himself (John 8:14, 5:31) are for Balthasar neither contradictory nor even dialectical. Jesus bears witness to himself insofar as every form, in revealing its content, shows itself to be form; but he does this only inasmuch as he bears witness to the Father who in the Son bears witness to himself. Looking ahead to the volumes of the theological logic still to be written, Balthasar can conclude:

> The truth is both the Father in himself and the expressive relation-ship between Father and Son as well as, finally, the Son in himself, in so far as he is the Word and the Expression of the Father.[57]

The witness of Israel

If the *Father's* testimony is an absolute necessity for Jesus (his own testimony is 'the Father's testimony becoming visible'),[58] the same is not the case for the witness of the *Hebrew Bible* (inspired summary of world history, in its saving significance), which is rather, for the sake of other men. As the incarnate One, Jesus 'constitutes one form with the history of the Old Testament'[59] not mainly because *any* human being is, after all, dependent on their prehistory, but owing to the obedience which brings him to perfect his Father's work. Not that the issue of Jesus' continuity and discontinuity with the Elder Testament is a straightforward one: Balthasar calls it, indeed, the 'central problem of the primitive Church'.[60] For Balthasar, the solution to the problem lies (as indeed many ancient theologians recognised) in the concept of *figura* or *typos* – 'figure' or 'type'. The deepest explanation of Israelite aniconicism lies in the fact that 'God himself was to become his people's Builder of figures and that, in his own divine way, he was to prepare *the* Master Figure, *the* Image *par excellence* (2 Cor. 4:4)'.[61] The promise is image, the fulfilment reality. The outline is shadow, fulfilled form comes only with Christ. We must take care neither to underestimate what is already given in the figure (Abraham's faith is the true faith, and even, in hidden fashion, Christian faith, just as in the Revelation of St John the twelve elders of the Old Testament stand before God's throne in the same row as the twelve of the New), nor to overestimate the figure, neglecting the novelty it could never invent.

> The form is fulfilled because it is eschatological, because it makes the leap but can only pre-figure it, in an existence that presses beyond the boundaries of the Old Age without nevertheless being able to leave it altogether . . .[62]

56 *GL* I, pp. 614–615.
57 *GL* I, p. 615.
58 *GL* I, p. 618.
59 *GL* I, p. 619.
60 *GL* I, p. 620.
61 *GL* I, p. 623.
62 *GL* I, p. 624.

If there is an exegetical Marcionism, ancient and modern, there is also a patristic (or neo-patristic) naïveté which concedes to the just of the Old Testament an immediate share in the grace of the New. The most original part of Balthasar's theology of Israel as witness to Christ, however, is his reinterpretation of *figura* as Israel's imagistic self-objectivation. Israel, alone of all the peoples of the earth (if also on their behalf), is called to transcend itself towards a future it cannot yet see. A priori, we can suppose that the pre-history of the Word Incarnate would require, in the perspective of theological aesthetics, some feature broadly of this kind: 'The history with which he can constitute one form must rise above the rest of history and must bear a stamp that points to him while originating in him.'[63] When assessing the great messianic images for 'he who cometh', in which Israel cast the hope that at once set her apart and impelled her towards that 'ever more incomprehensible historical destination', we must neither, with the History of Religions School, reduce their significance to the level of her pagan environment nor, with the Fathers, make Israel already the Church by anticipation. 'The essential point is that Israel as a whole and existentially is an image and a figure which cannot interpret itself. It is a sphinx's riddle which cannot be solved without Oedipus.'[64]

Balthasar investigates this more fully under two subheadings: the rôle of 'myth and prophecy' in Israel's witness and the relation to her of the unseen God in judgment and salvation. On the first, he writes sympathetically of the (Old Testament) Scandinavian school hypothesis of a subjacent complex of myth and ritual, centring around an 'enthronement festival', whereby in a royal figure acting representatively for God man is established over the created world as its viceroy. The king, issuing symbolically from the primal era of creation, fights and by divine aid conquers, the powers of chaos; on him hangs messianically man's salvation. If true, this thesis renders the Old Testament a wonderful prefiguration of Christ (far more successfully so than the sometimes forced allegorising of the Church Fathers), and links Israel to related mythopoeic expressions of the human predicament not only in the pagan Near East but in such far-flung cultures as that of China (here Balthasar makes use of Claudel's strange symbolist drama of the 'Middle Kingdom', *Le Repos du septième jour*). Unfortunately, (or perhaps fortunately) this 'dazzling construction' of a 'total typology' cannot bear the weight that some would put upon it. Attractive as is this way of making Christ the fulfilment of the nations' longing (and not that of Israel alone), it fails to do justice to what is distinctive in the Old Testament message, and notably its historical and indeed future-oriented character.

> The imaged form, which thus illuminates the relation of Old and New, does not result from a mediating movement that runs from the myth to the history that fulfils it; it is, rather, the contrary: the image is the product of a return to the myth. But this is tantamount

63 *GL* I, p. 625.
64 *GL* I, p. 628.

to a falsification of history, for Israel's centre of gravity quite certainly lies in its unceasing forward movement . . .[65]

Israel must shatter the mythical totality of which the Scandinavian scholars spoke so as to have to hand its fragments for the building of a new totality which she can in no way wholly anticipate, for it lies at a point of convergence in the future.

Her feasts are 'historicised', reapplied to temporal events; her prophets begin to speak of new things which God not only is doing but will do as well. That latter expectation of God's future decisive deed breaks the confines of 'inner historicity' itself and reveals the 'dimension of the eschatological as a step beyond time into the Absolute'.[66] Balthasar's emphasis, however, lies on the not merely *seeming* but *real* irreconcilability within the Old Testament of that range of 'forms' that results from these theological milestones on Israel's journey. A passage worthy of citation in full, despite its length, so important is it for Balthasar's theology of the Bible, reads:

> The terrible personal suffering of the servant of God in the Book of Consolation of Israel is something totally different from the cultic and mimetic suffering of the royal ideology. And, the 'coming from heaven' of the 'son of man' in Daniel, conceived as it is as a serious possibility, is something totally different from the divine sonship of the mythical king. The ethico-political actualism of the Prophets, which admittedly presupposes the mythical period as its past, is nevertheless irreconcilable with it since this actualism at the same time presupposes an experience of God of a new kind: the experience of a God who commands and creates freely and sovereignly, who cannot be inserted into a calendar of feasts, who has the power to burst open and relativise the closed religious world of myth and to transform it into reality at a wholly different level. This prophetic concept of God emerges as the most exalted and living reality which could be attained by a pre-Christian religion. But, in a very strange way, prophecy breaks off and produces from itself this last period that interiorly remains so ambiguous. On the one hand we witness in it a decay and a petrification into legalism, sapientialism, apocalypticism. On the other hand we also see an ascent to a final distance which is what made possible the final redaction of the Sacred Scriptures: an interiorisation that leads to the contemplation of God's 'great deeds' in nature and history; an abstraction and a universalisation that lead to a total theology and a unified conception of history; and, above all, the radicalization of the whole reality of a New Age which can be sighted but not grasped in itself and which, therefore, is totally misconstrued – witness the apocalyptic calculations, the lifelessness and lack of historical perspective, and the almost lascivious curiosity with which the pseudonymous authors set out to spy on the divine mysteries. How

65 *GL* I, p. 633.
66 *GL* I, p. 637.

could the 'son of man' in Daniel at the same time be the son of David? How could the glory of God in Ezekiel, which returns at the time of salvation, be one with the suffering servant of God in the Book of Consolation? How could the *kairos*-theology which the Prophets unconditionally demand be one with the contemplation of the wise men, which is wholly divorced from time? And how are we to harmonise Job's dealings with God, the almost Buddhist resignation of Qoheleth, and the ardent eroticism of the Canticle within this total form, which in every direction is pulled apart by intolerable tensions? Qumran's Book of Battles can be taken as an illustration of where such attempts at a synthesis can lead: for this book, the eschatological battle of the apocalypse must – with perfect logic! – be reconcilable with the realism of the holy wars of the periods of the Exodus, the Judges, and the Kings, and the divine battle on the 'Day of Yahweh', in which Israel will participate, must be both a mythico-sacro-cultic act and a prophetic and apocalyptic act; but this union results in a terrible vision of grotesque proportion, which is worse than all other known conceptions of 'holy wars' and crusades. No! The elements that Israel successively bears and gives to the world are, humanly considered, absolutely disparate and demonstrably irreconcilable. They constitute a chain of forms which are impressive and dramatic in the extreme, forms of a religious and ethical earnestness not to be found anywhere else in human history. But this succession of forms cannot itself produce the *one* form; rather, with all the urgency which the fragment of a form possesses, the succession of forms demands a transcendent fulfilment within this second prophetic perspective oriented to the future.[67]

Just as the bio-forms of the animal kingdom are neither simply preparations for each other nor, in their totality, an adequate explanation for the emergence of *Homo sapiens*, and yet the First Adam is unthinkable without them, so it is with Christ, the Second and Last Adam, in his relation to the forms, whether of life or thought, found in Israel. Israel has no finished *eidos* (form) of her own, and this very fact renders her a witness in history to something *more*.

But in a theological aesthetics we need to be told how Israel *shows* this to be the case – and so the dialectic of 'seeing the unseen' must be Balthasar's last halting-place in considering the 'witness of history' in the Elder Covenant.

If mythical time had been 'vertical time', where in the saving relation of God to the world, all sense of the need for 'horizontal' progress was disregarded, so Christian time – *eschatological* time – is vertical likewise, inasmuch as salvation has descended directly from God through Christ in the latter's glorification as head of humankind. Myth could and did represent its relation with God in visible fashion – in the Jewish (or Gentile) liturgy. Christ's strange work is on its Godward side hidden, his mediation of judgment and grace invisible – and yet in a real sense it too

67 *GL* I, pp. 638–639.

can be seen, for it appears in the very interrelation of the Testaments
which

> not only *represents* the relationship of time to eternity, but *bears*
> it within itself in the manner of a sacrament that contains and
> communicates what it symbolises in the likeness of what is
> seen.[68]

The Old Testament is, then, the sacrament of the New. The divine light
playing on its forms enables them, once read in the perspective of Christ,
to 'make the invisible visible', and notably in three ways. When New and
Old 'conjoin', we see first, what *man and the world are for God*; second, *what
their destiny is to be through God*; and third, and by way of this last, *what
God himself is for the world.* As to human *existence*, then, judging light falls
on man – in one sense mercilessly, but in another for his healing. All the
acts of No-saying are for the sake of a definitive Yes spoken in Jesus
Christ, for

> in the Old Testament God measured man with his own divine
> measure, but in the New Testament the divine measure itself
> became man: and these two measurements with the same measure
> can be seen in history.[69]

And as to human *destiny*, Israel is kept by God at the threshold of the
world beyond, told to take in the harsh reality of death, such that her
ruminations on an after-life appear shadowy and somewhat unreal. But
again the 'apophases' – the negative theological utterances – of the Old
Testament are ordered to the supreme 'cataphasis' – the essentially
affirmative utterance – of the New. 'This barrier, so strikingly implanted
and guarded, will be removed only by Christ as he descends into hell and
rises from the dead.'[70] And as, finally, to *theophany* – the manifestation of
who God himself is: in the entire form of this history of salvation, from
Israel to Christ, the God of all election is interpreting himself for us in his
freedom and love. If in the Old Testament we hear two voices, that of
sovereignty, as God judges, and that of humiliation, as he nonetheless
continues to pursue his people with the ardour of love, they are united
and kept distinct by an ineffable third voice (which in time we will
learn to call the Spirit). 'In the tragic history of God with his unfaithful
people . . . is prefigured the immanent Trinity which becomes fully
manifest in the Incarnation of God's Son.'[71] To those who love to
contemplate the form shown in Scripture it appears not only as the
most perfect harmonics, but also, then, as the 'most glorious drama'[72] in
the world's history – and with these words Balthasar points towards the
great interpretation of the divine action in the narrative form of revelation
which will be his theological dramatics.

68 *GL* I, p. 646.
69 *GL* I, pp. 650–651.
70 *GL* I, p. 652.
71 *GL* I, p. 657.
72 *GL* I, p. 659.

The witness of the angels

Meanwhile, however, he must consider the last of his 'witnesses' to the beauty of Christ – the *cosmos*, which means not least, on Balthasar's theological cosmology, the holy angels. The witness of the cosmos to Christ is not only the 'willingness of matter to receive and, express the saving signs of grace'[73] in Jesus' miracles; it is also found in the subjection, however unwilling, of the fallen 'powers and principalities' and the confession, by the heavenly angels, of his glory. For Balthasar the miracles of Jesus are 'necessarily located within the salvific and dialogical dealings of the Redeemer with man', as 'clarifications of his living form' in its communication to needy humanity.[74] On the demons and angels he must pause longer, for they are, to much contemporary exegesis and theology, more problematic still.

Balthasar's account of the evil angels makes use, for its interpretation of the biblical teaching, of the philosophical conceptualisation of these 'powers' – *Potenzen* – by Idealism. They are powers which, though deriving from God, did not remain powers in and through God – and hence subject to God – but willed to be autonomous, and found expression for that autonomous sphere of activity in the world and man. The human embodiment of the Redeemer in the cosmos means confrontation with this luciferian counter-power – but Balthasar succeeds in reformulating this encounter (for instance in the scene of the temptations of Christ) in theologically aesthetic terms.

> *Doxa* stands against *doxa*, beauty from below against beauty from above: beauty as entanglement and as a decadent, seduced sliding into the power of lust and the lust for power stands against the beauty of the adoration and service of the one God of glory, whereby the servant not only experiences glory but is himself wrapt about with glory: 'Then the devil left him, and behold, angels came and ministered to him'.[75]

Indeed the miracles themselves can be seen in this demonological perspective: not social concern but the epiphanising of the messianic fulness of power over against these wayward separated potencies are their essence. Here we strike, for Balthasar, 'foundational realities': no further 'demythologisation' is necessary – or possible. Jesus did not work 'signs' in Origen's sense, in the *Homilies on Matthew*, of symbols merely, of his spiritual deeds; rather he *was* what the sign manifested (bread, light, life-giving water, resurrection) and it is in this sense that, as he tells unbelieving Jews, he will perform no sign which can serve as a detached index to the truth or otherwise of his claims.

As to the good angels, Balthasar speaks of them in the context of the transfiguration of Christ which presents the form of humiliation of the Son of Man, on his way to the passion, as a function of his form of glory. Jesus' metamorphosis on the mountain reveals the Bridegroom as the

---

73 *GL* I, p. 660.
74 *GL* I, p. 661.
75 *GL* I, p. 662 with a concluding citation of Matthew 4:11.

Church, his Bride, sees him, for with the passion and resurrection, his divine form 'comes wholly to permeate the human form and to make it transparent in its functionality as love'.[76] In the twofold dispossession, of God into the human form by *agapē*, of man into the divine form by a transformed *erōs*, God and the world enjoy their ultimate meeting. And heaven itself – the realm of the angels – receives a share in this covenant of *agapē* and *erōs*, to its inhabitants' marvel, for as Gregory of Nyssa remarks in a passage in his commentary on the Song of Songs which effectively closes Balthasar's angelology in *Herrlichkeit*:

> It is through the Church that the heavenly powers will now be instructed concerning the variegated aspect of wisdom, which consists in the unification of contraries: they will now see how the Word becomes Flesh, how life becomes commingled with Death, how our wounds are healed by his ulcers, how the force of the Enemy is vanquished by the weakness of the Cross, how the Invisible becomes manifest in the Flesh.[77]

The work of the Redeemer will be, then, to render the world the body of God – not in a pantheistic sense but in one defined by the hypostatic union of humanity with divinity in his own increate person. All the forms of this world worthy of the name – and not the forms of nature only but of human culture and the literally gracious forms which holiness takes – must be perfectly completed by the Christ-form itself. On the tympana of the mediaeval churches of the West we glimpse what this process involves, as 'in the face of Christ's unique form, the icon of the Last Judgment levels all earthly forms: not only the worldly crowns, but also the mitres and tiaras roll in the dust'.[78] Yet Christ is never without his angels and his saints, the 'epiphany of his parousia' in the words of Paul's second letter to the church of Thessalonica (2:8). There is a bridal aspect to the Church, a part of her which is always filled with Christ's fulness; but for us to enter that marriage-chamber, our sinful side must die. As Balthasar ends the volume of prolegomena to his aesthetics, he lets us know, accordingly, that theological aesthetics will never be pretty-pretty: there is no room in the manifestation of sacrifice for sub-rococo kitsch.

---

76 *GL* I, p. 672.
77 *Homilia in Cantica Canticorum* 8, cited in *GL* I, p. 676.
78 *GL* I, p. 681.

4

❧❀❧

Constellation of Clerics

Balthasar's remaining tasks in the theological aesthetics are: first, to exemplify the richness of the theologically aesthetic reading of divine revelation in Christian tradition – something he does by a dozen essays (the apostolic *numerus clausus*!) on a variety of seminal figures; secondly, to trace both the emergence and the partial occlusion of the meta-physical preconditions of such a 'reading', from the ancient Greeks to the moderns; and thirdly, to round all off by a concluding return to the primordial and ever-fresh source of theological renewal that is the Holy Scriptures.

The principle of illustrative choice

The purpose of Balthasar's twelve 'studies in theological style' is to show how rich are the ways in which the 'glory of the Lord', delineated 'abstractly' in the opening volume of *Herrlichkeit*, has been beheld and experienced. Two criteria were at work in his choice of 'stars' with which to stud the sky of his theological world: intrinsic excellence and historical efficacy. In the first place, these will be

> a series of Christian theologies and world-pictures of the highest rank, each of which, having been marked at its centre by the glory of God's revelation, has sought to give the impact of this glory a central place in its vision.[1]

But secondly, these will not be supernova exploding unobserved but theologies which, as 'reflected rays of the glory' have also 'illuminated and shaped Christian culture through the centuries'. In point of fact, Balthasar appears to claim that these criteria coincide: there can be in this domain no efficacy without excellence.

> There is in the time of the Church no historically influential theology which is not itself a reflection of the glory of God; only beautiful theology, that is, only theology which grasped by the glory of God,

1 *GL* II, p. 13.

is able itself to transmit its rays, has the chance of making any impact in human history by conviction and transformation.[2]

His hope is that these luminaries, from Irenaeus to Péguy, will not just repeat each other, but will offer, in aggregate, a 'plenitude of perspectives', allowing him to grasp the main themes of theological aesthetics in their diversity.

The twelve writers selected span eighteen centuries of Christian thought; yet the year 1300 or thereabouts marks a significant boundary between them. Before then Balthasar's eye is on the clerics; after that date, he looks chiefly to laymen. As theology and spirituality drifted apart, he abandons the doctors for spiritual writers – an indication of his rejection of Baroque Scholasticism and the official theology of the Catholic schools (Scholastic or not) ever since. Balthasar's introduction to these twelve studies is filled with apologies: there are so many omissions, not only theologians and devotional writers, philosophers and novelists, but also artists and composers, as well as Christian poets from Synesius and Romanos the Melodist to Claudel and T. S. Eliot. Even so, Dante, John of the Cross, Hopkins and Péguy ensure that the poetic contribution is not neglected, though it is confined to those whose work bears directly on the biblical revelation and so may more easily be transposed into a theological key. Registering that glorious expression of the Church's faith which is the liturgies, Eastern and Western, would also have been possible – we have already seen the vital rôle played by the traditional Nativity Preface of the Roman Mass in the unfolding of the aesthetics. But as for Christian drama, that is another question, which Balthasar reserves to the central work of his trilogy, *Theodramatik*. Finally, Balthasar is obliged to admit that there *are* influential theologies, and excellent ones at that (such as Thomas') where the aesthetic values do not achieve a comprehensive theological form, just as there are theologies characterised by true greatness (such as those of the mediaeval German monastic women Hildegard of Bingen and Mechthild of Magdeburg) which have left little trace in Church history. There could also be an expression of the plenitude of Christian truth which its author was content to leave in paradoxical form – and this is the case of Chesterton. Nonetheless, despite this catalogue of omissions, Balthasar believes he has furnished the reader with:

> fascinating dialogues that open up between one and another, one greeting another across the centuries, grasping something and perhaps making expressible what was intended in quite a new form, completing what was fragmentary, and bringing to the one-sided a compensating counter-balance . . .[3]

In their totality these 'dialogues' constitute no system, yet their sound is music from an orchestra. Their internal harmony proves that 'they all play from the same score (which both transcends and embraces them)'.

2 *GL* II, pp. 13–14.
3 *GL* II, p. 22.

While arguing for the well-chosenness of his twelve aesthetic apostles, Balthasar also finds ways of indicating more schematically the range of authorial type from which theological aesthetics can select. His twelve preferred figures can be placed on a spectrum of forms of a theology of revealed glory, or on one made up of the possible styles in which theological beauty renders that glory newly articulate. For a given theology may centre its sense of glory on God himself (so that all else is lovely only insofar as he shines forth in it); or on his revelation in its mediating rôle in his regard (so that beauty belongs primarily to his self-displayal in creation and salvation); or on Jesus Christ as, in his two natures, the 'synthesis of God and the world' (here where redemption in the Son occupies centre-stage, it is the beauty of suffering love which, above all, strikes and overwhelms the observer); or on the Spirit of Christ, poured out on humankind from Father and Son as the gift of a share in their glory (and now the focus shifts to transfiguration by the Spirit in his 'all-consuming, dazzling intensity').[4] Alternatively, a variety of theological candidates may be interrogated less in terms of the formal object of their writing, and more in terms of its style of presentation. Brilliantly, Balthasar paints cameos of some choice sitters: Augustine 'whose whole work has become an infinitely extending, rolling sea'; Nazianzen, devoting himself to 'the cutting of tiny jewels of verbal skill'; Bonaventure, seeking to master revelation's superabundance by 'building dizzying towers, . . . gothic sacrament houses, all beautiful and possessed of an inner correctness, yet lacking any final necessity'; Clement of Alexandria opening up 'with the touching ardour of a connoisseur, a kind of treasury of antiques', so as to bring out the finest and fairest from the 'religions of all people and philosophers', and lay them before the Word made flesh.[5]

But this very luxuriance of stylistic growth gives Balthasar pause. With so disparate a set of styles before him, is it still plausible to argue for a correspondence between the glory of divine revelation and its mimetic expression in theological beauty? If we bear in mind the pertinence to this question of certain salient truths about human and divine self-expression, it is. First, it is typical of man's artistic expression that the beauty he creates comes about in *freedom*: great art conveys the simultaneous impression of disciplined necessity (no detail can be other) and sovereign freedom (the whole need not have been at all). Secondly, the divine freedom, in its choice of vehicle in the history of salvation, can hardly be *less* free than its human counterpart. The literary genres, for instance, found in the canon of Scripture, are in their accumulated unity at once wonderfully appropriate to the Word of God yet in no way its inevitable media: Balthasar speaks in their regard of 'a deliberate play with forms of expression that lie already to hand'. And so:

> the phenomenon of revelation is only truly encountered by those who, like Anselm, see the greatest freedom of the manifestation in the greatest necessity of the form of manifestation: whereby 'necessity' means unquestionably more than what theologians on

4 *GL* II, pp. 22–23.
5 *GL* II, pp. 24–25.

the whole understand by 'convenience' – which perhaps they are not able to understand any better precisely because of their neglect of the aesthetic analogy.[6]

We shall not be surprised at the variety of theological styles nor at the claim that these are all, in the last analysis, ways of expressing the same reality, if we bear in mind that a theology beautifully attuned to its own proper object, the divine glory, is

the expression of an expression: on the one hand, an obedient repetition of the expression of revelation imprinted on the believer; and, on the other, a creative, child-like, free sharing in the bringing-to-expression in the Holy Spirit – who is the Spirit of Christ, of the Church and of the believer – of the mystery which expresses itself.[7]

Balthasar proposes the following division of labour between the tasks allotted to unity and those given to plurality in theological aesthetics. On the side of *unity* come, first, the form of revelation itself, the 'unique content of Christian theology' which each theologian must seek to make appear as thoroughly as he or she can; and secondly, the teaching of the Church, which provides the 'binding ground rules' for all such inter-pretation. On the side of *plurality*, Balthasar, with evidently, a high doctrine of the (orthodox!) theologian's office, speaks of him or her as commissioned, by a special charism, to see and interpret the divine revelatory form – whether as a whole or in some vital dimension of itself – under a 'particular, perhaps up to now little noticed, aspect'.[8] The living revelation is not only possessed of form; in Balthasar's view, it is also creative of form, able to call forth in history a vast array of great theologies whose inner form it inspires.

It is these 'inner forms' (rather than the outward stylistic qualities which are their sacrament) that Balthasar will try to capture in what follows. And here – faced with, in effect, a dozen monographs, compact though these are – I propose to give the reader an inkling of what Balthasar attempts by singling out what seem the most significant points in his account of each of these writers. In this chapter, I discuss the five doctors of the patristic and mediaeval Church who occupy Balthasar in Volume II of *Herrlichkeit* – a 'Constellation of Clerics', while in the chapter that follows I survey the remaining seven figures, whom Balthasar regards as 'lay theologians'. Since two of these, John of the Cross and Hopkins, were priests, it is evident that Balthasar was not using the term 'lay' in its ecclesiological sense. He means, firstly, those who chose to write in their vernaculars (and thereby not to follow the line of professional theology); and secondly, those who give primacy to 'concrete personal existence' – the significance of both of which points he will in due course develop in relation to Dante.

6 *GL* II, p. 27.
7 *GL* II, p. 28.
8 *GL* II, p. 28. The reader might be interested to compare here my own similar yet distinct approach in *The Shape of Catholic Theology. An Introduction to its Sources, Principles and History* (Collegeville, Minn. and Edinburgh 1991), pp. 349–355.

Irenaeus

Balthasar begins, however, with 'clerical styles', and first of all with St Irenaeus: Greek Father of the Church, and early ornament of the primatial see of the Gauls, at Lyons. As we shall see, Irenaeus' principal contribution to theological aesthetics is, for Balthasar, his 'historical aesthetic', his account of saving history as a wonderfully ordered whole. But there is more to say than this. While admitting that Irenaeus' thinking *may* have been stimulated on various particular points by the challenge of *gnôsis*, Balthasar considers that Maritain could well have taken him as his first 'anti-modern' – the first Christian thinker who consciously opted to present the faith not in terms of its congruence with contemporary religious and intellectual aspiration, or even with 'perennial modernity', but inasmuch as its 'internal obviousness' is irrefutable, irresistible.[9] Irenaean thought circles freely in the space defined by the mysteries, exhibiting the beauty of their harmonious reciprocity as it does so.

Balthasar notes the predominance of visual metaphors in Irenaeus' writings: revelation and its human appropriation is *ostensio, manifestatio, visio*. What Christ appeared to be, that he was:[10] the manifestation of the Father through the Word takes place in the self-showing of the incarnate One in his life, death and resurrection, as pointed to by the Scriptures; in seeing these saving mysteries we begin upon the eschatological vision of God. Here 'seeing' is nothing pejoratively theoretical, but is 'identical with life-giving, nourishing, purifying and bliss-giving communication . . .' in the Holy Spirit.[11] Moreover, such seeing is through our own eyes, though healed and transfigured: it is the 'Father's ancient creation', as Irenaeus puts it, which through Son and Spirit gains access to the Father's glory. Here, in his affirmation of the fundamental goodness of the world, Irenaeus' critique of the Gnostics agrees (though Balthasar does not say this) with that of such Neo-Platonists as Plotinus.

The beauty of Irenaean salvation lies in its wonderfully *integrated* quality. As the fulfiller – the 'recapitulator' – of what humanity was meant to be at its origin, and of all the chief determining aspects of its subsequent experience, the Word made flesh has the power to 'give every emergent thing scope for perfection',[12] precisely by drawing it actively to himself, assimilating it to his own fulness. 'The ground of the advance of the inchoate is thus found in the fulfilling return of the definitive, by whose integrating power everything is decided.'[13] And yet this is no mere miraculous incursion of divine power, essentially unconnected to the pre-existing pattern of the human creation. For the created pattern already knew in Adam an integrating focus – which is why the interrelation of the two heads of humanity, Adam and Christ, is so important to Irenaeus, and why he considers it a theological necessity that the first Adam should, thanks to the second, be redeemed.

9 J. Maritain, *Anti-moderne* (Paris 1922²).
10 F. Sagnard, O.P. (ed.), *Contre les hérésies* III (Paris 1952), p. 328.
11 *GL* II, p. 47.
12 *GL* II, p. 52.
13 *GL* II, p. 53.

But if the recapitulation concept lies at the heart of Irenaeus' theological aesthetics, that heart itself possesses a centre. The 'still centre' as Balthasar terms it, of all Irenaean thought is the notion of the humanity which, borne as it is by God, is capable of sustaining the weight of the divine – a concept, incidentally, which will be crucial to the second volume of his theological logic, his 'Christo-logic'. Owing not only to the Creator's gift to man of his image and likeness but also to the supernatural gift of the Spirit, it is possible to think of 'man bearing and receiving and containing the Son of God'.[14]

From this midpoint of the incarnation – the God-enabled God-bearing which resumes and brings to perfection the origin, structure and history of humanity – Irenaeus' camera-work pans out in three directions. On Balthasar's analysis, three themes display the 'organising power and the blazing heat of the recapitulative movement':[15] the triune God, hidden and revealed; the Creator's relation to the human creature; and the salvific dispensation which binds together Israel, the gospel and the Church. Let us glance at each in turn.

Consider first the *Holy Trinity*. For Irenaeus, Father, Son and Spirit are joined in an eternal open trialogue: unlike the divine powers of Gnosticism, constantly seeking or finding, and hence enmeshed in ignorance, the trinitarian persons conduct their exchange in the everlasting light and freedom. Without prejudice to his unknowability, which is a function of his transcendence, the Father makes himself known – not in his greatness, which is immeasurable, but in his love – through the office of the Word by which 'we learn, if we are responsive, more and more how great God is and that it is he who through himself establishes and chooses everything and makes it beautiful and contains it'.[16] To be sure, the Word for Irenaeus does not exercise this office without the collaboration of the Father's other 'hand', the Spirit.

Consider next the *relation between Creator and creature*. This same triune Lord is the creature's absolute Source in whom inheres what Irenaeus terms: 'the substance of creatures and the pattern of his artefacts and the beauty of the individual life-form'.[17] The humanity he has made to his image and likeness he calls to communion with himself, as his perfect artwork, remade through the visible Image, Jesus Christ, in which the invisible Archetype is seen on earth. Since the 'true man is soul in body and grace in both',[18] the eschatologically whole man is not the disembodied post-mortem soul but the risen flesh, where the Holy Spirit is victorious over man's mortal wounds: sin and death.

The Creator's work is only properly seen at its mid-point, the God-man, in his crucified and risen glory. That God can do all things is clear, writes Balthasar by way of interpretation of Irenaeus, but that 'man together with God can also do all things had to be proved'.[19] As, in

14 F. Sagnard, O.P. (ed.), *Contre les Hérésies* III (Paris 1952), p. 282.
15 *GL* II, p. 58.
16 W. W. Harvey (ed.), *Sancti Irenaei, episcopi Lugdunensis, Libros quinque adversus haereses* (Cambridge 1857), II, pp. 212–213.
17 Ibid., p. 213.
18 *GL* II, p. 64.
19 *GL* II, p. 68.

Balthasar's favourite metaphor, the 'fruit' both of the world and of the Father, Christ united the Spirit with man, in his affinity with both leading them back – and here the language is once more that of Irenaeus himself – to 'mutual love and harmony'.[20] Anticipating his own theology of the atonement, both in *Herrlichkeit*, and in his extended meditation on the Easter triduum, *Mysterium Paschale*, Balthasar summarises Irenaeus' message of agony and glory:

> The same person must be glorified and abased, must penetrate heights and depths, in order to make up by his humiliation for Adam's arrogance, must live through all the ages of man in order to heal all. Salvation lies in the human life and fate of Jesus, and this includes his real death; really dying, however, means going down to the realm of the dead, to Hades, and not just leaving the cross to return to the Father. And if everything in the fate of Jesus is the revelation of his Father, so too is his Passion. It is the real suffering and dying man who, by what he completely and utterly is, glorifies the Father, and this man who suffers and is humiliated even to death is much more magnificent than all the bloodless patterns of the Gnostics. . . . Through the suffering flesh of Christ the Father's light reaches us; that is the essence of the *mystêrion*.[21]

And consider too the *salvific dispensation that binds together Israel, the Gospel and the Church*. In the first place, the order of salvation in the Old Testament is a *praeadaptio, praeformatio, praemeditatio* (in this context a preliminary *training*) for the coming of Christ. The child Adam is to learn wisdom through injury; his Fall, though not inevitable, had a kind of necessity about it. Had all goodness been man's inalienable possession from the outset he would not have valued the society of God as a prize worth great effort: 'Sight would not be so desirable to us if we had not learned how awful it is not to see . . .'.[22] The mutual accustoming of God and man – an idea already important to Balthasar in the first volume of *Herrlichkeit* – explains to perfection why the Redeemer came so 'late', after multiple generations of Israel's *educative* spiritual experience. And in any case, since for Irenaeus Son and Spirit are the manifestness of the Father, all the Old Testament theophanies (as Balthasar puts it) *are* the Son, just as all inspiration is the Spirit. Thus in the words of the *Demonstration of the Apostolic Preaching*, the Son 'was with our humanity from eternity, announcing beforehand the things that were to happen later and instructing men in the things of God'.[23] Any attempt to prise apart the two covenants, especially, in the horrendous example offered by Marcion, to ascribe them to different deities, means to 'undo all God's art'.[24] Originating in Abraham's free obedience, the ancient covenant helped

20 F. Sagnard, O.P. (ed.), *Contre les hérésies* III (Paris 1952), p. 326.
21 *GL* II, pp. 68–69, 70.
22 W. W. Harvey (ed.), *Sancti Irenaei, episcopi Lugdunensis, Libros quinque adversus haereses* (Cambridge 1857), II, p. 291.
23 L. M. Froidevaux (ed.), *Irénée de Lyons, Démonstration de la Prédication apostolique* (Paris 1959), p. 45.
24 *GL* II, p. 82.

men and women to find, through law, the way to love, and by the prophets, avoiding legalism, to seek the essence of the God-man relationship in the inwardness of hearts.

Irenaeus had to face, accordingly, the question of what, in such a context of ripe development, could constitute the 'novelty value' of the gospel. Though everything in the New Covenant might have been announced beforehand in the form of teaching, now, with the gospel, it becomes a person – and *therefore* is fulfilment. Balthasar writes:

> In addition to the correspondence and the intensification there is Christ's divine quality and his efforts to transpose everything verbal and symbolic into living existence and so to recapitulate it by giving it concrete form in such a way that its reality is enhanced.[25]

The moment of the incarnation is the moment of unsurpassable fulness.

> With this creative event in view the Father gave this 'hour' the character of the fulness of time. In this fulness not only the Old Covenant but also all human and physical nature is fulfilled, because now the Word is present within the flesh.[26]

And so, lastly, the Church steps into view, with her 'timeless newness' which Balthasar connects with Irenaeus' statement that, though the incarnation is a ripening into fulness it is also a return to – a now *un-*threatened – childhood, since the Word became a child like us. Balthasar captures Irenaeus' ecclesiology quite brilliantly in a few lines:

> In Irenaeus the Church . . . stands historically at the end of the early Christian era, the splendour of which still surrounds it, and at the beginning of the Catholic form of the world, the features of which it has already assumed. It is the esoteric mystery of the world and of Christ and yet the most public and anti-sectarian body known to history. It is fully the pneumatic and charismatic Church as in Tertullian; but Irenaeus avoids the dangers and disasters which befell Tertullian, because at the same time in his view the Church remains resolutely in the spirit of the apostolic kerygma and paradosis.[27]

Nor could this be for Irenaeus a privileged originating moment whose plenary freshness may not always be with us. The Spirit *perpetually* rejuvenates the Church, giving her 'eternally young beauty'.[28] By the continual refreshment which comes from abiding in the person of the fulfiller the Church's existence lies wide open to eternal life.

Balthasar emphasises then the way in which the Christian aesthetic of Irenaeus excels its Gnostic rival by its capacity to display the 'temporal art' of God, his beautifully proportioned ordering of time. For Irenaeus,

25 *GL* II, pp. 85–86.
26 *GL* II, p. 86.
27 Ibid.
28 *GL* II, p. 88.

the beauty of the cosmos, of *cosmic order*, can never be sundered from the artistic intention of its Creator, which is disclosed only in the recapitulation in time, in the *temporal order*. God creates by his 'artistic Logos', for everything was created in accord with the divine Word who alone has the measure of the Father's mind. Creative power, wisdom and goodness were disclosed from the beginning, but it takes that expression of the 'symphony of being and history' which is Holy Scripture, interpreted by the rule of faith, for us to hear the chords and cadences aright.[29] The supreme artwork of God is the human being – and here Balthasar locates the origin of that vital Irenaean concept, the mutual 'glorification' of God and man. 'Man, who preserves God's art in himself and obediently opens himself to its disposing, glorifies the artist and the artist glorifies himself in his work.'[30] The natural world, as found in the first moment of Adam's creation, is a promise of the supernatural order to come, yet each stage in the unfolding of God's plan must follow at its proper time, the *aptum tempus* – Irenaeus' version of the New Testament's *kairos*, or appointed hour.

> The 'times' and their 'fulfilment' are 'appointed' according to the Father's 'pleasure' so that 'his art might not be in vain', but this pleasure is always translated into the order of time by the Son and Spirit: 'and so, through this disposition and by such rhythms and with such guides, man, who has been produced and shaped, is led towards the image and likeness of the ungenerate God. In all this the Father approves and prescribes, the Son executes and forms, the Spirit nourishes and increases, while man gently advances and moves towards perfection, in order, that is, to approach the Uncreated'.[31]

Although Balthasar criticises Irenaeus for an excessively homogenising view of the relation between the two Testaments (which in reality should be treated as highly dramatic, dialectical – *Theodramatik* will bring this out in full measure), he regards his weak sense of historical context, almost inevitable in his period, as a venial offence:

> The elimination of this defect by modern historical exegesis is the removal of a defect which is accidental in Irenaeus; it is the true continuation and liberation of his basic purpose across the centuries.[32]

Balthasar is also minded to look mercifully on Irenaeus' millenarianism. Though his insertion of a transfigured earth into an apocalyptic space between general resurrection and general judgment was unfortunate (and the result of too literal a tendency to see the Church as re-entry on the inheritance – the land – promised to Abraham, recapitulation with a

29 *GL* II, p. 73.
30 *GL* II, p. 74.
31 *GL* II, p. 77, with an internal citation of F. Sagnard, O.P. (ed.), *Contre les hérésies* (Paris 1952), III, p. 382; and W. W. Harvey (ed.), *Sancti Irenaei, episcopi Lugdunensis, Quinque libros adverses haereses* (Cambridge 1857), II, p. 296.
32 *GL* II, p. 91.

vengeance!), much may be forgiven the 'anti-spiritualising tendency in his eschatology'.[33] Balthasar will return to the theme of the resurrection of the flesh, highly significant as this is for a theological aesthetics, in his account of Bonaventure, the last of his 'clerical' stylists in *Herrlichkeit*. It is, as he points out here, important for the dialogue with Judaism he attempted in his study of Buber – and for the debate with modern cosmology, as well as with the cosmic religiosity of a Teilhard de Chardin.

Irenaeus occurs first in the 'symphony of sources' of *Herrlichkeit* not simply because of the accident that he is the first in historical time of Balthasar's Christian witnesses. The appearance of the concept of salvation history, centred on Christ, as the 'art of God' in Irenaeus' thought, and the general structure and temper of Irenaean theology as Balthasar captures it in these pages brings these two 'fathers of the Church' together across the gap of centuries.

Augustine

How does Augustine's theology exemplify the theme of beauty *in divinis*? Balthasar regards Augustine's (long drawn out) conversion as essentially a turning from a 'lower' to a 'higher' aesthetics.

> No one has praised God so assiduously as the supreme beauty or attempted so consistently to capture the true and the good with the categories of aesthetics as Augustine in the period during and after his conversion.[34]

Balthasar agrees with Pierre Courcelle that Augustine's Plotinianism came to him through Christian Neo-Platonism: his early writings do not show a pre-Christian mind, though they certainly express a metaphysically attuned one. The two things – 'philosophical form' and Christian teaching as the content which that form 'frames and structures' – are equally well attested there.

In point of fact Balthasar treats the *De vera religione* of 390, rather than the *Confessions* (with their necessarily subjective emphasis), as the key to Augustine's theological 'seeing'. That work – essentially the 'refraction of the Creed in the temperament of a religious philosopher'[35] – presents God as the Sun of spirits, a Light which illumines all the intellectual objects the soul knows and does so, moreover, the more penetratingly where the soul is engaged in self-purification and recollection into unity. The divine, absolute character of truth is not there for the taking by cognitive *force majeure*; finite intellect must be prepared so as to *receive* this disclosure for what it is. Here Augustine's early philosophical theology is in perfect harmony with his later (anti-Pelagian) theology of grace. And in a litany of phrases from the *De libero arbitrio*, the *De quantitate animae* and the *Soliloquia*, Balthasar recalls how for Augustine God's truth 'shows its face', 'places itself at the ready', 'manifests itself when it pleases' and 'lifts up to itself'. Here Balthasar sees prefigured:

33 *GL* II, p. 93.
34 *GL* II, p. 95.
35 *GL* II, p. 97.

the later anti-Pelagian dialectic, which on the one hand must main-tain that the structure of the human mind and, in consequence, of its freedom has not been destroyed by the Fall, but on the other that man, as a result of his alienation, must be incapable of a return to authenticity, of a free choice of the supreme God in love.[36]

Balthasar explores Augustine's approach to the existence of God in a way which echoes his own reflections in his study of the 'truth of the world', throwing light (precisely!) on his *mélange* of realism and Idealism in the opening volume of the theological logic. The light of infinite, absolute mind is, in its informing of finite, contingent mind, the transcendental condition of the latter's mental structure – and Balthasar goes so far in the direction of Idealism as to say that the recognition of the need for such a conditioning principle is a recommendation of Kant's critical philosophy and Fichtean and Hegelian philosophical mysticism. And yet this all-conditioning light is *truly* absolute – free, and therefore personal: something which none of these gentlemen apprehended. Relation with the personal Absolute – by prayer, humility, purification – is essential to the act of coming to know being.

The spirit, once attuned in this way to truth:

> sees God in all things (which are what they are only by participa-tion in an unqualified being, life and mind), and it can see them in no other way than in their participation in God; but equally it sees God over all things, since God can be the ground of all things only because he is no one of them, which is why the supreme activity of human freedom is, when presented with the whole divinely established order of the world, to prefer God himself as the far better. When things reveal God, they point beyond them-selves to him; that is, they conceal him in themselves to reveal him in himself. The inner order of being is thus perceived by the same vision which sees also the transcendent freedom of the Creator and Orderer.[37]

Finally, in his skirting the foothills of Augustine's theology of beauty proper, Balthasar points out how the divine truth – as supra-subjective, neither thine nor mine for essentially unprivatised – is internally linked to goodness. The order of things understood is the order of love.

Such are the foundations on which Augustine can construct, the more safely, a theological aesthetic which will be saved from the charge of irrationalism precisely through this 'ostension' of a 'light-filled, light-giving essential truth', sacred and gracious in character, requiring purity and vigilance from the soul that would receive it, as well as the longing for it in love. Yet this can be no *Christian* aesthetic until Augustine has spoken of a definitive manifestation of the infinite in finite form, has adverted, that is, to the incarnational principle.

---

36 *GL* II, p. 112.
37 *GL* II, pp. 108–109.

The triune Creator provides form for what is shapeless – an activity Augustine associates with the *Son* – within an integrated order. Beings do not only possess a structured nature, they are also situated within a universal order – and this Augustine links to the *Holy Spirit*.[38] In the fulness of time, accordingly, the Son will become man, taking individual form, while the Spirit will bring the redeemed universe into harmony with that form.

Augustine's sense of the harmony of finite form is based – at any rate, formally – on ancient Platonic and, behind Plato, Pythagorean speculations about the significance of number. Balthasar's own favoured ontological key concept of *measure* has one of its own sources here, linked as it is to the notion of *numerus*. For Augustine, the concept of number applies analogously to all levels of being:

> from the usual mathematical sense in the material world through the sense of proportion (in space) and rhythm (in time) within the world of souls (external and internal sense and memory) to harmony and intellectual correspondence in the realm of the mind, and finally to the harmonies we can only guess at in divine wisdom, from whose numbers all form has flowed and in whose light it is seen and enjoyed as a beautiful copy of the eternal beauty.[39]

But the combination of Augustine's philosophical intellectualism and a nervousness, born of personal experience, when faced with the potentially overwhelming power of the imagination and senses, led him, in Balthasar's view, to set the latter at a lower price than a Christian thinker should. In Augustine, the incarnational principle is only really saved by the incarnation.

> The further Augustine penetrates into Scripture and theology, the more detailed and the richer become not only the figure of the Son as eternal wisdom and original likeness, through which and by participation in which all things can be traces and images of God, but also the figure of the incarnate, humble and humiliated Christ, disfigured to the point where no image is left.[40]

---

38 In a fascinating contrast and comparison of Augustine here with Aquinas, Balthasar points out how Thomas will later distinguish sharply between creation proper – which takes place in the order of being where the finite structure is composed of *esse* and *essentia* – and that of the in-forming of the formless – which concerns the order of nature with its elements of matter and form. For Augustine these still coincide since for him the supremely existent Being is understood platonically as absolute Unity. As a consequence, contingency and createdness can be adequately expressed in terms of the unity – striven for but never attained – characteristic of finite things: thus *GL* II, p. 115.

39 *GL* II, pp. 117–118.

40 *GL* II, p. 122. Note the twist in the tail here compared with the more 'standard' view that Augustine's faith in the Incarnation as theologian, preacher, bishop redeemed the somewhat disincarnate epistemology he possessed as philosopher and rhetor: cf. C. Harrison, *Beauty and Revelation in the Thought of Saint Augustine* (Oxford 1992), pp. 35–36.

He now sees the kenosis of the Word-made-man as the revelation in fulness of the beauty of God: 'the path itself is beauty'.[41]

> And so even that 'hidden sanctuary' of the eternal numbers is drawn back up into heaven like the linen cloth in Peter's vision, and being swept up in ecstasy to the heavenly numbers gives way to the simple following of Christ.[42]

Not that there is anything very simple about the account of the 'reality of the image' in Augustinian thought with which Balthasar follows this breathtakingly daring passage. For he at once launches into a profound analysis of the contrasting senses in which the Platonist tradition both abetted and hindered Augustine's vocation as a Catholic doctor. Negatively, Platonism is a 'dualism of world and God, sense and mind, not mediated as in Aristotelianism', and yet positively it is a 'monistically descending outpouring of the One truth-and-beauty and a monistically ascending eros moving towards this One'.[43] This passage provides students of Balthasar with a useful key as to what he opposed, and what he admired, and wished to salvage, in Platonism (and especially in Neo-Platonism).

Balthasar is keen not to misinterpret Platonism – least of all Augustine's – in terms of what he calls a *vulgar* dualism, a two-tier cosmos where the realm of the intellect and of truth sits atop the domain of the senses and of appearance. As he points put:

> The true cause of the lower world's lack of being is merely that it is not understood and construed in terms of the upper as is required for truth, for in fact the truth of being is not restricted to the upper world, but embraces the whole, though the whole as viewed from above.[44]

The trouble is that, in Augustine's judgment, the lower will rarely accept instruction from the upper, as he brings out in his little myth of Philokalia and Philosophia. Of these two birds, 'Wisdom-lover', soaring to the heavens, recognises 'Beauty-lover', singing in her cage, as her sister, but only rarely succeeds in freeing her from earth.[45] The notion that the whole (upper *and* lower) can be recognised as glorious from a superior vantage-point – ultimately, that of divine Providence – led Augustine to his 'aesthetic' theodicy, or attempted resolution of the problem of evil. To this, however, Balthasar shows himself much opposed. Treating not just physical evil but moral evil too as tesserae in a mosaic pavement where every piece is necessary for the overall splendour of the whole draws from Balthasar a rebuke of rare sharpness.

> It will be this aesthetic justification, and not Scripture, which will be the source of the shadows which from Gottschalk onwards darken

41 *De libero arbitrio* II. 45; *Enarrationes in psalmos* 123, 2.
42 *GL* II, p. 123.
43 *GL* II, p. 123.
44 *GL* II, p. 127.
45 *Contra academicos* II. 7.

the middle ages and, from Calvin and Jansenius, the Christianity of the modern period ... Augustine's concluding aesthetic theodicy represents a twofold reduction of the biblical data, first by interpreting its existential statements in aesthetic and systematic terms and again because this interpretation, in which immanent evil, considered transcendently, becomes good, is then used to close a gap left open by philosophy.[46]

To Balthasar's mind, neither philosophy nor systematics but only what he called a 'deeper biblical theology' can solve this one – a task to which he addressed himself in the closing volume of *Theodramatik*. Whether his eschatology is fully consonant with theological (and even doctrinal) tradition is another question.

Fortunately for theological aesthetics, Augustine's thought about beauty can be developed without deviating up the cul-de-sac of aesthetic theodicy. How so? There is, first, the notion of virtue as the 'eurhythmy' of the soul, at once goodness and beauty.[47] Balthasar takes from this not a lesson about the loveliness of the embodied (and hence visible) action of the right-acting person so much as a doctrine of how virtuous subjectivity, coming to itself, knows itself as inner light given from the Light of God. Here is where one can overhear the *melodia interior* spoken of in Book 4 of the *Confessions*. Already in Plato the unenviousness of the divine Light had made it supremely lovable and worthy of ethical mimesis; when with the gospel, it names itself as sovereignly free Love, the *erōs* provoked in Platonic love is deepened into sheer *frui*: 'settled and blossoming enjoyment'.[48] Only where God is understood as the Trinity is this possible (for only the Trinity is Love *in se*) – and hence Augustine's treatment of the triune structures in created reality can be called the conclusion not just of his metaphysics but of his aesthetics likewise.

> It is only in the light of such [trinitarian] considerations that the beauty of all being is fully justified, because here for the first time the inner vitality and dimensionality of being as such fully emerges and gives being the fulness and richness which neither the hierarchical pyramid alone nor the dynamic of eros alone was able to give it.[49]

Nor can Balthasar object when in the closing book of the *De Trinitate* Augustine takes a duster to rub out this wondrous pastel, for the God we would deal with is 'known by unknowing'.[50]

But what of the trinitarian Son made man? Is he – even, or perhaps especially, in his passion – to be called 'beautiful'? Reviewing the efforts of the Fathers to come to terms with the conflicting prophecies (more fair than all the sons of men, Psalm 45; no beauty or comeliness, Isaiah 53),

---

46 *GL* II, p. 128.
47 Cf. *Enarrationes in psalmos*, 58, 18.
48 *GL* II, p. 133.
49 *GL* II, p. 134.
50 *De ordine* II. 44.

Balthasar finds sympathetic Augustine's assertion that Christ's veiling of his beauty was inspired by a desire to make the ugly beautiful by his love. In the tractates on the First Letter of John, Augustine explains how the deformed soul can become lovely by loving the eternally beautiful; for as his love grows in the soul, it becomes itself beautiful.[51] In the *Enarrationes in psalmos*, the Church, moved by the voluntary deformity of the Crucified, confesses her guilt and becomes beautiful; or, as Balthasar sums up Augustine's train of thought, Christ is the 'ugly root from which the beautiful tree of the Church rises'.[52] The fruit is seen finally in the life of the resurrection, when the bodily senses will have their share in the vision of God.

Balthasar's conclusion on Augustine includes a helpful clarification of the basic notion of theological aesthetics. Like Pascal, Soloviev and Newman, Augustine rested the 'certainty of the ultimate rightness of the *vera religio*' on a 'seeing' of that rightness of a kind that can only be called, at any rate in a broad sense, *aesthetic*. At the same time, however, this is a vision which can bear rational investigation – and which will acquire self-evidence for the one who makes the mind's eye pure.

If the tone of Augustine's writing derives from an equilibrium between the 'pathos of rhythmical proportion' and that of infinity, his sense of theological harmony is invested above all in the relationship between personal development and the overarching divine Providence. This can lead him to speak in the accents of Irenaeus, as in that pot-pourri of a treatise the *De diversis quaestionibus LXXXIII*: 'All beauty derives from the supreme beauty which is God, but the beauty of the ages from the appropriateness of the sequence of things.'[53] Yet his Christian Platonism causes him to 'perceive always, through the flow of history, the relation between time and eternity' – and the danger of rendering otiose 'the great aesthetic turning-point of Christian history, the dialectic of the Testaments',[54] which all such Platonism carries with it, will surely recur when Balthasar turns to the third of his witnesses, the Pseudo-Denys.

Denys

To Balthasar, Denys is a monk who 'dying to the world, assumes the name of a saint, and lives in his encompassing reality', as in Scripture the continuators of Isaiah to a second and third generation (Deutero- and Trito-Isaiah) had done likewise. And his peculiar mystagogic idiom, the language of the Church's erstwhile 'discipline of the secret' and of the Hellenistic mysteries, is but a philological and aesthetic instrument used in the shaping of a 'unique creation of theological form'.[55]

In the context of a theological aesthetics, it has to be on such form that interest is focussed. Balthasar must necessarily come to terms with the eternity-centred thinking which had struck him as insufficiently tutored by Scripture when he encountered it in Augustine and now returns with

51 *Tractates on I John*, 9, 9.
52 *GL* II, p. 137.
53 *De diversis quaestionibus* LXXXIII, 44.
54 *GL* II, p. 143.
55 *GL* II, p. 153.

redoubled vigour. Denys claimed to draw all his wisdom from the Bible, and yet he consciously chose – as, so Balthasar maintains, an artifice, a strategy of art –

> not to follow through in thought the Biblical history of salvation, but from the viewpoint of timeless *theôria* to contemplate the essentially timeless (and only lately temporal) outflow of the eternally good God, or rather, as Denys never tires of saying, to celebrate it.[56]

By actualising the mysteries of salvation as their celebration by the Church, Denys casts his theology in the form of a liturgical action – and this is to treat its divine object as something supratemporal, to be fêted out of time and space by the aesthetic act of praise.[57] For art, like the game, is not within the ordinary continua of space and time.

Alternatively, Balthasar can describe the rationale of the *Corpus Dionysiacum* as a placing at the service of Christian theology of the religio-aesthetic character of Greek thought from Plato to Plotinus: namely, the experience of the cosmos as the 'representation and manifestation of the hidden transcendent beauty of God'.[58] As Balthasar explains, the being of God's creative and salvific movement is *manifestation of the unmanifest*: as manifestation, it is a coming forth, and as reference to the unmanifest, it is return. In other words, it displays, within the context of the God-world relationship, that same pattern – disclosure, and yet simultaneously concealment – which, in the first volume of the theological logic, Balthasar treated as typical of a phenomenological account of being at large. Being appears: but in disclosing, through appearance, its own depth, it also hides itself the more. This 'proportion', itself the fulcrum of all aesthetics, is, as Balthasar puts it, 'without being ruptured, infinitely transcended and, as it were, stretched out, when it is a matter of the relation between God and the world'.[59]

The dialectic of negative and affirmative theology takes its rise from here. For the more the aesthetic is transcended in profound, wondering experience of the unmanifest God (which goes beyond simply knowing him as manifest), the more possible it becomes to discern *what it is* that is manifest – and hence (by a merely apparent paradox) the truth of the aesthetic is confirmed.

> Everything lies in the circular movement between procession and return, the cataphatic and the apophatic, nothing can find fulfilment except by entering into this movement. No explanations can help him who does not see the beauty; no 'proof of the existence of God' can help him who cannot see *what* is manifest in the world; no apologetic can be any use to him for whom the truth that radiates from the centre of theology is not evident.[60]

---

56 *GL* II, p. 153.
57 Cf. Balthasar's comment that 'the "hymnic" is for Denys a methodology of theological thinking and speaking', *GL* II, p. 160.
58 *GL* II, p. 154.
59 *GL* II, p. 165.
60 *GL* II, p. 166.

But 'return' to God, in Christian terms can only be (once again) salvation, and as the treatise *On the Ecclesiastical Hierarchy* makes abundantly plain, the *saving* mystery of God is found for Denys in ministry and sacrament. If we then raise the question of the ethical performance of those who share in these realities – surely relevant to gospel living as this is, Denys will simply respond that, of course, the moral is *called to coincide with* the ontological. This is why, in his companion treatise *On the Celestial Hierarchy*, the angelic orders are 'forever set over the Church who must see herself as their earthly translation'.[61] By the same token, the 'private' praise of God by the mystics is not something different from her public liturgy – for is it not the developed expression of the Church's praise?

Balthasar uses the opportunity of his exposition of Dionysian thought to cock a snook at those contemporary Catholic theologians who would have it that 'the world sets the agenda', or at any rate always have one eye on the world. In Denys' own comparison, just as the earthly artist must look constantly to archetypal form if he is to depict the truth in the likeness, so those who would inscribe the divine beauty in their minds will find that only 'the constant and intent contemplation of [God's] fragrant and secret Beauty is rewarded by that manifestation which is unerring and most godlike'.[62] Denys is thinking of the saints – but Balthasar adds that all this applies equally to the theologian. *Can* the author of penetrating theological studies of contemporary novelists and playwrights have intended to dismiss so cavalierly *les réalités terrestres*? It is not a question of dismissing the world's needs but of prioritising the divine message which alone can both sift and meet them: what Balthasar opposes is the theologian's 'looking restlessly back and forth between the needs of his age and the apparently so uncontemporary divine truth in the Church', rather than giving wholehearted primacy to the latter in its (in fact) perennial pertinence.

The world of Denys, as Balthasar interprets him, is an iconic world, but one where the epiphanic power of the image is always to be measured by the analogy of being, in the mystical understanding of that concept which the Swiss theologian, following the cue of Przywara, consistently follows. Balthasar is pleased to find that, whereas Gregory of Nyssa spoke of the 'erotic' movement of man towards God, the desiring search of thirsty being for its fulfilment, as overthrowing all limit,[63] Denys keeps 'measure' (that favoured Balthasarian term) even in the striving of *erôs* for infinity.

Anselm

How does Anselm – best known for his attempted 'ontological' proof of God's existence, as well as his 'juridical' theory of the atonement come to be the next of Balthasar's witnesses for the claim that theological aesthetics are eminently traditional in Catholic divinity? The

61 *GL* II, p. 166.
62 *On the Ecclesiastical Hierarchy* IV. 3. 1.
63 See my 'Gregory of Nyssa and the Movement of Eros' in *A Grammar of Consent. The Existence of God in Christian Tradition* (Notre Dame, Ind. and London 1991), pp. 39–52.

first of Balthasar's two mediaeval 'clerical' theologians (the other will be Bonaventure) comes across, in his presentation, not as an incipient rationalist, but as a *contemplative reasoner*.

> Anselm contemplates the highest rectitude (*rectitudo*) of the divine revelation in creation and redemption; he discerns its truth from the harmony, from the faultless proportions, from the way in which it must be so (*necessitas*), something at once dependent on the utmost freedom and manifesting the utmost freedom, and this vision reveals to him absolute beauty: God's beauty in the freely fashioned form of the world. When he asks by what reason or necessity God was made man (*qua ratione vel necessitate Deus homo factus est*), the question appears to him 'very difficult, but in its solution it is intelligible to all and delightful both on account of its usefulness and on account of the beauty of the reason (rationis pulchritudinem)'.[64]

The subject Anselm's disciple Boso raises is *speciosa ratione*, fair with a reason beyond human understanding, just as it has to do with him (Christ) who is, in the words of Isaiah, applied to the Saviour by the Church, 'beautiful above the sons of men'.[65] Balthasar insists that the question, Did Anselm speak as philosopher or theologian?, is fundamentally misplaced (even though we can, using modern categories, assign some of his works more to the first, others more to the second category). Anselm understood the biblical revelation as the transcendental consummation of ancient philosophy which was itself in its principal concerns theological through and through. Revelation enables philosophy to find its authentic self – though at the same time it would be unthinkable to wish to dispense with reason and live 'from faith alone'. Here Balthasar remains faithful to the view of the interrelation of nature and grace (and so of reason and faith, philosophy and theology) laid down in the opening pages of *Theologik*.

The beauty of reason, Christian yet human, in Anselm is a differentiated unity consisting in three 'moments', each of which has its 'aesthetic' aspect. First, theology issues from life based on the revealed, salvific truth, a life which knows itself to be always dependent on the God of free grace. Faith's point of departure, which where faith is serious, makes reason catch up with it, is a being overwhelmed by the ever-greater God and the consequent (or concomitant) realisation that the sinful self is out of tune. Secondly, there comes the effort of conceptual understanding so as to achieve insight into faith's Object – an effort which, in Anselm's picture, mind, given dignity by the gospel, wants to make from very gratitude to God. 'To think' for Anselm is to make something perspicuously visible to spiritual sight. Or as Balthasar expounds Anselmian 'aesthetic reason':

> The foremost task for the thinker is to develop and use [the] power of synthetic vision, the capacity to gather together what is separated which is the root meaning of *legere, logos*. . . . This power of uniting

64 *GL* II, p. 211, citing *Cur Deus homo* I. 1.
65 *Cur Deus homo* I. 3.

in the *intuitus*, which raises one from a particular view to a universal vision, is judgment.[66]

The logic involved must have an aesthetic dimension, since the self-revelation of God in saving history, with Jesus Christ as its centre, unfolds not only with ordered necessity but also in unsurpassable freedom. The meaning of the ontological 'proof' is surely, opines Balthasar, that God is the presupposition for all (and so any) being, and all thought (and so any thinker). Not this, however, is the fulfilment of the act of philosophising for Anselm but rather:

> the revelation of the mercy of the Father in the suffering Son, in which in an incomprehensible manner all righteousness is satisfied . . . ; herein lies nothing less than the overwhelming of the aesthetic reason of faith by the incomprehensibility of the divine love, an incomprehensibility radiating in the form of revelation as it is exhibited . . .[67]

And thirdly, then, there comes delight and joy. This is not simply, in Anselm's *reportage*, response to the beauty of God's world and, yet more wonderful, his saving dispensation. Rather is it intrinsically related to the utilisation of aesthetic reason itself. As Balthasar explains:

> Because the joy of finding the harmonies hidden in the history of salvation presupposes the grace of faith and therefore supplicating prayer, it will at the same time be both satisfaction of the reason through the evidence that is offered and, at a deeper level, thankfulness for its being given in grace: thus the theological blessedness is found in the philosophical and beyond it.[68]

Delectable intuition follows, if God wills, the weary labour of thought. Note, however, that this is not in itself even the beginning of the joy of heaven; the light of God's truth is not the vision of his Face.[69] Thus the *Proslogion*, for instance, ends with faith's reflection on the joy of the End in which alone the full overwhelming by God's glory will occur. Then, as *Proslogion* 24–25 put it, it will be not so much the joy of God that enters the heart of man, as the hearts of the blessed that enter the joy of God. And finally, an account of Anselm's contemplative rationality would, Balthasar thinks, be incomplete were we not to mention that, for the *Meditationes* the harmony of the saving plan is founded on the suffering of the Son: hence the *gaudium* we desiderate is ultimately, 'Christ's Easter present'.[70]

66 *GL* II, p. 226
67 *GL* II, p. 233.
68 *GL* II, p. 234.
69 Here Balthasar makes use of Henri de Lubac's contribution to the Anselm centenary of 1959: 'Sur le chapitre XIVᵉ du *Proslogion*' in *Spicilegium Beccense. Congrès international du IXᵉ centenaire de l'arriveé d' Anselme au Bec* (Le Bec-Hellouin and Paris 1959), pp. 295–312.
70 *GL* II, p. 237.

It is a recurring criticism of the very idea of theological aesthetics that it cannot do justice to the freedom of God. A glorious icon signifies, so it is said, but it can hardly be called free. True, the theme of freedom belongs more with Balthasar's theological dramatics, where it will be developed at length, both as regards God and as regards man. But even here, in the midst of word-painting these vignettes of the aesthetic theology of past ages in *The Glory of the Lord*, he wishes to show how his chosen authors were capable of integrating the theme of freedom into their sense of the divine glory: for *what* the icon of the glorious crucified Lord signifies is the altogether unexpected – and so most free – divine love. And so before leaving Anselm to pass on to Bonaventure, Balthasar lingers on the former's treatment of the theme of 'concord' – in effect (at any rate as Balthasar interprets Anselm, very much by way of anticipation of the second volume of *Theodramatik*), an account of what for the creature freedom is.

> For the creature, freedom can only mean being allowed to enter into communion with the other (and thus participation in God's independent personal being), something, however, which can only be perfected as, through grace, creaturely freedom is drawn ever more strongly into absolute freedom, when it is free with God and in God, and simply wills, in freedom and not through being overpowered, what God wills.[71]

This Balthasar terms, on the model of the *analogia entis*, the *analogia libertatis* (or *personalitatis*). Human freedom can only be itself by sharing in divine freedom, which is to say graciously (for the will can will no rectitude unless it has the rectitude whereby to will it), and indeed eschatologically (for only the freedom attained by the creature through its penetration by the divine freedom can enable it to gain salvation). Hence freedom's 'radiance' in Anselm's writing, even when it is *human* freedom that is at stake.

That quality intensifies as soon as Anselm speaks, moreover, of the divine freedom, which he does with a reiterated use of the adverb *sponte*, 'spontaneously'. So far from meriting the sobriquet 'legalistic' with which a variety of critics, from Western liberals to the Eastern Orthodox have saddled him, Anselm's teaching is that

> the whole obedience of the incarnate Son depends entirely on the spontaneity of his love and simply unfolds the inner necessities of this free love, including the very mystery of Gethsemane, the heavy bearing of the guilt of the world and the death. The whole Trinitarian mystery between the Father and the Son – that the Son obeys really and to the end, and on the other side that the Father compels nothing but allows the Son's way of sacrifice – however one contemplates it, is such a mystery of spontaneous, unforced love.[72]

71 Ibid.
72 *GL* II, p. 246, with reference to *Cur Deus homo* I. 9–10; II. 1; II. 16–17.

To Balthasar, the heart of Anselm's doctrine of the atonement is not a calculation but an issue of ontological union: in the covenant, man is to remain God's authentic partner, and this means that man had to become free again *for* the covenant, free, that is, for absolute freedom. That is why God determined that the 'pearl' (cf. *Cur Deus homo* I. 19) would not remain blemished for ever. And surveying the wonderful prayers of Anselm, so ably translated into English by Sister Benedicta Ward, Balthasar concludes that, by an astonishing reversion of the commonplace rhetoric of the faith, for Anselm 'the final thing here below is not vision, but being seen'.[73] *Vides et scis, vide ut sciam*: You see and you know; see in order that I may know (it)'.[74]

Bonaventure

Anselm is often referred to as the Father of Scholasticism, thanks to his interest at once in logic, doctrine and spirituality. Of the great Scholastics themselves Balthasar elected to write about the Franciscan doctor, St Bonaventure, whose theological comments on the *pulchrum* are, he thinks, the most comprehensive, crucial and conceptually innovative of all. After tracing the sources of Bonaventure's theological aesthetic in Augustine and Denys, Bernard and Joachim of Fiore (whose literalistic re-creation of the Irenaean 'historical aesthetic' he renders, as Joseph Ratzinger showed, evangelical and sane),[75] Balthasar goes to the heart of the matter in an attempt to capture the quintessence of Bonaventure's contribution. The answer is that he is Franciscan – but something more.

> His world is Franciscan, and so is his theology, however many stones he may use to erect his spiritual cathedral over the mystery of humility and poverty, like another Baroque Portiuncula over the unpretentious original chapel. And yet, ... Bonaventure does not only take Francis as his centre: he is his own sun and his mission.[76]

So many themes of Bonaventure's teaching are pertinent to theological aesthetics that at the end of his lengthy account he will confess himself (at first) hard pressed to bring their luxuriance into some satisfactory order. But first of all Balthasar sets forth what he takes to be Bonaventure's 'fundamental experience'. And this is an experience – open in principle to every orthodox Christian – of the overflowing richness of the objective revelation. Bonaventure's primary metaphor for how revelation strikes us is the ocean, or mighty rivers that swell the sea's floods. If he displaces from centrality the image of the depths of the sea (*mirabiles elationes maris!* the psalmist had written), it is only because that of some great river connotes more strongly the idea of flowing movement. In his prologue to the *Commentary on the Sentences*, he advises his readers that the four rivers

73 *GL* II, p. 259.
74 *Oratio* 12, a prayer addressed in fact to St John the Evangelist: see *The Prayers and Meditations of St Anselm. Translated and with an introduction by Sister Benedicta Ward, S.L.G.* (Harmondsworth 1973), p. 169.
75 J. Ratzinger, *The Theology of History in Saint Bonaventure* (E.t. Chicago 1971).
76 *GL* II, p. 263.

of Paradise will be his subject: the Trinity, the eternal flowing of God
himself; the creation, itself as wide and deep as the sea proper; the
incarnation, when God in Christ flows issues from himself and returns
back again; and the sacraments, which are the stream of the water of life,
clear as crystal, that in the vision of the Seer of the Apocalypse, flowed
from the throne of God and of the lamb. In the prologue to the
Breviloquium, Bonaventure expatiates on the prayer of Paul that the church
at Ephesus may be able to grasp the 'length and breadth, height and
depth' (3:18), identifying as the goal of both revelation and theology that
'our fulfilment may bring us into the entire fulness of God'.[77] In its
luxuriance revelation is like a virgin forest, in its staggering richness like
a star-filled sky. Though a true Scholastic, out to bring order and clarity
wherever possible, Bonaventure, unlike Thomas, makes a virtue out of
the knowledge that he will be defeated. In Balthasar's own metaphor for
this, from card-playing, the last word is the experience of being 'out-
trumped'.[78] So far from depressing Bonaventure, however, this mastery
by revelation of the theologian's intelligence gives him the greatest
aesthetic pleasure – at the inexhaustibility of God.

> For there is great beauty in the construction of the world, and far
> greater beauty in the Church, which is adorned with the beauty of
> the gifts of grace of holiness, but the greatest beauty lies in the
> Jerusalem above, and the beauty greater than the greatest (*super-
> maxima*) is in the highest and most blessed Trinity.[79]

All of which sends the soul into *excessus*, making it ecstatic.

What, then, are the more particular themes of aesthetic theology which
this 'fundamental experience' of revelation carries? Balthasar enumerates,
in effect, five from which he will subsequently infer, in a closing passage
of great speculative brilliance, the structure of Bonaventure's concept of
theological beauty as a whole. The first theme is the most *sui generis*:
Bonaventure's understanding of the stigmatisation of St Francis by the
Crucified whom the Poverello saw as borne, seraph-like, by six wings.
Here for the first time we encounter those key-terms, personally coined,
of Bonaventure's aesthetic: 'expression' and 'impression'. In seeing the
seraphic Christ, Francis grasped that, since he was consumed by spiritual
fire, he would be changed into the 'expressive image' of the Crucified.[80]
Both his inner resemblance to Christ and the bodily resemblance
impressed upon him in the stigmata are equally the work of the crucified
God whose love sought its *own* self-expression in each of these forms.

> Permanently decisive for Bonaventure's aesthetic theology is the fact
> that the stigmata were impressed on the soul's body precisely in the
> soul's ecstatic *excessus*: just as it was there that the divine beauty was
> glimpsed, so it was also there that the same divine beauty took on its
> 'worldly' form.[81]

77 *Breviloquium*, Prologue, 6.
78 *GL* II, p. 266.
79 *Breviloquium*, Prologue, 3.
80 Bonaventure, *Legenda minor*, VIII.
81 *GL* II, p. 273. Author's own translation.

Bonaventurian ecstasy does not flee from the world, but opens the world to the kingdom of heaven, or better, shows that the Lord of the kingdom has already taken possession of the world. (In one meaning of the six wings of the seraph in Bonaventure's allegorical exegesis, they signify that sixth age of the world where, in his theology of history, the seventh already starts its course: 'through Christ [as Balthasar sums up] heaven is now in principle open'.)[82]

Bonaventure's second aesthetic theme is less narrowly Franciscan, for it is the idea of the twofold light of reason and faith. The light of reason – despite Bonaventure's alarm at the advent, in his time, of a more rational and secular theology – is a necessary condition for the communication of God's Word. Though the only true metaphysician be the man who knows the Trinity, and the only true general ethics that of him who knows Jesus Christ, neither faith nor grace would be possible in reason's absence. Still, the precondition (reason) is not the gift itself or rather *him*self, for the source not only of the incarnate Word but also of the inspired Word (in the prophets, in Scripture, and in the preaching of the Church) is the uncreated Word, the second divine Person. The light of faith is a mode of presence of the personal God who impresses supernatural knowledge on the soul, thus rendering it duly if imperfectly proportioned to the Lord who, in the charter text of Paul's theological aesthetics, as we behold his glory, makes us to be changed 'from one degree of glory to another' (2 Cor. 3:18) until that time when God will perfectly imprint himself on created spirit, in the Age to Come.

Then thirdly, Bonaventure's triadology – his theology of the Holy Trinity – is itself aesthetically conceived. For Bonaventure, every worldly expression – every creature – is directed to the end of God's perfect self-expression in Christ.

> Bonaventure's picture of the world is accordingly in the highest degree christocentric – because all the copies that are imperfect expressions must be brought into relation with the one perfect Image of the Father, which expresses him with the highest precision, and so be made transparent in order to be comprehensible.[83]

But first and foremost, expressive relationship is something which subsists in God himself, in the Trinity. Above all, the Father's relation to his Son, who is at once his Word and his Image, is both the condition of possibility and the means to full actuality for any and every created self-expression of God in the world. The reflective believer recognises (or should do) that the perfection of Being (which God infinitely is) requires the highest form of self-communication within a perfect communitarian love – and yet also that this must be compatible with the divine unity. The plurality of Persons derives from the 'highest originality of absolute fecundity', and this in turn means, so Balthasar goes on, that

---

82 *GL* II, p. 273. Cf. *GL* II, p. 315: 'the *excessus* comes about as an act of marvelling in the presence of God's nearness and immanence in the world.'
83 *GL* II, p. 283.

the old Platonic axiom *bonum diffusivum sui* now in the light of Christian revelation no longer refers simply to God's relationship with the world but to his absolute being itself: and this opens the way for an explanation of the structure that belongs to the natural kinds in the world, makes it possible to trace them back to their origin without absorbing them monistically into the rays of the light that is their source.[84]

Bonaventure's theology of beauty is 'always deployed in the framework of an ontology of expression',[85] where the latter is considered as the fruit-fulness (*Fruchtbarkeit*), surrendering self-giving (*Hingabe*) and love (*Liebe*) found in the triune Source of being as well as in its created efflux. The Father's fontal capacity is such that the One he generates is himself *Gott in der Weise des Ausgedrücktseins*, 'God in the mode of "expressedness"'. In his commentary on the *Hexaemeron*, Bonaventure describes the Son as the unifying centre of the Trinity.[86] He gives expression both to his own being begotten by the Father and to the Father's spiration of the Spirit, the term of the divine fecundity: it is in that spiration, and so in the Holy Spirit, that the Son is a 'centre' who leads back to the Father.[87] All this becomes highly pertinent to theological aesthetics when Bonaventure comes to speak of the Son as locus not only of truth but also of *beauty* in God. As expression of the Father's entire capacity, the Son is *ars Patris*, the Father's art.

> If the Father has really given expression in the Son to his whole being and capacity, then in the Son everything that is possible through God has taken on reality: if anything else outside God is realised through God, it can have possibility and reality only through the Son and in the Son . . . Bonaventure subordinates his whole teaching on the analogy of being . . . to this central proposition.[88]

The Word says better – and thus more beautifully – everything the creature as creature would say. The creature's self-expression succeeds, therefore, only when it is carried by the self-utterance of the Word. The Son indeed is beautiful both as the perfect resemblance of the Father, and in relation to all the beauty that is his image. And inasmuch as the Son who (as the New Testament witnesses) wishes to be nothing other than the image of the Father is the foundation for every creaturely attitude to God, such attitudes 'can be [true and] beautiful only insofar as they copy the attitude of the Son to the Father'.[89] On Bonaventure's reworking of the contents of Augustine's *De Trinitate*, therefore, the 'trace' (*vestigium*)

---

84 *GL* II, p. 285.
85 *GL* II, p. 287.
86 *In Hexaemeron* I. 12.
87 A point more clearly explained by Balthasar at *GL* II, p. 329: 'It is part of the essential humility of the Son, precisely because he is and desires nothing else than to be the expression of the Father, that he possesses no other midpoint than one that mediates: and therefore he continually makes himself nothing by pointing back in the Holy Spirit to the Father'.
88 *GL* II, pp. 292–293.
89 *GL* II, p. 299.

of the Trinity found in all objective being; the 'image' (*imago*) of the Trinity found in the structure of created spirit which in its native form of being reflects the relationship of the divine Trinity to its own Origin; and the 'likeness' (*similitudo*) of the Trinity achieved by sanctifying grace when that divine Archetype actually comes to dwell in the image – all this, is reworked in christological fashion, to produce the distinctive Bonaventurian theologoumenon whereby not only does the spirit of man find its sole fulfilment in (trinitarian) faith but more specifically that fulfilment happens to the extent that the human being is *ad Imaginem*: tending towards his proper Image, the divine Son.

> The world, for the Father who created it, possesses its full goodness and beauty only in the Son, and in so far as the Son embraces it in himself at its origin as exemplar, and as Bridegroom draws it back to himself in nuptial love . . .[90]

that final reference to the saving economy of the Son in time deriving from Bonaventure's treatise *De reductione artium*, to which we shall return.

The fourth and fifth doctrinal themes submitted by Bonaventure to predominantly aesthetic theologising are indeed anthropology and Christology: the First and Second Adams. His philosophy and theology of man emphasises the dignity of the body and the importance of the senses. In part, this derives from his view of matter as endowed with 'appetite' for form; thus prime matter is not for him, as it is for Thomas, pure privation, but already houses some spark of beauty. Human bodies are ordered to the noblest of forms in this world, spiritual souls, but by the same token to be the instrumental register of such forms bodies must possess, as the *Breviloquium* puts it, 'the greatest variety of organs endowed with the greatest beauty and skill and manageableness'.[91] Man, however, lives not only in nature but in history, and for Bonaventure the rhythm that joins matter and spirit in his constitution is echoed in the rhythm of generations and historical periods which creates meaning for time. And just as Scripture is needed if we are to read aright the sense of the book of nature, so, since no man lives long enough to experience the whole of history, Scripture gives us its meaning in outline likewise. Temporal disorder cannot overthrow the beauty of the total story-line which the Bible unfolds. Christ, the Second Adam, is the crown of the process of saving history, just as man, the first Adam, was the crowning of the development hitherto (Bonaventure's thought is here definitely proto-evolutionist).[92] Accordingly, he makes his appearance 'in order to establish in himself the harmonious balance of the cosmos towards which the cosmos itself was oriented'.[93]

The transfiguration of man, at which the Second Adam aims, cannot be a purely immaterial affair, for man is not his soul: it is the whole human nature, with its wondrous sensitivity of bodily perception, that is to

90 *GL* II, p. 308.
91 *Breviloquium* 2, 10.
92 See *Breviloquium* 4, 4.
93 *GL* II, p. 315.

receive grace and glory. In heaven, that body 'with its senses will have a full share in the overflowing of the joys of the spirit in God',[94] for in the unitary intellectual-material nature of the human being the powers of both sense and spirit have their ground. Through, moreover, the 'spiritual senses' (an ancient theme of Christian reflection on the experiential knowledge of God), sense experience is supernaturally extended (and transformed) as experience, for Bonaventure, of, more especially, 'the Word in his nuptial relationship to redeemed and sanctified man'.[95] For it is, finally, the Word incarnate who is the centre of all things, *medium omnium scientiarum*,[96] to whom all knowledge must be related if it is to find its place. He became our 'exit and entrance':

> our ascent to God and descent to neighbour, our looking outwards into the book of nature and our looking inwards into the spiritual truth. . . . But when he stands thus in the midst it is as the one who brings reconciliation, enlightenment, the one who leads back, who measures all things, who makes straight. In this mission lies his beauty: not only because he is the *rectitudo* of all that has deviated, but because he is able to make what has deviated come to resemble himself through the power of the radiance of his omnipotent heart.[97]

It remains only to pull together these strands into a statement of the 'structure' of beauty – or, as Balthasar will several times remark in this finale to *Clerical Styles* – the *analogy* of beauty. Bonaventure is one of those Scholastics who has no doubt at all about the genuine status of the beautiful as a transcendental determination of being.[98] As the expression of being's complete roundedness, its plenary character, all roads lead to it – from the one, the true, the good. It is because beauty is so clearly a transcendental determination of being in Bonaventure's work that the analogical structure of Bonaventurian beauty can be explored by such a student as Balthasar. The appropriation of beauty to God the Son hints at the 'midway' position of *pulchrum* at all levels of the real (since, as we noted above, for Bonaventure the *analogia entis* must be understood from *within* the doctrine of creation in the Word). By analogy with the beauty of being at large, itself analogically identified, then, in relation to the Son, Bonaventure also finds beauty in the contemplative soul – which he often compares to the Woman of the Apocalypse, clothed in sun, moon and stars. Lastly, there is beauty in the joy experienced by the senses as the macrocosm of God's creation enters the microcosm (the 'lesser world' of the human being) through their gateways, and the supernatural equivalent of this in the activity of the spiritual senses, for just as the eye perceives the *speciosum* (what is lovely), and ear and nose perceive the *suave* (what is sweet), and taste and touch the *salubre*, (what is healthful)

---

94 *GL* II, p. 319.
95 *GL* II, p. 320.
96 *In Hexaemeron* I. 11.
97 *GL* II, p. 329, 331.
98 See on this issue H. Pouillon, O.S.B., 'La Beauté, propriété transcendentale chez les scolastiques, 1220–1279', in *Archives d'histoire doctrinale et littéraire du moyen-âge* 21 (1946), pp. 263–329.

so do the spiritual senses behold the truth of the Word, enjoy his intimacy and receive his satisfying fulness.

And this range of analogical applications of the term 'beautiful', all held within a framework of christological reference, allows Balthasar to infer the trio of properties of theological beauty in its expressiveness, a trio subjacent to all Bonaventure's writing. Beauty is harmonious proportion measured *vis-à-vis* God in Christ – thus pointing to the relation of expression in the Godhead which is, as we have seen, the ultimate foundation of beauty. Beauty is disclosure of the depths of being, it is the epiphany of the Word, uniquely in the art of God incarnate from the crib to the resurrection but also, more diffusely, in all things. And beauty is disinterested self-giving, for God's creative self-effusion is not caused by anything outside himself. And here Bonaventure would insist that only the pure of heart can interpret aright beauty's appearing since there also does 'the potential sacrifice in the heart of the one who is addressed, touched and inflamed answer to the gratuitousness of the beauty which offers itself as a gift'.[99] And this, in conclusion, gives Balthasar the clue to what in Bonaventure remains peculiarly Franciscan. 'His sole concern is with the movement of love in the nuptial kiss of the Cross between the God who has become poor and the man who has become poor.'[100] That is not simply piety, or rhetoric for preaching, but the source of the deepest metaphysical theology:

> It is precisely in this act of pouring itself into what is nothing that God's heart glorifies itself, and thereby fulfils all the 'glory' of being, as this is based in the transcendental power of self-expression. 'He was glorious in what caused him to be despised.' This is the measure of all Christian and ecclesiastical glory.[101]

99 *GL* II, p. 349.
100 *GL* II, p. 357.
101 *GL* II, p. 359, with an internal citation of Bonaventure, *Sermon 1 on the Epiphany*.

5

❧

Landscapes by Laymen

Dante

Balthasar opens his series of 'lay' theologians with Dante – something we should not find in the least surprising given Balthasar's peculiar use of the concept of lay status in the theological aesthetics. To be lay is to write in the vernacular and speak to theological purpose by a deliberate, personal scanning of the contours of existence. On both counts – as an apologist of vernacular poetry and prose (in the *De vulgari eloquentia*) and as a theologian of personal – though far from individualistically conceived – experience, vocation and destiny (in the *Commedia*), Dante could hardly be left out of account. He is also a star, indeed a supernova.

> There is, of course, a long tradition, both in Antiquity and in the Christian era, of journeys to the hereafter, of transcendental adventure stories and reports of ecstatic experience. However, Dante should be seen in stark contrast to this whole literary tradition because of his awareness, both theological and aesthetic, that he was setting down something that had never existed before and that in its own way is inimitable, a work that raises him high above his own age, plants him in the future (*s'infutura la tua vita*), in eternity itself (*s'eterna*). His sense of mission is without parallel in Christian history, inasmuch as it is not only lived out (as in the case of many saints) but is energetically impressed upon men and is ratified by the greatest poets of antiquity as well as by the representatives of Christianity. How could Dante's sense of being a new constellation have been so real to him, if he had not experienced the mediaeval synthesis he represents as something qualitatively new, open to the future?[1]

For Balthasar, Dante is an extraordinary synthesis of elements Scholastic and mystical, pagan-antique and Christian, of sacral politics and spiritual Franciscanism, of courtly love and metaphysical wisdom, yet in such a way that 'his work is not a sum-total but an indivisible prime number'.[2]

---

1 *GL* III, pp. 12–13; with internal citations of *Paradiso* 17, 98, and *Inferno* 15, 85.
2 *GL* III, p. 13.

Before entering into the heart of that work, from the perspective of the *Glory of the Lord*, Balthasar expands a little his reasons for treating Dante as (in effect) the initiator of 'lay style' in theological aesthetics. Not only did Dante turn to the vernacular, concerned as he was with 'translating the knowledge of reality – hidden in the seven liberal arts, in philosophy, theology and history – from dead, fossilized Latin into the living spoken language', thereby ensuring that his 'learning' would be at the service of his 'action'.[3] He also, and of set purpose, drew the concrete history of institutions – empire and Church, supremely – into his theology in a more constitutive fashion (so Balthasar implies) than had been the case with Irenaeus, Augustine or Bonaventure – though these too, after all, had been theologians of history, each in his own distinctive way. The difference appears to be that Dante, by contrast to these figures, fully intended to *change* history by his writing, to leave an enduring mark on its future course. Perhaps owing to the contacts of his family with the successors to the last sovereigns of the *Deutsches-römisches Kaisertum*, Balthasar shows himself strongly sympathetic to Dante's superethnic, and supranational imperial idea.

> Just as in the order of things, the individual is related beyond himself to the family, the family to the village, the village to the city, the city to a particular kingdom, so the different kingdoms must be integrated in a universal kingdom of man, for *totum humanum genus ordinatur ad unum* . . . The emperor, who possesses everything and has no rival, is essentially disinterested and stands free above all as the supreme embodiment of justice, for he rules men as men and so can be the embodiment of selfless love.[4]

(Here of course Dante, and Balthasar, are speaking of the *form* which is the emperor's by office, not any individual's manner of realising that form.) The imperial order is, therefore, inseparable from the human rights given at the creation – which is why Dante can identify the 'tree of the empire' in the *Purgatorio* with the Tree of Paradise,[5] rejuvenated *de facto* by Christ's Church but *de iure* of its nature a mystery of creation, implanted directly by God and requiring no ecclesiastical intermediary for its validation. Part of Dante's argumentation for the latter view (strongly contested by papalists in his time) is that the *Church*'s form must reflect that of Christ who affirmed that his kingdom was not of this world.[6] Influenced by the spiritual Franciscans, Dante regards the Church's beauty as entirely a function of her lowliness – hence his excoriation of the prelatically ambitious. The incandescent anger with which his holiest figures treat a number of the popes

---

3 *GL* III, pp. 13, 15.
4 *GL* III, p. 18, with an internal citation of *De monarchia* I. 5: 'the whole human race is ordered to a unity.'
5 *Purgatorio* 32, 38–60.
6 Another factor is Dante's strange concept of the two separate yet final ends of man which Balthasar – incredibly for a supporter of de Lubac – allows to pass, *GL* III, p. 17.

has nothing sectarian about it, nothing of the heterodoxy of a Joachim; it springs solely from the loving zeal of a Christian layman, who sees himself cheated of his rightful inheritance of the Spirit and of the riches of Christ, and who, on behalf of those who have been led astray, indeed on behalf of the Lord of the Church himself, laments the dereliction of the holy city.[7]

But more important, even, than the conversion of Dante to the vernacular and to engagement in the historical process is his redirection of theological interest to the conditions of possibility for a truly authentic Christian life – for laypeople, above all. That life, Dante insists, cannot be lived without a foundation in natural 'nobility', for nobility – which has nothing to do with old money or correct manners – is, as the *Convivio* puts it, the 'heaven' in which the stars of the virtues (the distinctive fruitings of human nature) must shine. Now the virtues for Dante develop from seeds sown by the creative force of the (angelically governed) heavenly powers as the latter draw out living reality from the potency which is matter. But the process is not fully thinkable without at the same time the gratuitous infusion of the gifts of the Holy Spirit, itself the direct work of the Primal Cause, God. Dante's particular interest in all this, as seen by Balthasar, is its implications for *vocation*: the notions of charism, vocation, mission are always closely interrelated in Balthasar's thought.

> The noble soul, following its own flight, discovers that it must reach out beyond itself; its apparently natural *magnaminità* requires it to submit to the ways of grace and to take upon itself the burdens of its Christian vocation.[8]

The Dantesque understanding of the unity of human and Christian large-souledness, 'confirmed' as this was in the course of the *Commedia* by Virgil, Beatrice and the leading apostles of Jesus, makes an evident appeal to the Christian humanist in Balthasar. Balthasar's own heart goes out to Dante as lover of antiquity, for such love is a recognition of everything that is generous and fine in the best of paganism.

> Dante, the poet, like Aquinas, makes the ethics of Antiquity in its abstractness the broad basis of Christian morality; but he does more than that; he takes over all its historical and mythological substance as well. . . . There is no flowery rhetoric or 'conventional wisdom' about this (as there was so often in the preceding centuries); it is not even a matter of broadening one's 'cultural range'; no; it is the work of the *eros* in Dante's soul, that in the last analysis knows itself indebted to both worlds, that loves both with a positive and appreciative love, that, it is true, clearly recognises the relative

---

7 *GL* III, p. 24; 'Joachim' is the Calabrian abbot Joachim of Fiora whose prophecy of a 'third age', when, under the presidency of the Spirit, the structures of the Church of the Son would give way to a time of sheer spirituality, proved tempting to some contemporary Franciscans.

8 *GL* III, p. 26.

hierarchical positions of Christianity and Antiquity – Beatrice sent
Virgil to Dante, and Virgil takes him to Beatrice and then leaves him
– but that never repudiates the rightful value of nature to the
advantage of supernatural values.[9]

Such nobility, however, must be invested in the narrative form of
soul-making, in the story of a life, and though Dante's name appears once
only in the *Commedia*, at the climax of his meeting with Beatrice, the entire
poem is written in the first person – a fact to which Balthasar finds the key
in Dante's explanation of why Augustine wrote the *Confessions*: 'his
[Augustine's] assessment of himself was a lesson for others and so of great
benefit', And if, in Augustine's case, the earthly loves that figure in the
Confessions have little if any theological value, nothing could be less true
of their place in Dante's sense of personal identity, destiny, vocation.
Influenced here by the 'romantic theology' of the English 'poet of
theology' Charles Williams, Balthasar can write:

> The love, which began on earth, between two human beings, is not
> denied, is not bypassed in the journey to God; it is not, as was
> always, naturally enough, hitherto the case, sacrificed on the altar
> of the classical *via negativa*; no, it is carried right up to the throne of
> God, however transformed and purified. This is utterly unprec-
> edented in the history of Christian theology. . . . [But] why should a
> Christian man not love a woman for all eternity and allow himself to
> be introduced by that woman to a full understanding of what
> 'eternity' means? And why should it be so extraordinary – ought
> one not rather to expect it – that such a love needs, for its total
> fulfilment, the whole of theology and Heaven, Purgatory and Hell?[10]

Here Balthasar touches on one of his own favoured themes, the costing
incorporation of finite love into infinite.

It is in fact from the figure of Beatrice that Balthasar proposes to review
the *Commedia* in theologically aesthetic perspective. Like Williams,
Balthasar does not propose to let the warm-heartedness of romantic
theology become an excuse for the abandoning of clear-headedness.
Though in all the references to Beatrice Dante makes it plain that he sees
his 'whole Christian existence as resting on [this] unshakeable fidelity',[11]
and, as Balthasar remarks, for lack of evidence we do not know how there
enters in here the matrimonial covenant with Gemma, who bore him
children but refused to follow him into exile, there is in the *Vita Nuova*, by
contrast with the *Commedia*, a certain callowness in his recollections of
their relation. Balthasar speaks critically of the 'atmosphere of aesthetic
reverie' which afflicts the earlier work, and presents Dante's first attempt
at a Christian doctrine of love quite negatively as 'the hypostatisation of

9　*GL* III, p. 29.
10　*GL* III, p. 32. Cf. C. Williams, *The Figure of Beatrice. A Study in Dante* (London 1943).
　　For Williams' work, see G. Cavallero, *Charles Williams. Poet of Theology* (London
　　1983).
11　*GL* III, p. 36.

an enclosed, self-contained world of human emotion'.[12] Dante's sympathy with the damned soul of the sentimental lover Francesca da Rimini shows how the *dolce stil nuovo* of court poets could have enticed him down this cul-de-sac, as an earlier version, so Balthasar rather bitingly comments, of the English Pre-Raphaelite Dante Gabriel Rossetti whose somewhat wan artistic sensibility went hand in hand with personal promiscuousness. However, the *Convivio*, like Dante himself, is saved, humanly speaking, by the universalising impulse of philosophy, the *donna pietosa* who takes pity on him and by the hand leads him to the highest love. Under philosophy's gaze – and, Balthasar insists, 'we must take seriously the description of the erotic-anagogic beauty of philosophy, the description to it of all the praises of the *Minnesang*'[13] – the poet's *erôs* is at once kindled and redirected to the eternal wisdom that only loving intelligence can gain. And this means, so Balthasar explains, that Beatrice, whom Dante was unworthy to look on, and whom the angels and the blessed in paradise have bade God call to them, is refound in a new way.

> For Dante, looking truth or wisdom in the eyes . . . means not stop-
> ping before one has encountered the object of God's approval and
> love. But Beatrice is precisely the definitive object of God's approval
> and love, a part of eternal wisdom, and since one cannot really speak
> of a part where all things interpenetrate, she is that wisdom herself.
> In fact, now it becomes unimportant whether it is the *donna gentile*
> who symbolizes philosophy; all that matters is that the ineffable
> grace, which once and for the first time was encountered on earth in
> Beatrice, is the manifestation of that eternal grace, which loved us in
> advance, from eternity.[14]

And from the point of that discovery on, philosophy for Dante takes second place to revelation: all mediations between heaven and earth are seen henceforth as 'ways of grace, occasioned by Christian, not philosophical, powers'.

> Beatrice then proves herself to be a reality (not a symbol), for, in her
> *pietà* for Dante and in graciously sending Virgil to him, she is stirred
> into action by the highest creaturely sanctity: Mary is the one who
> has taken pity and who sent St Lucy to Beatrice in order to spur her
> into helping her beloved. Thus stirred, Beatrice descends into Limbo
> and beseeches Virgil to hurry to the aid of her 'friend': 'I fear he may
> already be so far astray that I have risen too late to succour him . . .
> Love moved me and made me speak.'[15]

Like Virgil in Canto 10 of the *Inferno*, Balthasar regards Beatrice as the key that unlocks the sense of Dante's journey. It was her love which led Dante to see and hear the dreadful warnings of hell, and to purification in purgatory, and brought him to the threshold of the divine Glory, where

12 *GL* III, p. 41.
13 *GL* III, p. 44.
14 *GL* III, p. 46.
15 *GL* III, p. 48, with an internal citation of *Inferno* 2, 64ff.

he must not only *encounter* love but *withstand* it (as Newman's angel tells Gerontius, 'the flame of the everlasting Love doth burn 'ere it transform'). As Balthasar excellently puts it, 'the thought of the eyes, smile and even laugh of Beatrice was enough to lead Dante to her; but the sight of her leads him to the vision of God.'

Balthasar is at pains to stress that, innovatory as such a romantic – or, as he prefers to say, 'existential' – theology may be, Dante does not intend to depart, in his account of how the *régime* of the grace of Christ is mediated, from the common doctrine of the Catholic Church.

> It is the grace of God flowing down to him through Mary, the mediatrix of graces. But this grace is also mediated by the whole of the 'Jerusalem above', by the community of the saints, who were and are entirely real, historical human beings, and from whose midst arises a multitude of helpers, guides and intercessors, each of whom, in his own way, expresses the community of love in its totality. Beatrice, formed by God as the poet's eternal beloved, has without doubt, the same degree of reality as the other saints. Here is no allegory or symbol; here we are dealing simply with the laws of the *communio sanctorum*.[16]

But what is the force of the term 'existential' in Balthasar's description of Dante's 'theology'? The protagonist of the poem comes to realise, through its course, what being a Christian means; the passage from perdition to salvation is executed. But this takes place with, in and through his 'discovery of how his first and deepest love can become, in a Christian way, truly eternal'.[17] This is no idiosyncracy for 'whoever wishes to be a Christian must keep his psychological experience open and allow it to be determined, to the very last, by the experience of eternal realities'.[18] Such an existential theology should not be considered in any sense a rival to the classical dogmatics of the Church, for it functions not by sidelining the theological virtues (Dante in paradise will be interrogated by the leading apostles on the orthodoxy of his faith, hope and love), but by realising them to the full.

> It would be ludicrous to say that Dante is indeed a great poet but 'still' bound by the dogma of the Middle Ages or of Catholicism in general: as a poet he can be interpreted only from the centre of this dogma; he identifies himself existentially with it, plunges his inspiration into its waters in order to receive that same inspiration anew from it. Thanks to the concrete, Christian reality of grace, his poetic pre-existence in the *Vita Nuova* and his philosophical explorations in the *Convivio* are subsumed without remainder in this new inspiration.[19]

16 *GL* III, p. 50.
17 *GL* III, p. 50.
18 *GL* III, p. 51.
19 *GL* III, p. 52.

From Origen to Bernard, the Catholic tradition has known of the *anima ecclesiastica*, described most typically in commentaries on the Song of Solomon, a soul whose 'experience and sensibility, thoughts and desires have been assumed into the universality of the *Sponsa Christi*, the bride of the Lamb . . . '.[20]

But even when we hear from Balthasar how Dante has 'full Christian authority' to identify Beatrice, whom he knows to be enjoying the vision of God in heaven, with 'the loving Church', and to this extent, expect to receive through her divine grace for his 'redemption, purification, illumination and union' (for this is not simply justification, but justifying grace working itself out most thoroughly through all the reaches of the personality with its faculties and powers), we can still stand amazed at the audacity whereby, in the *Purgatorio*'s earthly paradise, he describes Beatrice in her glory stepping down from the 'chariot of the Church' like the sun rising. For the chariot is drawn by Jesus Christ, and those who accompany it (a host of exalted biblical figures as well as the personifications of the theological and cardinal virtues) greet her with a paraphrase of the *Ave Maria*: 'Blessed art thou among the daughters of Adam, and blessed forever be thy beauty!' Objections leap to the mind at this apotheosis of Dante's *innamorata*, until (that is) we read Balthasar's sobering comment.

> If Dante has done everything he can to make us believe in the identification of his *antica fiamma* with the heavenly Beatrice now merged with the Spirit of the Church; if, consequently, he directs his earthly *eros*, in all seriousness, at this heavenly object, he is also willing to pay the existential price for it and to submit himself, in confession, to the sacramental judgment of his beloved who now – across the purifying water – looks down upon him from the heart of the Church.[21]

For Balthasar the triptych of the *Commedia* has the *Purgatorio* as its undoubted centre, and within that tableau, Dante's confession and subsequent absolution in the moment of meeting with Beatrice is crucial. This is not the first time Dante has manifested repentance – he has climbed the mountain of penitence, assisted by the intercession of the living, and conscious (as in hell) of his own complicity in some at least of the sins whose outworking he can now observe. (Balthasar notes how, in the *Commedia*, such walking can only be done *in the day* – the contrast with John of the Cross, the second of his 'lay' theologians – is acute, since the *via purgativa* is here already *illuminativa*.) The poet has also prostrated himself to beg mercy at the 'gate of confession', where the step leading to the threshold is porphyry-coloured, a reference to the all-expiating Blood of Christ. By the time Virgil takes his leave, at the entrance to the earthly paradise, Dante's will has been (so far as natural virtue is concerned) quite rectified, which is why Virgil – antiquity at its best – can let him go. But still there is something more, and it is in a supernatural context the *unum necessarium*, the 'one thing necessary'.

20 *GL* III, p. 52.
21 *GL* III, pp. 53–54.

The man now become autonomous has not yet been justified in the sight of God and of love . . . Dante has understood that . . . Purgatory after death can be no less than the final existential confession: confrontation with love, as it is, really and in Heaven, the total destruction of all on earth that presumptuously called itself by that name.[22]

Balthasar's recreation of the confession scene ('not just an episode . . . the dynamic goal of the whole journey'),[23] is a highpoint of volume III of the *Glory of the Lord,* though perhaps we shall not appreciate how it advances theological aesthetics as such until we read in the summary of the first five volumes of *Herrlichkeit* at the beginning of the sixth:

Glory is the intruding lordliness of him who comes to confront the world, both judging it and gracing it. It is this that distinguishes the biblical reality from the epiphanies of gods outside the Bible.[24]

Judgment and engracement are the words. To underline the nakedness of judgment, Balthasar's stress how much else that has occupied Dante hitherto in the *Commedia* must fall away. Ideas of destiny and tragedy are put aside; there are no side-glances at others who are sinners, maybe greater ones than ourselves, no consideration of mitigating circumstances, no anticipation of forgiveness to come. Instead, 'existence in its entirety must force itself into the judgment of confession like a river through a narrow gorge'.[25] Beatrice, as the embodiment of the Church, confronts Dante with his own lovelessness, though it is only when she turns to look at Christ that he collapses, morally stricken, to the ground.

No other part of the *Comedy* has anything like the force of this scene; it is the heart of the whole work. Here Eros has grown out of its subjectivity and into the objective form of a sacrament. On the other hand, here too we see sacramental, ecclesial form unveiled and justified and convincingly shown to be love . . . Supremely personal love breaks forth from the centre of the Church, but it will not tolerate subjectivity unless it has been purified, ordered, overcome and gathered up in the subjectivity of God himself.[26]

Upon which a fourfold engracement happens. First, Dante is ducked under the waters of the first of the rivers of paradise – the ultimate in absolution, where sin becomes not only forgiven but forgotten. Second, Dante begins to contemplate church history, for now he can become the 'father confessor' of the sin-stained Church in time. Third, he drinks from the second river of paradise which gives him memory recall of the good he has done on earth – the 'indispensable foundation',

22 *GL* III, pp. 59, 54.
23 *GL* III, p. 61.
24 *GL* VI, p. 14.
25 *GL* III, p. 55.
26 *GL* III, p. 61.

Balthasar stoutly remarks, 'of his existence not just as a poet but as a man'.[27] (Confession and absolution are not meant to demoralise, but if the neologism be permitted, to 'remoralise'.) Finally, Dante enters on a new intimacy with Beatrice *qua* living form of the inspiration which love brings.

> Love's inspiration takes this constantly recurring form, namely, that whenever Dante has before him a thought, word or deed to conceive or carry out, he first searches with his eyes for the gaze of his beloved to assure himself that it is right. And this turning towards love, well nigh imperceptible yet each time almost ceremoniously reported, does not mean for Dante that he is a stranger and slave, but rather that he is truly autonomous and free.... The beloved does not imprison the poet within herself; on the contrary, she opens up for him the perception of all reality.[28]

By comparison with his exegesis of the *Purgatorio*, we can deal briefly enough with Balthasar's comments on the *Paradiso* and *Inferno*. For in commenting their cantos, he has in mind just one question in each case. What shall we retain of the theological cosmology disclosed in the *Paradiso*, and how shall we regard the doctrine of hell to which the *Inferno* gives poetic expression? On the first question: though the extent to which Dante considered his own cosmology a play of symbols cannot be fully answered (but some episodes suggest it, like for instance, the physical quaking of the foundations of Mount Purgatory at the cry of *Gloria!* whereby the holy souls acclaim one of their number who has come to the end of his purification), he drew from the sources of ancient and mediaeval thinking about the cosmos a picture of the world *largely* helpful to a theological aesthetics but not in *all* respects. The cosmos is 'embedded in the glory and peace of divine love, shot through with angelic and spiritual powers that shine forth and are sent out by God as his living organs'.[29] The structure of the universe, in this world picture, actively confirms the saving intentions of God. Owing to his view that the soul, as the substantial form of the body, has attractive power over matter and can prefigure for itself a resurrection body even in its separated state (a position contrary to the opinion of St Thomas but not a million miles removed, as Balthasar implicitly points out in a footnote, from that of Karl Rahner), Dante is able to mount, on behalf of the inhabitants of paradise, amazing displays of verbal description, 'theatre, ballet, and fireworks rolled into one'.[30] But, and here we come to the infelicitous element in Dante's cosmology, he was forced to pay a high price for his borrowings from Antiquity in general and Neo-Platonism in particular. And this is the sheer geographical distance of heaven from earth – even though Dante works to overcome this by the missions of mercy which can join one realm to another. What Balthasar would take from the cosmology of the *Paradiso*

27 *GL* III, p. 62.
28 *GL* III, pp. 63–64.
29 *GL* III, p. 67.
30 *GL* III, p. 72.

is rather the way that *erōs* and form (two key concepts both for him and for Dante) are fulfilled in the vision of heaven, a vision evoked by Dante not only in symbolist scenarios but also, for what concerns its deepest reality, with apophaticism and restraint. Opposed to all meandering, irresolute infinity of desire, Dante's

> understanding of the will in terms of form is based on Aristotle's: the law of the form of being, with its living entelechy, is not aimless and uncertain; it is clear and definite and demands obedience. Man's *desiderium naturale* may tend toward God and the vision of God, but because it is nature, it has a goal to attain, at which to come to rest, beyond which it cannot reasonably strive.[31]

> It is to this mystery that the central doctrine of the *Paradiso* points, namely, of human subordination to the divine will, which is not only recommended to men on earth but actually constitutes the form of eternal blessedness. Every desire is taken up into the divine form; obedience coincides with a blessed fulfilment that is beyond desire.[32]

Not that this takes place through (pagan) submission to fate; rather is it (Christian) exchange of a loving 'Yes' between God and man. 'We are left with the final reciprocity of Eros and Agape, which for Dante are but two names for the same thing: Amor, God's most truly proper name.'[33]

And so to, finally, Balthasar's second question – the issue of the evangelical quality of the *Inferno*, on which topic he is severe. Here, as (so we shall see) at the end of *Lay Styles* with Péguy, there surface Balthasar's own difficulties about the notion of eternal damnation. As he puts it, in terms chiselled finely to meet Dante's case:

> What if the [divine] eros that shapes and governs all worlds also rules over a kingdom from which love is totally and eternally excluded? And if Dante's theological aesthetic is based precisely upon the resemblance of *amor* and *bellezza*, then is a poem about Hell at all conceivable?[34]

Such a poem is, for Balthasar, only possible aesthetically insofar as it is so theologically – which must mean inasmuch as it can be justified by love. But can it? What might, in the work of Augustine or Thomas, pass muster as conceptual theology could not but be undermined when, with Dante, it suffered translation into the terms of existential theology. How so? What Dante finds himself obliged by the theological tradition to portray in his infernal observations is the simultaneous 'establishment and break-down of communication'.[35] The damned are deprived by that very fact of all real relationship yet communicate through the form of their punishment which, in Dante's subtle portrayal of the varieties of sinfulness and

31 *GL* III, p. 77.
32 *GL* III, p. 79.
33 *GL* III, p. 81.
34 *GL* III, p. 83.
35 *GL* III, p. 85.

their logic, 'so lays hold of the sinner from within that the punishment becomes the complete expression of [that sinner's] guilt'.[36] This is, then, communication *through justice alone* – which means, among other things, that nothing can happen in Dante's hell, since, by his own doctrine, love is the 'interior force of all living things'.[37] 'It follows inescapably from this that in Hell the love of God is completely veiled by justice, and the divine beauty can only consist in the right proportioning of punishment to guilt.'[38] It also follows that, despite the profusion of figures with which Dante overwhelms us in the *Inferno*, and the finesse of the moral intelligence with which he describes them, at the existential level Dante's heart, though it can overcome its human limitations sufficiently to enter into the level of heaven, finds a similar act of transcendence impossible in the understanding of hell.

But, as Balthasar underscores, it is not as if Dante has here followed his personal inclination, making hell the depository of his own hatred.

> Dante's mission is to throw eternal light on temporal affairs, to place human destiny on the scales of eternity, to raise up to full and clear definition what is blurred and incomplete and therefore, from the earthly point of view, unintelligible . . .[39]

and this must mean 'the most terrible kind of moral exhortation to the whole of Christendom'.[40] At least as a kerygma, Balthasar appears to say, hell is objectively real. But is it more than that? It may be, Balthasar hints, the lack of much explicit Christology in the *Commedia* which allows Dante to be so sure. So much is the work a 'transverse section' of the cosmos that the substitutionary atoning act of Jesus Christ on the cross (which, as historical event, can necessarily only be shown in 'longitudinal section'), hardly appears.[41] We can reasonably doubt, however, whether reference to the atonement *simply as such* would guarantee in eschatology the untenanted hell for which Balthasar 'dared to hope'. Newman, for instance, in his sermon 'A Particular Providence as revealed in the Gospel', spoke otherwise, of how:

> doubtless, at the last day, the wicked and impenitent shall be condemned, not in a mass, but one by one – one by one, appearing each in his turn before the righteous Judge, standing under the full glory of his countenance, carefully weighed in the balance and found wanting, dealt with, not indeed with a weak and wavering purpose where God's justice claims satisfaction, yet at the same time, with all the circumstantial solitude and awful care of *one who would fain make, if he could, the fruit of his passion more numerous than it is*.[42]

---

36 *GL* III, p. 86.
37 *GL* III, p. 90; cf. p. 99.
38 *GL* III, p. 91.
39 *GL* III, p. 98.
40 *GL* III, p. 99.
41 *GL* III, p. 100.
42 J. H. Newman, *Parochial and Plain Sermons*, III (Oxford and Cambridge 1881²), p. 122. Italics added.

Balthasar has huge admiration for Dante's achievement – and his final comment, under the heading of 'The Eternal Feminine', is praise of the intertwining, in the *Commedia*, of ethics and aesthetics (no ethics without *erôs*, and so beauty, but no beauty without the good). Yet he ends his account of the *Comedy* a disappointed man.

> Glory here is indeed the glory of a Heaven aflame with the eros of God, but the distinctively Christian quality of this – God's descent into death and Hell, his humiliation to the point of complete kenosis, God taking our place and bearing the sin of the whole world – this kind of glory does not come into view.[43]

John of the Cross

The way Balthasar contextualises the second of his lay theologians, John of the Cross, is altogether unexpected, at any rate to readers of conventional histories of spirituality. To Balthasar, John's work is a (largely successful) response to the breakdown of the mediaeval world-view, based as that was on a transparent sense of the *analogia entis* (rather than the kind of hard-won philosophical recovery thereof we should attempt today). Furthermore, it was at the same time an answer to the 'German Reformation', itself prepared by that collapse of a picture of the world, for only with the latter did Luther's counterposing of the 'kingdoms' of law and reason against the realms of grace and faith become remotely plausible. Moreover, what St John responds *with* is essentially the 'theology of the Christian East': not so surprising, Balthasar maintains, in an ancient Order (Carmel) with roots in Palestine. We can note, however, that of the two patristic writers John most draws on (Denys and Gregory the Great), the latter, a Roman of the Romans, 'consul of God', is not exactly Oriental. We can, however, second Balthasar when he goes on to remark:

> The challenge and the scandal of the Carmelite response to Luther lie in the fact that it incorporates the whole of monastic tradition from the Greeks up to and including the Middle Ages into the new Christian radicalism; indeed, with its modern orientation toward personal, experiential and psychological categories, the Carmelite response makes the new radicalism more radical than ever.[44]

Balthasar's initial statement of John's teaching is so austere that we may wonder however the latter got into a work on theological aesthetics in the first place! For the radicalism in question consists, at first sight, of an 'unrelenting reductionism' (compared by Balthasar with Hegel's) which in the name of the axiom 'God alone suffices' knocks down everything that stands in its way. Not only the good things of creation but even the supernatural gifts of God come under this remorseless hammer.

43 *GL* III, p. 101.
44 *GL* III, p. 106.

Placed before the naked reality of the Absolute, which presents itself
to her in the mode of privation and dispossession, the soul endures
an 'infinite death' in her languishing and suffering, 'a living image
of that infinite privation' . . .[45]

and a reliving of the experience of the wrath of God and abandonment by
God described by the authors of Job, Jeremiah and Jonah. What the soul
experiences as hell is in God's eyes purgatory, and St John means us to
take with complete seriousness the claim to a true identity between
this-worldly and other-worldly reality at that point. And yet the 'fire' that
purifies is a 'dark, loving spiritual fire',[46] and, like fire burning wood, what
it consumes it transforms into itself. Here sanjuanist negativity begins to
show its true colours as super-positivity. And soon enough, Balthasar
finds the point of insertion of Carmelite mysticism into a theology of the
beautiful.

When the living flame of love in which the soul burns has reached
its goal, heaven is anticipated. It is, first of all, an earthly paradise
resulting from the purgation of the senses and of the spirit in which
the soul attains baptismal innocence and complete subjection to
God. But later it becomes an anticipation of eternal blessedness
itself, from the final perfection of which the soul is separated by only
a thin veil, while at the same time she is already bathed in its glory.
St John's work reaches its peak in the description of these explosions
of glory from the fire of unifying love.[47]

So Balthasar will write shortly after of John's mystical poetry: as the
gospel sword must pierce between the joints and marrow before the
gospel promise of the hundredfold harvest can be reaped on earth, so in
John's verse:

To bear witness to this, the poetry must . . . begin inside the division,
as the scream of the vivisected soul in the middle of the night, in
order to end in the song of praise of the soul, even more fully alive at
a deeper level, wounded in the fire of glory.[48]

Emphasising the priority of St John's poetry over the commentaries
(which are sometimes not at the level of their subject), Balthasar regards
the choice of this particular literary form for spiritual doctrine as in no
way fortuitous. The reformer of Carmel answers the negativities of the
Protestant reformers by beauty; to their 'destructive dialectical Word' he
opposes his own 'constructive poetic' one.[49] The poems are, in all essentials indeed, an interpretation of the Word in Scripture – and notably of

45 *GL* III, p. 110, with an internal citation of *The Living Flame of Love*, III. 22.
46 John of the Cross, *The Dark Night*, II. 12, 1.
47 *GL* III, pp. 111–112, with an internal allusion to *The Ascent of Mount Carmel* III. 26, 5;
     and *The Spiritual Canticle*, 31, 5 and 37, 2–5.
48 *GL* III, p. 127.
49 *GL* III, p. 120.

the Song of Songs, the Psalms, and certain Gospel texts, notably the Johannine Prologue. Using not only the words and images of the Bible but also primordial human symbols and an imagistic repertoire from a background at once classical-humanist and popular-national, John creates, under the pressure of infused mystical experience, verbal icons at once unified and unique.

> Who can divide the spheres of supernatural and natural inspiration? Why shouldn't the direct inspiration of the Holy Spirit at the same time awaken all of the powers of artistic enthusiasm and creative inventiveness where such powers exist? And who would want to maintain that such elevation of man's creative ability to the service, both passive and active, of the divine Word is impossible or inadmissible from a Christian point of view or incompatible with supreme holiness?[50]

Though the holiness could of course occur without the poetry, both 'originate from the same sphere of loving freedom in the soul's relationship with God; both are the overwhelming splendour of grace, an "inundation with glory"'.[51] Balthasar admits that the centre of the mystical action (or better, *passion*) lies deeper than the act of poetic creation, yet the more important point is that both together – the mystic in his poetry, the poetry of the mystic – attest the action of the Holy Spirit who interprets the biblical revelation existentially in the soul, thus implanting it the more deeply in the womb of Christ's Bride, the Church.

Now precisely because this mysticism, though lyrically expressed, must testify to the marriage of God and the world *on the cross*, its love-poetry must renounce everything that can be counted as 'aesthetic' in the eyes of a fallen world. Hence the terrifying world critique, the remorseless demolition which sanjuanist mystical theology entails.

> 'Creature' here always has the meaning of that which is radically other than God, which for that very reason must transcend itself, if it is to attain that participation in the Godhead that God bestows upon it.[52]

All forms and figures – *even* those which originate supernaturally – must be discarded so that the soul 'may hold exclusively to the theological virtues, . . . so as to hurl itself in complete nakedness into the naked reality of God'.[53] Although noting that this is not at all the view of John's co-worker, the great Teresa ('God deliver us from people who are so spiritual that they want to turn everything into perfect contemplation, come what may'), Balthasar for the moment reserves judgment on the point, contenting himself with the remark that, despite the negativity of the undertaking St John urges, the soul's 'achievement' (the word is used

50 *GL* III, p. 124.
51 Ibid.
52 *GL* III, p. 129.
53 *GL* III, p. 132.

in part ironically, for all is a response to God's elective grace) is essentially positive: it is no small thing to cause human *erōs* to be overwhelmed by divine.

A second factor – beyond the issue of the 'denial' of creatures and 'rejection' of images – lies in John's understanding of faith, which is not to be sharply distinguished from hope and charity, since he holds the trio of the theological virtues to be *au fond* the single reality of participation in God, rendered triune only by the powers of our own soul. Such loving and hoping faith, then,

> makes the world transparent to God, makes it disappear in its objectivity and configurated character. But because its light no longer strikes against anything, and because God himself is not an object, God can be experienced by the soul only as dark night.[54]

Subjectively this night feels like death; but objectively it is resurrection, such that Balthasar is at a loss to say whether the 'blessed night' John describes is better described as a *theologia crucis*, a 'theology of the cross', or as a *theologia gloriae*, a 'theology of glory'. (For Balthasar, these are in any case indistinct: the cross of the abandoned Son is, as seen by the Father, 'purest light'.)[55] What takes the place of subject-object relatedness in the case of supernatural mysticism is what John calls *toques sustanciales de divina union*, where substance 'touches' substance in a way that goes beyond all particular acts of knowing, feeling or desiring. Only the doctrine of the Holy Trinity can make sense of this breathing by the Spirit of the fragrance of the Son into the bridal soul. The 'substantial touches' are living flames which one might think would prove mortal to mere creatures, but instead they unfold the content of a life of love.

And then thirdly, if we are to grasp how such a severe – literally dreadful – mystical doctrine has an honoured place in theological aesthetics, we must see how for John the world, definitively abandoned as a necessary condition of the mystic's climbing the dark stair, is subsequently regained in God, in such a fashion that the poet will never again be able to lose himself in the world's beauty.

> For this lover of contemplation the world gains its beauty from above: from divine love, which, for its part, through the reflection of the persons, one in another, is the archetype of all beauty. The contemplative sees not only the beauty of God and in it the beauty of the world; he also sees in the moment of vision, as it were the *analogia entis* itself.[56]

Or, in John's own words in *The Living Flame of Love*:

> Although the soul in this state is indeed aware that all things are distinct from God in so far as they have created being, and sees them

54 *GL* III, p. 134.
55 *GL* III, p. 137.
56 *GL* III, p. 149.

in him with their power, their root and their tension, nonetheless she knows precisely that God, by his being all these things with infinite eminence is such that she knows these things better in God's being than in themselves.[57]

Here the soul could be crushed by glory, yet the breathing of the Spirit is gentle, as the Father of Carmel, Elijah, discovered on Mount Horeb.

And particularly the aesthetically sensitive soul could be crushed by glory, for as Balthasar points out, John was acutely aware of beauty; he could neither have renounced it nor refound it in God had he been blissfully unaware of what it is. The contemporary sources make perfectly clear his love for cosmic nature, both in its sweep and its detail; he had, moreover, played and sung in his time much music, and as befitted one apprenticed to both a woodcarver and a painter, he was a maker of crucifixes, not least the masterly sketch of the crucified Lord that still exists. But in point of fact, as Balthasar concedes, John's attitude to the Church's artworks was somewhat half-hearted: yes, the Church authorises and even encourages their use, but devotional aids can be too external, a diversion and even pure puerility.

And if one were to try to point out the primordial sacramental reality and efficacy of the incarnate Image of God, the Son, then John's answer would be: 'Our Lord was indeed a living image during his sojourn in this world; nevertheless, those who were faithless received no spiritual gain, even though they frequently went about with him and beheld his wondrous works'.[58]

A very unByzantine attitude? But as Balthasar explains, only against 'the dark night's golden backdrop of love, hope and faith [are] the finite forms illuminated in their true and everlasting beauty'.[59] So there is a theology of the icon here after all, but it is a highly oblique one. How will Balthasar finally assess John of the Cross' contribution? And (especially) what will he make of the claims to normativeness that have sometimes been advanced for his mystical teaching, the thesis that he is the 'mystical doctor' *par excellence*?

Balthasar has nothing against the idea that one figure in the history of Christian discipleship could be a norm, albeit of course a subordinate norm to Jesus Christ, the *norma normans* of all participation in divine Glory. But does the content and quality of John's teaching merit this status? For Balthasar, both as dogmatic theologian and as theological asethetician, the question arises, what has happened in this spirituality to

the religious value of all the figures of revelation – above all, of the form of God incarnate; then of the Church as a visible institution of salvation, as the communion of saints; and of Scripture in its objective, multiform facticity. Does not this mysticism fly past the

---

57 *Living Flame of Love*, IV. 5, cited at *GL* III, p. 149.
58 *GL* III, pp. 157–158, citing *The Ascent of Mount Carmel*, III. 36, 3.
59 *GL* III, pp. 160–161.

incarnate Christ as it plunges, without mediation, into the furnace of the triune love?

And Balthasar's answer to his own question is that, on all these points sanjuanist mysticism emerges from the critique triumphant – on all *save that of the Church*. The theme of 'through the darkness to the light' is in John christologically (not philosophically) determined on the basis of the paschal mystery and many raids on Scripture serve its articulation. His crucifix icon shows that his insistence on transcending 'configured imagery' must not be taken *au pied de la lettre*: it is, rather, concentration on this single image that he desires. Yet there is no feeling here for the apostolic significance of prayer and oblation (found above all in the little Thérèse, but already indicated in her namesake of Avila), and Balthasar – whose own doctrine of contemplation and mysticism was, as befitted the co-founder of the *Johannesgemeinschaft* – strikingly ecclesiological, considered this a definite lacuna. 'Why is the image of God and of Jesus Christ, the human thou in its misery and hidden glory, not taken up into transcendence, into the wind of the Holy Spirit?'[60]

Nor can Balthasar support John's identification of the utterly foundational theological virtues of faith, hope and charity with contemplation, especially when the latter is conceived according to one particular developmental scheme.

> The possible varieties of perfect faith and contemplation cannot be canonically determined by one single experience, and within this variety the various forms of active Christian life must be allowed to make their contribution . . . Christ, the archetype, is . . . beyond the ways of contemplation and action, and love can be perfect in both ways.[61]

Like the contemplative life as a whole, John's doctrine serves as a parable – a *poem*, precisely – which exhibits in a very pure way the form of Christian living, and it in this analogical sense (and not literally) that Balthasar can regard it as of validity for everyone.

Pascal

Pascal, the third of Balthasar's 'lay' theologians is, like Dante, one of the figures who fascinated his former master, Romano Guardini. And highly Guardini-esque is one of Balthasar's opening *aperçus* on Pascal that 'like all great creators of form [he] strives to get back to the *source*',[62] and his expositor further explains how this means not just a return to the patristic sources but 'a return to the life of Jesus and through the undistorted facts of that life to the mystery of the suffering love of God'.[63]

Balthasar highlights Pascal's famous distinction between the three 'orders' of body, mind and charity, arranged hierarchically as these are in

60 *GL* III, p. 167.
61 *GL* III, pp. 169–170.
62 *GL* III, p. 174. The emphasis is Balthasar's.
63 *GL* III, p. 177.

such fashion that the intelligible realities are dark to sense, and those for which charity is the proper epistemic organ intangible to both the senses and the mind, and finds in fragment 308 of the *Pensées* confirmation on this basis for his own aesthetic theology of 'The Glory and the Cross'. Pascal had written

> Great geniuses have their own power. . . . They are recognised not with the eyes but with the mind, and that is enough . . . [Analogously] with what great pomp and marvellously magnificent array Jesus came in the eyes of the heart, which perceive wisdom.[64]

and Balthasar comments on these disparate kinds of visibility

> But if the things of the mind are hidden and remain dark to sense, and if the things of the love of God are hidden and remain dark to the mind, then the glory that the enlightened heart beholds is no other than that of love, and therewith the glories of the hidden One and the hiddenness of the Glory.[65]

But then we naturally ask how one *can* see the presence of the God who hides himself? Balthasar's essay on Pascal is in essence an answer to that question. He prefaces his substantive interpretation by the salutary warning that the 'heart' for Pascal is the Augustinian *cor* not the *coeur* of sentimentalism, and Balthasar believed that, despite the undoubted influence on Pascal of Port-Royal, his use of Augustine's writings was fundamentally sound – differing importantly from that of Jansenism (despite agreement with the latter on many specific points) because of a more just retrieval of the spirit of Augustine's theology as a whole. At the same time, Balthasar admits that the apparent exclusion of a natural theology in Pascal makes him more exclusively a theologian of the *super*naturally enlightened heart than had been St Augustine.

> For him who derives his philosophical descent not from Plato and Plotinus but from Epictetus and Montaigne, the bridge over the gulf of the analogy of truth can only be built by the supernatural grace of the free, electing and reprobating God . . .[66]

And if that difference is the sufficient reason for Pascal's innovations in theological aesthetics when compared with Augustine, they coincided in regarding the beauty of *number* (of mathematics in Augustine, geometry and natural science in Pascal) as something significant, as we shall see.

I spoke above of the *apparent* absence of a natural theology in Pascal (notoriously, he leaves the question of the validity or otherwise of the traditional proofs of God's existence quite open), but as Balthasar points out, it is in Pascal's writing a certain sort of anthropology which provides the *preambula fidei* otherwise furnished in Scholasticism by the doctrine of

---

64 *Pensées* 308 in the Lafuma enumeration, cited at *GL* III, p. 180.
65 Ibid.
66 *GL* III, p. 187.

being. This is how 'a concept of sufficient metaphysical power could develop that could embrace the disintegrating parts of human existence and bind them into unity'.[67] Pascalian man, alerted by anthropological reflection, can look 'down' to the form of science displayed in the numerical values found in matter; but he can also look 'up' (in faith) to the form of the God-man that makes him, in his median position, intelligible to himself for the first time. This statement becomes more plausible when we take into consideration Pascal's mathematically defined theory of space where all intelligible figures presuppose a twofold infinite – the infinitely small of unlimited divisibility and the infinitely great of unlimited extensibility.

> The spatially infinite is for him only a pointer . . . to a metaphysical status in being that makes it impossible for the finite being to come to terms with its ultimate cause, so that all its being and knowing rests on a foundation of something that it neither essentially is nor grasps.[68]

It is the atheist filled with dread before this dizzy prospect (the modern equivalent, Balthasar thinks, would be the evolutionary materialist for whom the form of the universe has emerged from formless matter) that Pascal, as the 'first "dramatic theologian"', takes as his conversation-partner, and would convert.

And the solution can be found only from a vantage-point that looks from above down.

> This theological aesthetic rests therefore completely on a relation-ship that is established from above. *Rapport* and *proportion, measure* and *correspondence* are the key concepts . . . Man cannot understand God, but through God he can understand himself – but not, precisely, by means of the 'God of the philosophers' and the *analogia entis*, but through the free, living God of inconceivable grace, as he has been manifest in the Cross of Jesus Christ.[69]

What Pascal has to show is that only in the perspective of the historic revelation can the 'deformed' be integrated into true form, the living 'disproportion' which is man become comely proportion, the contradic-tion between man's *grandeur* and *misère* be overcome. For when Pascal calls humanity monstrous, he is not, despite Jansen, referring to our depravity but – most tellingly for a theological aesthetician – to the *indecipherability of the figure that we cut.*

Still, the doctrine of original sin is absolutely necessary to Pascal's revelation-based analysis. For

> It is not that man is as such incapable of comprehending God, but that he no longer has that dignity that would render him proportionable to the divine love. To have fallen from love is the

67 *GL* III, p. 190.
68 *GL* III, pp. 195–196.
69 *GL* III, pp. 200, 205.

mystery of original sin, something rationally insoluble and yet nevertheless the illuminating presupposition for an understanding of the human condition.[70]

But if original sin be *le noeud de notre condition*,[71] then its *dénouement* is Jesus Christ in whom God provides 'man's possibility of wholeness and the restoration of the proportion that resolves in itself all lack of proportion, embracing it and drawing it into itself'.[72] So far is Pascal's answer to the human problem from any '*doctrine* of immanence' – by which the truth found in revelation could be read naturalistically from off the face of the world – that 'if Christ is to be understood, he must [in striking contrast] be read as God's free act of grace that nothing in the world could demand or suggest or construct'.[73] And yet there is, evidently, some justification for a '*method* of immanence' (Blondel's term for an exhibition of openness to the supernatural based on the exigencies of human nature) since once the content of revelation is formulated it strikes the heart immediately (so Pascal predicts) as truth.

But the closest *rapprochement* between Balthasar's theology and Pascal's apologetics in the *Pensées* is their shared notion of divine hiddenness in, with and through divine manifestation. The increasing manifestation of what is essential to the God of revelation brings with it an increasing hiddenness of that same God, for what is essential is love. 'God, as love, wills to be found only by love; "perfect clarity would only help the mind. . . . Their pride must be humbled".'[74] It is God's love which elects to redeem man by 'fulfilling' and thus 'revaluing' the dialectic of *grandeur* and *misère*, as Christ sinks low from his majesty in the kenotic incarnation and is exalted through humiliation in his cross and resurrection. Moreover, all the figures of the Old Testament as prophecy of the New, and of the New as the religion of charity, only make sense when seen in the light of the love of God. For Pascal, the Old Testament is a cipher which could never generate the key to its own code, yet which, through the revelation of charity, is decoded in its own intrinsic meaning nonetheless.

It is the incomprehensibly encoded medium (*le milieu*) between nature and grace, between paganism and Christianity, which can produce no picture of itself except when it passes over into the truth to which it refers.[75]

The 'transfigurative' order of charity includes all images within itself as their 'source' and their 'justification': only by reference to the New Testament perspective can the internal disparities of the Old Testament be united. Here Balthasar underwrites Pascal's hermeneutical principle

---

70 *GL* III, p. 214.
71 *Pensées* 131 in the Lafuma enumeration.
72 *GL* III, p. 215.
73 *GL* III, pp. 215–216.
74 *GL* III, p. 220, citing *Pensées* 234 (Lafuma).
75 *GL* III, p. 226.

that 'to understand an author's meaning all contradictory passages must be reconciled'.[76] Noting how the great Dominican exegete Père Marie-Joseph Lagrange considered Pascal's biblical interpretation (despite his probably exaggerated view of the scope of the prophets' own knowledge) to be right in all essentials,[77] Balthasar will, in the concluding volumes of *Herrlichkeit*, make a Pascalian theology of the relation between the Testaments his own. When the love of God was manifested – in the Father's surrendering the Son for the life of the world – that love became manifest in *God*'s way, which is to illuminate everything else from his own hiddenness, *not* to place himself in the light.

And in this regard, Balthasar finds Pascal's theology of the poor an effective filling of that ecclesial vacuum in which the mysticism of John of the Cross seemed to unfold. Nor was Pascal's 'option for the poor' merely theory; Balthasar records, among other evidences, Pascal's reaction, on being told at the height of the controversy over the Jansenist 'five propositions', that his mortal sickness was not hopeless enough for him to be accorded Holy Communion. This being the case, he would communicate with the *members* of the Head, and accordingly, had one of the sick poor brought to be nursed with him in his house. Here Pascal 'unites the concept of incomprehensible grace (interpreted as election and reprobation)' with 'the concept of the universalism of love'.[78] When Balthasar declares that for Pascal the credibility of Christian truth is determined by an aesthetic judgment, we might well demur, until he explains that acceptance of the gospel turns on a 'conviction of its inner measuredness and its outward fitness'.[79]

Hamann

In taking as his next witness Jakob Georg Hamann, that eighteenth-century Lutheran writer whose oracular manner of utterance gained him the not altogether complimentary title of 'the magus of the North', Balthasar sets next to Pascal a figure whose basic idea would no doubt have been congenial to the critic of Descartes – namely, the unsatisfactoriness of abstraction. What made Balthasar select this member of his 'lay' septet – the only non-Catholic among them, if at any rate (with Balthasar) we credit the reception of Soloviev into the Church of Rome as more than a gesture – soon becomes apparent when we hear how

it was Hamann's belief that the act of *aisthêsis*, if it is not curtailed, is the original religious act itself, for all things are God's word and language, and therefore one who apprehends these things hears God himself speaking.[80]

76 *Pensées* 257 (Lafuma).
77 M.-J. Lagrange, O.P., 'Pascal et les prophéties messianiques', *Revue Biblique* 3 (1906), pp. 533–560.
78 *GL* III, p. 232.
79 *GL* III, p. 235.
80 *GL* III, p. 241.

The God who 'speaks' as Creator and creates as 'Word' establishes the proper meaning of both things and language, their *kyriological* sense which, for Hamann, includes therefore the important corollary that what is 'taken in its proper sense' is grasped according to the *logos* of the *Kyrios*, Jesus Christ. As with Claudel in his *art poétique* a century and a half later, Hamann presents the world as a poem, a thing made to be eloquent.

But since the creation, which shimmers with gleams of the divine Shekinah, is crowned by man as the image and likeness of God, so is humankind the 'highest word of the Poet-God'.[81] The Fall of man made chaos, however, of the ordered poem, leaving us, as the *Aesthetica in nuce* has it, with only a 'jumble of verses and *disiecti membrae poetae* for our use'.[82] Only if the fragments are reassembled and 'given a destiny' can man and nature be healed. Balthasar cannot but approve of a writer who treats beauty as a transcendental concept constituted by analogy in such a way that no aspect of existence is foreign to it – especially one for whom this all-embracing beauty is the glory of God with 'the revelation in flesh [as] the midpoint of everything, the meaning of the divine Word in its entirety'.[83]

The incarnate Word provides a 'canon', or rule of judgment, for aesthetics, in four respects. First, God appeared in Christ through an act of *gracious freedom*. Just so, humanly originated beauty always includes the free constitution of some expressive relationship – and this is not less true of man's interpretation of the 'language' of God in the creation where in fact he has abused freedom and can no longer read aright without the inner help of grace and the outer help of salvation history in the Scriptures. Second, this act of gracious freedom was also a supreme *self-humiliation*, and so the proof of his love and glory.

> It is [Hamann wrote] an aspect of the unity in the divine revelation that the Spirit of God abases itself through the human pencil of the holy men that it itself impels, divesting itself of its majesty just as much as does the Son of God through the servant figure, and in the same way as the [Father's] entire creation is a work of the highest humility. . . . The sublime in Caesar's style is its carelessness.[84]

Third, the free kenotic action of God was to have *embraced the flesh* through becoming flesh and only so to heal the spirit. Against the rationalism of the Enlightenment Hamann invokes Humian empiricism (though surely Aristotelian would better have served his purpose?) in order to reclaim for the senses their rightful place. It is by their means that we sense (precisely) reality. ' "Not just the whole warehouse of the reason, but even the treasury of faith, rests upon this staff", upon "the five loaves of barley", "the five senses"'.[85] The embodiment of the divine Word in

---

81 *GL* III, p. 244.
82 Cited at *GL* III, p. 244.
83 Cited from Hamann's *Biblische Betrachtungen* at *GL* III, p. 245.
84 In *Kleeblatt hellenistischer Blätter* 2, cited at *GL* III, p. 252; Balthasar acknowledges the help here of H. Schreiner, *Die Menschwerdung Gottes in der Theologie J. G. Hamanns* (Tübingen 1950).
85 *GL* III, p. 256, citing Hamann's *Brocken*.

human flesh, and the incorporation of the world into his divine life are the fulfilment of God's poetry in creating; increasingly, so Balthasar reports, Hamann would turn away 'his gaze . . . from an unattainable protology to the eschatology toward which man and the world are making their way'.[86] And fourthly and finally, the saving incarnation serves as a measuring rod for aesthetics by the way it returns man to *reality through the flesh.*

> The inadequacy of human judgment as such – 'since *summum ius* and *summa iniuria* are, like light and shade, inseparably related in time within the underworld of the senses' – is also superseded and justified in Christ's judgment, which brings the truth concealed in it creatively to light.[87]

And yet, though praising Hamann for his rediscovery – not easy for an Evangelical – of the principle of analogy which enables him to find correspondences between nature and supernature at so many points, Balthasar fears that he does not do sufficient justice to their difference – with disadvantages for both philosophy and Christianity. Still, had he – rather than Schleiermacher – become the 'theological mentor' of German thought in the nineteenth century, the future of theological aesthetics, Balthasar suggests, would have been rosier.

Soloviev

Only through the idea of the Antichrist, extraordinarily enough, does Balthasar's fifth lay theologian, Vladimir Soloviev, escape the same charge. Balthasar accepts the description of Soloviev's metaphysics as 'the most comprehensive statement of the Christian totality in modern times', but more enticing is the claim that the theoretical and ethical aspects of Soloviev's scheme culminate in a 'universal theological aesthetic'.[88] Appealing to the evidence brought forward by Heinrich Falk[89], Balthasar has no compunction about treating Soloviev as a Catholic thinker – though of course one for whom Russian Orthodoxy is the single most important background element. More typically Balthasar's own is his speculative reconstruction of how Soloviev arrived at his 'Catholic conclusion' which he situates at the intersection of two ideas crucial to the Russian writer's thought. And these were, first, the notion of *universality* which takes the form in Soloviev of distaste for the particularist and (not least) nationalist outlook – Slavophilia, he came to recognise, is an insufficiently 'catholic' attitude; and secondly, the concept of *development* whereby a relatively undetermined reality becomes at once more determinate and more plenary, integrating all partial viewpoints and limited forms of actualisation into an organic totality in, once again, a 'catholic' fashion. As Balthasar admits, both of these ideas were taken from Hegel.

86 *GL* III, p. 261.
87 *GL* III, p. 272, citing Hammann's *Zwey Scherflein*, I.
88 *GL* III, p. 281. ,
89 H. Falk, 'Wladimir Solowjews Stellung zur katholischen Kirche', *Stimmen der Zeit* (1949), pp. 421–435.

In this regard, Hegel's influence was salutary for an Eastern Christendom that had to some extent succumbed to the temptations of nationalist particularism and fossilised self-enclosure. But in Balthasar's eyes, Soloviev's thought is actually far more successful than Hegel's – above all, of course, from a Christian standpoint. The Wisdom of God, communicated to the creation from the beginning, receives through the incarnate Word of God her ('Sophia's') supreme embodiment as the Body and Bride of Christ, for the 'limitless fulness and determinacy of God' fulfils and renders wholly positive the 'cosmic potentiality' of the non-divine.

What is extraordinary about Soloviev's achievement is that, with consummate daring, he deliberately integrated into his account of the Spirit's work in history such alien schemes as those of Indian thought and Valentinian Gnosis as well as Platonism, while yet treating the historic incarnation as the one utterly decisive moment in the transformation of reality:

> Before Christianity, the firm foundation of life was human (the old Adam); the divine was the principle of change, motion, progress. After the appearance of Christianity, the divine itself, incarnate now for evermore, stands over against man as a firm foundation, as the element in which our life exists; what is sought is a humanity to answer to this divinity; that is, a humanity capable of uniting itself with it by independent action appropriating it for itself.[90]

On Balthasar's interpretation, it is Maximus Confessor with his commitment to the dogma of Chalcedon as the key to all natural and supernatural reality whatsoever, who is Soloviev's true starting point. All that Soloviev added to Maximus' 'cosmic liturgy' was the 'dynamic element of German Idealism – the evolution of nature towards man, of history towards Christ, and of the Church towards the Kingdom of God in its completeness'.[91] Here we find the key to that aspect of Balthasar's own study of Maximus which most perplexed pure patrologists – his insistence, in *Kosmische Liturgie*, that the Confessor's Christocentric cosmology provides the evangelical answer to Hegel stems from the circle of ideas outlined by Soloviev in his article on Maximus Confessor in the *Brockhaus-Ephron* encyclopaedia.[92] But if Maximus is the Christian antidote to Hegelianism, it is Hegel who, at the end of the nineteenth century gave Maximus, as Soloviev saw, his topicality.

Taken in its entirety, Soloviev's vision anticipates that of Teilhard de Chardin, and is superior to the latter in its speculative finesse (the impressionistic and distinctly unreliable character of Teilhard's epistemology and metaphysics – he is better thought of as a poet-scientist – is well-known). Above all, Soloviev's theology of the Antichrist acts as a 'salutary counterpoise' to Teilhard's evolutionism, a motif in which Balthasar's account will culminate.

90 From Soloviev's *Dukhovniya osnovi zhizni* (1882–84), cited in *GL* III, p. 287.
91 *GL* III, p. 288.
92 'Maksim Ispovednik', *Entsiklopedichesko slovar Brockhaus-Ephron* X (1896), 598.

So far, little has been said about theological aesthetics as such. It is, however, this very 'tension between progress and apocalyptic' which for Balthasar 'moulds the shape of Soloviev's aesthetic'.[93] The latter's programme of Christian integration departs quite drastically from the Hegelian scheme of world reason moving ineluctably forward into the state of absolute knowledge – departs from that scheme precisely because it recognises that evil is not just ignorance; it is saying No to love. Balthasar outlines Soloviev's contribution to theological aesthetics in the course of surveying the three main phases of his literary output: the early philosophical writings, chiefly epistemological and metaphysical; the middle period of the ethical and ecclesiological treatises; and the final writings, on beauty and the apocalyptic struggle of the End. On the first (logic and metaphysics), it must suffice here to draw attention to those aspects which are of importance for aesthetics. Soloviev held that both Western rationalism and Western empiricism had absolutised one aspect of the structure of cognition (either the concept or experience, respectively), turning one formal element into the whole of reality. But knowledge is in fact integral, and reflection on what is involved in its various constituent factors leads Soloviev to affirm the true existence both of the world and of the God who is beyond the world. That conclusion enables him to break with the Idealist identification of finite and infinite subject – and therefore to speak of the love of God for what is not himself, while at the same time permitting him to retain the Idealist conviction that the world is a self-integrating process, the developing creaturely form, as Soloviev would say, of the divine Sophia. And beauty is distinctly germane to the latter, for according to his presentation of the transcendentals: in coming forth from himself and prescribing a goal for the world, God is goodness; in knowing himself, and manifesting himself in Christ as the kingdom, he is truth; and in experiencing himself, and fully actualising his selfhood in what is other than him, he is beauty. Affirming the ideal as good he gives it through the mediation of truth realisation in the beautiful. Beauty is the fulness of imitability of the divine Essence, and as such intimately linked to Soloviev's concept of the 'Wisdom' of God.

Soloviev's Christology is to be found within his ontology, for the latter is a metaphysics of 'Godmanhood'. If Sophia is the representative presence of God in the totality of being, the Logos is the active moulder of that totality. At the moment of the incarnation, the Logos determines the human principle not *externally* but *internally* – making space for the other by a kenotic movement of self-limitation in order to assume what is human. For Soloviev it is extremely important that this self-limitation of the Godhead in Christ simultaneously sets free his humanity, by allowing the natural will of the humanity assumed freely to renounce itself in favour of the divine principle, considered as an *interior* (not, once again, *exterior*) good in which man can then come to share the good in all reality.

This twofold kenosis is the essence of the person of the God-man no less than of his work, his death on the Cross, and it is at the same

93 *GL* III, p. 296.

time absolute glory in twofold form – the self-glorification of God in his creation as much as the glorification in God of the whole man, the man who, in the voluntary death of love, is victorious over all the disastrous contingencies of the material world and so has achieved for himself and for all humanity and the cosmos the resurrection of the body.[94]

The glory and the cross: those are, after all, the twin master-themes of *Herrlichkeit*.

On the second phase of Soloviev's work – ethics and ecclesiology – Balthasar has already signalled the importance of catholicity – of a universalising plenitude. If sophianic beauty can only be realised kenotically – by the setting free of man for God and for himself through the process of God's becoming man, this process of the integration of humankind into the kingdom is unthinkable without the Church. What is striking in the context of theological aesthetics is to see how Balthasar accentuates, in his reproduction of Soloviev's ecclesiology, the notion of *form*.

> The Church is, on the one hand, the God-man really living on in a community of love, realised ethically as well as sacramentally; but, on the other hand, it is also, necessarily the pattern of the ideal universal form of the Kingdom of God. . . . Everything . . . depends on the integration of humanity into the Church, so that it can receive there a share in the form of the divine-human universality, and on the other hand, on the Church's integration into humanity, so that she can shed the abstractness that is foreign to her because of her essential centre, but which she still retains because of the refusal of men to accept her.[95]

The form of the Church, though derived from that primordial form which is the Godmanhood of Christ as the divine self-expression in the world, and ordered to that ultimate form which is the kingdom of God as the complete embodiment of Christ in humanity, is nonetheless itself universal – and in this regard stands in sharp contrast to any form originated purely from within this world. For the Church offers a universal faith, where the powers of human knowing are penetrated by the Spirit of Christ; a universal hierarchical obedience, which itself upholds a right relation to all human beings; and a universal eschatological quality of life, based on participation in the Eucharist, the firstfruits of the transfigured cosmos. At the same time, this universal form is utterly concrete, for its existence is grounded in the immaculate Virgin Mary, and its indefectibility in the glorious prince of the apostles, Peter. Soloviev freely concedes, of course, the limitations of the great majority of the Church's members, but those limitations are defined precisely by nonconformity to the Church's form! (Alternatively, speaking of the Church as a body, Soloviev can say that its members may be diseased yet

---

94 *GL* III, p. 324.
95 *GL* III, p. 329.

its central organs are invulnerable – since Christ is its head, and our Lady and all the saints its hearts, and so its perduring vitality is assured.) Yet in the historic schisms which have rent the seamless garment (East from West, Protestantism from Catholicism), he can ascribe a peculiar *cachet* for the past (tradition) to the East, for the present (the constant renewal of the presence of Christ) to Rome, and the future (the spirit of prophecy) to Protestantism, while however denying that either Orthodoxy or the Reformation preserve the true form of the Church which can only be universal (*pace* the East) and objective (*pace* Wittenberg and Geneva).

The reconstitution of their unity, Soloviev speculates, and this brings us to the third and final phase of his work, will only be achieved in the face of the supreme challenge of the Antichrist. In his (fragmentary) aesthetic writings, Soloviev makes much play with the idea of apocalypse as a final revelation of divine-human harmony at the consummation of history. Consonant with his theological ontology as a whole, he treats the idea of beauty as

> eternally real in God himself, in so far as he exists as the eternal actuality of all his potential in the fullest degree of freedom. It is, at the same time, the reality of the Kingdom of God in its coming to be in the world as it realises itself eschatologically through the ascent of natural and historical forms. Christ and Mary, the Logos incarnate and Sophia incarnate, represent in this process the ever-perfect primordial form of beauty, the norm by which reality as it takes on form can measure and align itself.[96]

But if Soloviev never supposed this could be, in the last analysis, achieved anywhere short of the world to come, with the resurrection of the dead, his somewhat optimistic account of cosmic process had tended to gloss over the element of radical rupture. Now, however, at the end of his life the reality of the kingdom of death, of violence, of evil, hits him with full force. In the theological fiction of his Antichrist novel (the genre will be continued in Robert Hugh Benson's *Lord of the World* [1905] and Michael O'Brien's *Father Elijah. An Apocalypse* [1996]), it is only with the slaughter of the last Christians that the Christ appears in purple apparel to bring the harvest of creation home.

Hopkins

To those who find that the rarified air of speculative metaphysics leaves them gasping for breath, it is a relief to turn to Balthasar's Hopkins. In him the imagistic and the particular come back into their own. The *imagistic*, because:

> where on the Continent ecclesiastical modernism sought to take over the ideas of the imaginary character of concepts and also of dogmatic *symbola*, thereby earning the sharpest of censures – so that the two worlds were violently split in two – just there English

96 *GL* III, p. 354.

theology, reared in an hereditary empiricism, sensed no danger and preserved the native rights of imagery in religious thought, and therefore in Christian theology, right up to the present day.[97]

And the *particular*, for 'a mistrust of the value of universal concepts, a consciousness of the irreducibility of the individual, be it material or personal is as old as English intellectual life'.[98]

And this is why Blessed Duns Scotus became (contrary to the Suarezian tradition of the Society of Jesus which Hopkins entered) his *maître à penser*, why he considered him, 'Of realty the rarest veinèd unraveller': 'In the unique, the irreducible, there shines forth for Hopkins the glory of God, the majesty of his oneness, to whose ultimate, creative artistry the incomprehensibility of worldly images bears witness.'[99]

Balthasar is well-informed about Hopkins' biography, his circle of correspondents, and the landscapes and seascapes, both English and Welsh, that are integral to the making of his verse. Stressing that here writer, theologian and priest are inseparable, he emphasises Hopkins' theological vision as the one thing necessary: 'with him, form and content stand and fall together'.[100] That vision, as Balthasar presents it, is not simply Scotism rendered lyrical, for too many other influences went into its making. The Oxford classicist already knew of the intimate conjunction of the beautiful and the good among the Greeks (*kalokagathia*), and his sensibility would hardly be explicable without the inspiration of Ruskin who, in his desire to discern the forms of the world, is as draughtsman and prosist, a kind of English Goethe. As early as 1867, in the essay *The Probable Future of Metaphysics*, Hopkins predicted that the concept of species-type would bounce back, since if all life is simply a continuum, as extreme 'transitionalists' among the evolutionary biologists would hold, talk of development becomes impossible. The impact of Aristotle is further apparent in his acceptance of the Stagirite doctrine of soul as itself form and shaping power – a notion he would retain in his own treatment of 'selving'.

As is well-known, the pair of metaphysical terms Hopkins coined and made current through his nature descriptions and literary criticism are 'instress' and 'inscape'. On Balthasar's interpretation, instress is, summarily spoken, the power of a thing, inscape its form.[101] More fully defined:

> *Instress* . . . is used by Hopkins for both the object and the subject: things express their instress, their deep, unique act, which establishes them, holds them together and holds them in tension, and there is required in the subject an answering stress, so that it can hold communion with the stress of things and experience them from within and can also through a feeling prepossession of their nature find the word that exactly expresses it.[102]

97 *GL* III, p. 354.
98 *GL* III, pp. 354–355.
99 *GL* III, p. 357.
100 *GL* III, p. 393.
101 *GL* III, p. 366.
102 *GL* III, p. 365.

Whereas what is intended by

> *inscape* . . . is not a separate form, resting in itself, but a form released
> from its creative source and at the same time shaped and held by it,
> radiating from a focus from which the whole form (whether it be a
> curve or a play of colours, or a landscape) can then be brought to
> completion.[103]

Yet what brought Hopkins to Catholicism and the Society was nothing
aesthetic. If anything, it was – leaving aside the quite separate issue of the
ecclesiological incoherence of High Anglicanism – a sense of negative
theology. The poems written prior to his conversion suggest a gap of vast
proportions between the glories of this world and the God who dwells in
the deep darkness.

> At his conversion Hopkins offered himself to the real God, the God
> who addressed him personally, the God of the Cross and the God of
> this fearful world, and with himself offered his love of beauty and
> his art.[104]

And though Hopkins considered that, as a Jesuit, he must make that
offering in a spirit of sacrifice (hence his unwillingness to publish that
poetry to – it might be – critical acclaim), the formation and study possibilities found in the Society enabled him to meet, respectively, St Ignatius
and Scotus, and enhanced his feeling for two interrelated ideas, 'selving'
and 'thisness' central to the concepts of instress and inscape. Indeed
Balthasar – ever on the look-out for signs of analogical thinking – sums up
Hopkins' philosophy in the formula *analogia haecceitatis et personalitatis*,
thus joining the Franciscan metaphysician (*haecceitas*) to the author of the
Spiritual Exercises (*personalitas*) by that favoured term (*analogia*) in the
theological grammar of Thomas Aquinas.

But there is more than one way of looking at the uniqueness of
personality. Ignatius Loyola saw it in terms of the electing grace of God
which should elicit from our side distinctive acts of choice in return. It is
from here, according to Balthasar, that Hopkins will develop, by
continued reference (despite the annoyance of his Suarezian teachers) to
Duns Scotus, what is really original in his poetic thinking. Concentrating
for the moment on Hopkins' notion of 'selving at pitch' – his version of
the idea of the irreducible uniqueness of the 'I' – as found in the meditation on the foundation of the *Exercises* and the sermon 'On Personality,
Grace and Free Will', Balthasar speaks of the person as, for Hopkins
perfected only when attuned to the 'innate sound and taste of this
individual' as 'preconceived and chosen by God from eternity', in
accordance with the Ignatian principle that the will must learn to choose
what God chose for it out of time. But, as Hopkins had no need to learn
from de Lubac:

103 *GL* III, p. 366.
104 *GL* III, p. 369.

if we are indeed from all eternity predetermined and called by God to be brothers and members of Christ, the core of our personal 'pitch' lies in the supernatural, and thus our self-choice can only be perfected concretely within the grace of God.[105]

And in a mixture of Scholastic vocabulary – *gratia praeveniens, concomitans, perficiens* – and his own idiom, Hopkins portrays 'prevenient' grace clothing the old self with a new gracious and consenting self at which, drawn by 'accompanying' grace, personal freedom must take aim, while 'perfecting' (or 'unifying') grace is God's own

finger touching the very vein of personality which, nothing else can reach and man can respond to by no play whatever, by bare acknowledgement only, the counter stress which God alone can feel . . . , the spiration in answer to his inspiration.[106]

But while Hopkins treats the new 'cleave' and 'pitch' of selfhood achieved through grace as the work of the entire Trinity, his use of the Scotist idea that the sacrifice of the Son is the Father's first thought for the world gives his theology of supernatural transformation a more especially *christological* stamp. Even if we leave aside Scotus' stranger speculations (congenial to Hopkins) on the eternity of the eucharistic being of the Son as following from the predestining of his sacrifice, on the fall of the angels from bliss as coincident with the whole of human time, and on the 'real fetching, presentment, adduction' of Christ and Mary into the aeonic realm that the angels may choose whether to 'realise in the eternal foundations of the world the spirit of the sacrifice of Christ',[107] we can still understand how it follows that where the world's creation is seen as an implication of the decree of the incarnation 'the cosmos as a whole possesses, either manifestly or secretly, a Christological form'.[108] It will be Christ, then, who determines the selving of created persons; their true 'pitch' is their victory over the natural self, for him. By contrast, the lost are 'like half-creations and have but a halfbeing'.[109] Conversely, if the believer lets grace work co-operatively in him, Christ is enselved in his member – which is how the poem 'As Kingfishers Catch Fire' will see things.[110]

Two corollaries follow. First, all beauty belongs to the Christ in whom all truth is grounded; more particularly, it is related to his eternal sacrifice – that total self-donation from which the creation of the world proceeds. Secondly, Hopkins' conviction of the gracious, christological form of the world cannot leave the doctrines of instress and inscape unchanged. God's grace is the 'stress' in things, and their true 'inscape' is Christ. And

---

105 *GL* III, p. 378.
106 Cited from C. Devlin, S.J., *The Sermons and Devotional Writings of Gerard Manley Hopkins* (London 1959), p. 158, cited at *GL* III, p. 380.
107 *GL* III, p. 382.
108 *GL* III, p. 384.
109 Devlin, *Sermons and Devotional Writings of Gerard Manley Hopkins*, p. 197, cited at *GL* III, p. 384.
110 W. H. Gardner and N. H. MacKenzie (eds), *The Poems of Gerard Manley Hopkins* (Oxford 1980⁴), p. 90.

thus Balthasar can write in a splendid statement of the sweep of Hopkins' 'sacramental poetry';

> The fact that all natures and selves are fashioned and determined for Christ, who is both their ultimate inscape and instress, means that there is no other possibility of reading them objectively and understanding them than in relation to this centre in which they are integrated. Hopkins does not thereby confuse nature and grace, but the concrete *telos* of natures and persons is none the less that for the sake of which they exist, and out of the glory of the Incarnate God there breaks forth the truest and most inward glory of forms both of natures and persons.[111]

And we are speaking here of the God-man in his majesty and yet sacrifice, heroic love and yet condescending mercy; grace comes not only from heaven but through the manger and the cross, and includes as a constituent moment of its coming the human assent given it in Mary, who thereby becomes comparable (in the title of one of Hopkins' best-known poems) to 'the air we breathe'. In reading Hopkins, one cannot say where natural description ends and supernatural interpretation begins, and this is, Balthasar points out, as it should be, since 'the Christological-Mariological has been understood as the inner condition of possibility of the whole natural order'.[112] In the wonderful exegesis of 'The Wreck of the Deutschland' which ends his essay on Hopkins, the shipwreck becomes a parable of the atonement: resurrection comes only through 'foundering in God'.

Péguy

It remains to consider Charles Péguy, in whom Balthasar sees not only the soteriogical but also the social and political truth that theological aesthetics can make available. Péguy was a man whom a passion for justice took out of the Church and brought back to her (though not, owing to the refusal of his wife to accept the Church's blessing on their marriage, sacramentally). He strove to unite secular truth with sacred by means he would not call 'development' – like Balthasar, he distrusted the word – but *approfondissement*, a 'deepening'.

> He is the Church *in partibus infidelium*, the Church in those places where the Church will be one day, and he is so thanks to the fact that he is rooted in the depths where world and Church, world and grace, meet together and interpenetrate to the point of indistinguishability.[113]

Péguy takes Joan of Arc as his model because she unites both solidarities – that of the earth, of one's fellow humans, and that of heaven, the communion of saints – in a mission which was at one and the same time

---

111 *GL* III, p. 390.
112 *GL* III, p. 397.
113 *GL* III, p. 404.

temporal and spiritual. She suited one who considered himself a sinner (one thinks of Joan's devotion to the sacrament of penance), but a sinner possessed of the treasures of grace.

Like Joan, Péguy sought 'an earthly revolution for the sake of eternal salvation'.[114] Congruent with that mission statement, Péguy describes the only great revolutionaries as simultaneously contemplatives, for a revolution consists essentially in 'a deeper entrenchment in the un-exhausted resources, the wellsprings of the inner life'.[115] Having already left the Church – owing to its clergy's preaching of a populated Hell, and the (to Péguy) connected failure in *solidarité* which was the patronising attitude of the Church's members to the working class, Péguy thus abandoned a 'shallow political socialism' likewise.[116] On his return to faith, he will not slacken this passionate concern with salvation over against damnation and with solidarity over against bourgeois charity but redefine it – above all, in the five masterworks that are the reworked *Mystère de la charité de Jeanne d'Arc*, with its attendant *Mystère de la porche du deuxième vertu* and *Mystère des saints Innocents*; *Eve* and *La tapisserie de Notre Dame*.

Balthasar stresses the importance for Péguy not simply of the Dreyfus affair (as the classic case of worldly injustice whereby a people or a State gambles away its chance of eternal salvation), but of Jewry as a whole. The Hebrew Bible remains as a standing indictment of a Christianity which would seek to assert the grace of the incarnation by denying the intrinsic value of the natural order – the *temporel*, the *charnel*. In neglecting the temporal city and the flesh, an excessively other-worldly and hyper-spiritualised Church has left behind, rather than fulfilled, the hope of Israel. The Hebrew prophets in particular demanded not only spiritual but also political decision, a point at which, on Balthasar's reading, aesthetic and ethical coincide for Péguy since prophecy (in post-biblical times as well as in the canon!) means 'knowing how, from the standpoint of God, to assign to things and to human beings, to events and their configurations, their place in the overall pattern'.[117] Truth is beauty because it is, in a trio of key adjectives in Péguy, *exacte*, *axiale* and *juste*. What is just is that which is exactly placed in relation to the axis of what is truly important, and it is therefore the beautiful coincidence of heaven and earth, time and eternity, flesh and spirit, grace and achievement, contemplation and action. It was especially important to Péguy that Jesus should be seen as emerging from a particular race with its specific history, for the Logos did not assume a deracinated humanity, licensing all those Gnosticisms which flee from earth and time. Nothing can substitute, then, for Israel's position as the go-between linking ancient naturalism and the gospel, and yet its finest statement, in Péguy's eyes, was fashioned by a post-Christian neo-pagan, albeit one brooding on the biblical narrative – Victor Hugo. In 'Booz endormi', which forms part of his poetic sequence *La Légende des siècles*, in an atmosphere of 'primordial, chthonic time' Boaz,

---

114 *Oeuvres en prose, 1909–1914* (Paris 1957²), p. 595, cited at *GL* III, p. 409.
115 *Oeuvres en prose, 1898–1908* (Paris 1959), p. 1388, cited at *GL* III, p. 410.
116 *GL* III, p. 410.
117 *GL* III, p. 424.

asleep in a cornfield beneath a crescent moon, dreams of an oaktree growing from his innards up to the azure sky:

> A race climbed up, as scaling a chain,
> A king sang below; above a God would die.[118]

Péguy could only suppose that thus to become a witness to revelation from the outside, testifying to a truth otherwise barely glimpsed by the peoples of the Book (the incarnation as the humanity of God emerging from creation), grace must have outflowed onto genius in Hugo's case. The mystery of genius, Péguy thought, can no more be rendered transparent by psychology than can the mystery of the two natures in one person of Christ.

We cannot imagine that Balthasar, who was so exercised by the hope that all might be saved, will leave alone Péguy's comments on hell, and indeed he could justify critically the claim that Péguy's theological aesthetic stands or falls with the issue of Christian exclusivity (better, *inclusivity*). Péguy's beauty is, like Soloviev's till disturbed by the Antichrist, eschatological harmony. Péguy's early abandonment of the doctrine of hell did not, however, release him from the hellish aspects of modern secular existence – lovelessness, disintegration, oblivion. Péguy returned to the Church because her notion of the solidarity and even complimentarity of sinners and saints – the sinner offering his hand to the saint, since the saint has already given his hand to him – provides a practical though not a theoretical solution to the possibility of everlasting loss. In the revised version of the *Mystère de la Charité de Jeanne d'Arc*, Gervaise represents (in Balthasar's interpretation) the Augustinian and mediaeval theology of perdition in its noblest form, with nothing cramped or crabbed about it. Yet her withdrawal, leaving Joan to her lonely struggle with God, may symbolise for Péguy the final inadequacy of that theology (in its bearing on human destiny), while the 'sign' for which Joan prays, the relief of Mont Saint Michel, may signal contrariwise that the redemptive Trinity will never take the human 'No' to God's purposes as the final word. Péguy's position in these matters, to judge by the most recent study – Père Thierry Dejond's *Charles Péguy. L'espérance d'un salut éternel* – is much the same as Balthasar's: a denial of the Origenestic notion of *apokatastasis* or certain universal salvation but a hope that all will yet be saved, since God has himself 'hoped' for all.[119]

If, in discussing Péguy's account of the interrelation of *spiritual* and *charnel* I have already had occasion to speak of how, for him the incarnation is not only founded in the divine eternal being, but also rooted in the humus of this world, it will come as no surprise that the reconverted Péguy gave much thought to the question of the *enracinement* of Christian identity. His first answer is that, by his incarnation, hidden life and public ministry, Christ assumed and sanctified all that is good in the natural order of family, people and *polis*. If Christ is the founder of the unique

---

118 Cited from *La Légende des siècles* II. 6 at *GL* III, p. 329.
119 T. Dejond, S.J., *Charles Péguy. L'espérance d'un salut éternal* (Namur 1989), pp. 113–114.

City of God, such that – with this difference! – Christian liturgy resembles that ceremonious worship which the men of antiquity offered to all founders of cities, he nonetheless gives the temporal order its due. It is in the name, then, of Christian humanity that Péguy protests against a *déraciné* modern world where quantitative progress has absorbed meaning in life, where the idea of interchangeable elements has replaced the classic geometrical concept of equivalence, where (in a striking parable of modernity) industrial concrete – adaptive, in its preset form, to any shape – supplants those resilient materials of wood and stone which teach respect for the nature of things, where a false internationalism suppresses love of homeland, and a false pacifism makes men overanxious and war more likely.

But the rooting of Christians is not only (even via the recreating Logos) in nature. It is also in history, not the history measured in documents, placed by Péguy under the patronage of its muse, Clio, but the history which lays bare the origin of event and destiny, for which Clio must yield place to a real human being, the mother of all the living, Eve. In his epic poem of that title, Péguy presents Eve as the woman who has experienced the difference between paradisial and fallen time and so can represent the measure of their difference. Yet Eve is more addressed than addressing, for only in the son of her 'daughter', Mary, is time lost subsequently regained, so that the ultimate measure lies with Jesus, the New Eve's offspring. Once the youthful plenitude of the world was spent, Eve is reduced to the continuous, never-finished tidying of a world whose disorder goes way beyond her powers. As an arranger and classifier in the *temple de mémoire* (here Péguy expresses his sense of the inadequacy to real history of the *wissenschaftlich* historiography of Modernism), she takes on the traits of Clio, her mythological sister, until Jesus restores the memory of her origin and *quondam* dignity, as well as showing her the true nature of sin's disorder and grace's incalculable outpouring in his passion. Balthasar calls Eve, accordingly, the theological redemption of that 'search for time lost' portrayed by Proust. And if in *Eve* eternal time speaks with fallen time, in *La tapisserie de Notre Dame* Péguy appeals from fallen time to the presence of proleptically redeemed time in the holiness of Mary.

> Chartres, standing amidst the limitless golden cornfields of the Beauce, is a symbol of the harvest of the world come to fruition around a Paradise made present. Péguy, the weary but indefatigable pilgrim on his solitary way, established and initiated the pilgrimage that today many thousands of Parisian students and intellectuals still follow. His prayers are nothing other than the surrender of the earthly, which can find no ultimate measure in itself, to that which is right without qualification, the measure of Paradise and the fallen world that gives to all things their true direction and their peace.[120]

But the final mode of *enracinement* of the Christian is in that most unlooked for of all originations – the broken heart of God on the cross of Christ.

120 *GL* III, pp. 487–488.

> The risky venture of the soul's *enracinement* in the material world is,
> in so far as the soul is free spiritual reality, a response to the deeper
> hazard of the eternal divine Spirit as it puts down its roots in the
> nothingness of the created world, the nothingness of creaturely
> freedom.[121]

God's grace coaches men and women in the exercise of freedom, else they
could not respond by a liberality congruent with God's own. But because
of the divine 'hope' for human salvation, the sinner is always borne up
by the heart of God, for God's heart 'remains a wounded heart, rendered
helpless by love, an exposed and undefended flank, where the enemy,
man, can force a way through',[122] with which thought belongs Péguy's
memorable image of the human 'prayer fleet' behind its flagship or
rather warship the tip of whose pointed prow is formed by the clasped
hands of the Father's only Son.[123] Balthasar rightly acclaims the wider
context of such images in the 'conversations' Péguy writes for the trinitarian Persons as the most extraordinary things in his work. Avoiding
both false sublimity and mateyness, no other writer has been able to make
God speak in such a fashion.

Péguy is certainly the climax of Volumes II and III of *The Glory of the
Lord*. The strongly Francophile Balthasar is willing to grant him that the
people of France are 'a garden loving people . . . best at ploughing both
soil and souls'.[124] Moreover, Péguy deliberately made of his poetry an
extension of the grace of the saints. If, on Balthasar's view of the *communio
sanctorum*, the missions of all the saints are reciprocally effective, the
vocations of the Christian poets serve such sanctity through artistic
representation. In the genealogy of theological beauty, they belong to the
legitimate line, for they are its witnesses.

And in fact Balthasar has identified in Péguy's theological aesthetic,
better than anywhere else (better, even, than in the Fathers of whose
doctrine and sensibility, however, he finds Péguy to be the extension),[125] elements he will take up in the final volumes of *Herrlichkeit* (on
Old and New Covenants) when he will speak in his own voice. Let us
briefly enumerate them. First, a key role will be given to the prophets of
Israel.

> The prophecy of the ancient prophets is a path toward the
> Incarnation, as the divinely just reality embodies itself in what is
> ethically and aesthetically just and right and manifests itself in these
> terms.[126]

Secondly, this is said in no purely biblicist spirit.

---

121 *GL* II, p. 496.
122 *GL* III, p. 501.
123 *Oeuvres poétiques complètes* (Paris 1941), pp. 334–344.
124 Ibid., pp. 272–273, cited at *GL* III, p. 508.
125 *GL* III, pp. 483; 493–494; and see on this more fully J. Daniélou, S.J., 'Péguy et les
     Pères de l'Eglise', in *Littérature et société. Recueil d'etudes en honneur de Bernard
     Guyon* (Paris 1973), pp. 173–179.
126 *GL* III, p. 511.

The more firmly the total Incarnation of the Word in Jesus Christ is established as the supreme norm, overflowing in its abundance, the more it becomes clear that what is humanly right and just is not simply and unilaterally inserted into the world from above, but is simultaneously drawn up from below, out of the roots of creation itself . . .[127]

(That is why, in his next volume, Balthasar will consider the contribution of the ancient world – classical humanity – to our subject.) Thirdly, the transcendence of Christ's Godhead emerges with the visibility of his human figure. In the case of a

Jesus (like the Jesus of so many theological systems) who is no more than the abstract . . . sum of 'perfections', or, more precisely, of the things that look like perfections to human eyes and that they thus attribute to the God-Man, . . . his image is bound to degenerate . . . for such a Christ does not take his place in a series, . . . so as to form an authentic figure along with prototypes and imitations alike.[128]

'Prototypes', because, fourthly, 'the relationship between Old and New Covenants is decisive for aesthetics',[129] even though that relation be no straightforwardly progressive, developmental one, but sometimes 'faithfully, exactly, inverse'.[130] Before tackling that relationship, however, Balthasar has unfinished philosophical business to perform.

---

127 Ibid.
128 *GL* III, p. 513.
129 Ibid.
130 *GL* III, p. 514, citing words of Péguy in *Oeuvres poétiques complètes*, pp. 386 and 415–418.

6

❦

The Metaphysics of Antiquity

Balthasar's symphony of sources could not be restricted to Christian theologians. Justice must be done to whatever in nature and its proper transformation, human culture, has also contributed to the – as, after scanning Volumes II and III of *Herrlichkeit*, we may surely say – *traditional* theological aesthetics of historic Christendom. Balthasar must look, therefore, at those elements in the theological vision that are solidary with the thinking of humankind at large, and (especially) rooted in what he will call 'general religious metaphysics'.[1]

Why the ancients?

There are, *au fond*, two reasons for turning to (by and large) the pagans before deploying the ideas developed in Volume I of *Herrlichkeit* (and by way of illustrative extension, Volumes II and III), in the ambit of the biblical revelation, stretched as that is between its Old Testament beginning (Volume VI) and its New Testament end (Volume VII). In the first place, without a grasp of the natural or finite pole of the analogy between beauty and divine glory we shall not be well-placed to understand the gracious and infinite pole. As Balthasar himself puts it:

It is only when there is an analogy (be it only distant) between the human sense of the divine and divine revelation that the height, the difference and the distance of that which the revelation discloses may be measured in God's grace.[2]

Here, then, as befits a theologian of the 'ever-greater' (*je-mehr*) God, to 'understand' revelation means first and foremost to grasp its going beyond all that the heart of man has conceived.

But in the second place, there is also an apologetic thrust lying behind Balthasar's concern that we should not neglect the pagan sources. In an age at once post-Christian and ametaphysical, the Church should not offer the biblical glory 'neat' to the world, without any continuity or mediation in terms of natural reality, but let the scriptural revelation refresh its sense

1 *GL* IV, p. 13.
2 *GL* IV, p. 14.

of the 'metaphysical depth of being' that is, in principle, accessible to everyone, believer or no.

To see what Balthasar is doing in the fourth volume of *The Glory of the Lord* I recommend readers to start at the end, with the essay – off-puttingly entitled, perhaps – on the 'theological a priori of the philosophy of beauty'. There we hear of three great themes, announced in the ancient world, which will pass, almost unchanged, into Christian philosophy. The ancients already spoke of the procession of creatures from God and their return to him; they knew about that fundamental yearning – *erōs*, *desiderium* – whereby the finite creature seeks its own self-transcending in God who is the supreme unity and beauty; they experienced the native beauty of the spiritual soul – which, contrary to much interpretation of the 'inner-worldly' or 'other worldly' turn of late antique philosophy, Balthasar sees as

a courageous, world-affirming theme, which does not mourn the passing of physical beauty in a melancholy vein, but dares to see it as the reflection and sensuous image of a deeper, indestructible glory.[3]

This last motif is linked, importantly, to the notion of the harmony of virtue, achieved – if we may look from Plato to Pindar – not without the assistance of the graceful nobility of nature (*phua*). This too, Balthasar appears to be saying, is a *preparatio evangelica*, the first glimmerings of a rectification ('justification'), a creation of right order, based on the free gift of God (compare Pindar) and the divine virtues infused into the soul with justifying grace (compare Plato).

It is the sheer amplitude of the presentation of the human in the Graeco-Roman sources of our civilisation which attracts Balthasar – not as a humane scholar, simply, but precisely when thinking as a theologian. This is not because of some secret fear that, really, the revelation to Israel and in Jesus Christ might be a trifle parochial. As he remarks, the reason why 'glory' is too rich a term in Scripture to permit of easy definition is precisely the *universality* of that biblical concept of glory for which God is glorious not only in himself but in his unspeakably manifold epiphany in the cosmos, in man on whom his favour rests, in law and grace, in the gift of redemption, and in the mystery of the Church. It is, then, not the narrowness of Scripture but its vastness which requires the theologian to seek out that other 'universality' to which its message is addressed. And this is *Geist*, the (human) spirit open of its nature as that spirit is to the being of all that exists.

The revelation conveyed to the Church via the Scriptures cannot manage without metaphysics – not because of its weakness, its insufficiency, but, on the contrary owing to its strength, its superlative sufficiency and more than sufficiency as a disclosure of the beautiful truth in action. And the primary lesson that Balthasar would have us draw is that an historical or 'positive' approach to the exploration of the truth-claims of the gospel will not *of itself alone* serve our turn. For while it is

3 *GL* IV, p. 322.

true that only concretely existing things are real (and this validates the appeal to history in its limited, if genuine, significance), it is no less true that only in terms of being is what exists universal in its implications (and this points up the need for the historical to be contextualised in metaphysics).

What Balthasar will stress, in his survey of ancient thought, is the desirability of preserving the link between metaphysics and mythical or mythopoeic thinking (in something of the way that, for instance, Plato does in his dialogues – a topic to which we shall return), and, concomitantly, the manner in which the metaphysician rightly scans the whole range of the true, the good, the beautiful. And this will surprise no reader of *Theologik* I. His study of 'The Realm of Metaphysics in Antiquity' will show these two key principles at work in a schematic sequence of highlights in religious metaphysics. From a period dominated by *myth*, where the human being encounters *to on*, 'what is' in, above all, the form of dramatic *images*, we pass into an age where *wisdom* predominates, as the nascent discipline of philosophy begins to produce instead *concepts* of reality, prior to entering an epoch of renewed *religiosity* (with Virgil in the West, Plotinus in the East) when concepts are relativised through a pointing to *mystery*. And the reference to Virgil there may alert us to the fact that Balthasar will not spurn the services of the poets and tragedians:

> anyone who speaks of [the] mythical-religious interpretation of being speaks also of *art* in its most original act of generation, art in the womb of its most favourable development.[4]

And though Balthasar never wrote his projected fascicule of *Herrlichkeit* on Christian iconography, we can get a ghostly flavour of this unproduced work when he adds

> All great art is religious, an act of homage before the glory of what exists. Where the religious dimension disappears the homage degenerates into something that is merely attractive and pleasing . . .[5]

What Balthasar proposes is, evidently, a vast undertaking. It is one that could only be carried out by ruthless selection from among the data for the myths of Hellas; ancient philosophy; and the religion of the Hellenistic, or late antique, world. Nor could it be wisely ventured without the clearest of departure points, a 'view' whose unity can help to organise what it sees. Balthasar makes no bones about his own position. Its qualities are: spiritual and intellectual liberty ('an unhindered freedom to see the glory of the Lord'), tempered by responsibility to ecclesial and theological tradition, and vindicated by that Catholic humanism which – over against dissentient voices – has cherished much in pre-Christian antiquity. The aim of his project is, in contrast to a theology preoccupied by redemption alone, to see covenant and creation together. Only in that way can a Christian be, like the Jewish psalmist, the 'responsible guardian

4 *GL* IV, p. 12.
5 *GL* IV, pp. 12–13.

of glory as a whole'. His guiding principle is that neither the cosmos nor humankind is the final meaning of revelation, but only the kenotic love of the Father revealed by his Spirit in his Son Jesus Christ. That meaning, as Balthasar puts it, must be left 'disinterestedly' to the love of God to determine, and the world and man understood by its light. (This is how Balthasar would interpret the axiom of Scholastic orthodoxy that, in the world's creation, God can have no other end than the proclamation of his glory.)

All of which implies that the only aesthetics with which the biblical revelation can open a dialogue is a transcendental aesthetics which asks, like the denizens of antiquity, after the radiance of the whole. Just as for much of the noetics and ethics of the ancient world, the fragmentary truth and goodness of this transient realm can only be understood in terms of their anchoring in a truth and goodness perfect in stability, so too the epiphany of beauty in things or actions we find momentarily stunning is founded, as so many of the poets and philosophers of classical civilisation understood, in 'an absolute beauty that does not pass away, a beauty that dwells in the whole *archai* [the fundamental principles] of being – with the "gods", with the "divine", with "God"'.[6]

The ancients grasped the transcendentals. They knew that each held sway over being in its totality. No horror could suppress the foundational beauty of existence.[7] They realised that circumincession of the transcendentals of which Balthasar had spoken in the opening volume of the theological logic. They provided structures of perception, forms of sensibility, which anticipate or echo in helpful ways the revelation to Israel and, through Christ, the Church. Balthasar notes three such more particularly. First, the world for the Greeks was an epiphany of the divine to man and man's waking to consciousness of this stupendous fact – a kind of model for the far greater epiphany which is the biblical 'appearing' of God and man's response. Secondly, for the ancients, the ordering of the world rested on *dikē*, what is just and right, such that only action in accordance with that foundation could bring human nature to appropriate expression – and what is this but an analogue for the redemptive gift of the divine law? Thirdly, in their poetry, the world was more intimately disclosed as *charis* – playful, charming, gracious, and here we have a preunderstanding of the free grace of its Creator.

Not that this is meant to *homogenise* antique perception with that mind which was in Christ Jesus. The truth of the world's *rapport* with God is more profound than pagans realised; the law of God holier and its transgression more deadly, God's grace both freer and richer than they could imagine. Still, without the (transcendentally) aesthetic sense of wonderment at the world (How terribly marvellous it is!), there would be no content for philosophy to criticise, and consequently, no aesthetic teaching about, transcendental beauty, and therefore, in turn, after due

6 *GL* IV, p. 19.
7 Balthasar's best comment on that is perhaps at *GL* IV, p. 29, when he speaks of how 'what is crude, what is explicitly ugly, what is painful to the point of meaninglessness, the experience of being handed over to what is vulgar and humiliating, can appear as assimilated into a totality which can and must be accepted positively – without artificial sweetening, just as it is'.

theological criticism in the light of revelation, no theologically transcendental aesthetics such as Balthasar himself is writing in the service of the gospel! As we have seen already, the need to integrate the realms of creation and redemption one with another entails the relocation of a (suitably criticised) metaphysics within theology, or as Balthasar can also say, the 'embedding' of theology in metaphysics. Volume IV (and indeed Volume V) of *Herrlichkeit*, the philosophical tomes, are necessary, accordingly, for a full account of what Balthasar presented in Volume I as the 'doctrine of rapture' – our being transported into the sphere of salvation by what we have grasped of God's self-appearing in the doctrine of perception. Put more philosophically, Balthasar must show how the human spirit can pass from its own metaphysical systems into the free 'system' of God. Between the most far-seeing of the ancients and the vision of the gospel there is both continuity and discontinuity.

> If it is true that God in his dealings with his own creation cannot abuse its transcendental laws of beauty, it is likewise true that the free opening of the heart of the innermost mystery of God cannot be anticipated on the basis of this transcendental lawfulness, nor, once this has taken place, can it be systematically fitted into its categories. . . . It is quite obvious that there exists a universal human transcendence to God (for example, in the *erōs* of Plato and Plotinus) which implies an ascetic refusal to absolutise a finite form, and there is no reason why Christians should not take over the movement of this *erōs*, which must be 'disinterested' when it is accomplished, and perfect it as *caritas*.[8]

'No reason', perhaps, and yet the attempt at an evangelical repossession of *erōs* – a notion whose importance to Balthasar the introduction to the present study stressed – can easily be botched. If *erōs* is irked by finite form, it is quite capable of betraying a religion of incarnation, where one finite form – the humanity of Jesus – is indispensable.

Inevitably, then, Balthasar has to underscore, in this new context, the importance of form, central to his aesthetics as this is. What he has to show is that there is something about form in its visible finitude which God in his invisible infinity can make use of in order to express himself. Since form, no matter how circumscribed and lowly, is a 'totality of parts and elements which for its existence requires not only a surrounding world but ultimately being as a whole',[9] such that the radiance with which it strikes us issues not only from itself but also from that wider being in which it is immersed, it becomes thinkable that

> the absolute being makes use of the form of the world with its duality of language – inalienable finitude of the individual form *and* unconditional, transcending reference of this individual form to being as a whole – in order to make itself known in its unfathomable personal depths.[10]

8 *GL* IV, p. 25.
9 *GL* IV, p. 30.
10 *GL* IV, pp. 31–32. Translation corrected.

A demythologising, positivist exegesis would be less 'petty' if only its practitioners realised how individual form is ultimately founded in transcendent perfection and thus can have metaphysical significance, and if they appreciated the fact that all such forms with implications for the destiny of man in the cosmos (Balthasar is thinking, for instance, of the readings of existence provided by the Attic tragedians) can be made to converge upon a definitive form of divine revelation in Jesus Christ.

Myth

What then *is* the pertinence of ancient myth, philosophy and religion for Christian faith? Worth noting at the outset is Balthasar's account of why he has chosen the mythopoeic thought of Hellas – and not its most sophisticated competitor, that of India – as his starting point, for this throws light on the nature of his concern.

> In India, an unformed Many stands over against the formless One
> ... and thus conceals rather than reveals the One; it is more outer
> appearance than epiphany and it cannot, therefore, prepare the path
> ... for a definitive incarnation of God in the way that the Greek epic
> can.[11]

Contrary to what is sometimes said about the superficiality of Olympian religion in the Homeric writings, Balthasar treats Homer as a religious mind of extraordinary refinement and power. (He leaves to one side the vast question of Homer's use of pre-existing cycles of epic material.) The *Odyssey*'s chief theme, for Balthasar, is 'the humbled holding-firm in obedience to the invisible will of the gods', from which it follows that Homeric man is essentially: 'one who is in need of God, and the real sin is the arrogance of wishing to lead one's life without God'.[12] The perspective of theological aesthetics proper is raised when Balthasar comments that, for the Homeric corpus, man experiences in 'the free indwelling of the god': 'a lifting up which fulfils him as the transfiguration of his mortal lowliness, bestowing on him good fortune, a meaning for his life, and beauty'.[13]

The proper place to understand *beauty* is the relation which joins the god to the human being who is thus lifted up into the light of his favour – even in misery, for there can be a good meaning in the allocation of an evil lot. On Balthasar's reading of the *Iliad*, the chief drama lies not on the plain of Troy but in the heart of Zeus.

> The real theme of the poet of the *Iliad* is the divinity caught between
> the prayers of men, rent apart by the tragic contradictions of the
> world (this division is expressed in the personal relationships of the

---

11 *GL* IV, p. 43 footnote. Translation slightly modified.
12 *GL* IV, p. 50.
13 *GL* IV, p. 51. Translation slightly amended.

individual gods to their *protégés* and their quarrels against each other) and at the same time raised above the contradiction, keeping it under control by inscrutable decree.[14]

In this ancient epic heaven accompanies earth: the gods have a will to share in the joys and sufferings of mortals. The gods take the initiative, yet human beings retain their spontaneity. The absence of clear conceptual expression for the fulness of the divine world (i.e. Homer's polytheism) does not rob the Homeric evocation of divine epiphany and human reaction of its capacity to prepare a way for the incarnation of the Word.

> In the rising up of the mortal being to the immortal god, the favour, grace and beauty of being are experienced, in an act of original admiration which opens the eyes for the wonder of being and attributes to it in its height and depth that which is light, seeing, happy and eternal – even where mortal existence remains fearsome, thankless toil.[15]

The human protagonists of *Iliad* and *Odyssey* were rare mortals, the heroes. The post-Homeric question is whether the glory of being grasped in their relation with the divine could be at any rate broadened if not exactly democratised. In Pindar we see that happening, at least for the gifted victor of the games, in some form of test or struggle. The excellence which is touched by the splendour of the gods implies virtue, but virtue is only demonstrated once visible, and therefore must venture itself in some dangerous way. For Pindar, grace is the joy which crowns the adventurous man in such a *kindunos* (feat). That joy is the victor's own achievement – but *through* the favour of the gods. Balthasar does not hesitate, then, to round off his interpretation of Pindar's *Odes* with a christological conclusion.

> The images of the *agōn* – together with the *kindunos*, the onlooking universe and the aristocratic election of the victor in the unity of free grace and highest endeavour – will enter the image world of St Paul. But by then the gleam of glory which marks Pindar's world will have deepened into the one God-Man who contains in his triumph both death and life, victory and defeat, anointed not for an earthly but for an eternal contest and celebration.[16]

The importance of the *Attic tragedians* for Balthasar's project emerges when we hear him make the – breathtaking! – claim that it was Greek tragedy, and *not* Greek philosophy with which early Christians chiefly entered into dialogue. The works of Sophocles, Aeschylus and Euripides which, at any rate at this stage in his *oeuvre*, Balthasar treats as the *only* high tragedy (with the possible exception of a brief recovery of the true

14 *GL* IV, p. 63.
15 *GL* IV, p. 70.
16 *GL* IV, p. 100.

dimensions of the tragic by the Romantics) are always played out against the background of the divine. Eschewing mere psychological self-understanding, the men and women of these plays step into the light of their own truth falling as this does from the epiphany of the god. These dramas, therefore, *both* contradict the 'philosophical tendency towards an enclosing of being in itself as identity', *and* resist 'any containment of man within himself'.[17] For the tragedies: 'the way of man to God and the revelation of the deep truth of existence passes directly through the most extreme form of suffering'.[18]

By an apparent paradox, with which Balthasar connects such key themes of Christian theology as the kenotic dispossession of the divine Father, the suffering Son of Man, and the idea of sacramentality, the tragedies announce the divine presence by means of a heightened form of suffering and therefore in the mode of seeming absence – but all in the service of redemption. Thus Balthasar concludes his comments on the *Oresteia* by remarking:

> in Aeschylus the name of the unifying god is finally no longer of consequence. 'Zeus, for thus I call him, be he whoever he may be, using every name which pleases him.' What appears and becomes visible is his *kabod*, his *shekinah*, which can only be designated with apparently abstract names, such as right, justice, order, retribution. . . . But, as in Pindar, it is the facelessness of the flowing light of the godhead. In this incandescent beam true expiation is possible and the streams of blood caused by the mythic vendettas can be stilled.[19]

The same soteriological intent can be surmised in Sophocles, whose hidden God ('Eternal night, how bright thy rays')[20] Balthasar compares to the black or ochre background of a Greek vase against which the hero – in the Sophoclean case, the *suffering* man – is outlined. Though the divine Father is veiled (and Balthasar in all seriousness speaks of Sophocles as a precursor of negative theology), the hero functions as a source of salvation and sanctity for others. Balthasar's delvings produce most ore in Euripides, whose handling of the themes of life, death, glory and fame, wrath and self-sacrifice leads to the judgment that

> The Greek miracle remains that men and women do not turn from life and from suffering on account of the extreme fragility of the beautiful, but endure the ultimate in horror, in the consciousness that being is worth an absolute and loving assent.[21]

And yet something is lacking. These humans cannot endure to the end because the gods themselves do not reciprocate to the end – and here there yawns a gap which only the *Christianum* can fill.

---

17 *GL* IV, p. 102.
18 *GL* IV, p. 103.
19 *GL* IV, p. 121, citing the *Agamemnon* at lines 159–161.
20 *Ajax*, lines 394–395.
21 *GL* IV, p. 153.

The transition, at roughly the time of the pre-Socratics, from a mythical to a philosophical world-view was fraught with difficulty. For Balthasar, the difficulty involved is not so much the painful attempt to achieve a critical or (even a constructive) rationality as how to carry the precious load of the mythopoeic inheritance into the new world of philosophical reflection. 'Can the light of reason bring the radiance and the glory of myth within its purview?'[22] Inasmuch as reason's mode is not doxological (reason . . . must at least . . . methodically suspend the act of glorifying God'),[23] its method is probably going to look like storming heaven. But in Plato we see how successful reason can be when such titanism is tempered. In Plato myth can be used, in ironic, reserved fashion, in reason's own furtherance of conceptual clarity.

Philosophy

The achievement of the ancient philosophers lay in their identification of themes that any transcendental aesthetics must sound: the claim to totality in interpretation (raised by the question of knowledge itself; the move from a posteriori, *de facto*, knowledge to an understanding of things a priori, in their causes (for this is the passage in which the philosophical act is performed); and finally, the motif of harmony (critical for the development of a concept of the beautiful as this will be). Thus Heraclitus heard the eternal music, whose accents Parmenides once over-heard in ecstasy through a transcending of the realm of mere becoming, in the meeting of contrasting sounds in harmony, and found the *logos* in the communicative unity of cosmic contraries. Plato will define the righteousness of the just man in terms of such harmony.

Placing himself in a long line of Christian commentators. Balthasar finds in Plato multiple adumbrations of fragments of the gospel. It is difficult to miss the covert reference to the Word who was with God but took flesh for our salvation when, interpreting the parable of the cave in the dialogue just mentioned, Balthasar writes: 'the philosopher orders reality from his vision . . . of the truth and understands his superiority as a service which necessitates for him a "descent" . . . to *praxis*'.[24] He firmly rules out any Kantian reading of Plato's epistemology, insisting on the ready submission of the Platonic knowing agent to objective reality. Here too, Balthasar's vocabulary hints at an analogue of that filial obedience which made possible the Son's communion as man with the Father. 'Spirit', for Plato, is 'to stand face to face with reality at every stage, right up to the highest Good'.[25] Again, the notion of *erōs* in the Symposium is no mere stream of desiring subjectivity but is defined in terms of the *eraston*, the beloved *object*, and that bibulous conversation even has a suggestion of the wonderful 'fruitfulness of the finite in the Absolute',[26] which will characterise, on the basis of divine grace, the life of charity in the Holy Spirit.

22 *GL* IV, p. 156.
23 Ibid.
24 *GL* IV, p. 173–174.
25 *GL* IV, p. 177.
26 *GL* IV, p. 191.

Plato is certainly a good choice when it comes to showing the serviceability of symbolic or mythopoeic thinking to conceptual or philosophic. Myth for Plato is 'where the lines drawn by philosophical reflection stretch beyond its grasp'.[27] Yet because Plato lacked the concrete revelation he could only find in 'poetry' a surrogate vehicle in which the intelligence can venture in a direction proposed by reason yet beyond its ken. Only the Christian revelation can 'synthesise' the mythopoeic and the philosophical, whereas a philosophy untutored by the former is, on ultimate questions, stuck in a groove. 'It must at once create myth as its own limit and yet critically take it back again.'[28] Plato did not intend all the myths he built into his treatises to be taken with equal seriousness. Nonetheless his work testified to a 'strange crisis': 'It is as if [philosophy's] standing as the queen of the sciences is undermined precisely where one views it in the context of divine totality.'[29]

And the beautiful is no exception to this limping insufficiency of philosophy for the evocation of the whole. As the *Symposium* witnesses, the beautiful is coextensive with the whole of being (it is a transcendental). We need to know, however, in what way the beautiful can be distinguished from the good, which is equally all-pervasive, equally constitutive of what can be loved. Balthasar's answer, speaking as an exegete of Plato's writings is that the specifying notion of *to kalon* is 'measure' or, as he sometimes writes, 'inner measuredness'. Gracefulness in the body; virtue in the soul; grandeur in the cosmos, are united in this, the common element in their analogical loveliness. What the *corpus Platonicum* leaves open, however, is whether the divine is merely the world-soul, giving measure to bodies universally as our individual souls by participation in it to their own, or whether it be the unique Source of beauty, bestowing measure on soul quite as 'condescendingly' as soul on body.

Religion

But if the Christian revelation was the marriage of the poetic and the philosophical which Plato, in the nature of the case, could never find, then late antique religion for Balthasar is the natural search for a way of combining philosophy with myth. Balthasar speaks of philosophy and mythology as two mismatched piers which will not make, in religion, the bridge their engineers hope. Philosophy wills the submission of mythology to its own laws of construction, thus robbing it of any independent force; uncontrolled by philosophy, myth becomes sheer fantasy, frittering its content away among gnosticising enthusiasts and mystical sectarians. Characteristic of the religion generated by philosophy alone are two tell-tale ideas – that of the divine as all-encompassing or all-pervading, and of its native kinship with the human spirit. Partially exonerating Aristotle from these criticisms, Balthasar concentrates his fire on the Stoics. While he speaks in large terms of the 'arrogance' of philosophy towards myth, his real complaint is about what he takes to be

27 *GL* IV, p. 195.
28 Ibid.
29 *GL* IV, p. 197.

philosophy's inveterate tendency to monism, for it treats all differentiation in terms of unity, and reduces the dialogical to identity. (It was, we
remember, the strength, in his view, of the religion of Homer and the
tragedians that it resisted such 'closure'.) The upshot is inglorious, for it is
finally of little consequence

> whether the identification of God and the soul is thought of and
> experienced as happening through ecstasy (the expansion of the
> soul to the dimensions of divinity) or 'enstasy' (the indwelling of
> the godhead in the soul to the point of absorption). Both forms
> lie close to the point of tilting over into atheism or at least radical
> scepticism.[30]

When, by contrast, myth attempts to project an ordered religion from
out of itself by means of philosophy, two routes may be followed, neither
wholly well-chosen. By the construction of a systematically hierarchical
world-view (taking its cue, typically, from the image of the Demiurge who
looks upwards at the world of Ideas), the mythical thinker will probably
end up with a bipolar concept of God. Here God is divided between the
Creator and the unnameable super-essential One above him, or again,
between the divine Source and its own energies as they reach down into
the world. If, however, a religion that has hitherto been developing in
mythical form would, in an era of conceptual rationality, adapt itself more
radically to philosophy, its likely plan will be the incorporation of a
rational metaphysics into its revelatory scheme. Here the divine Absolute,
simultaneously unfolding and enclosing itself, not only grounds religion
but furnishes the key concept in fundamental ontology. (Balthasar looks
ahead at this point to his treatment of Plotinus.)

Both the mythophile's attempt to pull himself up to the level of
philosophy by his own bootstraps and the philosopher's would-be reconstruction of the myths seem doomed to fail. A mythologoumenon is
always particular; philosophy cannot but be universal. So the mythical
bridgehead will never extend sufficiently to cross the divide. But the
philosophical work in progress on the other bank is no more satisfactory.
The system of 'identity' in which, lacking as it does the revelation of God's
absolute difference and equally absolute freedom, it remains ensnared
can never reach the midpoint of true religion, as the Christian theologian
understands it, for this is the *self-humbling of the divine being to serve
humans*.[31] To which the reader might comment: What, then, is the interest,
other than historical, of this subject? Balthasar's answer is brisk. This
material is irreplaceable by the gospel since the bearers of the gospel need
it for a grasp of the situation into which the gospel comes.

> Christianity well understood that in the essentially unfinished
> nature of the world's constructions it was confronted by something
> incomparably authentic, a definitive expression of the *humanum* of
> the world . . .[32]

30 *GL* IV, p. 229.
31 *GL* IV, p. 241.
32 *GL* IV, p. 242

It is a delusion to think that we can simply dispense with the myth, ancient religiosity and philosophy of Gentiles. Unless we are Jews, it is as Gentiles that we come to the gospel, and except in the case of a mission to Israel, it is to other Gentiles we are sent. In any case the incarnate One himself, unlike some of his modern disciples, did not flinch from religion, philosophy, myth. Christianity may not be *per se* a religion, a philosophy or a mythology. And yet:

> God would not have become human if he had not come into positive inner contact with these three forms of thought and experience. . . . Those who want to 'purify' the Bible of religion, philosophy and myth want to be more biblical than the Bible, more Christian than Christ. . . . Paul quotes Aratos, John speaks of the Logos, the Epistle of James uses the conventions of Stoic diatribe, the Deutero-Pauline letters take over the terminology of contemporary religious, cultic and political conceptions of *parousia* and *epiphaneia* without a trace of apprehension – to take only a few instances; and all this points clearly to the fact that human thinking does not happen without concepts (philosophy) and images (myth), and the relation between 'religion' and 'revelation' is thus bound to be an intimate interior penetration of just this intense kind.[33]

But while this certainly shows the *general* importance of 'the realm of metaphysics in antiquity' for Christian origins, and thus for the *res christiana* at large, Balthasar has not really justified his more *specific* contention that the late antique period gave a meaning to 'glory' which Christianity could not ignore. The claim that it did so is embodied for Balthasar in two names: Virgil and Plotinus.

What Balthasar finds absorbing about *Virgil* is not so much his presentation, in the *Bucolics* and the *Georgics*, of the glory of nature – nature's beauty, if also harshness, the latter illuminated by the hint of immortality subtly suggested in the portrayal, in the last book of the *Georgics*, of the bee. ('Who knows whether Protean Nature will not after all show us the right path to a magical resurrection beyond hope or conceiving?').[34] In the *Aeneid* such naturalism gives way to a perspective of human hope: an openness to a destiny requiring self-transcendence. The obedience of Aeneas to a mission of destiny offering glory only through renunciation and humility is 'an analogue to Scripture in the ethical-aesthetic sphere',[35] the central story-line of the biblical epic from Abraham to Christ.

The second offering of an expiring paganism to the new faith is the religious metaphysics of *Plotinus* whose scheme of the coming forth of all things from the One and their return to it furnished Christian thought with a formal structure for its doctrines *both* of immanence – the Beauty in the caravanserai of being, *and* of transcendence – the Beauty beyond all. Here, too, by courtesy of a personality not unlike Virgil in unostentatious

---

33 *GL* IV, pp. 243–244.
34 *GL* IV, p. 261.
35 *GL* IV, p. 266.

goodness, we stand at a *'kairos* of human thought in the mode of Advent expectation'.[36] While not denying that Plotinus' corpus *can* be read in Idealist terms, making him a forerunner of Hegel, Balthasar treats his thought as, rather, a theological philosophy opening casements to the world of the gospel. The Plotinus of Balthasar integrates the philosophical awareness of the ancient world with its many myths now referred to the 'single and complete theological revelation of being [which] appears in them'.[37] Of 'the One', the keystone of his edifice, Balthasar writes, finely:

> All intellectual activity in Heaven and earth circles around this unattainable generative mystery, all longing love ... struggles upwards towards it, as the beauty of the world is only a sign coming from it and pointing to it so that as he contemplates and seeks to understand the things of the world the philosopher is compelled at a deeper level to run away, to let go, to turn again ... to the uniqueness of absolute unity.[38]

Securing both God's transcendence and his immanence, for the One is 'a wellspring that has no source but itself, sharing itself with all rivers, yet never exhausted in this giving but remaining at rest in the streaming forth',[39] Plotinus can and does understand God's self-manifestation as the epiphany at once of his rationality (bound up with his inner necessity) and his freedom (the correlate of his unconditionedness). It 'just' needed the experience of the divine freedom in its self-expression in historical action in Israel and the Church for the concept of creation – determinative as that is for all Christian philosophy and already gestating in Plotinus – to come to birth. The intelligible universe of Plotinus is irradiated by inbreaking glory – and only when his epiphanic vision faded from men's minds did the task of finding God in all things pass (exclusively) to Christians to whom it was given, with the incarnation, that they should see the glory of God in very flesh. Strictly speaking, for Plotinus, the beautiful exists at the level of *nous*, *below* the One. And yet: 'this "proper" level of existence subsists only as an epiphany of the mystery of being itself and so as a summons back towards that mystery'.[40] The beautiful shines out from a point beneath the One and yet does so thanks to its illumination from the One. And this, so Balthasar points out, is that very 'formal structure' which, in the opening volume of the theological aesthetics, *Seeing the Form*, he ascribed to *pulchrum* on his own account. Its light breaks forth from within splendid form; yet form's splendour is only visible in its light. Returning to his exposition of Plotinus:

> The *fascinosum*, which is the radiance sent forth by beauty at every level of Intellect, Soul and nature, signifies beauty itself, yet also signifies that there is *in* beauty something *beyond* it. The structure of the Beautiful inscribes itself within the formal structure of a doctrine

36 *GL* IV, p. 291.
37 *GL* IV, p. 280.
38 *GL* IV, p. 282.
39 *Enneads* III. 8, 10, cited at *GL* IV, p. 289.
40 *GL* IV, p. 307, translation completed.

of God. The 'in' here is not voided of force by the 'beyond'; there is no reduction to 'pure appearance'. But the radiance of manifestation presupposes the One, from whose centre all the rays emanate and *become* manifest.[41]

From this ontological standpoint must Plotinus' (sometimes penny-plain) remarks on aesthetics in the narrower sense be viewed.

For Balthasar, Plotinus 'effectively silenced' Plato's criticism of art. In *Enneads* V. 8 he demonstrated that beauty is at home with form. Just as in nature the beauty of a living substance comes from something simple which streams out from within, catching up not only matter but outer form in its flood, so the inward spiritual intelligence of the creative artist imitates not outer nature (Plato's objection) so much as nature's manner of generating the beautiful object.

> It is always a question of some interior quality that excites us and the splendour of form resulting from this quality awakens our interiority by its own – awakens, as Plato has it, our recollection, and directs us towards that realm where outer and inner, what is thought and the act of thinking, the beloved and the lover are transparent to each other, and merge into each other.[42]

It is this aesthetic schema which Christian thought will make its own, deploying within its space its own themes of Trinity and Saviour, the sinner's conversion and the redeemed sinner's love for God.

What especially interests Balthasar, however, as he takes his leave of the world of antiquity, is how – for the moment – the ancient belief in the fundamentally divine nature of beauty, its epiphanic quality, survives. In recognising the 'theological a priori' at work in the philosophical (and literary) elucidation of the beautiful in the world where Christianity was born, the Church's earliest thinkers felt no need to disengage a purely revelational view of beauty from the philosophical. In an integrated ontology, the beauty of the world, and God's better beauty, grace, collaborate. They do not compete. For Boethius, the music of the spheres and the gracious harmony of the virtuous human being are one; for the early Latin monastic teachers, like Cassiodorus, 'majesty' is 'the basic word for God and for his manifestation',[43] and in the all-inclusive vision of that almost unplaceable late patristic Graecophile Irishman John Scotus Eriugena, the shimmering beauty of the cosmos is finally assumed into the glory of God in the risen Christ who 'as ultimate flame fills the whole world in the brightness of his appearance in all things'.[44]

The Balthasar of the closing pages of 'The Realm of Metaphysics in Antiquity' is nonetheless in something of a quandary. On the one hand, the almost effortless conviction of the unity of the orders of being and grace may suppress the novelty of the gospel: the message of the

---

41 *GL* IV, p. 307.
42 *GL* IV, pp. 311–312.
43 *GL* IV, p. 333.
44 John Scotus Eriugena, *De divisione naturae*, V, cited at *GL* IV, p. 351.

incarnated, kenotic, crucified Lord who is glorious precisely because he let all those adjectives be true. ('What distance there is between [Eriugena's] divine love in nature and its epiphany as *caritas* in Christ'!)[45] On the other hand, should the day arrive – as for Balthasar it did with another Celtic John, the fourteenth-century Franciscan Scholastic John Duns Scotus – when being is reduced to mere 'isness' and the divine outpouring of reality bereft of glory, then truly we can say, with sinking hearts, 'the beginning of the modern age' has arrived.[46] As the patristic era – Christianised antiquity – gives way to its successor epoch, the Middle Ages, and the world in which the Church was born becomes the world the Church has made, Balthasar ranges defenders of unbroken sacrality (the theologians of the School of St Victor, Hildegard of Bingen, Gerhoh of Reichersberg) against proponents of a speculative cosmology (the members of the School of Chartres, Alan of Lille, and that extraordinary theological physicist, bishop Robert Grosseteste of Lincoln). The emergence of a world seen theistically, indeed, yet not now sacrally, at the hands of such writers (and others) was powerfully aided by the arrival in the West of the works of Aristotle in their completeness. Still, as Balthasar points out, the victory of a profane view of the cosmos – the final expunging of the divine beauty of the ancients – was no foregone conclusion. There may have been an Aristotelian invasion. But there was certainly, and at the same time, a Dionysian renaissance. The Latin translation of the writings of that key figure of theological aesthetics (so Balthasar has presented him in the second volume of *Herrlichkeit*) could not but affect, to those who saw the 'disciple of Paul' as the metaphysical master of the apostolic age, the reception of Aristotelian naturalism. And here, though Balthasar mentions other congenial figures – Albertus Magnus and Alexander of Hales, Ulrich of Strasbourg and Thomas of York, it is another Thomas – *divus* Thomas, the 'divine' Aquinas – who captures his imagination as Volume IV of *The Glory of the Lord* ends, just as it retains it (so we shall see) when Volume V opens. The beauty of finite, dependent being, in Thomas' thought, reflects the glory of the infinite, subsistent being, from whom it receives its all. The Thomist doctrine of God as 'he who is', the One whose essence it is to exist, subsistent being, enabled the distinction yet unity of divine glory and worldly beauty to be, at last, affirmed. Had this high point of Christian reflection been sustained, then all that was worthwhile in the pagan inheritance (looking back to Volume IV) could have been preserved, while nothing of the innovatory impact of the gospel (evoked so many times in Volumes I to III) need have been traduced. In a passage fit to gladden Thomist hearts:

> The kingdom of *beauty* (of the Thomist *esse non subsistens*) is as a whole, as being, transparent to a divine *esse subsistens* only comprehensible as *mysterium*, which is, as a hidden primordial ground, radiant *glory*. The *elevation of God over being*, now at last established by Thomas (over against all pantheism), secures at the same time for the concept of glory a place in metaphysics. This place was always

45 *GL* IV, p. 352.
46 *GL* IV, p. 330.

intended and envisaged in every form of Platonism but ... the sublimity of God was not revealed [among the Platonist] as absolute *freedom*. ... The philosophy of the transcendentals was developed by early Scholasticism in a conscious approximation of classical ('natural') theology to a Christian understanding of the world, while by Thomas it would be methodically and neatly distinguished from Christian theology; all the same both of these remain close to one another as each other's shadow, and let the (natural-supernatural) theological *a priori* shine forth everywhere.[47]

And if in this way Thomas' achievement could have salvaged antiquity at no cost to the integrity of the gospel, it also anticipated what is worthwhile in the speculations of a 'separated' philosophy among the moderns. It is, Balthasar writes, the 'mediation between classical and modern metaphysics' and to that extent 'the most valid representative of distinctively Western thought'.[48]

The emphasis on 'Westernness' there is not fortuitous. For what the Greeks, from Homer to Plotinus, taught is that the world is not, as various Oriental systems are tempted to say, ultimately illusion. Though not God, and indeed utterly God-dependent, it is not for all that any the less real. In the last analysis, Balthasar thinks, only the doctrine of the Holy Trinity can explain this.

The doctrine of the Trinity is the final underlying guarantee of Western, transcendental philosophy; for only a triune God can render credible a world outside himself as true and good and yet in its free independence united with him, who is most free and most independent. The philosophical difference [between common being and divine being] points back to a revealed, theological *mysterium* and is most happily confirmed by it.[49]

A world which exemplifies the unity of the Father and the (distinct) truth of the Son can manifest goodness thanks to the Love – the Spirit – who joins that 'divine Original' and divine 'Copy'. And if, on the mediaeval account of how unity, truth and goodness range through all being, even in the difference of the created and uncreated poles, *beauty* can shift, at first sight confusingly, from attachment now to unity, now to truth, now to goodness, this is – Balthasar thinks – only as it should be. The Franciscans – St Francis first among them – may have discovered that glory of God coruscating through all the other transcendentals in the world's being, but it will be Thomas who here achieves 'final clarity'.[50] That 'real distinction' between what a thing is and its act of being, between essence and existence, which makes each and every thing totally dependent on the God who alone exists by simply being what he is, and makes everything in that sense the receptacle of God – this somewhat

---

47 *GL* IV, p. 375. Translation slightly amended.
48 Ibid.
49 *GL* IV, p. 376.
50 *GL* IV, p. 382.

derided doctrine, scorned in recent decades by Catholic divinity as an overestimated shibboleth of a tired Neo-Thomist Scholasticism, is to Balthasar, by contrast: 'what enables us to recover the true meaning of . . . glory as much for the ordinary believer as for the theologian'.[51]

It is the Thomas who knows how infinitely the divine Essence transcends common being, yet for whom that common being is no *commonplace*, but irradiated by glory, and who grasps, moreover, that revelation does not nullify a natural theology but raises and completes it, as the glory of the Son the beauty of the world, that Balthasar places at the axis of ancient and modern metaphysics.[52] He is the *kairos*, the classical and climactic moment, which can serve as a paradigm for the enterprise of linking philosophical and biblical aesthetics on which Balthasar is engaged.

The metaphysics of Thomas is thus the philosophical reflection of the free glory of the living God of the Bible and in this way the interior completion of ancient (and thus human) philosophy.[53]

Pagan sages: you may rest peacefully.

51 *GL* IV, p. 395.
52 Some would call this reading Aquinas as though he were Bonaventure. Romanus Cessario, O.P., has written, 'The custom of reading Aquinas as if he were Bonaventure is gaining increasing respectability, and therefore must be considered one of the evolutions to which Thomism submits', 'Virtue Theory and Thomism', in D. W. Hudson and D. W. Moran (eds.), *The Future of Thomism* (Notre Dame, Ind. 1992), p. 297.
53 *GL* IV, p. 407.

7

꼭꼭꼭

The Metaphysics of Christendom – and Beyond

The division of Balthasar's originally unitary account of the 'glory of the Lord' in the realm of metaphysics into two volumes in the English translation is fairly justified. For, as we have seen, St Thomas' general ontology – as the precious setting for an aesthetics at once meta-physically adequate and biblically controlled – is, in Balthasar's view, the door on which the division of the ages (ancient from modern) itself turns.

Metaphysics and mysticism, from Middle Ages to Baroque

With few exceptions, the Christian philosophers of the early and high Middle Ages had 'dutifully received and developed the classical experi-ence of a world which reveals God'. They had understood the salvific events attested by Old and New Testaments only within such a 'com-prehensive and cosmic context'. So much was this so that, in their work:

> the universal categories of beauty which we find in antiquity served largely as a conceptual language in which the total revelation of God – with its centre in Jesus Christ – was expressed.[1]

As if unwilling to break free from the fascination of so – in every sense – *salutary* a moment, Balthasar reiterates that Thomas Aquinas represents the acme of this development. His metaphysics of being gathered up all that was valuable in the ancients both pagan and Christian – not only Aristotle and Plato but Denys and Augustine as well. This was not just a triumph of recuperative integration. For, in the first place, Thomas' ontology is extraordinarily nice in its balance; especially in what concerns the interrelation of Uncreated and created, infinite and finite, existence and essence.

> Being (*esse*) with which he is concerned and to which he attributes the modalities of the One, the True, the Good and the Beautiful, is

1 *GL* V, p. 9.

the unlimited abundance of reality which is beyond all comprehension, as it, in its emergence from God, attains subsistence and
self-possession within the finite entities.[2]

Such an equilibrium could not be taken for granted; indeed, in the age
after Thomas it speedily collapsed, what with, first, the advent of Scotism,
for which being is univocal – the same sort of thing for both God and
creatures, and second, Eckhart, for whom being becomes again (as before
Thomas with Eriugena and Gilbert of Chartres) identical with God. On
each of these degenerate views, a transcendental aesthetics loses its
citizenship rights in the philosophic community. In the first case, being
turns into an idea simultaneously supreme and yet meaningless – a mere
registering of the happenstance of the stuff of existence, an anticipation of
the contemporary scientific outlook at its most sterile. And, so Balthasar
asks, 'How should the divine and mysterious *plērōma* radiate from this
empty space?'[3] But then in the second case, where God swallows being
up, it is hard to see how outside God a world can exist at all and thus 'the
glory of the Absolute is called into question by the fact that it has little or
no remaining space in which and through which it can become manifest'.[4]
And so the two false directions, contrary to one another though they seem,
actually turn into each other. Both prepare the way, to Balthasar's judgment, for later Idealism and rationalism, and hence the abolition of God.

But the ontological fine-tuning of Thomas' metaphysics is not the only
reason for treating him as a climactic moment in Christian philosophy.
There is also his achievement in interrelating so successfully philosophy
and revelation. As Balthasar points out, reason and revelation are likely
to come into conflict since by their very nature, each is an imperialism:
reason with its transcendental claim, and revelation with its no less
universal pretensions. Balthasar applauds the way Thomas brought them
together by a 'bold paradox'. For in Thomas' view (and here Balthasar
sums up and corrects Henri de Lubac's presentation of the relation
between nature and the supernatural): 'it belongs to the nobility of human
nature that we can attain perfection in our *desiderium naturale* for the very
Highest only through a free self-disclosure by God'.[5]

And here too it is not so easy to keep hold of both ends of the chain.
Mediaeval Averroism, like the Enlightenment and its Idealist successors,
treated philosophy as the sole comprehensive science, spurning revelation; an exaggerated Augustinianism, both Catholic and Protestant, gave
revelation (by the doctrine of double predestination) an anti-universal
cast which closed it off to the contribution of philosophy. The pieces, once
separated, are not so easily brought together.

Balthasar shows himself deeply unsympathetic, then, both to the
Scotist tradition (which he sees as continued in Ockham and, via that
eclectic Scholastic of the Catholic Reformation, Suarez, in Descartes and
modern scientism), and also to Eckhart (whose work, he thinks, had

2 *GL* V, p. 12.
3 *GL* V, p. 13.
4 Ibid.
5 *GL* V, pp. 14–15.

endless repercussions from Luther to Hegel). The 'being' of Scotus, a neutral essence pervading all distinctions, was consigned to the philosopher that the theologian may be unencumbered in his exploration of a *practical* faith (there are connexions here with modern Liberation Theology) in the God who acts. And this deprived the distinctively Christian perception of God's glory, for which Thomas had laid the intellectual foundations, of its own necessary medium.

> Since, on the one hand, philosophy is assigned to an undiffer-entiated and neutral sphere of 'existence' and the vision of God through the medium of the creation in its actuality (Rom. 1:18ff.) is obscured and cast into doubt, and since, on the other hand, as a consequence of this, the contemplative component of theology is relinquished in favour of one which is wholly practical and *gnōsis* yields to pure *pistis* ['faith'] – therefore . . . the element of glory, the *doxa*, does not truly become manifest; neither philosophical reason in its contemplation of existence nor theological faith in its practical, ethical and non-aesthetic orientation can any longer possess a sensorium for this.

Consequently, the philosopher, to whom the realm of being is surren-dered, will in the future work out the foundational principles of rational ontology 'without ever glimpsing theological glory'.[6] Ockham draws the conclusion from Scotus' *esse univocum* that only specific indivisible entities are real, for all description of the kinds and levels of being must be deemed subjective classification. Such Nominalism leads ineluctably to the viewpoint of the seventeenth- and eighteenth-century British empiricists John Locke and David Hume and indeed to that of their doughty episcopal opponent George Berkeley, for whom God can allow the immediate experience of the subject to persist even when its object has vanished – an epistemological smile on the face of an ontologically evanescent Cheshire cat. Furthermore, once the original Franciscan image of God as a love beyond all knowledge is married with the Scotist theology it readily turns into that of a potentially fearful monster, for a God of sheerest freedom could in principle 'posit and demand what is contrary'. For instance, as with Ockham, he might in theory damn the innocent and save the guilty. The double predestinationism of extreme Augustinianism found here propitious conditions for a comeback. And it will bounce back with terrifying force in the Reformers.

Not that Balthasar wishes to write off historic Franciscanism as a bad dream: far from it! But the spiritual charism of the Poor Man of Assisi failed to find its proper philosophical accompaniment in Scotus, just as – so Balthasar will now go on to explain – that of Ignatius was very imper-fectly represented by Suarez. The spiritual poverty embraced by Francis, the *indiferencia* so crucial to the *Exercises* of Ignatius, are but perceptive expressions of the fundamental Christian attitude to transcendence: the heart expanding till it is ready, in marian fashion, to love without limits, and enters God's 'ever-greater' glory of love, manifested on the cross,

6 *GL* V, pp. 18–19.

offered us now by grace. But the question is, How does this spiritual attitude find its counterpart in the *philosophical* thinking which (since it is not just Christian but also human) it cannot avoid accepting in one form or another? Alas, Christian thought has not proved up to the demands of Christian inspiration. Balthasar's indictment of Suarez is severe indeed. The planification whereby, along the lines of Scotus, he reduced reality to one level not only laid the foundations for the (questionable) enterprise of modern metaphysics from Descartes to Hegel. (Here Balthasar follows the historic analysis of a writer he enormously admired, Gustav Siewerth.[7]) By abolishing philosophical mystery it undermined theological, and ushered in an era of desiccated thought, preaching and prayer, of the kind Balthasar himself described so witheringly in his animadversions on inter-war Jesuit formation. Theology and spirituality, in the early modern period, go their separate ways, with the mystic – who, thank God, continues to experience glory – now identified as the odd man out, the recipient of an altogether exceptional subjective experience, whereas the normal rule must be the 'strictly logical and intellectualist metaphysics of the Church'.[8] And if the conceptual rationalism of the Neo-Scholastics (on Balthasar's harsh evaluation) has lost all feeling for divine glory, it should not surprise us that their epigones fail to resonate with the glory of the creation too. The capacity to sense created beauty as an efflux of the glory of God passes to the poets, from Dante to John Keats, and indeed to certain outstanding men of science, from Kepler to Teilhard.

Finally, with Suarez, the disastrous shift in the philosophical representation of the 'external' world whereby Being gives way to mental concepts has already taken place. Things are not so much in themselves as for me, and the road to the Königsberg of Kant lies open.

Here, with Siewerth's help, Balthasar offers an astonishing *tour de force* in the history of thought. In a passage of compressed brilliance he explains what happens once the human being begins to regard itself as 'legislative reason' in act. The rational subject

> pronounces judgment *a priori* in its luminous space over the initial concept of Being, which it has been given and which lies open to its comprehension, to which judgment other *a priori* and *a posteriori* judgments attach themselves. And it can assure itself of the correctness of this judgment through reflection upon itself in its action (the *cogito*), and then either seek the ultimate certainty in that kind of reason whose postulates are archetypal, in which it participates and which is God (Descartes), or understand this participation as an ultimate identity of the finite with the infinite subject and, in conjunction with it, project and creatively produce possible real essences (*concipere*): statically (as in Spinoza) or dynamically (as in Leibniz and Fichte), or both together (as in Hegel).[9]

---

7 In this case, especially Siewerth's *Das Schicksal der Metaphysik von Thomas zu Heidegger* (Einsiedeln 1959). For Balthasar's evaluation of Siewerth's work, see his glowing encomium 'Abschied von Gustav Siewerth', *Hochland* 56 (1963), pp. 182–184.

8 *GL* V, p. 26.

9 *GL* V, p. 28.

Beyond the realm of such 'projected essences' lies only the *res extensa* of Descartes, that 'matter' which was once, in Thomist Aristotelianism, pure potency in regard to form, but now becomes the 'last remnant' of external reality, the substratum of classical modern physics.

> This *res extensa* is the pure quantitative element, the unlimited empire of numbers, and it is here that the metaphysical origins lie for the ideal of mastering the whole of the external world through mathematical calculation. An ideal of this kind [viz., the world-view of scientific positivism which is largely our own][10] could never have arisen if the whole of reality had not already been stripped of its living depths and spontaneity, its own truth, goodness and beauty, and had thus been set in unmediated contradiction to the *res cogitans*. The foundations of our 'modern' materialism were laid long ago in the intellectual history of our Western, Christian tradition.[11]

And how do things fare when the primary influence is not Scotus but Eckhart? Balthasar has more time for the German Dominican mystic, considering his experience absolutely authentic, but his manner of expressing it in certain respects not just unfortunate but lethal. Like Origen's, Eckhart's is a pure Christian piety clothed in ill-fitting garments. We are dealing here with an experience of glory where all being, unity, truth, goodness are ascribed unconditionally to God himself, in such a way that the frontier between finite and infinite is lost and the pass sold unwittingly to the enemy. '[The] future will not think, as he does, with a worshipping heart, and so will misuse his words and insights for the purposes of its titanic idealism.'[12] Eckhart's message, to which Balthasar thoroughly subscribes, is the call to live in sheer transparency to the ever greater divine glory – the heart of *Herrlichkeit*! In Eckhart's own terms, the fontal being of God is ceaselessly happening, in the eternal now of the Son's generation from the Father. I must be born with the Son, by letting 'the Whyless' (Balthasar's formulation here of Eckhart's basic concept of God is indebted to his seventeenth-century expositor, Angelus Silesius) come to be in me through sheer passivity. I must not take hold of the God who happens in me *quasi in transitu*, 'as though in passage', and that same lability characterises all Eckhart has to say about the Christian life, for I do not even 'have' the virtues, which rather 'are in a state of permanent becoming like gleams of light in ether and reflections in a mirror'.[13] Only in an unconditional poverty of absolute self-surrender can the human spirit be receptive to the infinite Giver. Balthasar cannot fault the essence of Eckhart's doctrine, which he presents as christological (and indeed staurological – of the cross), marian and trinitarian. *Gelassenheit* is

---

10 One might have thought that *res extensa*, for Descartes, is by definition obedient to laws wholly explicable by *mechanical* description. Such laws, however, as now known, contain many fundamental numbers such as the size of the electric charge of the electron and the ratio of the masses of proton and electron.

11 *GL* V, p. 29.

12 *GL* V, p. 41.

13 Eckhart, *In Sapientiam* I. 45, cited at *GL* V, p. 33.

conformation to Christ in his passion; it is maidenly, and only when 'virgin' *can* be fruitful; it is the catching up of the creature by grace to be a moment in the trinitarian exchange. Unfortunately, Eckhart does not stop there. In his zeal to arouse a sense of this mystery Eckhart piles audacity upon philosophical audacity, reversing the order of the divine being and knowing – so that God is *because* he knows, and as absolute self-identity comes to be in thought.[14] In an infinite spiritual freedom *beyond* the trinitarian process (an idea anathema to so completely a trinitarian theologian as Balthasar) an uncreated spark of intellect *in us* has its ineffable home.

> All of this converges, against Eckhart's intention, towards the abolition of created natures and their proper operations, towards, in fact, an Indian kind of doctrine that everything is God. Eckhart clothes Christian humility and poverty without qualification in the mantle of pagan antiquity's doctrine of departure and return. In so doing, against his most deep-seated intentions, he gives Christian accentuation and enhancement to the pre-Christian religious systems later inherited by the post-Christian *Geistphilosophien*.[15]

Via Luther, for whom the creature remains sin and darkness though inserted 'outside' itself into the justice of God through Christ (here a forensic account of justification and a mysticism of ecstasy are not so far apart as might at first sight appear), Eckhart's own fascination at the 'absolute point of identity with the divine in the subject' is passed on to Fichte and Hegel. Barely having crossed the threshold of his subject, Balthasar can already look ahead to his final conclusion: one day, non-Christian humanity will stand before the 'yawning abyss of reason and freedom', first opened up by Christians, and face there the 'pseudo-*doxa*' of a self-glorifying absolute. Staggered by the confrontation with this void, men will turn back for consolation to pagan antiquity, where a touch of true glory still bathed the cosmos. But when this fades, as fade it surely will, the decision will have to be made: nihilism or 'self-surrender to the sign, in all its purity, of the glory of God's love revealed in Christ'.[16]

But for all Balthasar's praise of Thomas and his weighty reservations about Eckhart, there is a sense in which he regards the latter's deliberate self-distancing from the 'cosmic' mediation of God found in the wise and sane metaphysics of the former a golden opportunity. The desire for a contact with God unprotected and vulnerable in its immediacy *could* lead to thinking through man's relation with God, lived out as this is in a tragic world, in a way which gave greater emphasis to such themes of the Gospels as patience, endurance, destiny, suffering, and the positive significance of *despici a mundo*: 'being despised by the world'. Here the

14 Probably a consequence of his restricting analogy of attribution, where the real presence of the quality being attributed is confined to only one of the objects being compared. Thus if we attribute *esse* to creatures, we must call God something else, e.g. *intelligere*, or *puritas essendi*. It is the *intelligere* which, for Balthasar, points ahead balefully to Idealism.
15 *GL* V, p. 45.
16 *GL* V, p. 48.

acute insights of the tragedians into the human situation become relevant again, but within a metaphysical context with the events of Christian salvation at its heart. The 'metaphysics of the saints' – from the Dominican mystics of the Rhineland school to the seventeenth-century Jesuit *spirituel* Jean-Pierre de Caussade, is Balthasar's name for this kind of writing. He insists that, however lightly it may be regarded in histories of thought – and in point of fact the phrase 'metaphysics of the saints' comes not from any chronicle of the development of ideas but from Henri Bremond's *Histoire littéraire du sentiment religieux en France* – it is of the utmost importance for the emergence of a sense of the 'distinctively Christian glory',[17] which after all, is what Balthasar's project in *Herrlichkeit* is all about.

By evaluating the teaching (and to some degree the lives) of a host of spiritual writers from John Tauler to Jean-Pierre de Caussade, Balthasar shows how, first and foremost, the Eckhartian key-idea of *Gelassenheit* (abandonment) was salvaged from any kind of (essentially sub-Christian) spiritualist or Idealist misinterpretation; and secondly, how in the course of that rescue attempt, important contributions to a properly Christian theological aesthetic were made.

As Balthasar remarks apropos Tauler, there is a rather serious need to distinguish between, on the one hand, 'abandonment to the personal decrees of the Holy Spirit', and on the other, 'the empty impersonal transcendence of one's own spirit'.[18] Cumulatively, the men and women (the latter especially important) he discusses will furnish, so it transpires, criteria for such discernment set ultimately by christological and trinitarian dogma: the principle of selfhood is surmounted only in 'total self-giving prodigality',[19] on the model of the incarnate Lord's atoning work and, deeper still, the mystery of the trinitarian life itself. And the disengagement of this principle will assist us, in a second constructive, rather than simply critical, moment of the enquiry, in the making of a distinctively Christian theological aesthetic.

Tauler's contribution is above all to the first of this interrelated pair of tasks. Over against Eckhart the most important of his successors in the Rhineland school stresses how the creature is genuinely the initiator of its own activity, in which it carries the trace, indeed, of its Maker. That however, does not suppress the theme of *Gelassenheit*, for in Tauler's teaching, 'even this activity actively transcends itself in abandonment to God'.[20] Such abandonment includes most importantly (and here Tauler does not differ from Eckhart) letting oneself be removed from contemplation and sent to succour one's neighbour. The Christian who has really surrendered himself exists contemplatively by an inward movement towards God, and apostolically by an outward movement towards all sinners on earth and suffering souls in purgatory; in this the fruitfulness of his love consists. Though the last of the trio of Rhenish mystics, Henry Suso, adds to this an especial emphasis on the suffering this will entail for the would-be giver, for its model is the Christ of passiontide, where the

17 *GL* V, p. 52.
18 *GL* V, p. 53.
19 *GL* V, p. 62, by way of summary of the (anonymous) *Theologia Germanica*.
20 *GL* V, p. 55.

Word attained the height of his self-revelation on earth. For Balthasar, Suso's chief contribution lies in his portrayal of the divine Glory. The Wisdom of God in its radiant self-offering for our worship is above all the Wisdom displayed as folly and weakness on the cross. Accordingly the two great mysteries of self-sacrificial abandonment in Suso's work are the Eucharist (the sacrifice in a sign) and the co-suffering – compassionate – soul of the Mother of Christ.

It is in Christ's humanity that for the *Theologia Deutsch*, God 'acquires a place in the world where he can be completely himself as love and at the same time experience by suffering, the anti-godly, the sinful'.[21] Though its author can emphasise the *anhypostasia* of Christ (his 'lack' of a purely human subjecthood whereby to personalise his human nature) to the point that, so Balthasar fears, it trembles on the brink of Monothelitism (the erroneous doctrine of a single will in the Word incarnate), he nonetheless presents Christ's absolute abandonment to the Father as the model of all authentic human relationship with God. Above all, he redeems Eckhart's brilliant idea of 'whylessness' by attaching it to his Christology, where the humanity of Christ serves as our exemplar in self-surrender precisely by its participation in this crucial divine attribute. Just as the sun shines, so God in Christ wills and works the good because it is the good and for no other reason. And here, Balthasar comments,

> we are looking into the very heart of the theological aesthetic. We are looking at a 'why-less' ray of light from the sun of the good (as understood by Plato and Plotinus), which is given a deeper Christian meaning when it is seen to be absolute love.[22]

It is from this aesthetic, Balthasar continues, that all Christian ethics issues. That is why he can say it is (this) 'form alone which makes all emulation truly Christian'.[23]

But it is with the contemporaneous Flemish mystical divine Jan Ruysbroeck that we really enter 'the whirlpool of glory' – Balthasar's subtitle for this section of *The Glory of the Lord*. In Ruysbroeck's personal experience – for which, nonetheless, he claims a universal validity – a life lived in *Gelassenheit, indiferencia*, for God's honour and glory alone, turns out to be a volcano where the *kabod YHWH* (Balthasar insists on the 'Old Testament vehemence' of Ruysbroeck's characteristic utterance) erupts with overwhelming effect. A supra-rational contact, of such a kind, in such a context, is not only the 'supremely free bestowal of God's grace and thus the centre of theology'; it is also what 'gives meaning and fulfilment to spiritual nature, and is consequently the centre of [all] metaphysics'.[24] Since our created being 'abides in the Eternal Essence', as *The Adornment of the Spiritual Marriage* puts it[25] – for the spiritual soul is grounded in the personal God, and more specifically (as with Eckhart) in the generation of the Word, we have our archetype beyond ourselves. Put

21 *GL* V, p. 63.
22 *GL* V, p. 65.
23 *GL* V, p. 66.
24 *GL* V, p. 68.
25 J. Ruysbroeck, *The Adornment of the Spiritual Marriage*, II. 2.

more theologically (and biblically), our election is from before the foundation of the world (cf. Eph. 1:3). Here for Balthasar, looking quizzically at these authors with the eye of one trained to follow the eventual fate of theological ideas in various erroneous modern philosophisms:

> Ruysbroeck succeeds . . . in overcoming [in advance evidently!] Fichte's fundamental premise, the anchoring of the empirical in the absolute subject . . . He sees that the reflection of the finite subject on its own unity enables it to perceive that 'the foundation of his being is without ground, and he possesses it only in this manner'. Looking into his own ground, he sees beyond it into the eternal I, which for man is both the source of his own I as well as his eternal Thou, and in the final analysis this is because the eternal I is already in itself I and Thou in the unity of the Holy Spirit.[26]

But the nuptial encounter between the created I and its divine Counterpart is impossible, for Ruysbroeck, without the evangelical virtues of poverty, purity, humility, and a habitual seeking God's honour in all things – in which, however, man will always fall short. Such 'falling short' will end up later with the Idealists and the Neo-Kantian school as the notion of the 'infinite dynamism' of *Geist*, but Balthasar notes how that interpretation fails to recognise the way Ruysbroeck's metaphysics rest upon a theology of *dialogue* between the covenant partners, God and man.

> In the last analysis, it is the humility of the lover before the ever greater glory of the Beloved, which arouses this feeling of constantly falling short. And then again it is a lover's humility (and not a Gnostic light-mysticism) which is the motive for the beloved God's coming to meet man with so overwhelming a degree of *kabod, doxa, gloria*, majestic splendour.[27]

The immeasurable 'brightness' of the Trinity inundates the soul as the Father utters his Word in those who have been drawn into God, but this inundation of glory also sends out the soul on a mission of 'catholic' (universal) love. In a frequently rehearsed image of inhaling and exhaling Ruysbroeck takes on Tauler's emphasis, therefore, on the inseparability of the Godward and the manward, the mystical and the missionary. Like the Jesus who served both the Father and human redemption the 'catholic' man gives himself away both to heaven (in constant 'rest' – compare the biblical idea of Sabbath) and to earth (in constant activity). And, as always in this volume of *Herrlichkeit*, Balthasar emphasises the wider implications of such a spiritual doctrine not only for Christian experience and theology but also for *philosophy*. First of all, it indicates an interpretation of gospel living directly relevant to theological aesthetics:

> Indifference, for the Christian, means Catholic love, which lets itself be robbed of form in the movement from the world to God and

26 *GL* V, p. 70, with an internal citation of J. Ruysbroeck, *The Book of Supreme Truth*, 10.
27 *GL* V, p. 73. Translation modified.

transformed in the movement from God to the world. Through being rooted in a personal ('mystical') experience of God, this Catholic love illuminates the rhythm of life common to all Christians – contemplation and action.

But then secondly, it throws light on psyche and cosmos alike.

Psychologically, it illuminates the oscillation of life between the three centres of man: super-ego, mind (consciousness) and heart (active potencies). Metaphysically, it illuminates the cosmological schema common in Indian philosophy, Plotinus, Eriugena and Thomas Aquinas (the *egressus* of God to the world, the *regressus* of the world back to God), but it elevates it Christologically: the departure of the Son from the Father into the world and his return to the Father (John 16:28). But Ruysbroeck's understanding of Catholic love further elevates the cosmological schema by placing it in a Trinitarian context, since for Ruysbroeck God is not only rest (in his essence) but also activity (in the processions of the divine persons).[28]

Balthasar stresses that in the Flemish author this is not, as with Eckhart, a matter of the uncreated Essence *behind* the trinitarian processions, but an Essence which subsists as the 'resting ground' *in* those processions, the 'essential love which they are together'.[29]

But despite his encomium of Ruysbroeck, and certainly one would be hard pressed to find a mystical theologian in whom the *explicit* vocabulary of glory was more prominent, it is the Taulerian themes of (1) the passion of Christ as defining the condition and action of the post-lapsarian creature, for whom true transcendence can only be found through an entry into the 'night' of the substitutionary experience of the innocent Lamb upon the cross; (2) the femininity of authentic *Gelassenheit* – for humankind, considered as God's creation, is his handmaid, and considered as his covenant partner is his bride; and (3) the folly of the truly wise, which will occupy Balthasar's attention for the rest of this chapter and beyond.

He passes directly to the women mystics, from Angela of Foligno to Catherine of Genoa – though in point of fact his references stretch on in time beyond the later Middle Ages, for the prominence, if not predominance, of women in spirituality is a phenomenon not only of the Gothic but also of the Baroque. According to Balthasar, the discovery (by the Rheno-Flemish spiritual writers) of the extreme pertinence of the abandonment theme to the very idea of transcendence was a perfect opportunity (given the femininity of *Gelassenheit*) for women in the Church. Women establish devotion to the pierced heart of Jesus, as well as to the *Addolorata*, our Lady of Sorrows. For Angela of Foligno, Franciscan poverty is transformed into a metaphysical theme by its rethinking as an expression of marian lowliness: it is the soul that beyond its own perversity has become 'little' in God that enters into possession of

28 *GL* V, p. 76.
29 Ibid., with reference to J. Ruysbroeck, *The Book of Supreme Truth*, 9.

all truth 'in Heaven and Hell and the whole world'.[30] For Julian of Norwich, transcendence is reconceived in the light of Christ's 'plentiful shedding of his precious Blood' and 'the virgin who is his beloved mother', generating the insight that 'God is everything that is good, and the goodness which everything has is God'.[31] (Balthasar, with an eye, no doubt, on his own eschatology, notes her emphasis on the universality of God's saving work, to be continued in Marie des Vallées and Elisabeth of the Trinity.) And as to Catherine of Siena, her *Dialogo* is to Balthasar the purest and most comprehensive example of an 'aesthetic of Christian transcendental reason' with which the 'metaphysics of the saints' can supply us. The 'dialogue' takes place between infinite reason and finite reason – between the Trinity and that 'catholic' soul who, in Catherine, is above all, *anima ecclesiastica*, one who thinks (and feels and acts) with the universal Church. Her form of the 'Marian' attitude is to put herself at the service of the divine plan of mercy, in sheer obedience to the Word who seeks from men and women the imitation of Jesus' work on the cross. Terms such as 'desire', 'longing', 'thirst', in Catherine signify no longer, as they did for Augustine, the creature's ontological need for the Creator but rather an 'ardent desire to correspond with God's requirements and expectations',[32] and that, for Balthasar, is what distinguishes *erōs* (redeemable but in itself ambivalent) from true indifference. The soul is to be stripped of its own will and clothed in God's but this can only be done in the God-man who became the 'bridge' between earth and heaven:

> With God, in the crucified Son, it becomes possible for man too to love his neighbour infinitely, since he can place himself, infinitely and limitlessly, at the disposal of the work of Christ. This love is the heart of every fruit and every work that man can achieve. But because it is an imitation of Christ even unto the cross, it is also, therefore, essentially a humiliated love, a love exposed to insult, mockery, persecution.[33]

Sangue! It is the blood of Christ which makes the divine Glory visible, for it is the sign of God's mercy and charity.

When seen from the heights reached by the Sienese Catherine her Genoese namesake, the last of Balthasar's quartet, is something of a comedown, not least because at Catherine of Genoa's hands, the concept of indifference (with, as Balthasar, strongly influenced by Ignatius Loyola, would see things, its markedly *apostolic* potential) reconverts itself into the more *intimiste* (and therefore *individual*-centred) concept of *erōs*-under-grace. The simultaneity of love and judgment in Catherine's influential doctrine of purgatory (Newman's *Dream of Gerontius* expresses it to perfection when Gerontius responds to the personal Judgment with the plangent appeal for purgation – 'take me away, and in the lowest deep there let me be') is a metaphysical truth (God's glory in its plenitude

---

30 *GL* V, p. 85, citing Angela's *Book of the Experience of the True Faithful*, 157 and 121.
31 Julian, *Revelations of Divine Love*, 5, cited at *GL* V, p. 86.
32 *GL* V, p. 94.
33 *GL* V, p. 96.

coexists with the creature's poverty and indeed, after the Fall, shame); but it also led on to Luther's defective doctrine of justification, where man is at one and the same time just and a sinner.

Balthasar must come to terms with his former 'father', Ignatius, and the spiritual theologians of the Baroque age which Ignatius ushers in, but beforehand it is worth mentioning his use of *The Cloud of Unknowing*, which it would be easy to miss, for it is slipped in among his portraits of holy women. It would be difficult to imagine a spirituality less Baroque, less theatrical and 'representational', than the *Cloud*'s, but we can see why, with its author's emphasis on the discarding of concepts and judgments, the utterly unBaroque 'nakedness of intent' he recommends could be mistaken for some technique of non-Christian Oriental meditation. Actually, Balthasar is at least equally concerned that 'unknowing' could be a contemplative parallel to the abstractly univocal theory of being of Scotus and, later Suarez. Fortunately, the *Cloud* expressly forbids the metaphysical reduction of its doctrine, since it is, after all, by *love* that God shall be gained. Still, we can see, with Balthasar, the need for something more tangible, more (in a word) aesthetic.

And this the Baroque provides with superabundance, possibly excess, so much so that the forms of worldly beauty are *too* closely aligned with the power and glory of the Saviour God. But the truth grasped by the Baroque (and nowhere more clearly than in Loyola himself) is that 'to be a true Christian is to exist purely for the "ever-greater glory of God", to be immersed in that glory, to be at its disposal, to radiate it through grace'.[34] But how does this differ from what, say, Ruysbroeck, had already divined? It differs in the way the phrase 'at its disposal' is construed in terms of active service, the ready grasping and hot pursuit of the will of God in the world. 'The perfection of the kingdom of God ... can be pursued as the universal operation of God in the active co-operation of the creature'.[35] In Ignatius' *Spiritual Exercises*, we participate through grace and freedom in God's own elective act, choosing as Ignatius remarks, 'what God our Lord gives us to choose'. Consequently, for the transfigured humanism of the new age, man becomes a representative, viceregal in his dignity, of the God who sends him, and the more perfectly so the more absolutely he donates all his powers to his Lord's service. Ignatius, consequently, achieved the inner synthesis of, on the one hand, the Scholastic doctrine of secondary causality, the notion of the true causal instrumentality of effective agents, with, on the other, the mystical tradition and so made possible the best – the most Christian – aspect of Baroque culture, its sense of the glory of the receptacle of Glory, the manifestation in the human representative of the absolute sovereignty of the God who sends.

Unfortunately, the people of the Baroque age were not always good at distinguishing between the genuine pursuit of God's ever-greater glory and the apotheosis of man himself. Against the objection that the Catholic Church of Renaissance and Baroque behaved as if she had half reverted to paganism, Balthasar argues that antique forms were deliberately re-pristinated in the service of glory:

34 *GL* V, p. 105.
35 Ibid.

in a conscious act of faith and loyalty to mother Church, in a conscious rejection of the Protestant rejection of the idea that divine revelation can have any real visibility in the time of the Church's history or in the charisms of sanctity, which the Holy Spirit so richly poured out on the Church in this very century, and which the art of Tintoretto, El Greco, Zurbaran, Rubens and many others tried to represent visibly as the splendour of grace.[36]

Alas, that is not the whole story, for the revelatory icons of the Baroque have something contrived about them when one bears in mind the draughts sweeping around the room beneath the Baroque ceiling, the space where the spirit of critical philosophy and the new empiricism of the natural sciences was making its home. Only a total commitment to Ignatian *indiferencia*, and to that 'election' which shares in God's own allotting to us of our rôles, could save Baroque representationalism (for emperor and pope, as well as lesser mortals) from mere theatricality.

But Balthasar can find something to admire in 'the final systems' – his term for the spiritual theologies of the French *grand siècle*, from François de Sales to Jean-Pierre de Caussade. Here we are on the terrain of Bremond's voluminous *History of the Religious Sentiment in France*, twelve volumes, with their (theologically) appalling title, that give an idea of the rich diversity of the 'metaphysics of the saints' in the period, but not of the common threads that bind various writers together. And these are, for Balthasar, first and positively, a common structure (he would even say 'system') to be summed up in the words 'dialogue' and 'transcendence'; and secondly and negatively, a tiresome psychologising self-preoccupation. The jewel in the crown of the French Baroque is the ever more fully accentuated theme of *abandon* (*not*, Balthasar insists, a form of *erōs*, of religious striving, for it expresses the fact that 'God alone can lead man to union with him', so one 'just leaves it to God').[37] And as for the second, it is, Balthasar disapprovingly remarks, the mildew on the fruit, of rather, as he blisteringly adds, with a side-reference to the exaggerated manners of the age, the talcum-powder.

Some of his judgments are remarkably severe – and would hardly have occurred to anyone save that *rara avis*, an historian of spirituality who is also a philosopher. Thus on François de Sales while Balthasar praises the *Treatise on the Love of God* for setting out to show how the human will, by love and 'indifference', can 'enter' the divine will, he also stigmatises his work as an anthropocentrism naively imagining itself theocentric, not realising that, because the 'love' of its title is primarily our love for the divine goodness, it has succumbed to the Scotist-Suarezian concept of univocity of being, and so become a harbinger of eighteenth-century pietistic rationalism (itself of course chiefly Lutheran!). Here, one has to say, Balthasar's capacity for detecting hidden chains of causal connexion in the history of thought has run away with him.

The account of the Oratoire de France – its great figures Cardinal Pierre de Bérulle, and Charles de Condren, his successor as general – is more

---

36 *GL* V, p. 111.
37 *GL* V, p. 115.

satisfactory. To Balthasar, Bérulle in his description of the 'primordial metaphysical act' did well when he wrote of how God

> makes our soul adore the divine majesty, not only by its own thoughts and affections but also by the operation of his divine Spirit, who acts in our spirit and makes it bear and feel the power and sovereignty of his being over all created beings by the experience of his grandeur applied to our littleness and by the experience of our littleness incapable of being his grandeur; for it is infinite and infinitely distant and disproportionate to all created being.[38]

And if Bérulle echoes Balthasar *avant la lettre* in stressing the ever-greater grandeur of God, he also stunningly anticipates the Balthasarian notion of Christ as the 'concrete' *analogia entis*. The God-man is the 'bridge between infinite and finite, between absolute glory and absolute adoration, the mediator of the religious act . . .', the 'definitive proportion between God and man', found nowhere else.[39] Balthasar also welcomes Bérulle's most original contribution to spiritual theology: the doctrine of the *états* (states) relevant to our salvation which the Redeemer lived out. In Jesus:

> all the states of a truly human existence are experienced and shaped into a precise expression of his eternal adoration of God. According to Bérulle, all Jesus' particular states . . . are integrated in his general state as God and man, which, in precisely *this* integration, is the place of man's true transcendence towards God. In fact, here finite being's perfect act of homage to God (the foundation of all authentic knowledge of God) is performed with divine validity.[40]

Indeed, Balthasar presents Bérulle as having in blissful ignorance solved, whether prospectively or retrospectively, a good many of the problems of intellectual and theological history. Thus in the quotation just cited, the pattern of transcendence found in Bérulle's writing is that which the philosophers, novelists and poets discussed in *Apokalypse der deutschen Seele* sought in vain. The way Bérulle fits together the time-bound historical acts in which Jesus existed humanly in various 'states' and the eternal significance which attaches to everything that concerns him as the *God*-man, and *must* do if the mysteries he performed in time are to be of help to us, solves in advance the problem raised by the *Mysterientheologie* of the twentieth-century Benedictine theologian and liturgist, Odo Casel. The Saviour's temporal acts and states issue – temporally, then – from his abiding fundamental attitude as the 'perfect adorer' and are recaptured in that attitude both as a permanent disposition of mind (there Bérulle does justice to the eternity of One who is God) and also (and here the element of temporality recurs, but now integrated into that eternity) as 'the harvest of all the real achievements of Christ in time'.[41]

38 *Oeuvres complètes* (Paris 1856, Montsoult 1960), p. 1417–1418.
39 *GL* V, p. 120.
40 *GL* V, p. 121.
41 *GL* V, p. 422.

Finally, Balthasar regards Bérulle's religious metaphysics as giving a more satisfactorily Christocentric expression to the bipolarity of the 'transcendental' and 'categorial' aspects of revelation and salvation found in the theology of his main contemporary interlocutor, Karl Rahner. The transcendental ground of the Christian experience of both faith and grace (our spiritual 'capacity') is Christ's 'capacity' – as the Mediator and Substitute – for us. For according to Bérulle, he possesses 'two wonderful capacities: one for the fullness of God, the other for souls whom he contains in himself, and has in his authority, in his power, a capacity that contains, conserves and protects', and that, in him, gives souls 'life and subsistence'.[42] This transcendental determination of Christian existence overarches (or undergirds) all particular experiences of life in Christ, which, in their concrete shape in the biography of a Christian, Bérulle would ascribe to the free election of Jesus who chooses disciples for specific locations within his 'states'. And so one person may have a special call to share with Christ in his being the Father's child (one thinks at once of Thérèse of Lisieux, on whom Balthasar wrote at length); and another a vocation all their own to participate in his contemplation in the wilderness (an Anthony of Egypt, or Charles de Foucauld). As Balthasar points out, this idea greatly influenced Bernanos, and reworked as a christologically determined concept of vocation as mission, it will recur in important contexts of the theological dramatics.

Condren, whom Balthasar thinks underwent a strictly metaphysical experience, decked out in the Old Testament imagery of the glory of the Lord as a consuming fire, figures in *Herrlichkeit* chiefly for his doctrine of sacrifice. In comparison with the inexpressible glory of the God who is all, the soul wants to be nothing. The creature's 'consumption' by the Fire of God is also its fulfilment. In this way, Condren's exalted teaching on sacrifice as at once annihilation and vivification is, Balthasar remarks, ontological rather than soteriological. So radical is it, that he wonders how it passed muster when archbishop Fénelon of Cambrai's comparatively innocuous doctrine of the pure, disinterested love of God, seeking no reward, could lead his brother of Meaux, J. B. Bossuet, to start canon legal proceedings against him.

The idea that we should love God absolutely even without any promise of eternal life may sound Christian, and even super-Christian, but Balthasar has no time for it (and so really concurs – minus the politicking involved – with Bossuet).

> Does not this lead logically to Hegel, according to whom there is likewise no hope of eternity for the individual spirit, which is just one passing moment in the infinite ascendancy of Absolute Spirit? It is then a short step to materialism. Mysticism and atheism in a strange way look one another in the eye, for common to both is disdain for human finitude in the interests of an all-embracing Whole in which the little 'I' disappears.[43]

---

42 *Oeuvres complètes*, p. 968.
43 *GL* V, p. 130.

And again, bitingly, in Fénelon God's glory 'fails to shine as it should: the search for selflessness is far too self-concerned'.[44]

And so the one thing for which Balthasar *does* praise poor Fénelon – a philosophy of *abandon* with theological foundations sunk in the rock of Golgotha, must be extracted from its misleading setting and recontextualised – as happens in the last example of hagiological metaphysics and their summation: Jean Pierre de Caussade. Abandonment for Caussade is faith, hope and love, the entire *vie théologale* of the theological virtues, as founded on the infinite mercy and merit of Christ, and lived 'poorly', 'without all the accessories of sanctity which make souls a cause of wonder.'[45] In this night of faith God's will meets the willing soul, and the result is a 'perpetual feasting' – the nuptials of the cross. 'A God always given and always received, in everything earth has of weakness, folly, nothingness'.[46] And with an anticipation of Kierkegaard, Caussade speaks of God thus coming to us in each moment in a bewildering variety of disguises: the famous Caussadian *communion de tous les instants* in the 'sacrament of the present moment' in which the Holy Spirit is writing with his pen an exposition of the Word in the impact of each created thing on the heart. Balthasar compares this 'strange aesthetics' to the reverse side of a piece of embroidery: the tangled threads do not yet reveal the beautiful sampler, for the design is seen right way round only in eternity.

> Everything extraordinary that we perceive in the saints – visions, revelations, interior locutions – is but a reflection of the sublimity of their state, which is guarded and concealed in the exercise of faith. For faith guards everything in itself, since it knows how to see and hear God in everything that occurs from moment to moment. When this is perceptibly and externally revealed, nothing is happening that faith does not already contain within itself; only the grandeur needs to be made visible and the soul stirred to exercise.[47]

Just so the transfiguration of Christ and his miracles did not augment his grandeur; they expressed it. But if in some of the saints God makes his grace visible *pour encourager les autres*, many other saints 'remain hidden; destined to shine only in heaven, they spread no sort of light in this life, but live and die in deep darkness',[48] a darkness identical, so Balthasar comments, with the light of the Word.

Yet all this remains, after all, primarily a *theology for contemplatives*. The entire French school, moreover, seem 'so preoccupied with their personal encounter with God that Catholic openness to the world recedes into the background, or remains alongside contemplation as an isolated external

---

44 *GL* V, p. 132. One might compare the following judgment on Saint-Cyran: 'This indefinite study of self is tiring. The soul will always be obliged to read its salvation in the goodness of God. It will never find that salvation in itself', M. T. F. Louis-Lefebvre (ed.), Abbé Huvelin, *Cours sur l'histoire de l'Eglise* 11 (Paris 1968), p. 20.
45 *L'Abandon à la providence divine* (1691; Paris 1928), p. 104.
46 Ibid., p. 44.
47 Ibid., p. 63.
48 Ibid., p. 64.

factor'.[49] Integrating the two, Balthasar remarks with tantalising brevity, is something reserved for our time.[50]

To reach that time, he still has a way to go, and he will travel it in four chapters, traversing the holy fools of Christendom (from the Middle Ages onwards); Nicholas of Cusa's valiant attempt in the Renaissance to fashion a new Christian metaphysics; the would-be repristinisation of ancient sources in the classicism which reigned, in various phases, from Renaissance to eighteenth century, and finally the philosophical era ushered in by Kant which brings us to our own time.

Holy folly and learned ignorance

The relevance of holy fools – a recognised genre of sanctity in both East and West – to the task of a theological aesthetics may not be blindingly obvious. Holy fools become highly pertinent to Balthasar's enterprise, however, when he asks, what are the human 'classics' which the tradition of spirituality he has just described brought forth? (I use the term sanctioned for the way biography becomes related to theology in Father David Tracy's study *The Analogical Imagination*.) One might have thought such classics to be the saints *simpliciter*, but Balthasar has doubts as to the practicability of that appeal for the illustrative purposes that are currently his own.

> For a long time, in countless Latin and vernacular legends, the saints were the canonical image of man, but the heart of sanctity, abandonment in transcendence to the open will of God, cannot be put into epic or dramatic form; only the indirect, accidental effects – miracles, heroic achievements, strange behaviour – offered narrative material capable of gripping a reader.[51]

Christian literature did better, then, in its attempts to capture the essay of the 'representative fools and buffoons' about whom lingers a faint yet unmistakeable whiff of the *odor sanctitatis*. The fool is the 'unprotected man, essentially transcendent, open to what is above him', lacking the 'ponderousness' of the earth-bound, closer to the saint than the self-preoccupied moral achiever. At the same time, he is not exposed to the danger of 'purism' or 'exclusiveness' which – as the 'metaphysics of the saints' Balthasar has chronicled attest – the candidate for (as it were) 'normal' holiness can run. The fool, therefore, is for Balthasar the best picture of the Christian man or woman before God: these are, in John Saward's brilliant pun, 'perfect fools'.[52] And Balthasar finds the Spirit of holy folly (along with a great deal of dross besides) in such additional *literary* figures as François Villon and Johannes von Tepl, as well as the character of Parsifal (whose name means 'Pierce-through-the-heart') in the version of the Grail epic by Wolfram. Erasmus becomes the

49 *GL* V, p. 127.
50 *GL* V, p. 140.
51 *GL* V, pp. 141–142.
52 J. Saward, *Perfect Fools. Folly for Christ's Sake in Catholic and Orthodox Spirituality* (Oxford 1980).

(somewhat haywire) philosopher of folly in *Encomium Moriae* (1509). Here the 'deeper Christian meaning' is the way grace outplays sin, though for Balthasar Erasmus finishes, by his own (not especially gracious) act of folly in ending his treatise on the topic of flight from the body: blind, then, to the radiant glory of the true folly revealed on the body on the cross. And in *Don Quixote* the principle of folly embraces even ridiculousness, though, as Balthasar points out, some of his scrapes bear an uncanny resemblance to episodes in the life of St Ignatius. In a really beautiful reading of Cervantes' novel:

> In the first part the exterior foolish deeds predominate whereas in the second the author demonstrates more and more the interior supernatural rationality of his hero, so at the end, after the final defeat, all his foolishness, like a light garment, falls unresistingly from him. . . . Don Quixote is so much better a Christian because subjectively he makes no claim to sanctity, and because objectively it is never possible, at any moment or in any respect, to count his ridiculous doings among the solemn deeds of God and Jesus Christ. . . . It is precisely in this way that Quixote's life becomes a permanent monument of Christian existence and a reflected ray of the glory of God.[53]

And in its slightly later German picaresque equivalent, Grimmels-hausen's *Simplizissimus*, the 'holy rogue' who gives the tale its name despite all the vagaries of his course remains a 'defenceless heart' open to the mercy of God. In Balthasar's interpretation of the hermit's ode at night-time which begins the story: 'though we have to live in the dark, no night can prevent us from singing God's praise, and [with reference to the screeching of an owl which accompanies melody and words] it is not just beautiful sounds that harmonize in this praise'.[54] But what Balthasar finds most extraordinary – when we consider the philosophies that formed, or issued from, the nineteenth century – is that superlative epiphany of the fool-figure, Prince Myshkin in Dostoevsky's *The Idiot*. Whereas folly in the neo-classical age is educated into rational wisdom, as the *Bildungsroman* testifies, and for the Idealists represents a punishment for misunderstanding reality (not a prize for exposing oneself to it),[55] Dostoevsky produces in Russia a universal vision where beauty and folly combine. In *Raskolnikov's Diary*, Dostoevsky had saluted Christ as the 'eternal miracle, . . . this infinitely beautiful figure, . . . the only one positively beautiful figure'[56] – since beauty is not in any straight-forward way a transparence of the divine; it can be the devil's mask or sacrament as well . In Myshkin, the Russian novelist set out to portray not the miracle itself, but a reflection of it in post-incarnation time. In this unselfconsciously compassionate figure, who loves by overlooking, not only forgiving insult but forgetting, 'there, as it were by chance, to receive

53 *GL* V, pp. 177, 179–180.
54 *GL* V, p. 187.
55 Another contrast is with Schopenhauer who, as Idealism collapses in fatigue, makes aesthetics unmask intellect as a world of madness.
56 Cited at *GL* V, p. 190.

furious slaps in the face',[57] and whom people experience as disconcert-ingly unique, Dosteovsky portrays 'that simple love which is not really at home, cannot settle down or be classified here below'.[58] Crucial to Balthasar's interpretation of the novel is his account of Myshkin's epilepsy, the chief function of which

> is as a veil; it veils the Christian mystery from himself and from others. It is the mystery of the glory of absolute love descending from above, the love whose magical power lies beyond both disclosure and concealment, memory and oblivion. . . .[59]

And if Bernanos continues the theme of the Christ-like priest exposed to ridicule in *Journal d'un curé de campagne*, Graham Greene, for Balthasar, is far off the mark with his version in *The Power and the Glory*.

Balthasar's final variation on the theme is not novelistic but painterly. Rouault's clowns sum up the humanly grotesque but do so in their disfigurement in a Christ-like way, just as Rouault's Christ takes on the traits of clowns. A luminous use of colour turns the late landscapes into holy ground, but the dark world of the *Miserere* sequence is no less irradiated by the 'glory that streams from the face of despised and dying love'.[60] The solitary clown of plate eight of that series embodies all that Balthasar would say of the holy fools:

> The games of the fools from Parzival to Don Quixote and Simplicius were a merry prelude to the seriousness of the Idiot but now the destiny of that lonely individual has become the destiny of mankind, a destiny which, at the point where human existence was pro-claiming its senselessness and idiocy, has been taken up by the gentle divine Idiot on the Cross. He silently contains everything in himself and imprints on everything his form, the form of the divine mercy, for which it is a matter of sublime indifference whether its glory is manifested invisibly in earthly beauty or in ugliness.[61]

To investigate Cusanus entails, following such a conclusion, a major change of gear, and a necessary one, for the 'solutions' just described, though in their own way wonderful, hardly do justice to the *reality of the world as a whole*. Rather do they tend to withdraw from that reality as a 'nominalist–positivist scene of wreckage' and seek the 'gleam of the divine glory in an immediate supernatural'.[62] Reaction to *that* took, on Balthasar's assessment, three major forms. First, conscious of the *déracinement* of a 'positivistically uprooted reason', people tried to recover some of that antique patrimony whose strengths (if also weaknesses) Balthasar set out in the preceding volume of *The Glory of the Lord*. After the sixteenth-century Reformation this was all the more pressing since the

57 *GL* V, p. 99.
58 *GL* V, p. 201.
59 *GL* V, p. 200.
60 *GL* V, p. 203.
61 *GL* V, p. 204.
62 *GL* V, p. 206.

foundations of a unitary Christian culture needed rebuilding as well. Though the ancients had never ceased to have an influence on theology, with the Renaissance their presence intensifies as 'the revelation of Christ is understood as the pinnacle, summation and synthesis of the whole divine revelation in the cosmos'. And the result is that, from the humanist revival to the Hellenophile Hegel

> now more than ever are Plato and Plotinus 'baptised' as Christians before Christ, more than ever can the ancient gods be interpreted as partial aspects of God (as they seem to us in Homer) and be incorporated into Christian art and literature, more than ever the doctrine of the *Logos spermatikos* is seen to be valid not only in the case of the philosophies but in the religions inseparable from them, more than ever will the distinctively Christian be regarded as the highest example of the universal bridge between God and man.[63]

But then secondly, there could be in fact no going back: the Christian experience of the immediacy between the infinite 'I' of God and the finite 'I' of the personal self had launched onto history a speculative account of God in his relation to a human subject who is likewise a mystery with no determinable limit. As the Idealist philosophers and the poets influenced by them go to show, by comparison with the fascination – ethical, aesthetic, speculative and even erotic – of the infinite, the unbounded, the splendours of classical as of biblical glory grow pale and fade away.

And finally, so Balthasar suggests, there is a third response, which is that of the idea of evolution, the self-developing world-process – a theme already articulated, he maintains, thanks to the fusion of elements from the first and second 'responses', long before there was a Darwin or a Wallace to verify it experimentally. Putting those first and second responses together:

> the world can come to lie nowhere else now than in the gap between the finite and the infinite I, and because, as long as pure materialism is avoided, the infinite I, even if simply as an idea, has the primacy, the world and man can in the end be nothing more than the goal of its Odyssean voyage of self-discovery. With the insertion of God into the world-process, however, his sovereign freedom over man is lost; speculatively, man emerges as an absolute standpoint, and consequently remains . . . the unique *divinum* in the landscape of thought.[64]

And at the fissure where these streams of evangelically questionable metaphysics issue from the depths, there stands the philosopher-priest, cardinal Nicholas of Cusa whose work for Balthasar shows in advance how none of the three will serve our turn.

Combining the inheritances of Plotinus, Eckhart and Scripture, Nicholas comes up with a 'cosmic universal view of the glory of God'

---

63 *GL* V, p. 207.
64 *GL* V, p. 209.

where, however, what is biblically distinctive about the glory is in danger of being sacrificed on the altar of an 'aesthetic cosmic scheme'. The world is, as with Plotinus, the manifestation of the non-manifest God, but this God is, as with Eckhart, absolute freedom, and so the manifestation is utterly non-necessary: it is, as with Scripture, an act of love. And so far, so good. In his demonstration in *Beryl* that ancient thought, searching for the *quidditas* of things, their distinctiveness, was doomed to frustration unless it could reconceive them as intentions of a God who by creation communicates himself in freedom, Cusanus makes great play with *Herrlichkeit*'s master theme of glory.

> And so the teaching of the Gospel becomes ever more manifest, which gives to creation the purpose that the God of gods is revealed in Zion in the majesty of his glory, which is the manifestation of the Father in whom is all delight.[65]

But for the glory of God in the creation to be seen as the work of *love* God must disclose his inner mystery, which he does in the economies of Son and Spirit. Only through the Father's gift of the Son, even unto death, and the Son's gift of the Spirit (and so not by its own resources) can the spirit of man become *speculator maiestatis*, a seer of glory. And yet it remains true that universal being, for Nicholas, is an expression of the divine beauty.

Balthasar's question concerns the stability of this synthesis in the way the cardinal of Cusa presents it. When Nicholas speaks of the mind as 'a kind of divine number', so proportioned as to let the divine harmony enfold, by its mediation, all the lesser harmonies of the world, he ascribes to human intelligence a quasi-divine creativity, where our spirit is

> so much a reflection of divine spirit that . . . it takes over the divine features as a 'second god' and genuinely becomes the creator of a reflected world (that of numbers), just as God is creator of the real world of things. Nicholas himself never consciously steps over the boundary of the analogy to an idealism of identity, but for those who are determined to make such a transition everything is ready prepared.[66]

In Nicholas' account of the analogy of being, God is immanent to the creature as the *Non-aliud*, the 'Not other', for he is already in himself in simple totality everything the creature is in its individuated unfolding. God so masters the whole realm of being that he can be himself outside himself. Nothing is *gloriosius*, 'more glorious', than this capacity of his to be the ground of every ground. Yet the human spirit belongs in one sense on God's side of this divide between the finite 'explications' and the infinite 'complication', for, as God's image and likeness, the *mens* of man has the power to assimilate itself to any 'explication' – any finite reality – by way of judgment. In the *Idiota, de mente*, the spirit seeks in everything

---

65 *De beryllo* 36–37, cited at *GL* V, p. 216.
66 *GL* V, p. 210.

for its own measure but does not find it, save where all is one. In another of Cusanus' treatises, the *De filiatione Dei*, divine sonship can be understood in just these terms:

> Sonship is the annulling, *ablatio*, of all otherness and difference and the resolution, *resolutio*, of all things in the One, something that is at the same time the transfusion, *transfusio*, of the One into everything, and precisely this is deification, *theosis*.[67]

And surely, remarks Balthasar, this is not just the last mediaeval echo of Eriugena; it is also the first Renaissance anticipation of Idealism. For though sonship here be the fruit of grace, unavailable save by the God-man, it takes the form nonetheless of absolute knowledge.

> This aprioristically understood Christology ... was certainly meant in an Anselmian way, but it opened the way for Hegel, because the exact proportion between God and the world in the God-man – philosophically completely unmaintainable – is finally made accessible to reason.[68]

This is not how to depict the 'decisive glory of the God of Jesus Christ' against its (legitimate) backdrop of philosophy, religion and myth. Balthasar does not contest – on the contrary, he thoroughly approves – Nicholas' drive towards universality; but that universal outreach must be in the service – not to the detriment – of the 'biblical concept of glory'.[69]

It remains then, finally, in Volume V of *The Glory of the Lord* for Balthasar to unveil the consequences of the defective philosophical approaches to beauty which he has signalled, and to propose their corrective in the closing chapter of the work, 'Our Inheritance and the Christian Task'.

Starry heavens: glory in the cosmos

Seeking help from the ancients again ('classical mediation') and rethinking the relation between divine and human subjects ('metaphysics of the spirit'): these, along with the theme of developmental process, are the main motifs of European thought between Renaissance and twentieth century. In his survey, Balthasar is not setting out to provide a history of Western philosophy (his chapters would be impossibly esoteric if viewed

---

67 *De filiatione Dei*, cited at *GL* V, p. 242.

68 *GL* V, p. 244, with reference to the last book of *De docta ignorantia*; by 'in an Anselmian way' Balthasar means on the basis of *faith* seeking understanding. John Milbank offers a more positive, but equally brilliant, conspectus of Cusanus' thought in his essay 'Man as Creative and Historical Being in the Theology of Nicholas of Cusa', *Downside Review* 97. 329 (1979), pp. 245–257.

69 Actually, Cusanus' combination of ontological large-mindedness and special focussing on the historic incarnation was not, in his period, so unusual as Balthasar suggests if one can believe J. W. O'Malley, *Praise and Blame in Renaissance Rome. Rhetoric, Doctrine and Reform in the Sacred Orators of the Papal Court*, c. 1450–1521 (Durham, North Carolina, 1979), pp. 124–125.

in such a light), but to draw out the salience of a variety of key points for a transcendental doctrine of beauty. In point of fact, Balthasar considers ideas of natural process as evolution to be far from defining for modern thought: neither Aristotle nor Goethe would have scrupled to incorporate the development of species into their cosmologies. So really, it is the other two motifs - back to paganism, or forward into the absolutisation of man – that are crucial. Balthasar kindly gives us his conclusion in advance of the survey:

> The decision falls uniquely – and the history of the modern period has no clearer result – for or against the Glory of Being, and history has fashioned the Either-Or so simply that it has become a decision between Christianity and nihilism. The 'gods', the 'divine', hold sway still only where God's personal love in the Son of God is recognised and acknowledged, and the storming ahead of metaphysical speculation is bridled only where thought – in the same epiphany – confronts the not-to-be-mastered majestic freedom of the God of love.[70]

First, then, Balthasar explains how from the end of the Middle Ages, through the Renaissance and early modern periods into the age of Idealism, the interrelated notions of beauty and *erōs*, in their cosmological application, are always secretly indebted to Christianity. Marsilio Ficino may have thought he was writing as a good Plotinian when he interpreted all being as beauty, but by seeing the cosmos as not only the self-radiation of the Good but also the manifestation of eternal love, he is relying on a subjacent Christian level of sensibility and thought. Then again, he identified *erōs* with *caritas* – a procedure which, insofar as it can be justified at all, is legitimate only on theological presuppositions.

> If . . . the eros of the creature is always first of all an answer to the divine beckoning back of grace, so that, on account of the eternal prevenience of grace it can be called 'divine' or even 'daemonic', then this eros can, without further ado, be explained as agape, if only it is considered that the beckoning of grace to the chaotic sinner is accomplished in the incarnate love of Jesus Christ[71]

– as indeed Ficino, with his commentary on the Pauline letters could well admit. Again with the Jewish philosopher Leone Ebreo one can hardly speak of a covert appeal to Christian revelation, yet his account of the God of the cosmos as archetype of not only beauty but *erōs*, the 'First Lover', makes no sense on Platonist grounds: once more we 'see the hidden biblical a priori of this theology'.[72] And as to Giordano Bruno, one would hardly expect Balthasar to make a believer *malgré lui* out of that 'father of the modern religion of the cosmos' for whom the world is the all. What he does instead is to point out how, in Bruno's rejection of prayer

70 *GL* V, p. 249.
71 *GL* V, p. 255.
72 *GL* V, p. 259.

and rapture not only in their Christian but even in their Platonist form, we can 'already see that attitude emerging here which will be christened by the young Goethe under the name of Prometheus and of Faust'.[73]

The whole idea that the movement of *erōs* – of self-transcending desire to be united with what is beautiful in the forms of this world – could lead to a religiously (yet undogmatically) conceived salvation can only generate frustration unless its Christian assumptions are explicitly confessed.

> The Platonism of the Middle Ages, of the Renaissance and of Idealism, where the beloved form as an incarnate idea can attract upwards to reach God, is coloured and conditioned as a whole by Christianity; christologically, for only in Jesus Christ does a single human form make the Godhead present with complete validity and effectiveness – sacramentally; and in a trinitarian manner because only the God of Jesus Christ is in himself freely and personally eternal love.[74]

Erōs to which the divine characteristics of New Testament *agapē* have become attached can only be, Balthasar writes, a 'melancholy' thing. The expectation, derived ultimately from orthodox Christology, that a finite reality can yield an infinite meaning, an infinite satisfaction, is itself unreal when it would decant from the limited vessel of a lovely landscape or an attractive fellow human being the 'gracious presence of the totality of the divine beauty'.[74] Hence the theme of the deceptiveness of love, in Shakespeare's sonnets, say, and the bitter-sweet ambivalence of *erōs* in Torquato Tasso's *Gerusalemme liberata*. Not for nothing was the moth mortally attracted to the flame one of Bruno's favoured symbols for *erōs*, which he presents as simultaneously self-glorification and self-destruction. In Balthasar's far-seeing perspective, we are not so far here from Richard Wagner's *Tristan und Isolde*: 'The absolute self-glory of eros, which grasps eternity in a moment, if taken seriously, eliminates any accompanying thought of an individual immortality after death.'[76] And so the classical patrimony disintegrates *with* the Christian: the language of eternity becomes no more than a 'myth of the loving heart'. The 'self-consumption' of *erōs* robs it of glory; either it must be retrieved in Christian form, where as with Claudel's play *Le Soulier de Satin* it is allowed its flawed and finite beauty but redeemed by God's better beauty, grace; or as with Sartre it disappears from an existence that must be created out of nothing by sheer acts of human will if it is to have any sense at all.

And so just as the theophanous cosmos could not survive when the biblical glory faded, no more could the basic human orientation of *erōs* stand alone when deprived of *agapē*. Consequently, people abandon, in the early modern period, the sacred canopy of the cosmos and neglect the

73 *GL* V, p. 263.
74 *GL* V, p. 265.
75 *GL* V, p. 267.
76 *GL* V, p. 281.

dynamic structure of human nature. With the marginalising of the supernatural, nature – which, in the real order of God's working in the world, exists for a supernatural goal – cannot stand firm as what she is, the child of God, calling men and women back to their Maker. Religion becomes first pietism and then moralism; the humanity once codefined by the God of the cosmic context enters by stages the state of isolation which the liberal theisms from Machiavelli and Bacon to the English Deists doubtless regarded as splendid – where man stands out as free in a sovereign autonomy of his own.

This development will be further explored in Balthasar's chapter on that 'metaphysics of spirit' for which the human 'I' takes on infinite proportions, but for the moment he is concerned to show how a variety of thinkers and poets would not rest content with so blatant an 'anthropological reduction'. From Shaftesbury to Goethe they would claw their way back, if only they could, to a 'classicising, humanist–cosmic religion'.[77] Above all in England – from the Cambridge Platonist Ralph Cudworth and Joseph Butler, through the Fathers of the Oxford Movement to Austin Farrer and E. L. Mascall, though here Balthasar contents himself with a simple enumeration of names – and in Germany, to which he devotes a hundred and more pages, there is a desire that the revealed glory continue to be experienced, however imagistically and even vestigially, in the natural world. But if in Shaftesbury's *The Moralists, a Philosophical Rhapsody* negative theology and prayer have alike vanished, filling Balthasar with suspicion that here 'the glory of God, which, if we have eyes and heart, manifests itself to us everywhere in the cosmos, shines for us *primarily in the glory of our own love*'[78] this disproportionate emphasis on the divine immanence in man will become ever more transparent.

> The word *Gefühl* (feeling) which the whole Goethe-period – from Shaftesbury and Rousseau's confession of faith in *Emile*, to F. H. Jacobi and Schleiermacher, and to Faust's confession of faith before Gretchen – reserved for the relationship to God, could well characterise the 'feeling after him and finding him' of the Areopagus speech (Acts 17:27) and thus legitimately continue the *sentire* of the *sensus spirituales* (from Origen to Bernard and Bonaventure) if only it did not function with the hidden presupposition of a final, encompassing identity.[79]

Despite Balthasar's devotion – not only as a man of letters but as a metaphysician and even as theologian – to Hölderlin and Goethe, he has to include them within the sweep of this criticism, and so conclude to the ultimate self-contradictoriness of their work. In Hölderlin, in order to re-create the theophanous world, the gods of Hellas are invested with the revealed glory of the gospel. His poetic art expresses a 'total experience of God in the cosmos', contemplating his glory with Christian eyes as the

---

77 *GL* V, p. 291.
78 *GL* V, p. 295. Italics added.
79 *GL* V, p. 298.

glory of love. If Hölderlin was perfectly correct to see glory as the 'unity of the holy and the beautiful', in his work the distinction of the ancients between gods and men is transmuted, under the influence of early German Idealism, into a difference between absolute spirit and nature, such that 'the glorious is equally holy and equally divine when it is *Hen* [the One, i.e. spirit] as when it is *diapheron* [different from the One, i.e. nature], when "a god" as when "a man" . . .'[80]

The One, which is also the All, undergoes *kenōsis* in order to become nature and humanity; the self-sufficient Fulness becomes poor through love: but the question is, are these categories Idealist clothing for a Christian message, or, contrariwise, are these images Christian accoutrements of an Idealist truth-claim? Evidently, the answer makes all the theological difference in the world. The problem is not easily resolved for in Hölderlin's poetry the language of glorious divinity is used for what is earthly and human *insofar as the latter is seen in the light of the gods*, and the poems themselves are saturated with the spirit of reverence and worship. Hölderlin's thought posits a redemptive reconciliation between time and eternity (and so a Christology), and he never lost his conviction that the world-order as we know it, 'egoism in all its shapes', must yield to the kingdom of God, 'the holy glory of love'[81] (and requires therefore a pneumatology). But Balthasar's final conclusion on Hölderlin's work is negative:

> The tremendous intensity with which he thought to do justice to the glory of all being was, despite all the humility of its thanksgiving and praise, objectively hubristic; it reduced the freedom that is God's in his mystery of suffering to a law defining the nature of the One-and-All, a law open to be experienced. The Christ, having been dissolved into the cosmos, can therefore ultimately never be brought back. And immediately after Hölderlin the cold winds of nothingness come bursting into his glory . . .[82]

For in all identity-thinking, beyond the humanly construed world lies . . . nothing.

Goethe, whose influence on him Balthasar acknowledged as profound, is a more hopeful case because his 'essentially pious theory of nature' was developed in part by way of reaction to the deficiencies of Idealism. 'Something he had found in his cosmic experience was missing in the Idealistic version represented by Kant and Fichte, by Schiller, finally by Hegel.'[83] Consequently, he is the last secular manifestation in Western metaphysics of the heritage of glory. Paradoxically, though Goethe, rejecting prayer, is far more worldly than Hölderlin, he lives from the analogy of being, not the mysticism of identity. A major genre of Goethe's writing is the *Bildungsroman*, the kind of novel that describes the 'formation', *Bild-ung*, of a human being, especially of the genius. But the forms, or *Bilder* involved, are not just arbitrarily self-set, by human individual or culture.

80 *GL* V, p. 302.
81 Letter 222, cited at *GL* V, p. 334.
82 *GL* V, p. 338
83 *GL* V, p. 340.

They remain embedded in that 'nature' (creation) whence, as a poem has it, 'stream floods of heightened figures'. In this way, Goethe's explorations of the human condition link up with his theory of natural forms – mineralogical, botanical, zoological – for both are a morphology in which ultimately God is the hidden source of all ordered beauty in the world.

> His aim was to combine the cool precision of scientific research with a constant awareness of the totality apparent only to the eye of reverence, the poetic-religious eye, the ancient sense for the cosmos.

While the scientists had gone over to his archenemy Newton, the Idealist philosophers preferred to deduce nature a prioristically and the Romantic poets to wallow in irrational feelings in her regard, for Goethe – by contrast – objectivity meant uniting observation and study with a 'reverentially pious perception of the divine presence in the cosmos'.[84] That is essentially, after all, what Balthasar himself provided, in phenomenological-ontological mode, in the opening work of his own trilogy.

'Through the observation of an ever-creating nature', wrote Goethe, 'we make ourselves worthy of spiritual participation in her products',[85] and the twin works devoted to *The Metamorphosis of Plants* and *The Metamorphosis of Animals*, suggest how this is so, subject and object entering into one another in a manner beyond both Idealism and empiricism. Yet, as Balthasar remarks, with specific reference to Goethe's account of the beauty of an artwork as a miniature copy of the highest Beauty found in Nature as a whole, one cannot quite see how the human microcosm and the cosmic macrocosm fit together, except to say that 'their relationship is like a brotherly intimacy; there is no place in it for an act of worship'.[86] Glory attends the visible form, as it attends *erōs*, only *while it lasts*. 'The shining images of the world remain ciphers whose meaning ends in themselves ... Glory passes from God to the cosmos, to what Heidegger will call Being.'[87]

Despite his reverential attitude, then, Goethe left an ambiguous inheritance. The universe no longer 'points to a transcendent unity beyond itself', as it did with Plotinus, for 'Christianity now occupies this space, which metaphysics accordingly avoids'. But in the meantime, the 'classical substance increasingly recedes', and hence the philosophy both of nature and of spirit must 'increasingly live from Christian material, despite their contradiction and rejection of it'.[88] So is that transfer of glory to a godless world actually viable? There is not much sign of it in the 'innerworldly humanism' – whether scientific in the study of psychology, sociology and evolutionary history, or literary in the 'bourgeois realism of the Victorian novel, and its European counterparts – of the nineteenth century. (That novel-form, suggests Balthasar, had to have recourse to perverse forms of human experience so as to arouse a sense of tension

84 *GL* V, p. 363.
85 Cited at *GL* V, p. 369, from *Perception and the Faculty of Judgment*.
86 *GL* V, p. 380.
87 *GL* V, p. 408.
88 *GL* V, p. 409.

within its foreshortened perspective, a process that begins with Stendhal's *Tentation de sainte Antoine*.) Other writers – critics, philosophers, poets – 'believed that a revival of mythology might be the means for rejuvenating art from the spirit of religion.[89] Thinking of his own *Apokalypse der deutschen Seele*, Balthasar agrees that

> many classical myths retain symbolic expressivity, indeed take on a greater expressivity where the fate of modern mankind takes on a more tragic form – the myths of Prometheus and Dionysius for instance – but the titanic or divine figures themselves are not thereby reanimated. They remain at best 'names' with which we designate our universal fate, well aware all the while that this in its occurrence transcends all names.[90]

Balthasar does not wish to say that a generously conceived biology of nature, on the one hand, and on the other, the mythopoeic work of the creative artist had absolutely no inkling, in the modern period, of the transcendental *pulchrum*. There is, after all, the Henri Bergson of *L'Evolution créatrice* with its 'directly aesthetic, marvelling and participatory beholding of the leaping fountain of life'[91] – though this proved feeble enough in the contest with mechanism and materialism. And then to represent the mythmakers stands Rilke whose 'Platonic love . . . aims into the emptiness of space which perhaps ultimately, in the last days, warmed and animated by this love, will give birth to a deity'.[92] Rilke's famous angels, though not without relation to the pure intellects of Neo-Platonism and the Church's doctors, are, Balthasar points out, in contrast to their Christian counterparts *self-enclosed*.

> We do not find here the golden chain of emanation, hierarchies and sendings-forth which, despite everything, their domain discloses to the world of men, allowing human beings to partake in the heavenly totality.[93]

The 'descending chain' has snapped, and consequently *erōs* can no longer reach upwards. In Romano Guardini's interpretation of the *Duino Elegies*, which Balthasar had described in his eulogy of his sometime master, Rilke has transferred the divine attributes to the world.[94] For Balthasar himself, matters are not so simple. Rather is the (analogical) continuity between the beautiful and the glorious ruptured, so that the latter can only be *schrecklich*, 'terrifying', and the unattainable angels in their representation of God are a cipher incapable of engagement in true dialogue. Their function is simply to 'delimit' that other totality, the inner-worldly realm, in which modern man is enclosed.

89 Thus the critic Ernst Michel, in his *Der Weg zum Mythos. Zur Wiedergeburt der Kunst aus dem Geiste der Religion* (Jena 1919).
90 *GL* V, p. 412.
91 *GL* V, p. 414.
92 *GL* V, p. 417.
93 *GL* V, p. 421. Translation slightly adapted.
94 R. Guardini, *Rainer Maria Rilkes Deutung des Daseins* (Munich 1977³) cf. H. U. von Balthasar, *Romano Guardini, Reform aus dem Ursprung* (Einsiedeln 1995²), p. 89.

And yet Rilke points to that recovery of the true understanding of being to which despite his silence on the subject of God, Martin Heidegger, in Balthasar's eyes, partially attained. In the *Sonnets to Orpheus*, 'song is existence' (I. 3), and we are 'only just when we praise' (II. 23). In other words, things are wondrous – if also (and this is part-and-parcel of our experience of their preciousness) fragile signs of a greater mystery still.

> Everywhere where single forms are portrayed with the art of the *New Poems*, in the flowers and fruit, fountains and sarcophagi, the horse-rider, the dancer, the beggar, the gardens, the fallow earth in early Spring, in all these their clear contours are wholly transparent to the singing secret of being, whose fulness, wholly permeated by nothingness (*dessen durchnichtige Fülle*), is present in them and reveals itself there.[95]

In Heidegger's recovery of the sense of the mystery of being, the accents of which are already audible in this lyrical interpretation of Rilke's last offerings, the primordial experience of '"wonder" (*thaumazein*) in the face of the form of existent things, their order and radiant beauty' is reinstated – along with the rather more disturbing question as to why there should be being at all. Which is where that 'permeation by nothingness' of things enters the picture, for as Balthasar explains: 'since being is that which is non-essential in its distinction from the existent (essence), it attracts the kind of definitions which negative theology reserves for God'.[96]

Heidegger's thought recovers, for Balthasar, in extraordinary, unexpected fashion, a number of the motifs of an authentic theological (and especially biblical) aesthetics – the otherness of being as originating and all-encompassing; the truth of being as disclosure or revelation (*alétheia*) before which man's appropriate attitude is *Gelassenheit*, letting-be; human thinking as first and foremost doxology, an act of thanking on the part of one who can 'hear' being's 'silent voice', and be 'betrothed' to the being which 'entrusts' itself to him. Through the gift of being, its grace and favour, individual things are, by a presence to them which has no 'why or wherefore' save itself. And such is the glory of being in its manifestation that its continuing concealedness is itself hidden by this overwhelming light – which is why forgetfulness of being could afflict philosophy in the first place.

And yet Heidegger's ontology remains finally unsatisfying, incomplete.

> In the work of Heidegger, the true wonder at the fact that something exists rather than nothing does not run its full course, for it points to a freedom which he does not wish to perceive.[97]

What Balthasar means is something at once metaphysically subtle and yet, from a Christian point of view, all-important, and the key to it is

95 *GL* V, p. 428.
96 *GL* V, p. 436.
97 *GL* V, p. 448.

provided by St Thomas (and only by him: here we touch the most important sense in which Balthasar is a Thomist). It is a question of what later Scholasticism called – though Balthasar spurns the phrase as pedantic and reductive in tendency – the 'real distinction'; the distinction, namely, between the existing thing (*essentia, Wesen*) and the act of existence (*actus essendi, Seinsakt*) which allows something to be as it is. In Balthasar's own terminology, the difference is between

> the *actus essendi* as non-subsistent abundance which attains a state of rest and self-realisation from and within finite essences, and *essentiae*, which attain to reality by act, without however reducing or subdividing the infinite act.[98]

The consequent need to explain both how a *non-subsistent* 'abundance' which does not contain its own ground, its own ultimate foundation, within itself can nonetheless be, as well as how finite realities acquire the definite, stable form they do, *obliges* the philosopher to raise the question of God. For:

> how can a non-subsisting act of being generate subsisting beings from itself alone, and how are the essences to acquire a closed and meaningful form? Both these questions . . . point to a subsisting and absolute Being, God, who both offers a share in his abundance of being (the *actus essendi illimitatus*) and also from his absolute power and freedom (which as such presupposes nothingness as the locus of the ability to create) devises the forms of essences as the recipients of this participation in being.[99]

And here we see why Balthasar accuses Heidegger of being weak on freedom: for it is in the most perfect gratuitousness that creatures are made. Because Heidegger does not construe the ontological difference (between being and beings) in a Thomistic way – as the sign *par excellence* of our *creaturehood* – his thought can only fall back into a philosophy of identity (between infinite and finite) which will be the subject of Balthasar's final historical enquiry. Added to which, Balthasar has a purely practical – yet far-reaching – criticism of Heideggerianism:

> A philosophy which will not firmly answer the question of God one way or the other, lacks intellectual courage, and a pragmatic and realistic humanity will pass it by and get on with daily living.[100]

None of which prevents Balthasar from also maintaining that in the modern period Heidegger's 'project' is the most hopeful one from the point of view of re-creating a metaphysics of being in the service of glory.[101]

98 *GL* V, p. 446.
99 Ibid.
100 *GL* V, p. 450.
101 *GL* V, p. 447.

Trailing clouds of glory – the deification of man

But before setting out his own proposals, Balthasar must still deal with that other line of development from the crisis of Christian philosophy: the speculative union of finite and infinite in the Idealists (and its predictable consequence in Karl Marx). The attempt to renew an ontological vision of the cosmos from the classical sources failed (it could only have succeeded if antiquity had been understood as 'an Advent-like openness looking to Christianity').[102] But the other option – to tease out the implications of the biblical revelation in its disclosure of how *immediate* the relation between the infinite Spirit and finite spirit really is – also led (as Balthasar now explains) down a cul-de-sac.

The philosophy of spirit, in which the immediacy of

> relationship between the divine and the human spirit is no longer mediated by the universe – is on the one hand the fruit of Christianity and, on the other, its greatest threat . . .[103]

Lacking a doctrine of being, this sort of proto-Idealist speculation leads inevitably either to materialism, where the universe 'loses its hierarchic gradation and collapses into "matter"', or to a 'Monism of spirit' where awe and prayer become impossible. In each case, of course, glory vanishes.

> The Eckhartian position of the 'spark of the soul' as a point of identity beyond all analogy is reached in Descartes by a funda-mentally philosophical method and is developed in Kant's 'original and synthetic unity of apperception', in Fichte's *Ich*, in Schelling's point of indifference and in Hegel's process of the spirit. . . . Accordingly, the question must be asked: whatever could 'glory' still mean within the philosophy of spirit? From the point of view of the unity of apperception or of the logical subject, there can be only *one* spirit, only *one* lord: in the event that 'glory' is fitting for it, over against the material world which it 'glorifies', this can only be a 'self-glory'.[104]

As the reference to Meister Eckhart in this passage suggests, Idealism is for Balthasar a 'titanism of *piety*' which only realises too late the monster it has conjured up, and in words of Heidegger Balthasar makes his own, finds climbing out of its pit of error harder than was falling into it. Balthasar is one of those who think that this particular *descensus ad inferos* was initiated by Descartes. Though the Cartesian *Meditations* were composed for the glory of God, and Descartes punctuates them (at the end of the third *Meditation*) with an act of philosophical adoration of 'the incomparable beauty of this immense Light, at least insofar as the strength of my spirit permits me', the situation unhappily created by his

---

102 *GL* V, p. 451.
103 *GL* V, p. 452.
104 *GL* V, p. 453.

philosophy of the *cogito*, the thinking self and its discovery of the absolute Consciousness on which it depends, is that henceforth 'no way . . . leads to God via the being of the world and the human thou'.[105] To chart the subsequent history of *Geistesphilosophie* is to follow the trail of destructive consequences Descartes – with the best of intentions – left behind. The road to both pantheism and atheism (for Balthasar not necessarily to be contrasted, both posit a 'solipsistic universal subject') lies wide open.

And yet the thinkers concerned – Spinoza, Leibniz, Malebranche, Kant; Schiller, Fichte, Schelling, Hegel – are very different, and what Balthasar must show is how each takes up in diverse, and far from equally unacceptable, forms a flawed inheritance. We would not imagine him to have much sympathy for the Jewish monist Spinoza, where the distinction between God and the world becomes one between substance and the *modi* (accidents) substance contains, and that between God's knowledge and our own a matter of the difference that separates precise or 'spiritual' and obscure or 'sensual' concepts. Only as part of his infinite love for himself does God love humankind, and even this Spinoza would rewrite as *acquiescentia*, absolute assent to the intuition of his own truth. Leibniz, by contrast, was certainly a Christian believer, albeit at the same time the greatest would-be rationaliser of the words and ways of God the history of philosophy has known. The beauty of reality, for Leibniz, lies in the philosophically demonstrable pre-established harmony of its divinely decreed constituent 'monads'. The 'primal law' whereby God always chooses the best thing possible is not only fused in Leibniz's thought with St Paul's exclamation of wonder at the depths of the wisdom of God in the outworking of salvation history. That wisdom is, furthermore, itself already precontained *within* that law. It never occurred to him, Balthasar comments, that 'the Christian can know not only too little but also too much, thereby forgetting two things: in philosophy being, and in theology the Cross'.[106] Balthasar hurries over Malebranche with his 'pious theologisation of metaphysics' in which 'ultimately it is in Jesus, God's Word and Son, who comes to meet us *immediately* in all sensible and intellectual knowledge',[107] to get to Kant whose enormous impact on aesthetics Balthasar naturally feels impelled to weigh.

And to weigh judiciously. For on the one hand, Kant's philosophy – critical Idealism – no longer permits the being of the world to epiphanise as an expression of God's glory. But on the other hand, with Kant aesthetics emerges for the first time as a realm of philosophical enquiry both *sui generis* and serious. And here, unfortunately, the sheerly formal character of Kant's concept of the beautiful – the way that, for him, to call an object 'beautiful' is to predict that it will precipitate a satisfying harmony as between our inner faculties of sensuous imagining and intellectual conceiving – divorced it utterly from a proper ontology of *pulchrum*. As Balthasar remarks of the arguments of *The Critique of Judgment*:

105 *GL* V, p. 461.
106 *GL* V, p. 478.
107 *GL* V, p. 481.

Pure beauty is formal in a double sense here: in so far as it ignores the link between the true and the good (which is unheard-of with respect to the classical, Christian tradition), in order to distil in pure form the concept of the beautiful, and in so far as it correspondingly 'abstracts' (this word is Kant's own) from every object and every ethical interest, in order to enjoy the form, as unrelated and possessing meaning only within itself, by the pure formal harmony of our cognitive powers.[108]

Kantian aesthetics lead after this fashion to an ultimately frivolous standpoint of 'art for art's sake', as well as (by bifurcation) to the justification of that abstract art which – as some critics would have it – has precipitated so dire a crisis of credibility in the Western artistic tradition as a whole. But more happily: the concept of the beautiful is not Kant's aesthetics in their entirety; there is also the idea of the *sublime*. Aided by Edmund Burke's *Philosophical Enquiry Into Our Ideas of the Sublime and the Beautiful* (1756), he discusses the human sense of awe at the sublime in relation not just to nature or man's own spirit but above all to God in his sovereign holiness. Thus when Kant calls the Good 'sublime' since only through the 'violence' which reason wreaks upon our sensual nature does that nature come to accord with it, he shows that he has not – thank God – crossed

the threshold of German Idealism with its aesthetics of identity, since he refuses to interpret the 'violence' which must be inflicted upon man as a yet higher form of beauty. He retains a Christian sensorium which, however concealed, still has knowledge of the Cross.[109]

The writer who stands on that boundary, uncertain which way to turn, is, rather, Schiller. Fatefully, Schiller takes a step beyond Kant. He rejects the Kantian categorical imperative which, arising out of Kant's sense of the radical evil in man, orientates the will beyond itself to a transcendent sense of *Sollen*, 'what we ought', and replaces it by: 'a fundamentally achievable identity, a complete harmonisation of ethical man with himself, whereby in a radical anthropological reduction every apprehension of the theological dimension is made redundant'.[110] In his treatise *On Grace and Dignity* Schiller speaks accordingly of 'our divine nature' as the locus of our freedom, while in his *On the Aesthetic Education of Man* we read that 'man bears incontrovertibly within himself, in his personality, the makings of divinity'[111] – or, as Balthasar glosses this claim, 'the absolute point, where the Spirit and the senses bifurcate, lies within man himself'.[112]

---

108 *GL* V, p. 506.
109 *GL* V, p. 513.
110 *GL* V, p. 531.
111 *Ueber Anmut und Würde*, 5; *Ueber die ästhetische Erziehung des Menschen* 11.
112 *GL* V, p. 531.

The Schillerian ideal, a human being where Reason and nature are graciously – beautifully – united, is *worshipful* – a notion alien, Balthasar remarks, to antiquity and the gospel alike. True, Schiller recognises the pertinence of the question. But where does such 'graciousness' come from? Despite the philosophy of spirit to which in principle Schiller is committed, his theoretical writings would answer 'nature' and his plays 'fate'. Though the words 'God', 'the gods' and 'the divine' recur, their meaning is indecipherable since the distinction between God and man has disappeared, and as to the 'Catholic sacramental décor' of the dramas it is, for Balthasar, simply that – wallpaper. In *The Maid of Orleans*, Joan of Arc becomes a 'purely Kantian saint'.

> Rarely has there been a greater distortion of Christian sanctity than here, where that word, which in Christian terms expresses our participation in God's own sanctity, becomes the expression of moral self-sanctification.[113]

Only one feature saves Schiller from total enslavement to identity thinking, but it is crucial enough to elicit from Balthasar high praise. And that is the rôle played in the dramas by the concept of obedience – obedience not of the empirical self to his or her intelligible counterpart (their own being as immanent Spirit), but to other people in active, costing self-engagement. That intuition of 'unconditional love' shows that Schiller was, despite everything, not far from the kingdom.

So it is only with Fichte, Schelling and Hegel that the boundary is at last blasphemously overstepped. When Fichte decided that the starting point of thought should be man in his free and active self-possession, had he argued as a theologian dependent on the anthropology of Genesis where man is the *image* of God, he would have done well. But of course he spoke as a philosopher for whom the biblical revelation of God was nothing different from the general disclosure of being. The finite *literally* reveals the infinite. Schelling and Hegel will continue to draw on the language of transcendental aesthetics for their chief metaphors: the world is the expression of God, its form contains his light, its structure his life. But since Idealism remains a reading of Kant, the 'world' here cannot be understood in the realist sense of even so Platonising a philosopher as Eriugena, or indeed of a monist like Spinoza – the totality concerned can only be developed now from a consideration of the immanent conditions of possibility of the thinking and acting subject. And this means that

> even when the Idealist systems are at their closest to Plotinus (as the final figure of the classical age) the situation with regard to the open and Advent-like decision, which predominates in Plotinus, does not return; rather, everything is finally decided through the determination to conceive Christianity (in a post-Christian manner) as pure philosophy and ultimately as the potentiality of man, history and culture. . . . The die is cast . . . Man is himself the manifest God.[114]

113 *GL* V, p. 544.
114 *GL* V, pp. 547–548.

The titanic 'cathedrals' of Idealist thought will inevitably lack Christianity's *unum necessarium*. Though they absorb everything else from it, this they will not have – *glory*.

> 'Glory' stands and falls with the unsurpassibility of the *analogia entis*, the ever-greater dissimilarity to God no matter how great the similarity to him. In so far as German Idealism begins with the *identitas entis*, the way back to Christianity is blocked; it cannot produce an aesthetics of 'glory' but only one of 'beauty': and the 'aesthetics as science' which was rampant in the nineteenth century, is its fruit.[115]

What began with Eckhart has reached its climax in Fichte: the God-man relationship revealed in Scripture has been retrojected into the inner-divine generative process (the Fichtean 'self' is neither God nor man, but is nonetheless that from which both God and man must be conceived), and the result is used to give formal expression to the God-world relationship (it provides the very structure of Idealist philosophy). If the univocal (as opposed to the analogical) theory of being in Scotus and Suarez had made being something neutral as between God and the world, the same principle is now applied in the new context of post-Kantian thought to the relation of subject and object: hence Schelling finds it possible to construct conceptually both absolute being and the being of the world. While for Fichte the difference between the unreal and the real consisted merely of 'the inner vitalisation and filling out of an initially hollow idea',[116] in Schelling such conceptualism is overcome but only at the cost of inventing a new philosophical mythology of a God in process of becoming.

> The ideal is the universal, 'while contraction is the beginning of all reality'; by contracting himself from the 'universal' or from 'being' [*Sein*] to an 'existent', God becomes real, which contraction is also however his 'condescension' from the level of an ideal 'existent' to that of a mere ground or premise or basis for it, namely to 'being' [*das Seiende*] and thus the possibility appears of a 'created' world . . .[117]

a world which God needs as the basis of his own reality, such that the world-process is itself the full personalisation of God. God and man both evolve, each in his own way, out of 'their common depths into the light of ideality'.[118] And if in Schelling's system spirit emerges from evolving nature in man while rising above nature through morals and culture and transfiguring it, thus allowing distinction within an absolute identity to be transcended in its very postulation, Schelling's message is ultimately

---

115 *GL* V, pp. 548–549.
116 *GL* V, p. 550.
117 *GL* V, p. 561, citing Schelling's *Stuttgarter Privatvorlesungen* at pp. 429–430 in Volume VII of the collected works.
118 *GL* V, p. 563.

the *aesthetic* one of the beautiful harmony of finite and infinite. Christ for Schelling may be beautiful as the embodiment of that harmony of infinite and finite. But such beauty can never – within a philosophy of identity – be glory. It follows from this summary that Balthasar is of the party which holds that the later philosophy of Schelling, ostensibly a negative reaction to Hegel's pan-logism, and more open to the objective theism of a biblical God who acts, is in truth no new starting point, no escape from identity thinking.[119] And while Schelling struggles to return from *Geistesphilosophie* to authentic Christology, Hegel's youthful first steps in philosophy consisted in trying to make sense of Christ, and continued by the progressive construction of a supreme speculative system which would use what it wanted of Christology for its own purposes and leave the rest behind.

> In Hegel as in Hölderlin, Christianity is now absorbed into the element of the omnipresent kenosis of being in which, for both, the unsurpassable 'glory' of reality occurs. For Hegel therefore glory is nowhere to be found more than in the totality of the absolute spirit itself; absolute thought radiates it in a triumph which can be compared only with that of Leibniz, though it is now no longer theodicy [the justification of God], but noödicy [the justification of mind].[120]

Once again, the rejection of the essential contrast between God and the world, the free sovereign lordship of the Creator *vis-à-vis* his creation, which in Hegel takes the particularly clear form of a rejection of everything that is Jewish in Scripture, the revelation to Israel, makes an account of true glory impossible. Not that Hegel embraces a Marcionism which would exalt the New Testament by depreciating the Old for he is equally severe on the Church's divinisation of Jesus, that expression of inappropriately particular attachment to 'this insistently isolated ego with its unique (and thus historical and positive) experience of God'.[121] What the Church should have done was let the divine consciousness of Jesus give way to the all-unifying Spirit, to the total reconciliation that absolute thought can achieve.

> Precisely the *Aesthetics* – one of the richest – and most successful of Hegel's works – is virtually no more than the portrayal of an awareness of the radiant blessedness of absolute knowledge itself, which can comprehend all things (even the most difficult and the most painful), justify all things and approve all things.[122]

And the upshot is that 'the absolute philosopher contains the Word-Spirit in his head, but he no longer sees the man who stands beside

---

119 Balthasar was influenced in this negative estimate of the later Schelling by W. Schulz, *Die Vollendung des deutschen Idealismus in der Spätphilosophie Schellings* (Stuttgart 1955).
120 *GL* V, pp. 573–574.
121 *GL* V, p. 582.
122 *GL* V, p. 586.

him'.[123] It is the cry of human need that tears through the 'web' of Idealism. But however understandable the genesis of Marx's thought, its limitations are palpable:

> Marx ceased to philosophise when he renounced Hegel, and so the question of meaning in its entirety is no longer asked. The fact that man *is*, suffices. . . . The very thing which was alone excluded from the Hegelian synthesis, the people that resists integration into any world-historical synthesis, toppled him from his throne. Marx, however, did not enthrone the glory of God, but once again absolute man as the centre of the world and of being.[124]

When being, then, loses its intrinsic radiance, transcendental beauty is lost to view and aesthetics can survive only as a science – and this by definition falls outside Balthasar's field of enquiry which is the metaphysical *context* of inner-worldly beauty. A beauty which is materially speaking co-constituted by the true, the good and the one could never be this kind of (putatively) exact science. Balthasar believed, moreover, that he could point to certain *aporiai* in contemporary aesthetic theory for which the only resolution is precisely the sort of opening out onto a wider context that transcendental aesthetics provides. Thus for instance, the philosophy of (artistic) 'form' and 'value' raises the question of 'what being as a whole epiphanically heralds and brings into view';[125] the aesthetic deployment of the idea of the 'empathy' which must typify the 'creative artist' returns to the agenda the issue of a metaphysically conceived *erōs*; and the gracious loveliness which escapes exact scientific characterisation yet remains internal to the experience of art is still, even in a disenchanted world, a 'hook' with which the angel draws the bleeding heart towards eternity'[126] (a somewhat overblown metaphor indebted to Claudel).

The Christian as guardian of glory

In conclusion, then: on the basis of these well-nigh three thousand years (since Homer) of reflection, how *should* a Christian see a metaphysics of glory?

Balthasar's answer begins by locating the *sanior pars* of metaphysical reflection, in an account of the 'wondrousness of being', which 'admirable' quality turns out to require from us a fourfold distinction when thinking about this topic. Wonder at being is not just the chronological beginning of thought; it is its permanent state of mind. What we have to do, then, is to explore the implications of that state. At a stroke, therefore, Balthasar would eliminate all necessitarian schemes which may start by recognising how wonderfully ordered phenomena are (and the success of technology is not the least testimony to this) but go on to ascribe such 'beauty' to the necessary laws which hold the world

123 *GL* V, pp. 590–591.
124 *GL* V, p. 596.
125 *GL* V, p. 603.
126 *GL* V, pp. 609–610.

together. To think like that is to remove oneself from the condition of wonder before being, and the concept of beauty at which such thinking arrives is just a totalisation of what is involved in any particular 'beautifully ordered' relationship, and so can never attain the true dimensions of the theme of glory. Reflection must, therefore, find some other starting point.

Balthasar finds this happier point of departure in the contrast between the contingent, even haphazard character of the process of human reproduction, and the mystery that a baby, held secure in its mother's grasp, comes to consciousness through 'being granted entrance into a sheltering and encompassing world', so that, when its own sense of identity begins to develop, it is always as an ' "I" which awakens in the experience of a "thou" '. An infant *playing*, Balthasar thinks, would be an impossible sight if its primordial experience were not (in the widest sense) one of grace. 'Admission' is the first reality it knows (to begin with, indifferently as admission by *being* and by a *human being*), and experiencing itself in this fashion as an object of love, it takes existence to be both 'glorious and a matter of course'.[127] And the person can no more ascribe a necessary character to his or her own existence than to that of the world – the two poles of this first 'distinction'.

But then secondly, there is a distinction between existents (such as myself) and being, for in grasping that there are others like myself, I see that while existents share in being none exhausts it. The 'beauty' of (even) the totality of the things that are does not equal the 'glory' of the being that is outpoured in them. And yet being is found only in existents: in that sense, it is itself dependent and 'non-substantial'. Here Balthasar would correct Heidegger: when considering his celebrated 'ontological difference' between being (*Sein*) and beings (*Seienden*) it is not only being which elicits wonder; it is beings as well.

From this it follows, in a third step, that being as such is no sufficient ground for the way that beings possess essential form. The forms of things, rather, 'bear the mark of an unconditionedly original imaginative power'. It is unpersuasive of the Neo-Platonists to teach that things in their totality are simply the self-explication of being, or of Idealists to treat being as the 'non-subsisting epitome of all entities [actualising] itself dynamically through a world'.[128] We can and should, with the ancients, pay homage to being and its radiance – but we cannot treat it as the *raison d'être* of the world. That would not do justice to the freedom which we implicitly ascribe both to being and beings in treating them as glorious, gracious, rather than necessary. The distinction between the being of beings and their form (that key word throughout Balthasar's aesthetic ontology) means that we must take a step further.

The fourth and final distinction is that between the world and God. Being is not just a given; it is *given*. It is not simply a 'datum', it is a *donatum*, a donation. The sole sufficient ground both for being and for beings in their form-possessing character must lie beyond not only beings but even being. There subsists an

---

127 *GL* V, p. 616.
128 *GL* V, p. 620.

ultimate Freedom which neither being (as non-subsistent) could have, nor the existent entity (since it always finds itself as already constituted in its own essentiality). And so on the one hand, the freedom of non-subsisting being can be secured in its 'glory' in the face of all that exists only if it is grounded in a subsisting freedom of absolute being, which is God; and so, on the other hand, the dignity of an essential form evades being threatened by the encompassing act of being and thus being swallowed up and devoured as an invalid 'stage of being' only if its valid contour can be referred back to a sovereign and absolute imagination or power of creation.[129]

> But if the most precious thing which must be preserved in being can only be preserved by God, viz its miraculous and glorious character, then must not God be pre-eminently the guardian and the shepherd of this glory: in direct contradiction to what the finite spirit imagines as necessity and absoluteness?[130]

That 'absolute freedom' is revealed in its utterly free – spiritual, personal – character only in the Bible. But, it is not enough to interpret God's free action personalistically, as a matter of the inter-subjective relation, simply, between God and myself. Rather – and this is the relevance of Scripture to metaphysics, and metaphysics to Scripture – the 'personal and free depths of self-giving absolute being' are what 'first bring the mystery of creation, the 'fourth distinction', into the light.[131]

And so a chain of self-giving, of outpouring, runs from God to existents – God in his fulness rendering himself 'poor' by communicating being; being delivering itself to existents, and existents themselves experiencing both the power to shelter being and yet also their own limitedness – from which they should learn the lesson that they must let being be further handed on through them, in which alone will they find fulfilment. The analogy of being proves itself to be in the last analysis an analogy of giving, an analogy of love. This is how man, for Balthasar, is, metaphysically, the image of God: the finite subject

> constitutes itself as such through the letting-be of being by virtue of an *ekstasis* out of its own closed self, and therefore through dispossession and poverty becomes capable of salvaging in recognition and affirmation the infinite poverty of the fulness of Being, and, within it, that of the God who does not hold on to himself.[132]

It is at this ontological level (and not just at that of psychology) that election, justification, sanctification and glorification proceed.

If the God–world distinction, understood in this way, is a piece of metaphysics necessary to the understanding of (and in that sense prior to) the biblical revelation, that revelation may also be necessary in practice for the maintenance of just this distinction. Seeing being as derivative,

129 *GL* V, p. 625.
130 *GL* V, p. 636.
131 *GL* V, p. 626.
132 *GL* V, p. 627.

dependent, involves a spiritual difficulty. Adapting the words of the Johannine Prologue about the Baptist's relation to the Logos Balthasar says of being that it is not the light, yet gives witness to the light insofar as by means of its non-subsistence it points to the light. To see being's radiance as a light from the Good beyond even being there is needed a degree of poverty of spirit – what earlier philosophy would call *apatheia* or *Gelassenheit* – but *not* a spirit of renunciation which would harden itself against pain and death, and therefore, adds Balthasar, against love.

> Only rarely do metaphysicians escape this danger, but Christianity by its own nature possesses the power and the responsibility of arming the spirit against this kind of abuse of detachment and to disarm the heart so that it becomes purely receptive – even, and precisely, to pain and deprivation.[133]

A right understanding of the structure of reality is not possible without what Balthasar calls 'metaphysical love'. What a difference there is, after all, between Augustinian *desiderium* – a 'love which powerlessly and longingly yearns, and which disposes itself for the reception of free grace',[134] and the Fichtean 'prayerless self-glorification of spirit'.[135] In Idealism, indeed, metaphysical love comes to an end, and Balthasar finds it unsurprising that in succeeding generations love between human beings becomes something one is supposed to 'see through', in cynical or at any rate melancholy fashion, for 'the glory of love can flourish only within the context of an at least intuited glory of being'.[136] Being and love, inseparable as they are in the 'metaphysical act', stand or fall together.

> Love loves being in an a priori way, for it knows that no science will ever track down the ground of why something exists rather than nothing at all. It receives it as a free gift and replies with free gratitude.[137]

In this sense, the Christian, the recipient of biblical revelation in its fulness, is the 'guardian of that metaphysical wonderment' which is all philosophy's origin;[138] and Balthasar will go further and say, at any rate in our age she is the guardian of metaphysics *tout court*.[139] Metaphysical *erōs* is ordered not to beauty – not to the attractiveness of the world, or the harmony of its inner organisation – but to glory. And it is Christians above all who can grasp this distinction, known though it was to the Greek tragedians and the Virgil of the *Georgics*.

> The special word of God in Jesus Christ ... lays down that the preferred place for the manifestation of God's love and thus for his

133 *GL* V, pp. 632–633.
134 *GL* V, p. 640.
135 *GL* V, p. 643.
136 *GL* V, p. 644.
137 *GL* V, p. 647.
138 *GL* V, p. 646.
139 *GL* V, p. 656.

emergent glory is precisely those areas of darkness which seem to fall out of every aesthetic contemplation. Areas of darkness which are otherwise excluded from any aesthetic view of the world (and thus prove the limitations of these views), or which lead the observer to look with stony gaze at nature and being, themselves as hard as stone, and which now become precisely the critical touchstones of love and glory: both of the love of God which glorifies itself even and especially when it shows its light in the darkness, and also of the love of man, which then corresponds to this aesthetics of God's glory insofar as it recognises God's love there in its highest glory and worships it accordingly.[140]

Christian faith unveils the metaphysical dimension – without being identified with it. It requires Christians, in times above all of metaphysical darkening, to affirm being in a representative vicarious fashion, so that its 'primal light' can shine out for the world. And what this amounts to is something so simple as almost to be commonplace, and yet all-demanding.

His [the Christian's] duty is to experience the presence of absolute love, and himself to actualize it, and to make it visible, within his love for his neighbour; it is his task to effect the miracle of the multiplication of the loaves precisely out of this poverty ('What is that for so many?'). . . . The Christian love for our neighbour is therefore something quite distinct from a good and morally upright model for interpersonal conduct; it occurs always as the focal point, as the demonstration (*Erweis*) and realisation (*Vorweis*) of a love which itself wholly transcends man, and thus also as an indicator (*Verweis*) to that love which man cannot appropriate for himself as it has long since shown itself to him to be that which is ever greater than himself.[141]

This is not moralism, but a way – and the Christian way *par excellence* – of drawing attention to the ontological difference in whose light alone the world can be theophanous. The gratuity of absolute Being is signalled in gratuitous living. And if Christians look, with the Balthasar of Volumes IV and V of *The Glory of the Lord*, down the tunnel of philosophical history they will note how the scriptural revelation of the God who is 'greater than anything that can be conceived' (Anselm) illumines an often dark place.

They will note the extent to which pre-Christian thought in all its complexity preserved an Advent-like openness of the coming of something greater than itself by which it could be determined, and how much post-Christian thought, whether it will or not, has been determined by that which is greater than itself.[142]

---

140 *GL* V, p. 648.
141 *GL* V, p. 649.
142 *GL* V, p. 655.

There is a lesson here for the metaphysician at large:

> the way in which Jesus Christ lives in openness towards the Father and in this openness shows both the supreme exposure of the love of God and the supreme decision of man for God, can cause the metaphysician to ask himself whether he already thinks and enquires sufficiently openly, or whether perhaps he has come too quickly to an end.[143]

---

143 *GL* V, p. 656.

8

⁕

The Elder Testament

The key ideas of biblical aesthetics

The three key ideas of biblical aesthetics for Balthasar are: glory, image and grace.[1] His account of the way they illuminate not only each other but also all reality in the Judaeo-Christian tradition constitutes the biblical and dogmatic substance for which all else in *Herrlichkeit* has been (more than sufficient, the reader may think!) preparation. Though the first volume of *The Glory of the Lord* already gave us the bare outline (without which we could have little sense of what Balthasar was up to in the four volumes that followed), that volume could only be, as he once more underlines, 'provisional' – since the 'form' cannot fully shape the 'theological act' until it is filled with its own proper 'content'.[2] And now for the first time – at least with such clarity – Balthasar tells us that the glory of God is actually nothing other than his divinity itself, and this being so, it must be accorded a constitutive rôle in the making of that act in which theology consists.

> Nothing can be the formal object of the believer's perception of revelation except God *in so far* as he is *God* and not, for instance, in so far as he is the horizon of the world's origin and goal, since in this respect God is the object of philosophy or 'natural theology'. It becomes evident, therefore, that even though God uses creaturely guises to speak and act throughout Holy Scripture, what is essentially at stake is solely men and women's encounter with the divinity or glory of God.[3]

In a German pun untranslateable in English, the *Herrlichkeit* ('glory') of God is both his 'sublimity' (*Hehrsein*) and his 'lordliness' (*Herrsein*), sovereignly in act as these are both in God's being and in his self-disclosure. (The overall title of the English translation of the theological aesthetics, the 'Glory *of the Lord*' does, as already mentioned, the best it can to bring this out.) And so God's glory is what distinguishes

1 *GL* VI, p. 88.
2 *GL* VI, p. 9.
3 *GL* VI, pp. 9–10.

him everlastingly from everything that is not God; it can be shared out only by being shared in – if we may render thus the useful formula *amethektōs metechetai* which Balthasar borrows at this point (as others) from the pagan Neo-Platonist philosopher Proclus. This is God's *aseitas*, his being as *Ganz-andere*, which God can 'communicate only in such a way that, even as it is communicated, it remains his and only his'. And if those philosophical terms sit uneasily at the outset of two volumes on Scripture, precisely, Balthasar immediately states their biblical equivalent.

> In a biblical sense this means that, the deeper a creature is allowed to encounter God's glory, the more this creature will long to extol this glory as being exalted over itself and over all creation.[4]

And in phrases reminiscent of all he had learned from Przywara, Balthasar predicts that the wider open God throws heaven, the more the person peeping in will see grace to be just that – sheer gift, while the better he or she understands the divineness of God the more will they realise that his love surpasses knowledge, as suitable texts from St Leo and the Letter to the Ephesians confirm.

The beginning, then, of the Christian religion is the self-communication of the wholly other God, and its end is the thanksgiving offered by the creature which knows itself to be 'overtaken' by what it has received. Writing in a Western European land two years after the closure of the Second Vatican Council, Balthasar is well aware that many readers will not only comment with Mozart's Papageno 'Das ist mir zu hoch!' (that's above my head!), but treat such metaphysical paradoxes as social irrelevance. And taking the bull of post-Conciliar horizontalism by the horns he warns that by such a reaction a person would have 'stepped outside the proper sphere of revelation'. With one eye, perhaps, on the less happy aspects of Rahnerianism, he explains:

> A Christian encounters his neighbour in a Christian sense only when he has experienced in the 'fear of God' something of the wholly-other measure of the love of the Lord God and then attempts to love his neighbour with all humility according to this unattainable measure.[5]

For – and here Balthasar is at his most Barthian – God's Word and its truth are their own witness: there is no neutral plane where man can dialogue with God on the topics of ethics and religion. Unless one is first overawed by God's divinity all conversation could only rest 'on a foundation of untruth'. And the priority of God's divinity (which equals his *glory*) over the communication he delivers is just what we find in the structure of biblical revelation, at certain crucial moments in the giving of the Word of God.

4 *GL* VI, p. 10
5 *GL* VI, p. 11.

It is significant that at decisive places in Scripture God's glory (*kabod*) manifests itself *before* God's word is heard. This is the case with the great epiphany on Sinai, the vision in the burning bush, the visions through which Isaiah and Ezekiel received their vocations, the visions on Tabor and at Damascus, and finally the apparition of the Son of Man at the beginning of the Apocalypse.[6]

The witnesses of the glory, in these episodes, fall to the earth, their faces cast downwards, or otherwise shielded or veiled, or in Paul's case, with blinded eyes. But all is known to be grace as the Spirit of God brings them from a kind of death once more to life. Nor are these merely isolated – if also, as any student of the biblical history must admit, strategically placed, occurrences.

> The biblical scenes we have enumerated show . . . what happens to every hearer of God's word: he perceives God by being transported outside of himself; he hears and grasps God in and through God.[7]

And so the recipients of these visions of God are 'expropriated'. They are no longer their own men, but are 'conscripted for total obedience' as instruments of the divine Word and action in the *mission* which invariably follows the manifestation of glory. For the epiphany of God's all-holiness not only finds the witnesses wanting; it reveals the wider unholiness of the world which God cannot, without critical judgment, draw savingly to himself.

> It is not possible to enjoy a reposeful aesthetic contemplation of the divine glory, a contemplation that would consider God 'in himself' and thus could dispense with the opposition between God's holiness and the unholiness of the world . . . Glory is the intruding lordliness of him who comes to confront the world, both judging it and gracing it. It is this that distinguishes the biblical reality from the epiphanies of gods outside the Bible.[8]

That Balthasar would have to come to terms with the Old and New Testament employment of the language of glory was, of course, apparent all along. What needs a word of explanation is why he now appends to the theme those of 'image' and 'grace'. These for him are not indeed appendages so much as internally connected ideas. He gives three reasons for including here that fundamental topic of biblical anthropology: man as made in the 'image and likeness' of God (Gen. 1:26). First, adopting as he does Barth's analysis of that much disputed text from Genesis, whereby in constituting man his image God essentially ordains him (and her) to be his creaturely co-respondent, Balthasar maintains that such an action is *par excellence* an expression of the lordship of God. Secondly, if this image (man) is genuinely to resemble its archetype then it must bear

6 *GL* VI, p. 12.
7 *GL* VI, p. 13.
8 *GL* VI, p. 14.

certain traces of glory which is what Psalm 8, one of the few texts of the Hebrew Bible to take up explicitly the Priestly Writer's creation account, will say in so many words. Thirdly, the goal of the 'entire movement of revelation' (and at this point Balthasar lets us see for a moment the full set of cards in his hand) consists in making image (man) and glory (God) coincide in Jesus Christ so that in the embodied human form the supra-formal divine fulness may dwell (compare the Letter to the Colossians 2:9). The incarnation (and atonement) will resolve in archetypal fashion the burning issue of all aesthetics, which is, in Balthasar's opinion, the relation between 'measure' and 'the measureless' – how (so we might paraphrase) an infinite significance may be found, if at all, through a finite vehicle. 'Grace' is, in this context, the missing link: it concerns the shaping of the image to reflect the glory. The grace of the divine giving of the Ten Commandments, for instance, following immediately as this does on the Sinai theophany, reveals how

> human life must be shaped to be considered 'righteous' and 'godly' in God's sense and to be found acceptable and permissible by God – and this beyond the abyss that divides divine standards and claims from inner-worldly and even sinful ones.[9]

A theological aesthetics cannot do justice to such grace on the basis of the Old Testament alone for only in its successor covenant does the image of God come to coincide (in Jesus) with God's Word, and thus become 'subsisting grace', subsistent righteousness.

That statement already assures us that Balthasar will treat Old and New Testaments, however differentiated they may be both internally and in their distinctness from each other, as more primordially a unity, and he now goes on to make this plain.

> The transformation in the idea of divine glory, which runs from the Pentateuch right through to the Johannine writings, is remarkably great, and yet the intermediate steps are so interconnected and they so clearly point to one another that in their very variety these phases constitute a whole, the parts of which support and substantiate one another.[10]

And after showing in summary fashion how the different theological traditions in Old and New Testaments condition, and connect with, one another in this respect, Balthasar finds their confluence in the Johannine Apocalypse and the key to decanting their meaning in the Johannine Prologue. John understands the *glory* which belongs to the Father's only Son as entailing both the fulfilled truth of the *image* and the fulfilled *grace* of the covenant – and by the close of the Gospel which the Prologue opens will be able to 'behold God's glory in the unity of the cross and the resurrection'.[11]

9 *GL* VI, pp. 15–16.
10 *GL* VI, p. 17.
11 *GL* VI, p. 19.

While Balthasar's writing is profoundly indebted to the tradition of the Church, as expressed in the Fathers, the liturgy, Christian art (verbal, musical, visual), the mystics, and the orthodox doctors of all the post-patristic generations, we should not overlook the way he gives Scripture (read, certainly, with an ecclesial temper) the primacy. So much is this so, that in a retrospect on the twelve aesthetic theologians of Volumes II and III of *Herrlichkeit* he can now remark:

> Only biblical theology can and must necessarily become the standard by which to judge the whole range of the historical developments in question, and by using this standard we can see that not all these systems have remained in equal proximity to the source, and that not all of them have portrayed the innermost concerns of biblical theology with equal success.[12]

However, Balthasar warns against treating the theological components found in Scripture as a super-theological system from which subsidiary systems are rationally to be constructed:

> The glory of God's love in Jesus Christ remains the omni-dimensional reality, and its utter transcendence of everything that can be known or systematised can itself be known only very dimly.... It is only the Holy Spirit who can expound, for the consciousness of the Church throughout all ages of history, the breadth and height, length and depth of the glory of God's love in Jesus Christ...[13]

which may well mean that, deaf though we be to the evangelical music of one or another historically given theological aesthetic in the Church's tradition, that music is nonetheless being played.

Old Testament glory

Taking in order, then, the trio of themes Balthasar has identified in biblical aesthetics, glory is, first and foremost, his answer to the question, How can revelation happen? Human creatures, as the history of religions tells us, express their sense of the 'undecipherable Meaning' behind even the apparent meaninglessness of their existence through a huge variety of sacral projections – inventing gods, elaborating qualities for them, ascribing to them actions and giving them words.

> But suppose that these pious attempts of humanity to penetrate into the region of the inscrutable are all pushed aside by a contrary movement whereby the Abyss and Ocean of all reality, on its own initiative, presses in upon humanity in order to disclose itself, in order to reveal itself as 'what' it is: if this *could* happen, how *would it have* to happen?[14]

12 *GL* VI, pp. 20–21.
13 *GL* VI, p. 21.
14 *GL* VI, p. 31.

An answer might begin by noting that typical of beings in the world is their enjoying a mysterious power of manifesting themselves to each other not just in their 'naked existence' but also in their 'potency' – and the latter is often enough something rather spellbinding, as we recognise at once with a 'powerful' personality. And this is something which Scripture grants, referring to it as man's *kabod* – his 'weight', that which makes him imposing. Then the question arises:

> Can we also . . . speak analogously of a *kabod* on God's part, in so far as he, too, in an incomparable and yet comparable manner, manifests and engages his 'I' over against man, along with its own 'weightiness' and spellbinding preponderance?

Since Scripture is in point of fact full of the language of *kabod YHWH*, Balthasar can at once go on:

> If this is the case, then the mightiness of this 'I', which is the Absolute, would at once assume the character of majesty, and its spellbinding power (which holds others simultaneously at a distance from and in close proximity to itself) would assume the character of lordliness and – to the extent that God's absoluteness is here made present – also the character of sublime glory.[15]

But how can the invisible God so show himself? Only through what Balthasar terms a dialectic of 'sensuous indications' (*sinnliche Anzeigen*). Just as one human being will catch another's attention in some way – by a movement of the eye, or gesture of the hand – before beginning to speak, so by some analogous sign or symbol in the realm of the senses the absolute Subject too can call to attention. The sign must not be confounded with the Subject, but neither should the two be separated, though there is a distance between them. The one refracts the Other – and so is but a fractured appearance of it.

> Appearance must always be spoken of in a broken way, especially when what appears is a free subject. It does indeed present itself by appearing but it does not thereby abandon its freedom to be able to appear also in some other way. . . . How much more will this be true of the appearances of the eternally free God, who cannot be naturally contained by any worldly form.[16]

Balthasar refuses, though, to contrast the glory of the sensuous sign as 'concrete' with the 'abstract' glory of the Subject presented – agreeing with Hegel that, contrary to common speech, it is sensory perception that is abstract since 'the content of the being becoming manifest has in no way been integrated in such perception'.[17]

---

15 *GL* VI, p. 34.
16 *GL* VI, p. 36.
17 Ibid.

Balthasar tries to expound what is *truly* concrete in the divine Epiphany in a series of apparent paradoxes which bring out the quality of such fractured yet continuous manifestation: knowing and not knowing, seeing and not seeing, form and non-form, light and dark, abode and event – all culminating in a 'dialectic of fire', the latter one of the great biblical symbols for the divine glory. Thus at the burning bush the divine Name is at once revealed and concealed, for the Hebrew connotes not simply 'I am who am' – the 'metaphysics of Exodus' so important for Thomism – but, in more nuanced fashion, 'I will be who I will be for you'. On the mountain, Moses both sees (in Numbers) and does not see (Deuteronomy) the Lord's 'form'. While the Exodus narrative identifies the vision of God with seeing his 'face' and his glory, it declines to cut the Gordian knot by ascribing to Moses a view of glory rather than of God himself, preferring to capture the dialectic (once again) of the situation by the perhaps deliberately naive image of seeing God 'from behind'. The alternation of light and darkness imagery in the Sinai accounts can give the impression that the 'sensuous indicator' during that crucial epiphany was in fact a volcanic eruption; but as Balthasar points out, the divine fire in the J Source, the Yahwist (Balthasar assumes that the classic late nineteenth-century source analysis of the Pentateuch is correct) does not erupt from inside the mountain but comes down from above like the cloud of the E Source, the Elohist. For Balthasar, the fire is the *tremendum*, the cloud the *fascinosum* aspect of the divine glory. The image of fire takes us deep into not only Balthasar's theology of revelation (the aesthetics) but his theology of salvation (the dramatics) as well:

> The word burns only because God himself burns in his jealousy; and with this a glance into the heart of God becomes possible as never before: if this jealousy communicates so much about his spiritual being, this is because it is the jealousy of a unique election, and this directs us to the uniqueness of the living, free and sovereign Subject involved and already lays open the point where such election can become both a consuming love and the consuming fire of punishment.[18]

As Balthasar's comments on glory as judgment and engracing should have warned us, the landscape of theological aesthetics is not by Watteau.

The sensuous indicators may be equivocal in themselves but they are perfectly clear in the self-revealing God who is their subject. His infinitely exalted being, signalled in the term 'glory' and the family of semantically related terms over which it presides, qualifies everything the biblical God does to express his nature by word and action. Accepting Barth's account of the divine attributes (in their fundamental root) over against that offered by Gregory Palamas (where the divine Essence, unknowable, is counterposed to the knowable divine Energies), Balthasar maintains that 'in his self-disclosure God becomes ever more manifest as the Incomprehensible One'.[19] Under the heading of 'glory', he will now go on

18 *GL* VI, p. 48.
19 *GL* VI, p. 57.

to speak of God's power and word, his holiness, name and face. The power goes with the glory, for it reveals the lordliness of YHWH in nature and history; more profoundly, it means that

> the divine Subject is no empty, indeterminable point; he has the whole space of freedom, which allows him to be present wherever he will: in the world, in his enemies, but especially in the covenant with his chosen friends.[20]

But it would be wrong to think of the word of God as any less lordly, and indeed:

> The signal of the *kabod* calls attention to the fact that the word which resounds is that of the absolute subject whose particular 'cadence' all by itself can sufficiently prove that it is the Lord's.[21]

The word commands; the proper human response is, accordingly, obedience, but not 'blind' obedience, for so Balthasar stresses, even if *the* commandment *par excellence* – the 'one all-encompassing and form-giving commandment' – is that the created 'I' shall be at the disposal of the Uncreated 'I', the reverse side of the coin is the truth that

> the more deeply the human self awakens in the answer it gives, the more boundlessly do the heights and depths of the absolute 'I' open out before him in the glorious lordliness of the divine word.[22]

It is by the 'transport' of the human spirit into the Spirit of God, or (to put the same thing in different words) the engrafting of God's Spirit into man's, that the glory of the word is humanly experienced. In Israel, that datum of religious anthropology called the 'holy' is increasingly concentrated onto God himself since, at least eschatologically, the whole earth is to be lifted out of the realm of the profane – so Zechariah 14:20 where even the bells of the horses are to be inscribed 'holy to the Lord'. And this in turn means, then, that God does not hug his divinity to himself but 'offers it as the space . . . in which Israel is henceforth to dwell after being transported out of itself'.[23] It is by his glory, at the consecration of the Tent of Meeting, that primitive locus of the encounter between God and Israelite man, that God hallows what is not himself. Conversely, to 'sanctify' the holy God (Num. 27:14) is to glorify him – and this is no external act alone, but a making room for his grace. Here too Balthasar can look ahead to the culminating volume of *Herrlichkeit*, on the New Covenant.

> The mutual interpenetration of 'holiness', 'name' and 'glory' will be maintained in the New Testament, where Jesus' task is summarised

20 *GL* VI, p. 54.
21 *GL* VI, p. 57.
22 *GL* VI, p. 59.
23 *GL* VI, p. 63.

as the glorification of the name of the Father. . . , and where he places the prayer for the hallowing of this same name on the lips of his disciples.[24]

What, then, of the *face* of God? From God's countenance there streams, for the psalmist, only light (89:16), yet the Lord's face can either be turned to or away from his people, or indeed his creation – and the notion that when God hides his face everything created dies away, whereas when he shows it again creation springs into new life – is so much the antithesis of the view of God found in deism that Balthasar goes so far as to call it 'anti-theistic'. Balthasar is quite opposed to the exegetical tendency to attenuate the Old Testament concept of 'seeing' God by treating it as a metaphor for participation in the worship centred on ark or temple. 'The mythical analogies are too far removed and the ceremonial analogies too shallow to explain the intensity of Israel's longing to see God.'[25] The passion for a face-to-face vision of God explains, to Balthasar's mind, the equally passionate aniconicism of the Hebrew Bible. And yet by the same kind of reversal of terms we encountered, in his company with St Anselm, he finds that where this tradition of thought culminates, in the letters of Paul, 'seeing God' means above all *being seen*. The apostle of Jesus Christ will 'anchor every aspect of man's vision of God in God's all-embracing and ever-surpassing vision of man and in man's awareness of being thus seen'.[26]

These divine attributes, then, enrich the meaning of the glory that is their common nexus, the glory which flames out in the many theophanies of the Old Testament – many yet distinguishable, Balthasar thinks, as *historical* (above all, at Sinai), *prophetic* (as in the call experiences of First Isaiah and Ezekiel), and *cosmic* (in the nature psalms, Job and the Book of Sirach). But though distinct these manifestations are also intrinsically interlinked:

> In the theology of Israel the historical experience of God occupies first position, serving as foundation for everything else; this experience primarily presents itself as including a sensory element, and then, for further clarification, it draws on both natural and mythical images. The prophetic experience . . . can blend insepar-ably with the historic-natural experience, and the vision of God's glory in the cosmos is at bottom the vision of those who know God's historical word and action and who, with enlightened eyes, see the Creator in the creation.[27]

And if in the course of coming to this conclusion Balthasar had perforce to review a good deal of Israel's imagery for YHWH as the *warrior* Lord of glory, he ends his account of the Old Testament God of glory on a very different note: the rainbow which closes Ezekiel's vision of the brightness of the divine form (1:28). That same rainbow, which the Judaism of post-

24 *GL* VI, p. 66.
25 *GL* VI, p. 71.
26 *GL* VI, p. 73.
27 *GL* VI, p. 85.

biblical times discouraged Jews from contemplating (for one should not seek to see God's glory unless one is sure of withstanding God's holiness) appears for the last time in the pages of Scripture in the Apocalypse of John: the aureole about the One on the throne, bathing even the angels in radiance.

Old Testament man as God's image

To turn from glory to image is to turn from God to the work of God's hands. Consonant with his Barthian view of the *imago Dei* as God's co-respondent in the created realm,[28] Balthasar places marked emphasis on the *freedom* of the human person before God.

> The creature, in its identity as image, can be understood only through its origin from God and its consequent return to God; and yet, we must add at once that the creature is also granted a certain space to be at home within itself before God; indeed, a sphere of autonomy is allowed it over against God that it may be a 'world' of its own with respect to God.[29]

Here, then, Balthasar wishes to lay down a marker indicating a certain humanism (this is after all the lover of Mozart!) before going on to speak of divine grace and the offer of the covenant: in a word, the *initiative* of God in the 'world' of his image. And yet since for Balthasar, humanism – even a humanism lived out in the conscious presence of the Almighty – could never be the last word, he insists on the way the human creature hovers between its being in the image and the call to covenant grace, finding its identity in a *relation* between the two. The Church Fathers (or at any rate many among them) in distinguishing between the *gift of the image* and the *project of the likeness* to God in man well understood the wider picture of the theological anthropology of the Bible even though the Hebrew words of Genesis 1:26, *selem, demuth*, are to the etymologist's eye more or less synonymous.

Balthasar does not spend much time on the question: In what precisely does man's imagehood of God consist? He acknowledges the origin of the key words in a vocabulary for cultic artefacts – a metaphor of the artwork. The choice of the metaphor, moreover, affirms a similarity between God and man which raises man above the other creatures. Invoking the epiphanic quality of the image in antiquity, Balthasar ascribes to the biblical writer a view of man as, accordingly, God's representative, and appeals beyond Protestant dogmatics to Protestant biblical scholarship for confirmation of the claim that there must be here a subjacent ontology. A special relationship must be built into man's being. The deliberative plural of Hebrew grammar ('Let *us* make man according to our image') may originally have reflected the Lord's consultation with his angelic court (in later generations the Fathers will find here an anticipation of the

---

28 This idea of 'responsorial existence' serves as a created foundation for Catholicism's primary understanding of grace as God's calling of man to the supernatural order.
29 *GL* VI, p. 88.

disclosure of the Trinity). Balthasar finds in the phrase a suggestion that a portion of 'heavenly dignity' has been accorded man – which is what Psalm 8, 'You crown him with glory and honour' (v. 6) will go on precisely to say.

> The crux of the matter here is the incomprehensible oscillation between lowliness and exaltation, between God's glory, proper to God alone, and the reflected splendour of the glory that emanates from God and enfolds man, without the human form ever being able to contain this splendour within itself.[30]

It is the whole human being, body and soul, who is thus irradiated by the primal beauty and likewise the whole of human kind, male and female, for as Balthasar is concerned to stress, the differentiation of the human creature into genders proceeds in Genesis not simply at the biological level but at the level of the divine image itself. *Erōs* and beauty belong together in theological aesthetics.

Most of all, however, Balthasar underlines the *provisional* character of man's divine imagehood in the Old Testament. The Ten Commandments would have included no prohibition of images if man's own imagehood were something already achieved; it is the danger that, in his fluctuating condition, he may so impart his own glory to the works of his hands as to lose the glory of God that explains the aniconicism of the Hebrew Bible. If the divine imagehood in man had been stabilised through a full and definitive appropriation of the meaning of its own origin (something that will not, in point of fact, come to pass until the *New* Testament), that *Bildverbot* would not have been necessary.

The unfinished character of man's imagehood emerges from four facets of biblical anthropology which can be expressed in four sets of paired terms – male and female; nature and grace; being and act; Adam and Christ. With regard to the *genders*, male and female are to exist for one another, and yet man is to be the partner of God – a puzzle dispelled only with the New Testament when marriage 'transcends itself to become the virginal and eucharistic reciprocity between Christ as the Man and the Church as the Woman'.[31] In connexion with *nature and grace*, the God of the Hebrew Bible has often to charge man with his sinful condition, yet no return to Paradise is possible – a riddle only solved prospectively when the 'definitive image . . . appears with Christ and gathers up into itself the meaning of all suspended fragments of the image that is man'.[32] And if we put these first two expressions of the incompleteness of the image together we find, in relation to *being and act*, a disparity between on the one hand man's fundamental constitution (the Old Testament never indicates that the Fall has *destroyed* the image) and on the other human agency which is grossly impaired. Only when man is renewed after the image of his Creator (cf. Col. 3:10; Eph. 4:24) – only with the Redemption

---

30 *GL* VI, p. 94
31 *GL* VI, p. 100.
32 *GL* VI, p. 101: here Balthasar's *Das Ganze im Fragment* (Einsiedeln 1963, E.t. *Man in History: A Theological Study*, London 1968) is clearly signalled.

– will 'the tension between being and act be resolved in [Christ]'.[33] And so finally the polarity between *First and Second Adam* turns out to be the all-essential one.

> The Son appears before the whole world as the 'icon of the invisible God, the firstborn of all creation; for in him all things were created' (Col. 1:15ff.), so that henceforth the task at hand is the 'proclamation of the glory of Christ, who is the icon of God' (2 Cor. 4:4).[34]

The christological 'fixing' of the fluctuating image has, most importantly, the effect of redefining the kind of 'dominion' which man, as image of the Lord, is to exercise in the world – a dominion characterised henceforth by the paradox of the God-man who, existing in the divine form, found nothing incompatible therewith in taking on the form of a servant.

The exploration of that christological crowning of the image is, evidently, a task for the final volume of *Herrlichkeit*, on the New Covenant. So Balthasar rounds off his account of the Old Testament foundations by pointing to the liveliness of the (verbal) image of man presented in the pages of the Hebrew Bible. Here his aim is to show that all human life is there, all the dimensions of the *humanum* registered in expectation of their christological reintegration. In all the variety of Old Testament narrative and reflection, we 'see man interpreting himself against the background of God'.[35] Thus from the story of David, Balthasar can conclude:

> This is indeed the theatre of the world; the action, however, is enveloped by a God who not only remains a spectator of the play, in order afterwards to reward and to punish, but a God who, in the actions of his 'images', remains the archetype that also participates in the action, both in hidden and manifest ways. He lets man explore the extremest possibilities of his freedom, and yet he conducts events as a play of his manifold elections and directions.[36]

Within the canon as a whole, from the *Königsnovellen*, the stories of the kings, to Ecclesiastes, the whole gamut of human experience is displayed, but with a particular eye to the human image's refraction of glory. The figure of the king, for instance, makes for both fear and joy, like the *kabod* of God; the wise man is in contact with the manifestation of divine lordship in the order of the world; the author of the Canticle of Canticles explores erotically the beauty bestowed by God. In each case, a dimension of worldly being – power, knowledge, beauty – is at stake, breaking through into the consciousness of the elect nation to ambiguous effect. As Balthasar remarks 'man is released to develop his possibilities with freedom; he is led "on a long leash" . . .'[37] but the upshot of all affirmation of an *autonomous* glory for the world's being *vis-à-vis* God is Ecclesiastes,

33 *GL* VI, p. 102.
34 *GL* VI, p. 103.
35 *GL* VI, p. 105.
36 *GL* VI, p. 114.
37 *GL* VI, pp. 122, 135: the statement is repeated in virtually identical terms.

where 'the scene of the world is all the splendour of spring is inevitably transformed into a panorama of trees stripped naked by the great wind'.[38] Balthasar comments incisively on the author's donning the mantle of Solomon:

> There is a particular appropriateness in this late Hebrew wise man's putting on again the persona of Solomon (1:1, 12) and his book takes pains (ch. 2) clearly to explain the internal logic of this: the experiment in worldly power, worldly culture and worldly enjoyment has led its subject precisely to the point where wisdom bites its own tail and completes itself by abolishing itself. Why? Because the wise man who has tried to comprehend the finite things of the world in all their existential fulfilment has, in fact, been driven about by them in circles and, in so doing, has become aware of his own gyrations.[39]

The conclusion of a scanning of the historical and sapiential books of the Old Testament, seen as the deployment of the virtualities of the human image, can only be that while man is wise enough to register his own finitude, he is impotent to transcend it. God subjected his image to vanity so that through experience, it might learn the need for his grace.

Old Testament grace

The theme of 'grace and covenant', is indeed, after 'glory' and 'image' the last of the trio of basic ideas crucial to a theologically aesthetic reading of the Elder Covenant.

The image of God can give itself unambiguous meaning, and receive its glory, only by recourse to its original. And for this to happen, says Balthasar, the inspired writers were well aware that the beautiful and the true must be complemented by the good.

> This relationship [q.v., that between Archetype and image] can become visible only when . . . the word which God addresses to the world . . . appears as the rich self-disclosure of God that invites us to share in what is his own, i.e. when the abstract 'beautiful' of glory that blazes up and the abstract 'true' of the divine presence are complemented by that 'good' which alone, as grace, makes the beautiful beautiful and the true true.[40]

Just as the truth of God, his truthfulness and reliability, is made known in his grace, so that grace of his has its beauty, which belongs essentially to the divine glory.

> The God of glory is experienced by Israel so powerfully as the God of all grace that the mighty splendour of God is never experienced as being terrible, something from which one is repelled: fear of the

38 *GL* VI, p. 137, with a reference to Ecclesiastes 1:2 and 14.
39 *GL* VI, p. 138.
40 *GL* VI, p. 144.

Lord and love of the Lord shade off inseparably into one another. The light of grace which streams forth from God is not broken or called into question by any darkness; it is pure, unmixed, undisturbed . . .[41]

Beauty and goodness, as truth, like all 'God's qualities', are (to combine the language of the nineteenth-century metaphysics of subjectivity with that of thirteenth-century Scholasticism) 'integrated fully in the freedom of the absolute Subject and become there the radiant fulness of the divine simplicity'.[42]

How does Balthasar present the grace of God? In common with all the theologians of *ressourcement* he emphasises not the 'accidental' (in the technical Scholastic sense) qualification of the human soul – grace as *habitus animae*, but the divine action of which that modification of our being is the result.

The primary meaning of grace must be, not that God bestows on the creature, from the far distance of his heaven, a new 'quality', but rather that he bends down to the earth and raises man up to himself, making space for him in God's own realm in a manner that goes beyond all his qualities and possibilities, in, that is to say, an act of 'rapture'.[43]

And if the introduction of the term 'rapture' (*Entrückung*) there is intended to cast back our minds to Balthasar's initial exposé of the idea of theological aesthetics in *The Glory of the Lord*, his account of 'grace and covenant' by and large follows, nonetheless, the well-trodden ways of 'biblical theology'.

Though admitting that the practice of covenant (in its various forms) in the ancient Near East throws some light on the unique covenant between YHWH and Israel, Balthasar's emphasis definitely falls on the *sui generis* character of the latter.

The 'covenant' is directed exclusively to the sovereign free 'I' who cannot be captivated and controlled through any name used in magic. This is a dizzying, terrifying adventure for the finite human person, something that can be answered only by stripping one's own 'I' down to the naked kernel. This 'I' is demanded and must be presented in sacrifice (all sacrifices in Israel will be borne by the 'intention of presenting oneself in sacrifice'); this 'I' must make the appropriate answer. The prophets will always have this immediacy in view, going as far as the 'Servant of God' who gives the total answer (Isa. 50:4–5). and who thus stands in the direct line to Sinai.[44]

41 *GL* VI, p. 148.
42 *GL* VI, p. 148.
43 *GL* VI, p. 149.
44 *GL* VI, p. 155, with an internal citation of Martin Buber's 1932 study *Königtum Gottes*.

Balthasar explains the coexistence, within the Old Testament Scriptures, of texts which seem to imply, contradictorily, both unconditional and conditional views of the covenant (or covenants) by ascribing to the gracious initiative of God in establishing the covenant community an utter *unilateralness* which, however, founds a total *mutuality*. Israel as a whole, and the individual Israelite within her, must return an obedience of love on the basis of the unsought for divine gift. When the righteousness of the covenant Lord interrupts the order of the world to create salvation, it 'shows all the characteristics of glory',[45] as in for example Psalm 97:6 'The heavens proclaim his righteousness; /and all the peoples behold his glory'. It fits with this that anyone who lives within the covenant must await his 'definitive being right'[46] (his *justification*) as something that can come to him only from God.

In entering the inner realm of the covenant – the sphere marked out, Balthasar says, by such 'totality words' as kindness, favour, mercy, justice, right, truth and peace – the creature is 'snatched' from

its own dwelling in the land of servitude into a 'land' that belongs to God, and all [its] concepts are transformed thereby: a ray of God's glory touches them all, and this makes them more beautiful, but also heavier. Everything is now measured against the standard of divine rightness, [in terms that Balthasar had been taught to use by Péguy] his ethical *justice* and his aesthetic *justesse*. In God's covenant, grace and demand are inseparably locked into one another.[47]

Within what Balthasar terms this 'theological ontology of the state of being taken outside oneself',[48] some – the 'poor of the Lord' of the Psalms and elsewhere – are more expropriated than others, and hence give privileged expression to the covenant knowledge of God. Israelite faith, so understood and lived, takes on a specially pure form, for Balthasar, in the Deuteronomic attempt to lead back

all of Israel's religious instruction, praxis and tradition to the sole fact of the covenant – as election by God in pure love, and as the answering love of the people in obedience – and so to confront the people with equal inexorability with the fire of the primal event by casting them back to it at each moment . . .[49]

And if the faith of the *ebiyon*, the 'poor man', already anticipates traits of the climactically Christian form of transcendence as total dispossession of self so that God in Christ may reign (the 'I live now, not I, but Christ in me' of Galatians 2), it is in Deuteronomy that forms of expropriation point forward most palpably to a new dispensation. This may be negatively,

45 *GL* VI, p. 166.
46 *GL* VI, p. 169.
47 *GL* VI, p. 177.
48 *GL* VI, p. 181.
49 *GL* VI, p. 184.

through the setting of goals that cannot otherwise be attained, or by way of positive prophecy. Thus the impossible attempt to return Israel to a condition of contemporaneity with Sinai is contrasted with the way that in the new covenant the eternal will be 'incarnated in time in such a manner that the historical event can lay claim to validity for all time'.[50] But then again the book positively predicts a new prophet like Moses – which must mean, in context, the mediator of a new covenant, one who, as Balthasar spells that out in a pastiche of Deuteronomic terms:

> will have withstood the glory of God to the uttermost, and what he will communicate will be this glory, no longer as a glory seen by the senses, but in an interpretation of which the innermost principle is: God has loved you groundlessly, so you must love God wholly, be wholly faithful, wholly with God. From Deuteronomy onwards, the true kernel of glory emerges from the *kabod YHWH*: absolute love.[51]

And since for Deuteronomy Moses had to die vicariously, on account of Israel's sin, the portrait of the coming eschatological prophet merges into that of the Suffering Servant of YHWH in Second Isaiah.

But central as Deuteronomy (and the wider 'Deuteronomic History') is for the Hebrew Bible and for Balthasar's own theology of the Old Testament, it is not the whole story. Under the heading 'Reaching Backwards and Forwards' he also considers the way that Genesis in its 'prehistory' illuminates a 'centripetal' movement whereby the lines of earlier history converge on the God of Israel (the theophanies to the patriarchs are functions of something more important, the word of promise; in the Joseph narrative, so transparent is God's loving guidance that he 'appears almost as incarnate');[52] and, before even the pre-history, lays out a primordial history where

> with its eye made keen by the history of the covenant, Israel has been able to distinguish as far back as the event of creation the free, personal God who is not dependent on any matter nor oppressed by any chaos, the God who has created man by admitting him to the intimacy of his own breath and who, despite man's failure, accompanies him even in punishment with forgiveness and grace . . .[53]

And precisely the form of this reaching *back* – with its awareness that 'the intention of the exclusiveness of the covenant was from the outset the inclusion of the whole world at its end'[54] justifies the manner of the reaching *forwards* in a hope for cosmic salvation. Israel was always meant to be the exceptional form of something universal, and so a 'centrifugal' movement from the Deuteronomic centre to the world's end is altogether to be expected, above all in the context of doxology, where a figure such

50 *GL* VI, p. 184.
51 *GL* VI, p. 188.
52 *GL* VI, p. 197.
53 *GL* VI, p. 198.
54 *GL* VI, p. 199.

as the author of Psalm 119 bears witness in rapture to the truth that only YHWH is the king of glory. (Here Balthasar confines himself to the Zion theology of the Psalter and, to a lesser extent, Trito-Isaiah, since he is keeping back the great bulk of the prophetic material of the Hebrew Bible for purposes which will soon become clear.) His last words under the heading 'Grace and Covenant' are devoted, in fact, to the topic of doxology as such. By returning to God his own word in the form of praise, Israel's response to God can itself be revelation, for 'God's revelation contains not only the statement about himself, but also the divinely-constructed dialogue between the partners of the covenant'.[55]

And this thought evokes from Balthasar one of his most remarkable passages on the mystery of Israel.

> Israel's true 'originality' lies in the fact that it is able to transform everything into praise, to invite everyone to join in its song of glorification, and even to draw them into this whether they wish to take part or not. It has employed its best powers in this endeavour, thus the 'incarnation of the word' as holy scripture is Israel's true fruit. Israel's blood sticks to the pages of the Bible. The correctness (*justesse*) of its praise cannot be formally surpassed by the New Testament, and this is why the Twelve of the old covenant stand before God's throne with the same right as the Twelve of the new covenant who are beside him. Israel's apostolate lies in *confessio*.[56]

Israel's delectation in YHWH and his revelation means that for her the *beautiful* can never be disassociated from the *covenant*, and so Balthasar can conclude, in a passage that gathers up the three essential themes of his Old Testament theological aesthetics – glory, image, covenant grace –

> Israel is happy when it sings. By giving back his glory to God, it fulfils itself as God's image, and also understands why it is not permitted to make for itself any carved image of God. In the exchange of the divine word, the archetype and the copy must stand uncovered in each other's presence. Only so is the space made ready in which God's Word can become flesh.[57]

Old Testament obedience

And yet all this is excessively optimistic for Israel broke the covenant, and broke it repeatedly. Glory must be brought into confrontation with evil – which is what the *prophets* achieve. Evil for Israel is not simply ethically or even metaphysically defined (as, for instance, lack or absence of due reality). It is theologically defined as turning away from the covenant God, the 'incomprehensible refusal of an answer of love to the

55 *GL* VI, p. 207.
56 *GL* VI, p. 208.
57 *GL* VI, p. 211.

incomprehensible offer of eternal love'.[58] And the fire of the love spurned and offended burns. Evil as infidelity knows the divine glory as blazing wrath.

What has gone astray as evil must be redeemed, the 'must' here referring to the nature of Israel's Lord precisely in his universal claim. But Balthasar's way of putting this is distinctively his own, and looks forward not only to his ultimate assertions – christological and trinitarian in character – in New Testament soteriology, but also more immediately, to his theology of the prophetic office.

> It is clear for Israel that God does not need to struggle against the realm of death, any more than he needs to exert himself in the chaos at creation in order to bring it into order through his struggle. And yet: can it suffice that Yahweh is enthroned 'gloriously on high', indisputably superior to all the regions of death and of reprobation? Must not God also subdue the chaos from within and from below, in some kind of analogy to the Sumerian and Babylonian concept of the descent of Innana or Ishtar into the underworld – but now stripped of the mythology? Does not God owe it to himself to 'glorify' his glory even there (Ezek. 39:21) and to 'sanctify' his holiness even there (Ezek. 28:22, 25) where all glory has been extinguished since all is empty unholiness?[59]

By the obedience of the prophets, God can, Balthasar explains, 'construct for himself a stairway' that will 'lead him down into the god-less darkness'.[60] The prophets will in some way gesture, in other words, towards the kenotic incarnation, and its climax (or nadir), the atonement.

It is the quality of their obedience to the divine Spirit or word which sets the prophets aside as a group from the generality of Israel. But in Balthasar's presentation their consciousness and manner of life (itself, as he admits, a variable factor) undergoes a mysterious enlargement, leading in the first place to direct encounter with glory (as in Elijah, Micah, Isaiah and Ezekiel) and thence to acceptance of a mission to an errant people. The pathos of God towards his people – love or wrath, mercy or judgment – becomes visible in the prophet's deportment as well as audible in his speech, and in his suffering or even death God himself is exposed to his people's hate. And in all this, there is a decisive shift in the temporal orientation of the word of God:

> the glory of God, which essentially belonged to yesterday for Israel as it celebrated the cultic feasts, can change unexpectedly in the focal point of the prophetic present to become tomorrow.[61]

Balthasar then illustrates this understanding of the prophetic enterprise by reference to Amos and Hosea, Isaiah, Jeremiah and Ezekiel, the author of Lamentations, of Job and of Deutero-Isaiah, where his

58 *GL* VI, p. 216.
59 *GL* VI, p. 222.
60 *GL* VI, p. 223.
61 *GL* VI, p. 236.

account breaks off. He draws attention, but in no forced manner, to the way the prophetic corpus is a house with many doors opening onto the covenant to come – whether this be with Hosea's declaration of the foolish love that would run after a faithless harlot, as God will do on Golgotha,[62] or Isaiah proclaiming that everything that would exalt itself must be humbled till God's sublimeness has become manifest in his judgment,[63] or Jeremiah bearing the supra-temporal burden of divine judgment and divine love, whose mutually conflictual effects in man could only be resolved by the gift to him of a 'new heart',[64] or Ezekiel, the prophet of theophanic glory *par excellence*, whose mission is the union of 'highest spontaneity and highest availability to the Spirit of God',[65] a foretaste of the incarnation. Ezekiel unites the divine wrath as it strikes the faithless people which has sullied his glory, and that corporate Israel on whose head this righteous anger falls.

> He unites these two natures in his person, and their unification reveals the absolute contrast between the transcendent glory of the absolute Lord and the weak, tortured bundle of humanity that Ezekiel is, as he stands at the head of his guilty fellow sufferers . . .[66]

but a step away, via the Suffering Servant of the Second Isaiah, from the New Testament 'Son of Man' himself. The Book of Lamentations would conjure up an 'absolute suffering',[67] measured not by the capacity of the human heart to suffer but by the darkness that comes to be when God turns away from Israel. But the poignant question which emerges from a personal – yet not unrepresentative – experience of that darkness, in the Book of Job, is how there can be so un-aesthetic a disproportion between a man's life and his suffering. And here the indices for the future divine resolution become more telling, for this – the Book of Job – is a

> poetic parable that projects the sketch of an unattainable totality. Its significance is that it rejects every solution that would too quickly transfigure harsh reality, while giving a very exact outline (in negative form) of the conditions of possibility of a redemptive synthesis, which will not be available at any price lower than Job's experiences of abandonment and his terror – and than his total inability to understand.[68]

Only God himself can achieve the unification of godlessness and Glory. Balthasar ends his survey of the pre-exilic and exilic prophets, however, not with Job but with Deutero-Isaiah. In Job (who in any case occupies a no-man's-land between Israel and the Gentiles) one key building-block remains to put in place – the idea of vicarious representation, and notably

62 *GL* VI, p. 245.
63 *GL* VI, p. 249.
64 *GL* VI, p. 262.
65 *GL* VI, p. 266.
66 *GL* VI, p. 269.
67 *GL* VI, p. 279.
68 *GL* VI, p. 289.

of the vicarious representation of all sinners by a 'servant who can embody Israel as the covenant-partner of God. And this 'is the one in whom God "will glorify himself" (Isa. 49:3) but in such a way that the Servant feels "the weariness of futility" and the "fruitless abrasion of his strength" (49:4)',[69] as the divine plan of expiation cuts right through him (53:10) – even if the task of delineating the Servant's image in definitive fashion exceeds the Old Testament's power.

Transition from Old to New

As evening falls on the revelatory epoch of Judaism there are distinct, yet possibly distracting, glimmerings of glory in an otherwise overcast landscape. Devout Jews could look forward for glory, in messianism; they could look upwards for glory, in apocalyptic; and they could look around them for glory, as in the last of the Wisdom books. All three phenomena have positive significance for Christianity in that they provided not only the climate of the incarnation but conceptual and imagistic elements with which to convey the truth of the incarnate One. But considered as Jewish attempts to solve the 'problem' of Israel bequeathed by the major prophets, they are, Balthasar thinks, a failure – a fruitless effort to force the glory of God into the open. Messianism, apocalyptic and wisdom theology are, before incarnation and atonement, premature; they would integrate the shadow side of Israel (and the creation) at a level of insufficient depth. They are in the negative sense stigmatised by Luther *theologiae gloriae*. In terms more personal to Balthasar himself, they tempt us to ignore that necessary twilight which Israel endured for the half-millennium before the Christian era.

> At the end of the long twilight, the seals will be broken for a moment in Jesus the Christ, who accomplishes what is impossible for the Old Testament and reveals the glory of the Father in the abandonment of the Son. But precisely this long twilight, with the distance it created, was necessary in order that the definitive sign of salvation in Jesus might be set up over and in the history of the world and that it could be understood as such (in the midst of the scandal); the twilight is both failure and opening. Failure, because it compels the acknowledgement that man is not able to establish the synthesis of the covenant idea and the historical reality of the covenant; opening, because in the half-millennium of prophetic silence, the event of salvation from Moses via David to the 'Servant of the Lord' draws closer to an historically recognisable form . . .[70]

And so, more positively, the new developments provide features that, if rightly integrated in the opportunity provided by the 'time of silence', can both illuminate the original form of the revelation to Israel and prepare its consummation in the gospel. Consider first *messianism*. If the figure of the king to come, endowed with a maximal share in God's justice and Spirit,

69 *GL* VI, p. 295.
70 *GL* VI, p. 302.

is suitably blended with those of the suffering Servant and the Ezekielic, 'two-natured' Son of Man, messianism can bring out the apocalyptic element in all prophecy, and accentuate the sense that humiliation and glorification are interrelated.[71] *Apocalyptic*, opening up, as in the Book of Daniel, the space between heaven and earth makes available, through the affirmation of a society of angels and humans that spans that space, the idea of a possible resurrection for the dead. Yet the constituent elements of this canonical apocalypse cannot fuse coherently without Christology, while the non-canonical versions which pullulate in the inter-Testamental period are, to Balthasar's eyes, distinctly degenerate, 'making enquiries about the heavenly realm like tourists',[72] and spawning, through their willingness to locate the impious outside the hope of Israel, the (to Balthasar false) opinion that the damnation of some of the brethren, at any rate, is theologically certain.[73] *Wisdom*, in its later incarnations (Ben Sirach and the Book of Wisdom itself), represents a 'broadening out' to the general metaphysics of Hellenism, which would be well enough if at the same time the authors showed an equal passion for an *immediate* relationship with the electing God. And though, once again, Balthasar finds elements that will be serviceable to the gospel – thus, for instance, Ben Sirach's 'compenetrating' use of both sacred and secular senses of *doxa* (glory) and *charis* (grace), and the author of Wisdom's profound thought (refuting in advance Hegel's attack on the God of Judaism as falsely defined *against* what is finite) that the Holy One both remains in himself and yet can be, by Wisdom, 'his own emanation, reflection and image in the world'[74] – his wider conclusion is that the glory these writers praise seems somewhat 'ethereal and bloodless',[75] and from nowhere is that more clearly seen than from the cross of Christ.

> The concealment of the New in the Old (*novum in vetere latet*) remains tightly sealed: the scholar of Wisdom does not put his shoulders under the Cross, but under something that puts him to the test because it 'educates' him in the Hellenistic and late Jewish sense. But fortunately, he knows that the standard in accordance with which and for which he is being educated is no anthropological standard; all wisdom comes from God alone (Sirach 1:1) and therefore remains unfathomable (1:2–3, 6) and hidden (11:4); and what man knows of Wisdom is even now too great for him.[76]

The 'urgent need for glory' which such messianist, apocalyptic and late-sapiential writings attest implies, says Balthasar, a soteriological deficiency of a massive kind.[77] The time of silence, the 'present day

---

71 *GL* VI, pp. 311–320.
72 *GL* VI, p. 324.
73 *GL* VI, pp. 339–343.
74 *GL* VI, p. 362.
75 *GL* VI, p. 346.
76 *GL* VI, pp. 357–358.
77 *GL* VI, p. 365. Balthasar will explain in *The Glory of the Lord*, VII how thorough a 'conversion' these elements need: 'Judaism's three forms of reaching out for the missing glory of God can find a home in the unity of the new covenant only by way of their total dismantling. The image of the coming Messiah must be broken

without glory', enables Israel to take stock of all that God's salvific activity in special revelation has *not yet accomplished*. The historical manifestation of his glory must be transposed into a universal sphere if it is to be the beauty that, as Dostoevsky remarks, will save the world. The inter-Testamental period is, accordingly, a time of testing for Israel.

> Israel's entire knowledge of the glory of God suddenly seems extremely threatened. The object of this knowledge withdraws continually, never becoming a present reality: it is at once past and future. Israel comes from some place to which it can no longer attain, and is en route to some place which it cannot yet reach. What it possesses is a faith – in its election, in the covenant, in the promises – and a hope that inviolably knows that, through all the experiences of night and through all judgments, the end which must necessarily come lies in the gift of the beginning.[78]

Still, there remain in Israel the 'speech event' and the 'blood event': an abiding, indeed intensifying, insistence on the Word of God as that divine event (on Sinai) which generated a language capable of endless interpretative adaptation in saving instruction for the life of the Jewish people (speech event), and an increasing emphasis on the expiatory rôle of the sacrificial cultus (the blood event), for 'true seriousness means commitment of one's entire bodily existence, and therefore includes the blood . . ., in this rich sense Israel is bound to God in blood'.[79] Yet Balthasar finds obedience to Torah in post-exilic Judaism, like obedience to the demands of its sacrificial cultus, to be 'naked' obedience, stripped of the attributes of glory – in which sense 'speech event' and 'blood event' are related.

They find their point of convergence, however, only in the mystery of Jesus which alone can shower them with glory. There 'the two lines converge':

> the perfect vicarious bearing of guilt (going to the point of bloody death) becomes identical with perfect faith or (the same thing) with the perfect acceptance of being poured out into death . . .[80]

And that is simply, at the end of the *praeparatio evangelica* of Judaism, one example of the true 'argument from prophecy' which is, on Balthasar's view, not a matter of understanding sayings from the Old Covenant as made with direct reference to the Christ, but something far more splendid. *The whole history of Israel is prophetic.*

---

through the image of the suffering Servant of Yahweh (which, for the Jews, could not be united to it); apocalyptic must undergo a complete transformation of signification, and be humbled to the role of a function of the dying and rising of the man Jesus; the sapiential teaching can be utilised only when it lets itself be measured against, and brought into alignment with, the scandal of the Cross and of the 'foolishness of God' that appears therein . . .', p. 39.

78 *GL* VI, pp. 371–372.
79 *GL* VI, pp. 391, 398.
80 *GL* VI, p. 400.

This is the covenant history of the chosen people with God, a history with a greatness, a catastrophe and a self-transcendence that drives forward to a fulfilment that cannot be clearly seen or constructed: that which brings fulfilment can be understood only together with *what* it fulfils.[81]

In a way that no Israelite could have predicted beforehand, all the forms constitutive of Israel's faith, hope and life converge upon the midpoint of the Word incarnate, in relation to whom alone their total configuration can itself be grasped as form. The Church of the gospel is legitimated by Israel, and yet what Israel means can only be seen from the Church of the gospel where Israel comes truly into her own.

> A statement such as the one that Christ was to rise from the dead 'in accordance with the Scriptures' (1 Cor. 15:4) presupposes, beyond all individual quotations, a total vision of the relationship between old and new covenants. But the individual images occur to the one who contemplates the Christ event in such abundance and with such facility, and with such a clear appropriateness . . . that the theology of promise and fulfilment, of type and antitype, which comes into use at once, arose as it were of its own accord, as the expression of a great wonderment.[82]

The 'long twilight' of late Judaism was an historical necessity if the qualitatively other, eschatological event of the incarnation, life, death and resurrection of the humanised Word was to be grasped in this relation of fulfilment to all the previous forms, images, types, of Israel.

And of course this does not announce the passing of Israel's revelation but on the contrary eternalises its relevance. There is no Christian supersession of many of the 'elements' that make up the covenant life of the ancient people of God – and this includes much that Balthasar has had occasion to say in Volume VI of *The Glory of the Lord* about, precisely, glory, imagehood and covenantal grace – the three chief themes of the theological aesthetics of the Hebrews. But looking ahead to the final volume, we can say more:

> God's becoming flesh was to be much more 'fleshly', was to penetrate the flesh much more deeply, than Israel could ever dream of. All its historical images were more or less capable of being seen and interpreted in a spiritual sense. But the descent of the divine Word into the flesh will leave all 'form and beauty' behind it and force its way down into an inconceivable formlessness – which for this reason is also incapable of being seen and interpreted, since it is hidden – in order to display the lordship and glory of God even in territory which hitherto had been out of bounds.[83]

---

81 *GL* VI, p. 403.
82 *GL* VI, p. 406.
83 *GL* VI, p. 411.

In retrospect we can see that one 'arrowhead' could have brought to a point all that was perpetually valid in the Elder Covenant. That arrow-head, the Suffering Servant, was however 'blunted' by the 'evasive' post-exilic theologies of glory.[84] And looking back more panoramically still, from the vantage point of the exaltation of that Servant in his true identity as Jesus, we can also see that, since Israel's experiences of revelation were real history, and yet history with the true God, their consummation could only have lain in a descent of the eternal into time which was also an ascent of the temporal into eternity. For such history could never, like secular history, be left behind, yet neither could it be fulfilled in anything short of eternity itself.

> Thus the Old Covenant is inherently oriented towards a temporal ending which, however, cannot be thought of as timelessness but only as the mystery of the coincidence of genuine time and genuine eternity: the entry of genuine eternity into time (the incarnation of God), the entry of genuine time into eternity (the resurrection of Christ and of the creation in him).[85]

So without the New Testament the Old is not, in theological aesthetics, well formed: 'only the entire biblical revelation mediates in a total form what God wanted to communicate to us of his glory'.[86]

84 *GL* VI, p. 411.
85 *GL* VI, p. 412.
86 *GL* VI, p. 416.

9

꿍꿍꿍

New and Everlasting Covenant

New Testament prolegomena

Balthasar's preface to his volume on the New Covenant gives an idea of the subtlety of what he will undertake there. The attempt to write a New Testament equivalent to what he has just completed for the Old is more, not less, difficult for a believing Christian, and that for two reasons. First – and, if we can throw back our minds as far as the opening volume of *Herrlichkeit* we are prepared for this – with that end (and fresh beginning) of time that is the paschal triduum of Christ all our temporal categories enter into crisis, and therefore, to the *prima facie* dismay of the theologian, the destiny of the central figure of the Gospels, and the Christian living that would apply that destiny to the world seem to slip through our fingers. But for Balthasar this is not so much a setback as a salutary warning against excessive cataphaticism:

> It is not our concern to get a secure place to stand, but rather to get sight of what cannot be securely grasped, and this must remain the event of Jesus Christ; woe to the Christian who would not stand daily speechless before this event![1]

And the second reason why this new subject is so hard, if also so rewarding, concerns Balthasar's aim in studying this unique (and to that extent, in the most literal sense, *incomparable*) material. While admitting that none of the theologies internal to the New Testament lack *droits de cité* there, each making its own contribution to the Church's entertaining of revelation, Balthasar wants to show them all as positioned on a trajectory whose final New Testament expression is Johannine (he is thinking here, I believe, more of the place of the Johannine Apocalypse – so important to the theological dramatics – in the canon than of the chronological dating of the Fourth Gospel, though the latter is not excluded). At the same time, he wishes to regard the 'categories' of Johannine theological thought (as of all its New Testament neighbours) as simply means to an end, that end being the reality of God, in the endless meditation of the Church.

1 *GL* VII, p. 10.

211

These caveats entered, he begins, in his own metaphor, the final stage
of the ascent. With trepidation, for now he has to describe the One who
receives the 'entire inheritance' (Heb. 1:1), in whose case the distinction
between the 'archetype of divine glory' and its 'reflection on the human
image' is transcended in the single person of the Word incarnate, even
though the two natures are, as the celebrated Chalcedonian formula has
it, altogether unconfused in their unbreakable union.[2] And not only the
incarnation will be involved, but the resurrection too, in which the man
who not only represents but *is* both God and the world rises into life
eternal. Here the basic laws of transcendental aesthetics reach their
astonishing fulfilment and more than fulfilment. For not only is the
general principle that the more transparent to absolute being's radiance
a form is, the more precious it is, triumphantly vindicated in an unsurpassable way. More than that, it is fulfilled in a way which leaves the
metaphysician – and here we mean the practitioner of a sound, correct
and otherwise adequate metaphysic – gasping.

> This general 'metaphysical' law is so superabundantly fulfilled
> through the unique event, the initiative of which lies in God's
> absolute freedom, that it is totally subjected to criticism [Balthasar
> refers ironically to Kant's would-be sifting of metaphysics, and to
> the well-known exigencies, likewise, of the historical-critical
> method]: the One, whose name is Jesus Christ, must go down into
> the absolute contradiction of the glory of the Lord, into the night of
> abandonment by God and the formless chaos of Hell, so that,
> beyond everything that man can see as form, he may be and
> establish the imperishable and indivisible form which joins God and
> the world in the new and eternal covenant.[3]

Here Balthasar looks for support to the conclusion of his own survey of
Western metaphysics: divine reality, like reality as a whole, requires that
poverty of spirit which is the peculiarly fruitful evangelical version of
Gelassenheit. And perhaps, in that spirit, he too can become a 'simple eye'
that will glimpse something of the cognate simplicity which the multiplicity in the final form of revelation attests. This is the notion of
Einfaltigkeit, of a unity unfolding itself in a manifold which in turn can be
made to return to a unity, an idea Balthasar invokes most fully in the essay
collection on the unitary self-identity of the Church's faith which bears
that name.[4]

In any case, the form taken by God in Christ in the definitive covenant
union with man in Christ *has to* exceed our understanding or it would not
be divine. To realise that, we can be dispensed from putting questions
about the historicity of the Church's Jesus and just ask ourselves what,
phenomenologically, such a form would have to be and do for us were it
to measure up to this 'job-description'. Evidently, such a form would of
its nature disclose to us as nothing else in the world can that 'supra-form'
which is the divine Essence itself.

2 *GL* VII, p. 13.
3 *GL* VII, p. 14.
4 *Einfaltungen: auf Wegen christlicher Einigung* (Munich 1969); E.t. *Convergences: to the
    Source of Christian Mystery* (San Francisco 1983).

Although God does not need the form of Jesus Christ in order to be the perfect triune God in himself, and thus does not achieve his own full reality through the world, there is nothing accidental to his act of making himself known in Jesus Christ: what seems to us to be 'the accidental truth of history' is the revelation of his absolute freedom, as this is in God himself, the freedom of eternal self-giving out of unfathomable love.[5]

At the same time, there could be no more ultimate justification of the world's being than to say that its right to existence follows from its incorporation in the eternal dialogue of Father and Son in the Holy Spirit. And so we should *further* expect that

the arguments of New Testament theology all have this structure: they point to an unsurpassable *rightness*, without giving reasons for the articulations of the form of revelation in accordance with the style of human logic through 'necessities', for the whole form has its being, fresh in every single one of its articulations, in the element of gratuitous love.[6]

And, in both respects, where better than in the kenotic yet exalted, incarnate trinitarian Word *could* we see the glory of God – whether, in the manner of Greek theology, suffusing Christian doctrine as a whole or, in that of Latin, radiating out into its many articulations from Christ as its centre? In this widest possible perspective, what warrants the exclamation 'Beautiful!' when looking at the form of Christ's being and work will not be so much the harmony between Old Testament promise and New Testament fulfilment, but the hope of the fullest manifestation of glory in that heavenly transformation of the world which we call the kingdom.

All this was well-spotted by Karl Barth in the section of the *Church Dogmatics* on the glory (and hence beauty) of God; but Balthasar wants to reappropriate it in his own way. And this means, most immediately, against the background of the theological aesthetics of the Old Testament as he has described it, culminating as that description did in an account of the 'present day without glory' of Judaism between the Testaments.

As we saw in the last chapter, it is only proper that there should be a pause, a 'caesura' between the Old Testament experience of glory and the New – both to allow the contemplative reappraisal of the divine *kabod* in the Hebrew Bible and to sketch out the fuller dimensions the Jewish experience of glory would need to take on were it ever to come to fulfilment. And what we find in the Synoptic Gospels is precisely, so Balthasar claims, the sense of a new start in the perception of the divine 'weightiness' – this is how he interprets the 'astonishment' and even 'astonishment beyond measure' which greets in St Mark's Gospel Jesus' display of potent authority in teaching and miracle-working.

5 *GL* VII, p. 17.
6 Ibid.

Only after the pause that the Synoptists have thus inserted, can John consider the transposition as fully achieved, and lay claim once more to the word *doxa* wholly for the New Testament glory (John 1:14): so much so, that he explains the vision of Isaiah in the temple (and thus the *doxa* of the old covenant) as a proleptic seeing of the glory of Christ (12:41).[7]

And John casts back the origin, *archē*, of the glory of Christ to something more foundational (even) than Sinai: to the trinitarian love itself (1:1).

Balthasar's 'programme' in this concluding volume of *Herrlichkeit* will be: first of all, to consider him to whom the name of glory is to be applied, Jesus Christ; secondly, to investigate the application of that name; and thirdly, to explore the world's response, as the New Testament portrays it – the 'glorification of the glory'. That concluding section on 'existential glorification' will show us, Balthasar predicts, how theology and anthropology are coinvolved.

> Where man is so 'dispossessed' through God's transcendent love that he himself is empowered to genuine transcendence, he wins access to his own true being, which was intended for him always.[8]

We would not be far wrong in seeing here an oblique answer to Karl Rahner's less salvation-historically determined version of the same interrelation – a sign perhaps that in his aesthetic Christology Balthasar is also addressing alternative or even counter theologies on offer in the market-place of the contemporary Church.

In the first, sheerly christological section of this tripartite closing volume, Balthasar divides what he has to say under five headings. After, first, considering the prelude to the public work of Christ constituted by the emergence of John the Baptist and the Baptism of Jesus at the hands of John – to which Balthasar's comments on the infancy Gospels (before) and the temptations (after) are appended, he offers his readers, second, a hermeneutical theory of how he reads the Gospels – a justification of his methods. Thirdly, he confronts head on the claim that, in St John's stunning language, 'The Word was made flesh', prior to, investigating, fourthly, the unique mode of inhabiting time which was Christ's and lastly, that supreme crisis into which his time entered with the cross and descent into hell. (The reader may recall that at the outset of the theological aesthetics, Jesus' sense of time and the *pro nobis* or public significance of his dying were selected as the keys that gave preliminary access to the uniqueness of Jesus.)

A New Testament prelude

In the 'prelude' to the public ministry, Balthasar presents the holy Forerunner and Baptist John as a real renewal of the classical prophetic

7 *GL* VII, p. 27.
8 *GL* VII, p. 29.

faith of the Old Testament yet someone who, in himself, is impotent to gather together the many pieces of the Elder Covenant's jigsaw.

> No one, not even the Baptist, could unite the many faces of the God to come found in the Old Testament, into one single face: wrath and absolute division are coming, the corn and the chaff will be separated in the wind of God – and yet the commission to make a way for God in the wilderness is a call of salvation, the return home from exile with the God who goes ahead through the wilderness to reach the homeland.[9]

And that will mean, above all, that John could not put together the two key pieces of a 'synthesis possible for God alone, yet absolutely indiscoverable for man':[10] namely, both the divine Word in its project of establishing righteousness on earth, and the surety from the side of earth that his will *shall* be done – the providential emergence of a figure who can stand guarantee for the covenant, by embodying in definitive fashion the functions which biblical Judaism ascribed to 'go-betweens' (be these judges, kings or prophets) on the model of Moses; to the priest of the sacrificial cultus, and not least, to the sacrificed animal 'whose blood flows in atonement, and which is consumed in the whole human offering to the glory of God'.[11] How could the Baptist, even if in him prophecy spoke again in all its ancient urgency, 'synthesise' God's own Word with his suffering servant, the atoning human mediator? For it is in the personal union of the Logos with the man Jesus, and the vicariously substituting death from love of the resultant God-man that the wrathful judgment and merciful salvation of the Father will become one.

John cannot offer the synthesis of judgment and salvation, but only a halfway stage from the one to the other. Appealing both to the twentieth-century German exegete Joachim Jeremias and the fourteenth-century Byzantine fresco of the baptism of Christ at Mistra in the Peloponnese, Balthasar positions the baptism John practised betwixt and between 'the Flood or the Red Sea in which men drowned, and the Christian eschatological sacrament of salvation'.[12] Nonetheless, John's position is crucial, since in his *recognition* of Jesus' rôle

> he is himself the old covenant which transcends itself, and in this act of transcendence discovers the new covenant which already lay hidden in it, . . . and precisely in the act of giving itself up and disappearing and making room is taken over and given an interpretation by the new covenant.[13]

Jesus in turn recognises John's martyr fate as the signal for the beginning of his public ministry: suffering in obedience is the unmistakeable hallmark of those called to represent the divine pathos in the world. In

9 *GL* VII, p. 47.
10 *GL* VII, p. 33.
11 *GL* VII, p. 34.
12 *GL* VII, p. 46.
13 *GL* VII, p. 49.

this, John is the new Elijah, which means not only that classical prophecy speaks again, but that – in accordance with the popular belief in Elijah's rôle in the consummation of God's plan – John sums up his predecessors. Their voices, as Augustine says in his wonderful *Sermon* 288, cited by Balthasar, resonate in the sound-chamber of John's speech, for he bears the *persona* of them all. Jesus too, the Word, accepts a place in the series of prophetic destinies not however, merely to echo them but in likewise 'assuming them all at once' to 'give them a fulfilment that lies beyond them'.[14]

Jesus makes his own epiphany, on Balthasar's reading of the fourfold gospel, in terms of a triptych of scenes: here the baptism is central but it is flanked on its farther side by the narrative of the temptations 'in which the abyss of the physical water changes into the spiritual abyss that interprets it',[15] and on its near side by the infancy Gospels of Matthew and Luke. Everywhere an impelling divine Spirit and a responsive human obedience make their presence felt. But what these powers of initiative and response bring about is a recapitulation of salvation history as in the theophany of the Jordan the promises to Israel are gathered up (at once from above, by the Spirit, and from below, by human obedience) for their fulfilment.

If for Balthasar the central scene in Christ's earliest epiphany is his *baptism*, this is because, in the first place:

> Jesus' descent into the river is at one and the same time solidarity with all who confess their guilt and dive into the waters of judgment and salvation, and – as solidarity – obedience to the voice of God which sounds forth from the prophet's voice, and this obedience in history.[16]

That combination of obedience and solidarity tells us in turn that incarnation is 'the encounter, to the point of identification, of the Israel who has been made ready and the God of the covenant who descends to Israel'.[17] Not that the divine address to the Christ who reascends from the waters ('This is my beloved Son') is an extract from a treatise on the Trinity (no more is it a proclamation of adoptionism). The divine voice speaks of soteriology – by allusion to the Servant of YHWH, the 'concluding image of the old salvation history'.[18] But the descent of the dove onto the Servant tells us that this obedient ransomer of the people will be limitlessly filled with the Spirit in contrast to the partial measure served out to the prophets. As the One baptised in the Spirit Jesus will himself baptise in fire, and this gives Balthasar his final theme in the theology of the baptism: Jesus' mission is to be a holocaust in the fire of God's wrath, the 'Lamb' of God (John 1:29, 36) – that Deutero-Isaianic designation of the Servant (Isa. 53:7).

14 *GL* VII, p. 50.
15 *GL* VII, p. 54.
16 *GL* VII, p. 56.
17 Ibid.
18 *GL* VII, p. 57.

To the baptism scene the portraits of the *infancy narratives* just had to be added, maintains Balthasar, if the idea that there could be something *fortuitous* about the baptism was to be excluded. While the two family trees, in Matthew and Luke, carry the notion that Jesus would be recapitulating all Israel, the same point is conveyed more impressionistically in Luke's stories of the childhoods of John and Jesus: compared by Balthasar with a bud that displays its form only on opening, which it will do in the commissioning at the Jordan. And here Mary's place is key. She is the embodied 'daughter of Zion' of the Hebrew Bible, and at the annunciation the divine overshadowing makes her the *living* ark of the covenant where the Glory dwells. At the visitation she brings the quickening Spirit to her cousin Elisabeth and so to the forerunner John. And as to her relation with the Fruit of her womb, that cannot be evoked, Balthasar maintains, without reference to the theme of her 'pre-redemption' through the Immaculate Conception. An adequate correspondence (note here the recrudescence of the language of aesthetics) between the faith of Mary/Zion and the Word of God coming to take up his abode there is thinkable 'only on the basis of a purity bestowed on Mary, a purity which owes its origin to the Source of all purification, which is to flow down from the cross'.[19] Luke's story is 'supple' enough to leave room for that.

In that Lucan appendix to the infancy Gospel telling of Jesus' loss and finding in the temple, however, the theme of the hard obedience of Jesus makes its appearance, and with it the 'dream-like' glory of the nativity and the encounter with Simeon gives way to the 'real presence of . . . the "weight" of God',[20] and the sword of the Word begins to cut through the soul of the Mary who is also Zion. The motifs of suffering and persecution-to-come are predominant in Matthew's version of this flanking panel of the 'triptych'.

On the far side of the baptism, comes the facing picture of the *temptations* of Christ. Satan is allowed to probe the depth of the obedience through suffering which Israel ought to have rendered as servant and son but which now falls on her Messiah. As anticipation of Christ's passion, the temptations express

> the essence of the Covenant, stripped of all accretions: on the one side is only God, the 'highest good' with no earthly reward, God to whom one must adhere only because of God himself – on the other side, the pure obedience in faith of the partner, who wagers absolutely everything on the God whose covenant he enters, because God has laid himself bare to him, even to the depths of his heart, and has made known to him, in his loving election of him, the incomprehensible weakness of his condition as one bound to men.[21]

By identifying himself absolutely with the divine Word, the obedient Jesus annihilates any distance that may remain between that Word and his human mediation.

19 *GL* VII, pp. 63–64.
20 *GL* VII, p. 66.
21 *GL* VII, p. 73.

New Testament principles of interpretation

However, Balthasar will not present the Word made flesh the true bearer of glory, in his mission, until he has duly expounded the 'hermeneutic', or interpretative basis, of his reading of the Gospels at large. If the New Testament presents itself as fulfilment of the Old this is not, for Balthasar, because the preaching of Jesus simply rounds off – and in this sense fulfils – the teaching of the prophets who preceded him. By foretelling his own death (which no prophet had done), and consciously taking death upon himself, Jesus 'displaced' onto that death the full burden of his actions and words – actions and words in which, moreover, he 'appointed himself as the standard gauge of the Law',[22] raising himself above both Torah and its giver, Moses. Indeed, inasmuch as his fulfilment of the Elder Covenant arises harmoniously out of the promises made in the latter so straightforward a completion is – Balthasar goes so far as to say – quite secondary. To bring out the rupture between the Covenants, the amazing, wondrous quality of the 'fulfilment' in question, he writes:

> The death of Christ is . . . silence, the silence and death of God as the fulfilment of the speaking, promising, living God. . . . Its truth does not lie primarily on the level of . . . the comparison between the form of the promise and the form of the fulfilment, but on the level of an invisible collision of the absolute weight of God with what is other, with what has nothing in common with God.[23]

Only through the formlessness of the disaster which overtakes Jesus are the images of the Old Testament freed to reconfigure themselves in relation to this strange climax – itself an extraordinary testimony to the 'power of the *triduum mortis* to bestow form'.[24] When the Word falls silent, the true message is communicated: the message of 'the heart of God, broken open',[25] in the wounded side of the Saviour's corpse. Only so does Jesus become the 'synthesis' of the Scriptures. The 'unifying impetus of his death'[26] as the covenant with Israel's true goal, makes him efficaciously the Word in relation to whom all the previous words of God can be heard as they were meant.

It is in the light of these affirmations that we must understand the distinctly limited rôle Balthasar will accord the historical-critical method in theological aesthetics. That method

> maintains its theological justification as long as it lets itself be understood, and understands itself, as a moment in the process whereby the intuition of faith comes to itself. [But] historical-critical exegesis is substantially incapable of explaining the absolute newness that comes into being through the synthesis . . . ; it is

22 *GL* VII, p. 80.
23 *GL* VII, pp. 81, 83.
24 *GL* VII, p. 84.
25 *GL* VII, p. 86.
26 *GL* VII, p. 87.

incapable with its own methods of seeing the synthesis at all, for this act of seeing presupposes the eye of faith.[27]

And what the eye of faith actually sees is the *novelty* of Jesus Christ crucified and risen, in accordance with the Irenaean dictum, that 'he brought all newness, by bringing himself, who was foretold'.[28]

That 'novelty' means the pouring forth of the glory of God onto man, and hence the recasting of all (philosophical and) theological aesthetics.

> Who could have had an inkling that, by bringing himself as newness, he would make a breakthrough to a wholly new image of God – to its true glory, of which the *kabod* of old was only a shadowy pre-figuring – and to a wholly new image of man – and the gleam of glory of old (Psalm 8) was likewise only a 'reflection of the coming' image of man?[29]

In the *New* Covenant, what was never dreamed of by Israel has happened: the Lord, united with the Servant, is not ashamed to call those in human flesh and blood his brethren. The Word, becoming immanent among the people of God, furnishes that people for the first time with a transcendent Head. The body of the new Israel, the Church, and thus the existence of each member of that body *qua* recipient of the New Covenant, derives from the Head, and takes its form from him, as the Pauline letters bear witness. Being one flesh, Christ and his new people can be spoken of, then, as groom-with-bride. (To speak of the Church as the 'people' or 'house' of God after the incarnation can only be done, Balthasar thinks, analogically – hence his criticism of the formulations of *Lumen Gentium*, the Second Vatican Council's Dogmatic Constitution on the Church, in this regard.) And the bride here must be the *spotless* bride on which Ephesians waxes lyrical.

> Now that the righteousness of God has become man in Christ, the exact response (*justesse*) that corresponds to the incarnate righteous-ness of God (*justice*) is required also from the bride that is his body.[30]

Somewhere in the realm of the Church there must be, in other words, a fiat with 'no internal boundaries', made 'in the name of all mankind', and one that 'goes all the way to the end with God's Word in unreserved agreement',[31] and this is our blessed Lady, who must, be, therefore, the principle of the Church, and the 'core' around which the structure of the corporate ecclesial recipient of the revelation of the New Testament is constituted. That recipient *can* be described 'statically, as "the Church of Christ"', but in fact exists only in a perpetual passage from the particularity of Israel to the universality of the human – and indeed the cosmic – world.

---

27 *GL* VII, p. 89.
28 Irenaeus, *Adversus Haereses* IV. 34.
29 *GL* VII, p. 89.
30 *GL* VII, p. 94.
31 *GL* VII, p. 94.

> This visible Church is constituted in its kernel by the summons to
> follow Jesus, and thereby is both a training by Jesus in the perfection
> of the faith of the Old Testament, and a training which is so much by
> Jesus that he is the one who has authority as custodian and mediator
> of this faith; and thus obedience to God modulates unnoticed into
> obedience to him, and the proclaimer Jesus modulates unnoticed
> into the proclaimed Christ[32]

– though, as Balthasar stresses, Jesus commands in so total a way only
because he obeys the Father so totally through the Spirit.

> If the Church found itself after Easter, at Pentecost, filled with the
> Holy Spirit of God and of Christ, this means that it grasped precisely
> the spirit of the universal mission of Christ based on his universal
> love to all (and therein to me), that it felt that this had been given to
> it and said yes to the gift. . . . Thereby, in the daily living out of love
> to him and to the neighbour, the Church after Easter brings to its
> goal the logic which had begun before Easter in the act of 'leaving all
> things (for his sake)'. This, and nothing else, is the Church, whether
> considered statically or dynamically.[33]

It was only natural, then, that the post-Easter Church began to work out
the filaments of connexion which join the events and texts of the Old
Testament to Christ, and his pre-Easter sayings and doings to each other:
all could be co-ordinated in the light of his pasch.

And that is as much as to say: in the light of that powerful love which
the 'new' *kabod* has disclosed as its own essence. In the unfolding of the
Church's faith, from the apostles to the Fathers, the rôle of knowledge,
Balthasar tells us, is to make present the 'central mystery of love'[34]. That
programmatic statement serves more than one end. It suggests a way of
grounding the rights of authority *vis-à-vis* knowledge, prepares us for the
fact that dogmatic truth will always be found only in an ecclesial context,
and explains the literary peculiarity that in, for example, the letters of
Paul, doctrinal and exhortatory styles of address interweave. Gospel and
Church, in Balthasar's hermeneutic, are mutually interpreting. At least
allusively and proleptically, the gospel tradition presents Christ as
surrounded by the Church of his disciples, and the Church repays the
compliment by producing Scriptures as the 'spontaneous expression of
its experience of the in-breaking of absolute love'.[35] The Church, in her
succeeding, post-biblical generations of preaching and teaching, tries to
live up to this model of her constitutive generation by exploring further
the treasures of wisdom and knowledge hid in Christ (as well as by
defending the same riches from misprision). The same key idea of the
manifestation of glory as love also throws light on the *structure* of the
Church (and not just the content of her message). The love of God in

32 *GL* VII, p. 95.
33 *GL* VII, p. 97.
34 *GL* VII, p. 99.
35 *GL* VII, p. 100.

Christ is incarnate, eucharistically present, in the 'womb' of the Church, in those inner depths of hers where she is 'bride, wife and mother'.[36] But whereas personal values ('subjective spirit' in the Hegelian language Balthasar oftentimes makes his own) in all other contexts suffer at any rate a degree of denaturing when they enter the framework of institutional living (and become 'objective spirit'), with the Church this is not so. Her corporately sponsal character achieves outward translucence in a 'holy city' of which the papal and episcopal office-holders are the sacred guardians: 'Peter' serves 'Mary'.

Naturally, the author of *Schleifung der Bastionen* – Balthasar's plea for a radical 'shake-up' of pre-Conciliar Catholicism through a razing of too high bastions between Church and world – does not mean to say that the Church is thus perpetually guaranteed against all need of reform, not least in her inherited theology. But the question is, In what direction should reform – and hence theological renewal – be sought? Balthasar writes:

> It is in the continuity of her looking to the mystery of the Trinitarian, incarnate love of God that the Church has her ontic, historic, theological and existential, unity: this is instituted in her depths as 'immaculate' and 'infallible', but in the empirical form of the Church it can experience threats and distortions which disfigure it so that it is unrecognisable. Every reform that strives to recover the unity of the subject that receives revelation must hold fast to what has been instituted in the Church (once for all in Cross and Resurrection, and ever new in the event of the Eucharist), which belongs immediately to the event 'than which nothing greater can be thought'.[37]

At the same time, this orientation to the divine and historic Source of her faith (Church reform and theological renaissance is always return to the origins) does not mean that here there is nothing new under the sun. What is given with the Church's founding cannot be used up or exhausted, but on the contrary, the more it is lived and reflected on, above all by the saints, the more inexhaustible – *and therefore, the more at home in the future* – it appears.

Because love-*agapē* is greater than knowledge-*gnōsis* it is only right that there should be a plurality of Gospels, a multiplicity of New Testament theologies: these testify to that very inexhaustibility of the true 'mid-point'. Later theology can only prolong this essential feature of Christianity as such. The Church of apologists and fathers takes the crucial step from the thinking of the Bible to the thinking of the world, both challenging philosophy and yet (after the resolution of the Gnostic crisis) harnessing it to revelation's service. Not irrelevant to Balthasar's aims in the remaining pages of *Herrlichkeit* is his balance sheet of the loss and gain involved. *Gain*, for the Councils from Nicaea I to Chalcedon ensures that

---

36 *GL* VII, p. 101.
37 *GL* VII, p. 102. Compare H. U. von Balthasar, *Schleifung der Bastionen. Von der Kirche in dieser Zeit* (Einsiedeln 1952; 1989[5]; E.t. *Razing the Bastions. On the Church in this Age*, San Francisco 1993).

the distance (recognised only with the help of the Bible) between the living God and his creature can be decisively . . . ensured, and can be recognised in the final christological unifying . . . in the reason for its existence – as the indispensable presupposition for the unifying work of absolute love, which can share itself and mark its name on what is other, what is not love, only on this basis . . .[38]

And moreover:

No matter how defective philosophical concepts may always remain in the attempt to come close to this mystery and describe it . . . , the translation of the conceptuality of the . . . Bible which serves predominantly to speak of events in history, into a conceptuality of the fully open horizon of being, behind which our questioning cannot penetrate, was a valid expression of the fact that, with Christ's death and Resurrection and with the outpouring over Church and world of the Spirit who is within the Godhead, the highest disclosure of absolute being (inaccessible to philosophy) has taken place.[39]

Loss because there might in the future be those who

could no longer distinguish between the level of the living revelation of the old and the new covenants, and the level of the theological expression of this revelation, as though any theology, even a conciliar theology or (above all) a theology of 'definition', could ever be anything other than a pointer to the reality which, by definition, will always elude every conceptual formulation.[40]

And this tells us that the theological rereading of the New Testament Balthasar is about to give us will respect that necessary duality whereby the best of the Church's thought is *simultaneously* conciliar-doctrinal *and* exegetical-biblical. He will be guided by dogma, but what he will contemplate is Scripture. In this regard, he ranges himself with that stream of theological interpretation of the Bible – respectful of the letter, yet absorbed by its (internally differentiated) spiritual meaning, christological, tropological, anagogical – which flows from Origen. According to that exegesis, a 'threefold transcendence' arises out of the events of biblical history:

opening out upon Christ as the presence of the triune God in the world, upon the receiving subject Israel – Church – myself – cosmos, and upon the consummation of Christ in his total body or kingdom.[41]

It is difficult to think Balthasar is not envisaging how his own theological aesthetics (above all in this its closing volume) will be viewed by spiritual posterity when he writes:

38 *GL* VII, pp. 106–107.
39 *GL* VII, p. 107.
40 *GL* VII, p. 108.
41 *GL* VII, p. 109.

This biblical theology has at its heart the leap first from promise to fulfilment, but more deeply, from death to resurrection, and draws its life from the constantly renewed accomplishing of this leap; this theology can and must dare to offer itself to dogmatic systematics as its inner form.[42]

It is as thinking which reproduces the exaltation of the One who was crucified that such theology can serve ('tropologically', as a spur to our living) the life of corporate proclamation and individual witness in the Church, and treat the Christ-event ('anagogically', for it is a spur to our hoping) as always in front of us as 'our future and the future of the world'.[43]

Despite his high doctrine of the significance of the theological plurality in Scripture and Tradition, Balthasar is not to be counted, however, among those who are happy to see the unity of the canon shattered into a thousand fragments, suitable reading for the members of an irremediably pluralistic Church. The plurality Balthasar recognises is, rather, limited and coherent: coherent because limited, limited because coherent. He speaks of the *interrelation* of the New Testament theologies, of their mutual greeting and acknowledgment, even in the concern of one to balance a seeming unilateralism in another. Above all, they are united in a 'common looking upwards to the one personal centre of all theologies, to Jesus the Christ of God, the appearing and exposition of the love of the Father'.[44] The genesis of the New Testament is traceable to the earliest lapidary formulations of dogma (Jesus is Christ, Son of God, Lord), around which the various theologies of the Christian Scriptures crystallise, just as will the later dogmatic theology of the Church. What needs to be justified is not the many theologies but their initial dogmatic starting point and the a priori consideration that can so justify it is the logic of love, which is also the logic of glory. 'Jesus is Lord' means that the glory of everlasting love has appeared to the Church through him.

The Word incarnate: his self-presentation

Balthasar's own theology of the incarnation, under the shorthand title 'Word-Flesh', considers three aspects of this 'Christ of history' and 'Jesus of faith' – authority, poverty and self-abandonment. It is, first, the authority of his glory which provoked and irradiates the many New Testament interpretations of his status. Jesus' 'claim to decide about men' is for Balthasar the chief impression he left, the 'formal *Leitmotiv* of all the Gospels'.[45] In him the judgment of God is present. Moreover:

in order that everything in man, the external and the internal, and indeed the demonic may lie before him fully transparent, it is necessary that Jesus, who is the bearer of authority, be himself fully transparent before God[46]

42 *GL* VII, p. 109.
43 Ibid.
44 *GL* VII, p. 111.
45 *GL* VII, p. 118.
46 *GL* VII, p. 125.

– and that is the point of the Johannine emphasis on his perpetual doing of the Father's will, looking to him, listening to him, all of which, however, has its Synoptic anticipation in the tribute paid to Jesus by the Pharisees and Herodians when they remark as if speaking of a well-known characteristic, 'we know that you are true' (Mark 12:14). Such truth, as transparence to God, links up, for a thinking tutored by the Hebrew Bible, with holiness and righteousness likewise. The Apocalypse, which turns these abstract nouns into names for Christ (cf. 19:11), makes of him, in the letters to the seven churches which form its prologue, the judge not only of his own contemporaries but of the present Church and future time as well. Bearing witness both to God and to his own absolute unity with God, Jesus' claim can only be fully explained by reference to *trinitarian* presuppositions.[47] Finally (on the topic of Jesus' authority), if in him there has come about the fulfilment of all the promises made by Israel's Lord in salvation history, then the analogous 'words of promise' that the Creator has set within his creation reach their acme too. 'A "Redeemer" who did not make the claim to be the One who fulfilled God's intentions in creation would be unworthy of belief.'[48] And that palpable hit at Gnostics ancient and modern leads Balthasar to conclude:

> It is not only the Word of promise of YHWH that has become man, but also 'his Word of power, through which he upholds the world' (Heb. 1: 3): therefore Jesus' claim can ring out with the sound of the Creator's voice, summoning man precisely to what is most human in himself.[49]

'Poverty' may seem a strange *idée-clef* with which to follow up 'authority'. But it is not merely the antithesis to the thesis which allows Balthasar to produce his synthesis. He has already alerted us, at the conclusion of his volumes on metaphysics in *The Glory of the Lord*, to the epistemic significance of the concept of evangelical poverty for the interpretation of reality in its deep heart's core.

> Right from the start, [Jesus] goes to those 'poor ones', as the beati-tudes show, and if he requires men to imitate him in the programme for life that is developed there, then this requires that he para-doxically combine the claim to be more than a prophet with the complete attitude of poverty.[50]

The bearer of the absolute claim is unconditionally vulnerable; he is equipped 'only to pass on what he has to others', not to keep it for himself.[51] His demand that disciples should leave all to follow him, he

---

47 Cf. *GL* VII, p. 160. 'The paradox of Christ, an absolute authority (occupying even the Father's position in judgment) in absolute poverty that goes as far as total self-giving, reveals the essence of the pure "relationality"... of the second divine person.'
48 *GL* VII, p. 129.
49 Ibid.
50 *GL* VII, p. 130.
51 *GL* VII, p. 131.

first meets in his own person, 'archetypally, representatively and inclusively'.[52]

> He has entrusted his cause so exclusively to the future which belongs to God that he can dare to do what is humanly speaking irresponsible: he can make others exclusively dependent upon himself, and thereby expose them to complete poverty, in order to give them in return the absolute promise of God as responding gift and guarantee.[53]

The poverty of Jesus is manifest in his *prayer*; all the great events of his mission, as Luke in particular presents them, transpire in prayer, and the *Abba* prayer which reveals the inner quality of Jesus' praying is, as the *Our Father* shows, a prayer for the Father's sustenance day by day, not for a stock to be laid by. It is also evidenced in the 'archetypal faith' of Christ: the adjective ('archetypal') being necessary as a marker that Balthasar is not ascribing faith to Jesus in that sense of the word proper to a Christian disciple.[54] *Fides Christi* for Balthasar means Christ's total confidence in the Father. Finally, Jesus' poverty makes itself known in the way he is 'propelled' by the Holy Spirit to meet the future God has in store, interposing no resistance of his own. This incarnation of the solidarity of the Word with those who are (in various senses) poor, has Balthasar notes, a 'catastrophic logic': if followed through to the end, it will take him to the cross, since the self-identification with people who have nothing must not stop short of those without the Law.

And if, then, the authoritative Word becomes abjectly poor, in order to lead the lost to the Father who comes to meet them, the third trait of the Word made flesh must be *self-abandonment*: this is a 'Word that abandons . . . and dissolves itself'.[55]

Though man is a speaking animal, utterance is only one of his activities, and it is not unbounded. When the Word becomes flesh he takes on an existence which begins in the silence of the womb, and ends in the silence of the tomb, passing from one to the other by way of an existence which is naturally incapable of *infinite* eloquence, for it is mortal. Yet it might be possible to think of a human being making over the expressive possibilities of their existence as a kind of keyboard for the Word to play on. The 'haste' – yet not *precipitate* haste – in which Jesus lives belongs to one conscious of a commission so to live as to be capable of yielding an infinite interpretation within the confines of a mortal life. Balthasar will return to this theme later, but meanwhile he notes how the intensification of this sense of mission produces in Jesus not (as growing awareness of commission would in us) an attempt ever more fully to control his life to this end, but on the contrary, increasing self-abandonment to the God who alone can draw out of his life whatever is needed to complete the new and

---

52 *GL* VII, p. 133.
53 *GL* VII, pp. 133–134.
54 Cf. 'Fides Christi', in *Sponsa Verbi. Skizzen zur Theologie II* (Einsiedeln 1960), pp. 45–79; E.t. *Spouse of the Word. Explorations in Theology* II (San Francisco 1991), pp. 43–80.
55 *GL* VII, p. 142.

eternal covenant. The Son of man goes ever more consciously to that hour only the Father knows.

And this should not surprise us, for the Word emptied itself of the form of God to take on the form of a slave and 'the slave has no form of his own, but has to take on, in pure obedience, the form that his lord imposes on him'.[56] In a 'formlessness' reminiscent of the wastefulness and careless excess in which his parables picture the divine generosity, he 'has emptied himself out, so that he may be formed and filled by God alone'.[57] Only on the death of the cross, with his resurrection ('*therefore* God exalted him, the Philippians hymn has it), will Jesus receive 'on the far side of himself' that form which God would bestow.[58]

Balthasar finds many signs of that self-abandonment – in the historic ministry, by way of the disjunction between the 'I' of Jesus and the 'he' of the Son of Man; in the first preaching of the apostles, by way of the notion that God made his servant Jesus Lord and Christ, for here is renunciation of self-mastery *par excellence*; in the Holy Eucharist, which is the distribution by Jesus of his flesh and blood; and in the entire process of 'reverbalisation' of the Word whereby in the course of formulating kerygma and gospel, dogma and Scripture, the Son leaves to the disposal of the Spirit 'what is mine' (John 16:22), so that the Spirit may be the definitive utterer of the truth concerning Father and Son.

Such self-abandonment is possible in this form only for one who has the sheer relationality of the divine Logos. The disciples are to be as the Master; but God empowers and legitimates such obedient imitation 'without promoting the imitators to the position of the God-man'.[59]

> The form that God gives to Jesus' increasing poverty and self-abandonment in the Passion and Resurrection, when Jesus submits his destiny to the Father, allows the Word that has disappeared into the flesh to become truly *the* Word that 'was in the beginning with God' and that as the Alpha is now to be also the Omega-word that fills the creation.[60]

The recurrence of the language of 'form' shows that Balthasar has not departed here from the perspective of theological aesthetics, even if in these chapters he is more concerned with the exegete's delineation of the figure of Jesus Christ whom the language of glory will subsequently describe. The fundamental character of the 'Word that expires on the Cross' became visible, so Balthasar recapitulates,

> in the triad of claim, poverty and self-abandonment, since the authority that comes from God was to take effect strictly in the sphere of powerlessness, and more radically still in the handing-

56 *GL* VII, p. 146.
57 *GL* VII, p. 147.
58 *GL* VII, p. 148.
59 *GL* VII, p. 160. This is said, of course, by way of opposition to an unhappy construal of the writing of Karl Rahner.
60 *GL* VII, p. 161.

over of the entire existence, including its death, into the disposition of God who was to give it form.[61]

The Word incarnate: his destiny in time

Balthasar will now go on to suggest how, in the light cast by such a cross-centred Christology, so much does this appear the basic character of Jesus' existence that it determines even the form of his *duration*, his participation in time. The chapters on the 'momentum of time' and the 'momentum of the Cross' which show the incarnate Word hastening to his destiny, wherein he becomes the subject of glory, will be greatly expanded in a theodramatic context in the christological and staurological volumes of *Theodramatik*. We can note that here he already has much to say – audible too in the exactly contemporary *Mysterium Paschale*, originally entitled 'Theology of the Three Days' – about the implications of that destiny, in time, on the cross, for the Church.

In these sections Balthasar is preparing for that (justified, not, *pace* Luther, misconceived) theology of glory in which his New Testament volume will climax. He emphasises not only the way the 'interval' between death and resurrection is unmeasurable in our time categories but also the quasi-simultaneity, in what must be the unique experience of temporality on the part of one who is universal Saviour, of the resurrection and parousia of the Crucified.

> It must not be forgotten . . . that it is not until the Passion that Jesus experiences what it means to bear the sin of the world, and that before this, he sees its fearsome 'timelessness' as it were threatening in outline, from the outside; it threatens as an endless end, that sinks into the eternal timelessness; it is objectively impossible and theologically false to allow this endless end a place in the 'chronology of salvation history', and to situate in a temporal succession the radical change of the Resurrection which, seen from Hades, is impossible, the unthinkable, unlocatable moment when 'death is swallowed up in victory' (1 Cor. 15:54) in divine 'suddenness' and the perpetuity of eternal life 'begins' (but this 'beginning' too must be cancelled, for despite the character of event which belongs to the Resurrection, Jesus soars up into the glory which 'he had before the world was made' [John 17:5]).[62]

And again, though the 'proper time of what is endless' achieved by Christ's exaltation may be, as the ending of St Matthew's Gospel implies, continuously present to the world's time, that does not mean that in and

---

61 *GL* VII, p. 202.
62 *GL* VII, p. 172. Cf. the 'little while' of the non-time of the cross in John 16:16–19, which Balthasar calls 'an absolutely qualitative, non-chronological designation', p. 173. Balthasar's ruminations on these themes go back, indeed, beyond *Theologie der drei Tage* (Einsiedeln 1969, E.t. *Mysterium Paschale*, Edinburgh 1990) to the wider, yet markedly Christocentric, *Theologie der Geschichte* (Einsiedeln 1959, E.t. *A Theology of History*, New York and London 1963).

of themselves resurrection, ascension and parousia are temporally separate.[63]

But the unique time of Christ also affects our time, thus bringing about the 'time of the Church'.

> The inclusive character of the time of Jesus lies in his 'having been chosen in advance before the foundation of the world' (1 Pet. 1:20) to appear in the last times as the 'Lamb without spot or stain' so that the earthly time of Jesus is from the outset already taken up into the plan and the disposition of the created world, and belongs to the eternal contents of the providence that governs the world.[64]

Just as the Word made flesh requires its response, which it receives in Mary and the Church through her, so too the time of Jesus leaves, through a grace which does not cancel freedom, its imprint on history in the time of the Church. For the nascent Church the Easter appearances are not definitive epiphanies but establish her in an interim time between resurrection and parousia, a time neither of promise nor total fulfilment. The best phrase Balthasar can find for it is 'indescribable anticipation'.[65] (Balthasar is of the opinion that the 'problem' of the delay of the parousia for the early Church has been much exaggerated by the scholars: only in 'a few peripheral passages' is it felt as a 'theological question'.)[66] That 'anticipation' must be understood perfectly realistically as a share even now in Christ's 'eschatological perpetuity and supratemporality'.

> If the time of Christ contains in itself the whole momentum of the eschatological act of God, then the time of the Church can give a response to this momentum only in so far as it projects itself wholly, in believing and loving hope, towards this perfected time as towards its own goal – the existence of the one who bears the impress of this form must shape itself into a flying bullet. . . .[67]

– Balthasar's more contemporary (but hardly more attractive!) substitute for Paul's metaphor in Philippians of the runner straining for the prize at the Games. And this enables him to clarify what is the matter with the manner of formulating futurist concern in progressivist or liberationist theology:

> The believer has been made Christ's own, and therefore the absoluteness of this forward movement which results transcends every other absoluteness, however utopian, of human hope or of the programming of the future. Simply by being lived, this absoluteness can take its place at the spearhead of all worldly hopes for the future, and can preserve them from acquiescing in the established present.

---

63 *GL* VII, p. 172; note how 'coming again' and 'seeing again' in the same section of John's Gospel refer to both Easter and parousia, p. 173.
64 *GL* VII, pp. 174–175.
65 *GL* VII, p. 178.
66 *GL* VII, p. 179.
67 *GL* VII, p. 181.

In this sense, it can indirectly exercise by itself functions of 'social criticism', but without letting itself be led astray from the straight line of its own flight-path by such criticism or by preoccupation with worldly projects of evolution. For this reason, it will 'keep awake and be sober', because it has already been bathed in the light and does not need to search for light (1 Thess. 5:5ff.). It knows that its 'home is in Heaven' (Phil. 3:20), and that we are 'pilgrims and strangers in this world' (Heb. 11:12; 1 Pet. 2:11).[68]

The sacraments and ministerial offices of the Church are congruently shaped to this, her pilgrim character. Baptism, Eucharist and penance, above all, bear the mark of the suffering and risen Lord, and the apostolic ministry to which they are committed is strong only in its weakness.

The all-sufficiency of the redemptive sacrifice of Christ means, further, the breaking down of the wall of separation between Israel and the Church.

> Unlike the particular time of Israel, which had boundaries separating it from the Gentiles, the time of the Church in its manifest character can be only what the *time of mankind* is through Christ. . . . The apparent brackets – between Cross and Parousia – that surround the time of the Church are in reality the opening of all brackets, since God has acted in Christ 'once for all' . . . and thus for all times and places before Christ, and not as the redeemer of a little group or of one single people, but as the Creator of the world . . .[69]

The righteousness of God ceases to be simply Israel's temporal rescue through her enemies' condemnation, and becomes 'the eschatological rescuing of all sinners that takes place through the *krisis* [judgment] of the one Cross'.[70]

In this new time of the Church there is, despite all difference from the time of Christ, a kind of contemporaneity with Jesus. Though the 'hiatus' of the cross creates a gap which man cannot overleap the reconciling grace of the cross itself can overcome this distance. This begins to be apparent in Paul, but comes into its own with John. For Pauline faith, God has reconciled the world to himself on the cross without the collaboration of any believer – yet the same faith unites the apostle to his Lord, so that he can make up in his body 'what still remains of the sufferings of Christ' (Col. 1: 24), for the sake of the Church. The Fourth Evangelist, as his portrayal not only of Mary but of the beloved disciple shows:

> lives so much in the love of the Lord that he knows himself to stand at the place where he is borne away by the Lord over the abyss of the Cross. . . . The grace that radiates forth from the Logos when he is

---

68 *GL* VII, pp. 181–182.
69 *GL* VII, p. 184. Note, however, that the time of the Church is not simply identical with the time of the world; the former is not determined by the latter but informs it as a 'subordinate material element'. Just so the continuing chronological time of salvation history, on Balthasar's understanding, could be and was comprehended within Christ's eschatological time: *GL* VII, p. 187.
70 *GL* VII, p. 186.

'raised up' – but raised up on the Cross, as much as raised up into glory – allows the Church characterised by Mary and John to accomplish the accompanying through the hiatus to the other side.[71]

The grace of following Christ takes its power of propulsion from the weighty 'momentum' of the glory of the cross.

Nowhere is the root of the Hebrew word for glory – *kbd*, 'weight' – more in evidence than in Balthasar's theological aesthetics of the cross. The *mysterium tremendum et fascinans* which makes us shudder on Good Friday is the 'momentum of the collision of the entire burden of sin with the total powerlessness of the kenotic existence'.[72] With the latter, the 'abyss of the unfathomable love' (the Father's in sending the Son, the Son's in consenting to be sent) has entered the sphere of the former ('the abyss of the meaningless hatred') and there concealed itself.[73] Here the dreadful momentum of God's wrath at the broken covenant (and God 'owes it to himself and to his loving covenantal righteousness' to reply with a 'No' to the world's 'No' to him)[74] is taken up into the (as it proves) still greater momentum of his love. The Word made flesh becomes the medium in which the Father acts, at once to meet the wrathful demands of his judgment and to realise the saving righteousness that is the abiding divine attribute against whose foil his rightful anger must itself be seen. And in proving capable, on the cross, of being this medium – of bearing out of love the universal burden of sin – the Word shows itself to be divine.

For the source of Jesus' obedience is the eternal relation of Son to Father. Balthasar seeks to find for the kenosis of the Son, in incarnation and atonement, a condition of possibility in the selflessness of the divine persons whose life composes the divine nature. Though the philanthropy of redemption is totally gratuitous, nevertheless

> if the mystery of the divine love is once disclosed in Jesus Christ, then we may argue that God could do what he did in reality do, and that his self-abasement and self-emptying were no contradiction of his own essence, but corresponded precisely to this essence in a way that could never have been thought of.[75]

Here Balthasar's position is that of the Russian Orthodox dogmatician Sergei Bulgakov, but shorn of the latter's 'sophiological' excesses. Unlike such seventeenth-century Dominican soteriologists as Thomas Leonardi and Louis Chardon, however, Balthasar will not allow that the kenotic character of the incarnation meant that the Son's life was of set purpose

---

71 *GL* VII, pp. 196, 197–198. This is one of the key points where Balthasar regards Johannine theology as leading on to the *Spiritual Exercises* of Ignatius Loyola, in which the following of Christ takes place in *disponibilité* to his call, by sharing in all the episodes of his life, including cross, resurrection and his coming to be in the Church.

72 *GL* VII, pp. 208–209.

73 *GL* VII, p. 210.

74 *GL* VII, p. 206.

75 *GL* VII, p. 215.

unmitigated suffering from cradle to grave. As he robustly remarks, a life of suffering with no joy intermixed at all would not be human just as one who had never known human love could experience solitude but not loneliness. The point about kenosis is not that the Son made man must always be miserable, but that he is ever ready to do the Father's will in the form of his human existence and its God-given destiny. Within the existential conditions of fallen humanity, he takes up the 'Adamic' attitude of the free human creature before God into that uncreated relation of obedience to the Father which the Logos, the archetype of freedom, everlastingly is.

> The Incarnation of the Son of God involves his assuming of this pure 'Adamic' act into his own readiness for the Father's will, accomplishing this act more decisively and spotlessly than any other; but this act can institute what God intends *only* because it is carried and transmuted by the act of the kenotic readiness of the Son for the Father's will, the act that penetrates deeper than every created state and is the foundation of the whole existence of Jesus.[76]

This ultimate foundation of the cross and so of the mission whose culmination the cross is can only be a hidden reality. For Balthasar such motifs and devices of the Synoptic Gospels as the Marcan 'messianic secret' betray this consciousness on the part of the New Testament writers – and come to their climax in the Johannine theologoumenon of how even or especially in his revelation as light and life, the Logos is unrecognised and so concealed.

Consonant with the theological doctrine stated in his *Theologie der drei Tagen* (his contribution to the multi-volume post-Conciliar dogmatics, *Mysterium Salutis*) Balthasar emphasises in particular the aspects of Godforsakenness, judgment, and descent into hell – though the material is presented here with a view to a wide-ranging theology of glory, and not just as an account of the *dénouement* of the paschal *triduum* on Easter Sunday. The 'collision' of the cross necessarily entails the most absolute abandonment – by God via men, for Jesus carries the sin of the world.

> No faith or hope can ward off the lethal momentum of the blow; and for this reason, within the unique form of Jesus' time, the experience of such an abandonment can be only an experience in timelessness and definitiveness.[77]

But in the judgment which is that definitive condemnation of sin, the old world – symbolised by the temple's star-studded veil – is torn up, and – figured this time in the earthquake's opening of graves – Sheol despoiled. True, the resurrection when it comes will be

> a new act of God the Father, but [it will be precisely] one demanded by the inner logic of the act of judgment on the Cross, and to this

---

76 *GL* VII, p. 218. Balthasar notes, moreover, that 'Mary's *fiat* too, uttered vicariously for all and founding the Church as the bride of Christ, is empowered to institute this only by this kenotic *fiat* of the Son' (in the 'pre-redemption' of Mary), ibid.

77 *GL* VII, p. 225.

extent contained within it: so much is this so that in John the raising
up upon the Cross and the raising up into glory are one single event,
just as for Paul no one is raised up apart from the Crucified.[78]

And in sinking down into that as yet eschatologically undifferentiated
'hell' of the Fathers (and Mothers!), Christ reaches (on Balthasar's interpretation) the nadir of his kenosis, for the disarming of the evil powers
follows only from that ultra-efficacious 'proclamation' which is, by an
ultimate paradox, the absolute passivity of the Word made flesh among
the dead. But precisely because this is the lowest point reached by the
kenosis it is also the maximal identification of the Son made man with the
essential will of the Father, and so 'the journey into the furthest depths of
Hell can change timelessly in the absolute instant of the Resurrection into
the uttermost intimacy of Heaven'.[79]

The Word incarnate: his endless glory

The Johannine Prologue says of the humanised Word whom Balthasar
has now described, 'We saw his glory'. In explaining how this could be
so, Balthasar has reached the true climax of *Herrlichkeit* which does not
wish to be a theological aesthetics save in that Christocentric – but not
Christomonistic – fashion Balthasar had learned from Barth.[80] The terms
'glory' and 'glorify' appear over one hundred and seventy-five times in
the New Testament so Balthasar will hardly be the first person to
comment on them. But he is the first perhaps to grasp that

> 'glory' here has a meaning, distinctive and unique, yet at the same
> time transforming and integrating everything that went before and
> bringing it to completion, a meaning that must disclose itself
> immediately out of the momentum shown in God's act in Jesus, a
> meaning that must be nothing else than the self-interpretation of this
> momentum.[81]

As (in Old Testament terms) the free manifestation of the unique 'I' of the
Lord, and (in philosophical terms) a transcendental qualification of being
that governs everything that exists, and thus (theologically) a synthesis of
absolute freedom and analogically ordered universality, glory has three
qualities closely relevant to its New Testament ascription to Christ. First,
it can 'hold sway over all the works of God while shining out more

78 *GL* VII, pp. 227–228.
79 *GL* VII, p. 234.
80 Cf. *GL* VII, pp. 262–263, where Balthasar defines the 'path' of theological aesthetics
    as leading from theocentrism to christocentrism, since any other would risk
    producing an aesthetics that was merely quasi-philosophical (rather than strictly
    Christian-theological) in character. And yet, as he points: 'Christ himself nowhere
    controls his own glorification, that is to say, the relationship between his obedience
    to the Father and his own glory, but once for all entrusts himself, in what concerns
    his glorification, in prayer to the Father, from whom the Spirit goes forth into
    Church and world to accomplish conviction, vindication and glorification'.
    Christocentrism must be transposed, therefore, into a *final* trinitarian theocentrism.
81 *GL* VII, pp. 240–241.

brightly at certain points than at others'.[82] Secondly, it can make itself known in diverse ways, for

> it would not be a statement about God unless it were the expression of his hiddenness just as much as the expression of his manifestation, possessing dimensions enough to make itself known in Cross and death just as much as in Resurrection and 'return to glory'.[83]

The distinctive advance of the New Testament over the Old is that glory now appears as able to 'embrace "transcendentally" even these uttermost contradictions', and hence need not be brought up short even by Sheol itself.[84] And thirdly, insofar as a theological *transcendentale* must bear some resemblance to the philosophical *transcendentalia* of being (for the God of theology is the source of the being which philosophy studies) everything that is glorious will be so to the extent that it is also good and true – echoing in this the unbreakable *perichōrēsis* of *pulchrum, bonum, verum*, which Balthasar set forth at the outset of *Theologik*.

And the last of these three points is the really decisive one for New Testament faith.

> What God's glory in its good truth is, was to be revealed in Jesus Christ, and ultimately in his absolute obedience of Cross and Hell. The unique ray of the divine majesty of love is to become visible from the unique momentum of this event, establishing the norm for everything that can lay claim to the predicate 'glorious', at whatever distance and periphery it may be.[85]

Balthasar opens his account of the glory of Christ with the prayer of the Johannine Jesus, 'Father, glorify thou me' (John 17:5a), made by Jesus during the Last Supper discourse prominent among whose themes is Jesus' own claim to have glorified the Father on earth. We are dealing here, then, with a dual glorification, in which the obedience of the Son, giving glory as that does to the Father, is the inner ground of the Father's prospective glorification of the obedient one.

The first phase of this twofold movement – the Father's glory manifest in the obedience of the Son - is, Balthasar explains

> John's transcription of the idea, common to the whole New Testament, that the 'majesty' and 'ruling authority' of the Father takes effect in the 'lowliness' of the obedient and serving Son. . . . He is the one who in his entire existence seeks only the *doxa* of the Father, the one who identifies himself with the execution of the mission . . . of the Father . . . to such an extent that the entire 'majesty' of the Father can appear localised in him.[86]

82 *GL* VII, p. 242.
83 Ibid.
84 Ibid.
85 *GL* VII, p. 243.
86 *GL* VII, pp. 246–247.

As Balthasar had only noted in the first volume of *The Glory of the Lord* but now can make more fully comprehensible: in the Son made man, authority – the majesty of the Father – and self-abnegation or 'poverty' – the refusal to seek his own glory, coincide. And in the last of the signs worked by the Son, the opened heart on the cross from which flow blood and water, the Father's commission and the Son's abnegation reach their simultaneous fulfilment, in such a way that, by the consequent revelation of God as love 'the space opened up by the utterly obedient Son suffices to make known the whole "name" of the Father and to make completely efficacious his sovereign power'.[87]

Whereupon, the second phase of the mutual glorification of Father and Son begins: God being glorified in the Son of Man, God will glorify him in himself and at once (John 13:32). The Son requests this glorification, but does so with all the assurance of one who is making an infallible statement; yet in the inner-trinitarian dialogue, such a 'statement' can only be made in the form of a request. That is how Balthasar makes sense of the Fourth Gospel's use of both impetratory and indicative syntax while the addition of the phrase 'at once' adds a note of urgency to this 'trinitarian logic'.[88] What Jesus asks is, in terms of the *economy*, the saving dispensation, that the salvific fruitfulness of his glorification of the Father become apparent; what he asks in terms of the *theology*, of the inner divine life, is that the Son enjoy again that glory he had with the Father before the world was made. But the glory that is common to Father and Son is the radiance of their eternal reciprocal love while the fruitfulness of the Son's work lies precisely in the entry of that love into visibility in the world. That is what Balthasar means when he writes:

> The glorification of the Son by the Father is understood as the proof brought by the Father that every glorious fruit that has resulted from the mission of the Son has its final foundation in the perfect, absolute obedience, and gives glory to this obedience too as the perfected revelation of the eternal love of the Son. The ray of the supra-mundane love (John 17:5) does not only fall upon the obedience of the Cross to transfigure it: it breaks forth from within this obedience too.[89]

So far there has been no mention – or at least no explicit mention – of the Holy Spirit. But Jesus says (John 16:14) '[The Spirit] will glorify me, for he will take what is mine and declare it to you'. The Spirit exhibits the identity between the eternal glory of the Son's communion with the Father in love and his obedience unto death on earth. As the Spirit of their love, both its bond and its fruit, no Other can perform this task. And since, in his 'accomplished obedience', the Son is 'wholly one with the Father as possessor of the Father's love' ('all that the Father has is mine', 16:15), not only the Father but also the Son can send the Spirit – though for this to

87 *GL* VII, p. 248.
88 *GL* VII, p. 249.
89 *GL* VII, p. 250.

happen the Son must first die (7:39; 16:7; cf. 20:22), a *sine qua non* rendered theologically perspicuous when Balthasar comments:

The Spirit of love is set free for the world where the love of the Father in the handing-over of the Son for the world has become free, where the love of the Son in his 'self-consecration' . . . as 'sin offering' . . . has reached its completion in the opening of his heart.[90]

To 'take what is mine and declare it to you', on Balthasar's interpretation means not just an external interpretation, through the Spirit's guidance, of his words and actions but, much more than this, the outpouring of the 'substance' of the Word made flesh – not in the sense, of course, of a literal evacuation of the being of the God-man but by way of a 'revelation of the fruitfulness that dwells within this substance'.[91] And so, if the Father is glorified in the Son, the Son is glorified in the working of the Spirit in the Church. Nothing will *be* fruitful in the Church, remarks Balthasar accordingly, unless it derives from 'christological obedience'.[92]

When Jesus says that he is 'glorified' in the Church (John 17:10), he sees that he has succeeded in revealing the Father's love in such a way that men have accepted it (17:6–8). The divine love has taken root on earth[93]

– notably in a habit of love of the brethren differentiated from humanitarianism by a law of self-renunciation and by the dependence of its efficacy on the Church's embodiment of the Trinity's unity-in-love. As Balthasar puts it in an important passage where he heads off one possible (mis-)interpretation of the text (17:5) where the Son prays for the recovery of his *premundane* glory:

The context of John's Gospel as a whole shows that this is no mere restoration of an original state, but rather the integration of the obedient love, lived out in the separation undertaken for the sake of bringing salvation, into the original intimacy and 'perfect joy' of the dwelling with one another of Father and Son. And the final request, drawing the Church and the redeemed world too into the light of the trinitarian love, belongs essentially to this integration.[94]

And so the Son's request for glorification in the Fourth Gospel enables Balthasar to approach the *substantive issues* of New Testament glory. A theological aesthetics of the New Testament Scriptures will be concerned with the 'correspondence' between obedience and love, and between kenotic hiddenness and exalted manifestation; it will have to do with the perfect 'proportion' Christ established between the Father's will in heaven

90 *GL* VII, p. 252.
91 *GL* VII, p. 253.
92 *GL* VII, p. 258.
93 *GL* VII, p. 259.
94 *GL* VII, p. 260.

and his own on earth; it will investigate the new 'equilibrium' established by the Son's creative obedience, between the divine archetype, God, and the human image, man.

What Jesus Christ reveals is 'the substance of glory', the God of glory's own *ousia*. Or, in the ontologically more oblique language favoured by theological aesthetics: 'it is always the radiance of the Unutterable that we shall see upon the face of the Son (John 17:24; Apoc, 22:4) and *thus* see the Ineffable 'as he is' (1 John 3: 2), 'face to face' (1 Cor. 13:12).[95]

Now the foundation of God's lordly splendour (his *Herrlichkeit*) as Scripture would see it lies in the fact that the God who by his immanence has already set signs of his power and wisdom in the world remains nonetheless in his transcendence utterly free over against his creatures, and 'precisely this free elevation above what is not God gives God again the freedom to reveal himself in his free divinity in personal fashion – in the "Word" – to what is not God'.[96] But within the distinction between the natural and the supernatural – a distinction which, Balthasar maintains (in conformity to Catholic doctrine but contrary to what some of its interpreters say of him!), is 'never wholly reducible' – God can manifest his glory in a variety of intensities. These range from his creative action *tout court*, through the creation of his personal image, man, to what we are now discussing: 'the definitive expression (*charaktēr*) of his invisible "Face" (*panim*) in the visible face of Christ'.[97] It is of course true that, thanks to the divine simplicity – which Balthasar prefers to speak of as the circumincession or interpenetration of the divine attributes – the glory of God is not to be separated from his power or his righteousness (and Balthasar mentions these attributes in particular because of the divine *power* to 'give comprehensible and appropriate expression to the utter otherness of his being',[98] and the way the divine *righteousness* manifests God's lordliness when he elevates sinners into the glorious freedom of the children of God). What Balthasar accentuates, however, is God's freedom to 'create for himself a valid expression of his incomprehensibility'[99] and not simply the unfathomable quality of his lying beyond all distinctions drawn from this world. And here lies the deepest meaning of Israelite aniconicism:

> The prohibition of images in the Old Testament had passed over the sphere of images and left them out, in order that God might of himself set up his valid image in the world.[100]

As the true Image, Jesus Christ is the epiphany of the divine Glory. Only the Conciliar dogmas can make sense of this.

> The Word of God is so personal that it itself is a person; but as God it is so essentially one with the Father, and as man so transparent to

95 *GL* VII, p. 266.
96 *GL* VII, p. 268. Translation slightly altered.
97 *GL* VII, p. 269.
98 Ibid.
99 *GL* VII, p. 272.
100 *GL* VII, p. 273.

the Father in obedience, that it becomes the visible presence of God's acting and speaking in the world.[101]

The New Testament is filled, in christological contexts, with *epiphany-words*, words for appearing, showing, disclosing, seeing (were it not, *The Glory of the Lord* would hardly have got under way in the first place!). Consonant with his account of faith as both seeing and hearing in Volume I of *Herrlichkeit*, Balthasar insists that this language of the visual must not be counterposed to a vocabulary of the aural. On the contrary, the high significance of their New Testament unity must be perceived.

> When the Incarnation brings a new emphasis on 'seeing', this does not relegate 'hearing' to the background; the reason for this can be given neither in purely philological nor psychological terms, but only theologically, for what appears and becomes visible is in its entirety 'word': everything in the One who appears, is an intensified address, as grace and as demand.[102]

And the *content* of this visible-audible Word is, as the Letter to Titus has it, 'the goodness and loving kindness of God our Saviour' [which] has now 'epiphanised' among us (3:4). It is the intrinsic interrelation of revelation and love in the New Covenant which allows the supreme epiphany of glory to be the cross.

If epiphany is the act of the divine appearing in the flesh, a family of words – *eikōn* (image), *homoiōma* (likeness), *homoiōsis* (similarity), *schēma* (shape), *charaktēr* (imprint), *morphē* (form), *apaugasma* (radiance) – express its effect. Balthasar points out how these terms were already inter-connected not only in Jewish Hellenism (in the sapiential books and Philo) but also (at any rate to some considerable extent), in pagan Hellenism too. There was indeed in late antiquity an entire 'image-cosmology' with its origins in the Platonic dialogues (above all, the *Republic* and the *Timaeus*). Only through Christian soteriology and ultimately through trinitarian theology can this image-cosmology be brought to a 'final and ... un-equivocal fulfilment'.[103] For while the pre-evangelical version of this cosmology could posit the consubstantiality of image with Archetype (as a 'ray' or, better, 'mirror' of the Source of reality), it could not of course grasp their hypostatic ('personal') distinction.

> This comes about when, for the first time, on the basis of the personality of the historical Jesus and his personal relationship to the Father, it is seen that the (quasi-)hypostases of the outgoing Old Covenant and their relationship to the God who is the Source of all may be understood in the sense of 'personal-standing-over-against' one another. But this step can be taken only when the relationship between Father and Son is disclosed from the point of view of

101 *GL* VII, p. 274.
102 *GL* VII, p. 276. Cf. the brief theology of revelation offered in A. Nichols, O.P., *Epiphany. A Theological Introduction to Catholicism* (Collegeville, Minn. 1996), pp. 30–33.
103 *GL* VII, p. 283.

soteriology as the act of the Father's love in the Son: this act is ultimately accessible only to a loving faith, and if it is to embrace effectively and completely the world that is to be saved, it presupposes the 'cosmological' status of Christ as the archetypal image standing over against the whole creation.[104]

And that transcendent fulfilment quite overshadows the prehistory of the concept in Hellenism, so that when Paul, for instance, calls Christ the *eikōn* of the invisible God not the slightest doubt arises as to the full personality of the imagistic Expression, nor that of the Father whose Expression Christ is.

God's 'epiphany in the word and the image of his essence'[105] must be seen in a way appropriate to itself. Here Balthasar can in large part be content with summarising what he had to say about 'Seeing the Form' in the initial volume of the theological aesthetics which bore that name. Yet we have also learned something(!) *en route* to the end, and so 'seeing' may now be redefined as 'the ability to interpret a person and a destiny as the epiphany of absolute love',[106] just as (another discovery) the 'enrapturing power' native to all genuine form 'goes so far' in the case of Jesus Christ, that 'it not only draws to itself those who believe and love, but lets them share in its own birth from its origin, from God' (cf. John 1:13).[107] Indeed, this form *gives* form, configuring human beings to itself, if they only let themselves be remade by the shaping power of God in his incarnate Son.

And in this correspondence between creation and Creator through Christ and the grace of Christ, righteousness is realised in the whole realm of God's lordship: here is Balthasar's opportunity to serve out a theology of justification, so important as that is to the entire Reformed tradition, drawn from wells he had drunk in studying Barth – and which might otherwise be thought to have little connexion with a theology of beauty.

> The New Testament nowhere speaks of the recovery of a lost glory
> of the original state, but rather of the eschatological achieving of the
> righteousness and glory of God in his cosmos, in which ultimately
> no other 'word' and 'image' speaks of God and gives light, than the
> eternal Son of the Father[108]

– and notably by that act in which, as Pauline theology asserts, God reconciled the world with himself through Christ as his atoning instrument in the Son's 'absolute, eschatologically adequate act of taking the place of all'.[109] Without in any way mitigating Paul's doctrine of justifying faith, Balthasar resituates it within a Johannine Christology of glory, and re-expresses its content in theologically aesthetic terms.

104 *GL* VII, pp. 282–283.
105 *GL* VII, p. 286.
106 *GL* VII, p. 291.
107 *GL* VII, p. 292.
108 *GL* VII, p. 297.
109 *GL* VII, p. 298.

This fact – that faith, as the acceptance (brought about by God himself) that God works in us, has christological measurements and dimensions – [is what] brings about the correspondence which God . . . established in the New Covenant between his righteousness in him and in us, and truly sets in motion our configuration to God's image, which is the Son.[110]

This faith cannot, then, be defined without charity, as we see from Ephesians, where the Church-bride submits to (precisely) the measurelessness of the love shown her; from the Lucan Mary whose hand-maidenly fiat is what is required of the true believer; and from the Paul of the Corinthian letters for whom faith without love is nothing. Nor does Balthasar neglect (in a tacit correcting, once again, of Protestantism) the rôle of baptism and Eucharist in the making of the 'act of abandonment' to configuration to Christ which is Christian faith.[111]

What such faith gives access to is the mutual indwelling of Father and Son in the Holy Spirit, a superabundance that can be put into words 'only in ever new expressions of profusion, of preponderance, of the priority that can no longer be measured and that shatters all proportion'.[112] Still, this does not imply that the notions of 'measure' (*metron*) and 'measuring rod (*kanōn*) are deprived of all soteriological value in the New Testament writings. They retain a validity not, however, as characterisations of the fulness of God's salvation (which is precisely unmeasured, unmeasurable), but in terms of what the saving God calls those justified to do in his Church. And so in an 'aesthetic' version of what he will lay out more fully in a 'theodramatic' context elsewhere, Balthasar explains that

whereas the mission of the Son (and therein his Spirit bestowed on him by the Father) is 'without measure ' (John 3:34), the mission is measured out to the individual as 'grace in accordance with the measure of the gift of Christ' (Eph. 4:7), thus expressing both Christ's free sovereignty over the body and the allocation of the member to its rôle in the building up of the body as a whole.[113]

That dialectic of the measureless profusion of grace and the measured allocation of tasks enables Balthasar to present the divine expressiveness as both an unmeasurable light and a fulness of order – and so the fulfilment of those first sketchy yet irreplaceable elements of all aesthetics which he identified in the opening pages of *Herrlichkeit*, *lumen* (or *splendor*) and *species* (or *forma*).

Are we to suppose that tangible glory attended, then, the Jesus of history at all points of his career? Not at all, yet glory in the mode of hiddenness has left its mark nonetheless. Even when allowance is made for the 'paschalisation' of texts that irradiated the remembered figure of Jesus retrospectively by the light of Easter, we are still left

110 *GL* VII, p. 305.
111 *GL* VII, p. 306.
112 *GL* VII, p. 310.
113 *GL* VII, p. 313.

with the phenomenon of the *sovereignty* with which Jesus made his presence felt.

> Jesus' words were truly the words of omnipotence (Mark 13:31), of the definitive demand for decision, of the bestowal of grace and promise – concealed beneath a quite unremarkable human situation. . . . The experience of Jesus' sovereignty in his refusal to make any display of himself or advertise himself (John 7:4) must have seemed so central to the disciples that they used every means at their disposal, when they began their interpretation from the starting point of the event of Cross and Resurrection, in order to make this sovereignty perceptible; they were sometimes tempted, while doing this, to trespass over the boundaries of the strict hiddenness, of the incognito.[114]

But Balthasar does not regard such post-Easter reconstruction as *over-interpretation* (and here lies his difference from the liberal-radical historical-critical exegete).

> One should always bear in mind that God's incognito in Jesus was simultaneously his appearing in Jesus' mission and task, and that this unity of disclosure and concealment was absolutely unique, without any point of comparison in this world.[115]

On the other hand (and here we come upon Balthasar's difference from the traditional exegete mindful of the demands of classical apologetics where argument from the – detailed and precise – fulfilment of prophecy is crucial), if Jesus' sovereignty is 'the appearing of the free abasement of God's glory in the . . . obedience of the form of a slave',[116] the obedience of his sovereign freedom was owed to the Father alone – and not to the historical structures of the prophecies as such.

> It was precisely this freedom – as the superiority to all the forms (or figures) made ready by the Old Covenant – that allowed him to be at one and the same time the 'superior form' that embraces all 'forms' in itself and the 'lack of form' that disappoints on the basis of the conceptions previously shaped. . .[117]

Only christological faith, which establishes right proportion to this unique object, can do justice to the 'sovereignty in the abasement',[118] though Balthasar feels confident that no section of Jesus material in the gospel tradition succumbs to 'custom and ordinariness'; on the contrary, 'the sovereignty provides the unifying atmosphere to such an extent that it makes itself felt at each individual point'.[119]

114 *GL* VII, p. 321.
115 *GL* VII, pp. 321–322.
116 *GL* VII, p. 323.
117 *GL* VII, p. 324.
118 *GL* VII, p. 326.
119 *GL* VII, p. 325.

Balthasar chooses three aspects of the gospel tradition – Jesus' miracles, his parables and his transfiguration – so as to explain what a 'sovereignty in concealment' might look like when the effulgence of the Easter light is deliberately toned down. Thus the faith Jesus requires of those for whom miracles were wrought was not yet faith in himself. Rather did he 'actively mediate faith between the human person and God, making himself the source of the faith that is indispensable for that person and letting it well up from [their] heart.'[120] Indeed 'all the miracles are but a reference and a pointer to the One [Jesus] who is concealed, who is deciphering himself . . . in the symbols.'[121] The parables too are in the historic ministry merely *'en route* to their own realisation'.[122] Before the event of the cross, and so the coming of the kingdom, it is 'not yet possible to hand over the key to the whole'.[123] *Some* ecclesial rewriting of Jesus' teaching was a necessity after the resurrection of the Crucified, when that Easter judgment to which Jesus had looked in his earthly life becomes for the Church the universal judgment of the parousia. Lastly, the transfiguration of Jesus is also a testimony to the hiddenness, before the resurrection, of his glory.

> The astonishing thing about the transfiguration is that, in this night on the high mountain, the ever elusive *doxa* of the Old Testament becomes present for a moment in all its stages and forms, and attains its immediate fulfilment in its Old Testament form in Jesus and at the heart of his prayer to the Father . . . in . . . a moment in which the Old Testament glory concentrates itself in a single point, so that it may enter and cross over into the glory of the New Testament.[124]

And yet:

> All this takes place in the deepest concealment – in Luke, in a scenario that is strangely close to that of the temptations on the Mount of Olives – far from men, before three witnesses who are half asleep and who must seal up in strict silence what they have seen![125]

Balthasar shows considerable ingenuity in bringing various features of the Synoptic Gospels under the heading of literary devices to evoke this 'sovereignty in concealment' of miracles, parables and the transfiguration episode.[126]

Even the resurrection appearances belong in one sense with the theme of the hiddenness of the manifested One for, strikingly, the word 'glory' never occurs in their course. (Balthasar ascribes the risen Christ's question on the Emmaus Road, 'Was it not necessary for the Christ to suffer these things and thus to enter his glory?' [Luke 24:26] to the evangelist's redaction: an example, one fears, of a theologian critical of critical method

120 *GL* VII, p. 331.
121 *GL* VII, p. 335.
122 Ibid.
123 *GL* VII, p. 337.
124 *GL* VII, pp. 346–347.
125 *GL* VII, p. 347.
126 *GL* VII, pp. 348–354.

invoking it without *arrière-pensée* when it suits his turn!) In these 'simple narratives' only the resurrection angels convey the *doxa* dimension. The appearance narratives show 'deepest reserve' – though Balthasar has some trouble in bringing the Pantokrator Christ of the end of Matthew's Gospel and the Risen Christ of Paul's Damascus Road experience under this rubric – not to mention the 'cloud' of the ascension, which he insists, on the basis of E. Pax's 1955 study *Epiphaneia*, is *not* a '*kabod* cloud', unlike that of the transfiguration. What Balthasar wants to guard against in interpreting the resurrection appearances is too undialectical a presentation of the risen glory. As he writes, expounding in the first instance the theology of Paul:

> God's glory in light and power possesses a visible component: this glory is objectively visible on the face of Christ, i.e. in the whole event of his death and resurrection, *although of course* this is the case only when the objective call of God, 'Let there be light!', finds an answering creative call in the subjective depth of the hearts that are given the power to see.[127]

An icon necessarily implies visibility – and yet 'must not the visibility of what is essentially invisible also bear in itself an element of invisibility and hiddenness?'[128] The visible Icon of the invisible God 'leaves it to the Father who raises him to "see to" the relationship between the openness and the hiddenness of God in the Son'.[129] And what is the result?

> In the concealment of all *doxa* in the one abandoned by God on the Cross, he enters the most immediate relationship to the concealed *doxa* of the Father, and when at Easter he rises into this divine, hidden *doxa*, he is presented by the triune God to the world, in the 'gospel of the glory of God', as the one he is through the few eye-witnesses who have experienced him as the living One. The Gospel, the proclamation of Jesus the Christ, is fully open, unconcealed and free of dialectic: it proclaims the openness of God and of his love in the event of Jesus, and summons the proclaimer to the risk of speaking freely (*parrhēsia*) and the hearer to the risk of faith. Here, every cover is withdrawn, and this openness is effected by the [Spirit]; thus the one who proclaims can stand forth with great *parrhēsia* (2 Cor. 3:12), and together with the believing hearers 'see' (or 'reflect') 'with uncovered face the glory of the Lord' (2 Cor. 3:18), although both the exalted crucified One and the Christian who suffers on earth live in hiddenness.[130]

The visibility of the glory, then, is for the *eyes of faith*. Though for St John glory envelopes the Word incarnate in his historic ministry (here he takes a step beyond Paul – but not for Balthasar a *vast* step, since 'the life

127 *GL* VII, pp. 358–359. Italics added.
128 *GL* VII, p. 366.
129 Ibid.
130 *GL* VII, pp. 366–367.

of Jesus makes sense and comes to light in his cross, which however takes on its inner meaning only from the light of the resurrection',)[131] to say that the Word became *flesh* is to reaffirm the aspect of hiddenness of this glory. 'Flesh' names that factor about the human person which 'decisively distinguishes him from God, his weakness when compared to the One who is mighty'.[132] Moreover, it is in his *relational* being that the Son manifests the Father's glory, not by his own weightiness in the created order – and hence he is, as Revealer, the 'One who is concealed, indeed unknown', as inconclusive discussions with 'the Jews' of the Fourth Gospel on the topic of his provenance bear witness. The visibility of the glorious Son is, therefore:

> equally a hiddenness, since all that can be seen in the Son is his relatedness to the Father; but the Father is seen by no one (1:18; 1 John 4:12), except in the emptiness of the Son that is ready for him and in his own self-attestation in this emptied out space (5:36ff.; 7:6, etc.).[133]

As the *déroulement* of the Gospel of John shows, the more love reveals itself in its signs, the more hidden it becomes for those who do not love. Here *judgment* is all.

And so it remains to consider only what should count as appropriate response to New Testament glory: the 'way in which man has to glorify the glory of the love of God in his existence, without himself being in the glory of God for the present'.[134]

Response to Glory

Balthasar gives the concluding section of the theological aesthetics a title drawn from the Letter to the Ephesians, a phrase central to the spiritual theology of Elizabeth of the Trinity, to whose 'mission' in the Church he had devoted an entire monograph: *in laudem gloriae* 'to the praise of [his] glory'.[135] This concluding section is essentially a pneumatology, for 'since the Spirit himself is the glorification of the love between Father and Son, wherein God's true glory disclosed itself to us, it is likewise only he who can bring about glorification in the world'.[136]

In a miniature commentary on the Letter to the Ephesians, Balthasar makes use of a successor of Paul as distinguished correspondent with the Ephesian church, Ignatius of Antioch. The doxological blessing of God by men, which in Israel was done on the basis of the Creator-creature relation (and its extension in the covenant), is in the New Testament, founded rather on the Holy Trinity. As Ignatius writes to the faithful at Ephesus, 'In every way glorify Jesus Christ, who has glorified

---

131 *GL* VII, p. 368.
132 *GL* VII, p. 374.
133 *GL* VII, pp. 379–380.
134 *GL* VII, p. 317.
135 *Elisabeth von Dijon und ihre geistliche Sendung* (Cologne–Olten 1952); E.t. *Elisabeth of Dijon* (London 1956).
136 *GL* VII, p. 389.

you'[137] – proof enough, because with Balthasar all Christology is understood to be thoroughly trinitarian in character. In the Pauline letter, indeed, it is the 'Father of our Lord Jesus Christ who has blessed us in Christ with every spiritual blessing in the heavenly places' (1:3). In other words:

> a trinitarian God who is not himself called 'Lord' but 'Father of our Lord' bestows the fulness of his Spirit-blessing on 'us', not in our condition of creatureliness in the world standing over against him, but in a place that transcends the quality of the world (*en epouraniois*, ['in the heavenly places'] 1:3) and is more precisely defined for us as the place 'of Christ'.[138]

And since we are *predestined* to become sons in Christ to the Father for the praise of the glory of his grace – since, that is, God has placed the flow of time within the power of his 'Beloved' – then this 'place' – God in Christ – and no other is where our creaturehood was always meant to find its true home.

> Since God does not alienate himself from himself by becoming incarnate (for the obedient Son of Man is only the illustration of the eternal relatedness and selflessness of the divine Persons), Christ does not alienate man from himself when he raises him from the apparently closed substantiality of his personal being (in which he thinks he definitively stands over against God) into the open relatedness of the life within the Godhead. Rather, Christ brings him into the genuine truth of his origin; he is a distant image of this (*imago trinitatis*) in the love between human persons.[139]

But it is more especially by means of the Holy Spirit, as in Augustine's phrase *Donum Dei*, the Gift of God, or, in Balthasar's own vocabulary, the 'Handing-over' of God, that the Father chooses us, calls us, and brings us to birth with his Son.

From this Balthasar draws three inferences for 'glorification' – which is how, in the context of theological aesthetics, he presents Christian living. First, 'glorifying' (*doxazein*) is not simply the worship of our lips. Rather,

> we must praise him through our existence, inasmuch as this is an existence that is in him and therefore what it truly ought to be: an existence in the love that hands itself over.[140]

Secondly, since human existence is now to be defined *vis-à-vis* that ultimate glory which is in every sense the 'end' of the world, the 'entire horizon of human existence has been disclosed in a way that can never be surpassed'.[141] And thirdly, divine glory is now not simply the object of

---

137 *Ad Ephesios* 2, 2.
138 *GL* VII, p. 393.
139 *GL* VII, pp. 408–409.
140 *GL* VII, p. 397.
141 Ibid.

our praise, but its inner principle, since through grace we are drawn into the glorious love made visible in Jesus Christ, his dying and rising.

In the perspective of pneumatology, one 'possesses' God only by being (through the Spirit) 'handed over' to him: from now on, *appropriation* means *expropriation*. Extending the circle of his Pauline references, Balthasar describes the effect of the action of the Trinity in bringing us, through our faith, into the realm of its own circumincessant handing-over, its 'expropriated Love'. It is

> the expropriation of our privacy, i.e. in concrete terms, of our sealed-up egoism, of our addiction to the desires that seek to draw everything to ourselves; it is the liberation that brings us into freedom (Gal. 5:1), for 'where the Spirit of the Lord is, there is freedom' (2 Cor. 3:17). This freedom is the opposite of addiction: it is the possibility for those who have been set free 'to live, no longer for themselves, but for him who died and rose for them' (2 Cor. 5:15), and therefore, as an act of handing over, it is essentially service – service first of the self-expropriating love of God, and, coming directly from this, service of all those for whose sake God has expropriated himself.[142]

Much of the rest of what Balthasar has to say in this 'pneumatology of Christian existence' will be devoted to those last two topics, 'returning fruit to God' and 'loving the "brother for whom Christ died"'. But for the moment Balthasar is more concerned to underline how in this process 'all is grace'. In this context, he speaks of the believer's need to be dispossessed even of his own acceptance of Love's expropriation – something which takes place in baptism which 'introduces the "yes" of his faith into the "yes" of the whole Church, who herself speaks her "yes" only out of the power of the obedient *fiat* of the Crucified',[143] and the Eucharist where, initiated baptismally into the sphere of Spirit and in Church as we are, we 'move – in hope proleptically, and definitively at the Resurrection – to the place of perfect sonship, incorporated in the great body of those who are redeemed'.[144]

By expropriation, then, we appropriate the Saviour. Because we live 'in Christ', Christ lives 'in us'. Balthasar finds this exemplified most palpably in the confident speech (*parrhēsia*) of the Christian whose prayer is a participation in the trinitarian dialogue.[145] The rôles of this and related terms in the New Testament

> converge to show that the consciousness of the only Son, their Lord, is made over to be the inner possession of believers, and all embarrassment in the presence of the infinite God disappears (although this does not affect reverence and adoration, Eph. 3:14).[146]

142 *GL* VII, p. 403.
143 *GL* VII, p. 405.
144 *GL* VII, p. 406.
145 Something most fully developed in his *Das betrachtende Gebet* (Einsiedeln 1955); E.t. *Prayer* (London and New York 1961).
146 *GL* VII, p. 410.

The same *parrhēsia* is intimately involved in the exercise of apostolic authority in the Church – where it is strictly to be distinguished from *kauchēsis*, 'boasting'.

But expropriation must show its *fruit*: perhaps the most pervasive metaphor in all of Balthasar's writing. Just as in Isaiah's Song of the Vineyard, unfruitfulness is ingratitude, so the thanksgiving which is glorification cannot be separated from fruit-bearing.

> Jesus' *eucharistein* (Luke 22:17, 19) is a thanksgiving to the Father that takes the form of self-giving and consecration of self into the redemptive death, and in this thanksgiving he definitively becomes the grain of wheat that falls into the earth, in order to bear much fruit; and the commandment for the cultic repetition [of the Eucharist] includes as its centre the presence of this event, both demanding and bestowing inner participation in it (1 Cor. 10:16; 11:26ff.). Christian thanksgiving, giving back to God the gift that he has given, is impossible other than in the Christian bearing of fruit.[147]

It is God who is the source of such fruitfulness – as the Johannine Christ remarks, 'without me you can do nothing' (15:5), yet precisely by this union wrought in grace the human person is 'empowered to a new fruitfulness of his own, which was previously unknown to him'.[148] Once again, expropriation and appropriation go hand in hand.

> And this is the essence of the Church. Thus the glorification of the Son by the Father, who permits the fruitfulness of the dying of the Son, is converted into a conclusive glorification of the Father by the Son: 'In this is my Father glorified, that you bear much fruit and [thus] show that you are my disciples' (John 15:8).[149]

The Pauline Letters emphasise above all the superabundance (*huperperisseia*) of the fruitbearing capacity of the divine source. In this they reflect that prodigality which so often characterises the Jesus of the Gospels – at Cana in the conversion of water into wine; at the house of the Pharisee, where the limitless forgiveness of sins draws forth an uncalculated flow of repentant love; in the multiplication of the loaves, itself a sign of the 'boundless eucharistic self-distribution of the Son of Man for the life of the world'.[150] In Second Corinthians the theme of grace abounding is orchestrated for the strings and woodwind of Christology and triadology. Both spiritual comforting of the afflicted and material donations to the needy – the classical spiritual and corporal works of mercy of the Church – flow from recognising the gracious act of the rich Christ who made himself poor so that by his poverty men might become rich.

147 *GL* VII, p. 418.
148 *GL* VII, p. 420.
149 *GL* VII, p. 421.
150 *GL* VII, p. 425.

The paradox that beggars can enrich others, when they give their heart to the Lord . . . depends ultimately on the greater paradox that Christ, although rich, contrived to become utterly poor . . . disposing of his riches as a whole in the kenosis, so that he might then give what he had disposed of (or more precisely the act of disposing itself) as 'the proceeds to the poor' (Mark 10:21). This is something that only Christ could do, because in him his riches . . . and his act of giving away are one: the riches of selflessness in the triune divine nature . . .[151]

The disciple who believes and loves – not in words only but in actions – becomes in his own person the glorification of the glorious grace of God.

And this means brotherly love – but a love that is always rooted in the trinitarian being and act. The 'final point of the outpouring of God's love is . . . the dawning of the divine I-Thou-We in the worldly-creaturely I-thou-we of human fellowship'.[152] Though in Israel the command to love one's neighbour had been a limited thing owing to particularism, that was, on Balthasar's view, a matter of (faulty?) human deduction from the election of Israel: the point of departure had always been in reality the *goodness* of God. But in any case, Law and prophets are oriented towards the perfected Word spoken in Christ who willed to bring home the very last of the lost sheep of the Father.

The protological, apparently impartial love of God has arrived, by way of the Old Testament predilection of the 'chosen', 'beloved', Israel, to its eschatological end: each individual who can be addressed humanly as 'thou' is raised to the status of a 'thou' for God, because God's true 'Thou', his 'chosen' and 'beloved' 'only Son' has borne the guilt of this human 'thou' and has died for him, and therefore can identify himself with every individual at the Last Judgment.[153]

Only the doctrine of the Trinity permits the human 'thou' to be embraced in this way by the Father, in his address to the Son in the unity of the Holy Spirit. In electing the human individual in the Christ who died, God ascribes to him or her endless value – and this is in turn only feasible if the 'I-Thou-We' relation has divine worth, which of course in the triune Being it does. Christ's incarnation and atoning work encompass each and every 'neighbour', each human 'I'. With his strong animus against theologies he regards as 'predestinationist' and 'Jansenist', Balthasar writes:

The horizontality of the open and universal love of neighbour . . . derives from the verticality of its institution (on the Cross) and comes into being in the common eschatological orientation in the same Spirit to the God and Father who has established all love and unity in the institution of the Son and of the Cross.[154]

151 *GL* VII, p. 429.
152 *GL* VII, p. 432.
153 *GL* VII, p. 439.
154 *GL* VII, pp. 443–444.

So far as our own relations with 'the brothers for whom Christ died' are concerned, Balthasar shows due modesty about the help the theologian can give. So long as we are living by the 'rhythm' of Christ's self-giving, it does not matter so very much whether we are conscious that preferring others to ourselves is Johannine glorification, much less that – in the technical Balthasarian understanding of such 'giving glory' – we know ourselves to be christologically expropriated! On the other hand, we are not to be content with an unreconstructed humanism. When the New Testament letters exhort us to the practice of virtues which embody fraternity they must be read as they were written: 'not ... against a background of merely interpersonal relationships and motivations for conduct, but against the background of a unity that lies above the persons, overlapping and embracing them all'[155] – the unity, in fact, of Christ's headship of his body of which all are at least potential members.

> Christian faith is in no sense primarily a self-understanding of Christians, or even of the Church as a fellowship; it is rather obedience, acknowledgement that one is expropriated by being made over to Christ who has expropriated himself for all in his dying and rising. Thanks to this obedience, which roots the being of the Christian outside of himself, in Christ, love – which descends vertically and spreads itself horizontally – is made superior to all knowledge, even the most absolute![156]

Not for nothing are those Pauline epistles where the doctrines of justification and the Church most prominent (Romans, Galatians and First Corinthians) simultaneously those where the apostle is most anxious to convey the superiority of *agapē* to *gnōsis*. In the Johannine writings likewise, on the basis of our loving God we must love as brothers all those begotten by him – though by the same token, one cannot love the Father's beloved children without being disposed in the same way toward the 'loving primordial Source'. *Pace* the disciples of Rahner, loving God is not merely the 'transcendental presupposition' for loving one's brother, for the brother is loved precisely as the one for whose sake the Father handed over the Son.

What has been said so far might seem, through a heightened concern for the human community as a whole, to imply a somewhat low ecclesiology, a rather unenthusiastic appraisal of the theological significance of the specifically churchly society within the world's midst. Nothing could be further from the truth. By his self-gift Jesus Christ establishes the Church as the place where his glory comes into being, and since that glory implies expropriation and fruitfulness, she is necessarily *communio sanctorum* in the personal sense of that ambiguous Latin noun, the 'communion of saints'. The Church herself, then, is irradiated by glory.

> Since Jesus prays the Father to permit those who belong to him to dwell where he is and to see his glory (John 17:24), and the Church is

---

155 *GL* VII, p. 447.
156 *GL* VII, pp. 452–453. Balthasar's last words here are intended as mockery of Idealism.

already the place where he is, the personal and social life of the Church permits one to see into the glory of Christ and of the triune love.[157]

The fruitfulness of the branches, in the Johannine image, is for Balthasar of the same kind as that of the Vine from out of which they grow. And this, if true, justifies him in a high estimation of the 'co-redemptive' power of the saints.

> The distance between the 'Head' and the 'body' must be maintained under all circumstances, so that Christ as the Head is the sole Redeemer of all, even of his 'proleptically redeemed' mother; but at the same time, the one Redeemer takes up the 'body' of the Church into his redemptive activity, and this becomes yet more fruitful the more a member conforms itself to the selflessness that is Christ's disposition, and the less he exercises reserve in putting his existence at the service of universal redemption.[158]

Adamic solidarity could only be, with the Fall, a solidarity in what is not love and so a contradiction in terms as well as an existence without glory, so that it is

> only the Church, in the love of Christ and of God, that remains as the surpassing model of solidarity, in which the One who is other – as our brother – displays to us both that the divine Love transcended itself by entering what was other than itself in order to bring us back home, and that it yet did not abandon its own being in doing so, since it always embraced in itself otherness, as *triune* Love.[159]

Nor is this union of love *simply* solidarity: it is also nuptiality, and so more intimate, for here, as by a miracle, 'divine love and human love not only look upon one another, but sink into one another'.[160] Christ is God's human face, his *prosōpon*, and the latter Balthasar takes to mean his 'spiritual presence in a total embodiment', which is what spouses enjoy. That the canon truly culminates and does not simply happen to expire in the Apocalypse of John is nowhere clearer than in this realm, where the Pauline teaching that Christ 'has presented to himself a glorious Church without spot or wrinkle' (Eph. 5:27 – and it is *woman* who is 'the glory' of man, 1 Cor. 11:7) becomes a panoramic vision of the imminent End, with the Church as Bride calling 'Come!' and the multitude of virgin saints following the Lamb wherever he goes. The 'two faces' – humankind's as female to God, and that of God the Creator and Redeemer – 'will unveil themselves fully at the nuptials of the Lamb'.[161]

> The insoluble puzzle of the gnostic dualism (between the heavenly syzygy ['couple'] and its earthly sexual imitation) is solved only

157 *GL* VII, p. 467.
158 *GL* VII, p. 465.
159 *GL* VII, p. 469. Italics added.
160 *GL* VII, p. 472.
161 *GL* VII, p. 476.

when the genuine creaturely sexuality of man and woman is thought of as fundamentally related over and above itself to an eternal, holy and spotless standing before God in the love of the incarnate Christ for his bride, which is the Church that consists of human persons.[162]

Human sexuality, in its sacramental sanctification, 'serves' this mystery, yet finally passes away, entering the greater realm whose mysteric image it is, as the Church passes, with the End, from the order of marriage to that of virginity – into the 'eschatological nuptiality'.[163]

The 'hope of glory' is 'Christ in [us]' (Col. 1:27), and so this future consummation is already present in seed here and now. Christian life is 'eschatological existence'. We see that in the very nature of the *Catholica*, the Catholic Church, as she abandons the 'protection' offered by restriction to one (the Jewish) people and opens herself in an 'unprotected' way to the universality of the world.[164] That has to be, if she is to continue Christ's work in communicating divine reconciliation to all. The 'existential self-consecration' of all believers – that is Balthasar's paraphrase of Paul's reference to 'reasonable worship', *logikē latreia*, in the Letter to the Romans (12:1) – is 'placarded' in the mission of the Catholic priesthood whom Balthasar eulogises as explicitly expropriated representatives of the new people of God, sent by God for the eschatological service of the world through the incarnation of the gospel in the 'liturgy' not only of teaching but also of the 'gift they make of their lives'.[165] (All of which is Balthasarian résumé of Second Corinthians, with its *Leitmotiv* of the glory of the apostolic ministry *qua* service of the gospel.) Like the apostle, the whole Church, as Bride of Christ and his Body

comes to the world from the activity of God, making proclamation, giving example and proferring invitation – in a position over against the world that is absolutely required in order for her to be able to address the world.[166]

– yet without for all that abandoning solidarity with a world that is, after all, the aim of her mission.

And what would she do with the world? The Church's mission is to fashion on the basis of God's reconciling act in Christ and his Spirit, an *oikoumenē*, an all-embracing realm that will carry the world within itself to God. The future of man is eschatological citizenship with God in his new *polis*, as created by cross and resurrection, with the redeemed bodiliness these offer. For Balthasar the glory of this New Jerusalem casts its refulgence in Church but not State. The latter he sees with Augustine in primarily negative terms, as existing primarily for the lawless. More persuasively, its structures

---

162 *GL* VII, p. 482.
163 *GL* VII, p. 483.
164 *GL* VII, p. 488.
165 *GL* VII, p. 489.
166 *GL* VII, p. 495.

embrace neutrally both the citizens of heaven and the citizens of earth, and cannot be affected by the all-important decisions between the two forms of freedom ... [namely] ... innerworldly self-determination ..., personal or collective, ... and a freedom of self-giving in faith's obedience to the free love of God.[167]

The Church, by contrast, is the place of glorification, and we have seen how interiorly connex this is with the revelation of glory itself. Not that the Church's members (and officers) do not need admonition, for they continue to exist in the old aeon. Yet such *paraklēsis* takes as its goal their holding fast in, or return to, the 'sphere' where they made the decision of faith, for this 'is the sphere in which God has his glory, just as he has his glory in Jesus Christ'.[168]

The Church's task is, however, to render herself superfluous in the kingdom, by the in-breaking of the world as a whole into the glory. Unfashionably, and somewhat reminiscently of the Russian philosopher of religion N. F. Fyodorov, a theological influence on Dostoevsky,[169] Balthasar regards the resurrection of the dead as the first thing to be said about the kingdom.

> When history's vanguard penetrates into the Kingdom, this does not involve forgetting what it has been, as if this were 'building materials' now lost to sight. The solidarity that no form of socialism can know, and which is likewise forgotten or undervalued by an existential and a merely historical interpretation of Scripture, hopes for those who belong hopelessly to the past, and only then for itself.[170]

Hopelessness is indeed the opposite of eschatological existence, which is essentially existence in the form of hope. Anticipating his own *Theodramatik*, Balthasar points out that for the Seer of the Apocalypse the One who is fighting in the present struggle is already the Victor, yet this same Victor is still really fighting – which means that the patience of his followers is never just a matter of waiting. Like Péguy, Balthasar can speak of not only man but also of God as hoping. In Romans 8

> the divine [Spirit] sighs together with the unsure and powerless 'sighing', for what is definitive, and gives this 'sighing' depth and accuracy: it is precisely the 'wordless sighing' of the spirit ... that is the adequate word of prayer to God that can be understood and will

167 *GL* VII, pp. 502, 501.
168 *GL* VII, p. 505.
169 Fyodorov's *The Restoration of Kinship among Mankind* is anthologised conveniently in A. Schmemann (ed.), *Ultimate Questions. An Anthology of Modern Russian Religious Thought* (London 1977). The primary meaning of Christianity – without which it would not be itself, i.e. world-wide love – Christ not Son of Man, i.e. 'the son of the departed fathers', and not 'heart and soul in the grave of the fathers' (viz. in hell) – is the resurrection of the literally dead and the spiritually dead among the living into a single family of brethren.
170 *GL* VII, pp. 508–509.

be answered ... just as the inarticulate dying cry of the crucified Logos became the definitive human word that broke through the whole realm of darkness to pierce God's heart.[171]

And what do world, human heart and Spirit of God sigh for? For *mellousa doxa* (8:18), the 'coming glory', on which Balthasar comments that everything glorious from Sinai to the gospel had just the right amount of glory to kindle in us the unquenchable hope for this superabundant definitive glory. Here there is no gradual introduction of the eschaton (*pace* the later Edward Schillebeeckx); not all the evolution of the world (*pace* the Teilhardians) or its work (the theologians of *les réalités terrestres*) will suffice to bring it about. The object of 'a hope that is constitutive of everything' can only exist (*pace* Ernst Bloch) on christological and trinitarian presuppositions – something that the closing volume of the theological dramatics will spell out in some detail and depth.

The middle and last volumes of the theological logic become pertinent too when Balthasar asks how we can know what we hope for without (like Hegel) converting God's promise into 'absolute knowledge' and so ceasing to hope for it. The answer is that God not only speaks out in the incarnation and crucifixion of the Logos but hands over his Spirit who is also Christ's 'mind' to our spirit (1 Cor. 2:16) – not however in such a way that it becomes our autonomous possession but that we may always be surprised by God's ever-greater grace.

> That is why Jesus points the mature persons who wish to enter the Kingdom back into the unquestioning readiness to receive that belongs to the children who live in the condition of love's gift[172]

– the theme of the small book Balthasar left finished at his death.[173] Yet this childhood is no Arcadian idyll: within it is 'something that burns'. In the cross, the rose is one with the fire.

> The loving Church assuredly lives, with Paul, on the basis of Easter and has the right to rejoice at the redemption that has been given to the world; but the loving Church, with the Marian-Johannine *fiat*, is always on the path that leads to the Cross, which we never leave behind as a 'fact' of the past, but which is the eschaton to which the whole course of the world's history is directed ... 'They shall look on him whom they have pierced' (Apoc. 1:7).[174]

In the world's rhythm, joy and suffering *alternate*, but not in that of the Church.

> The Jews refused to look on God's glory, because this was said to bring death. The Christians look on it in faith, and say 'yes' to the

---

171 *GL* VII, p. 512.
172 *GL* VII, p. 528.
173 *Wenn ihr nicht werdet wie dieses Kind* (Ostfildern 1989); E.t. *Unless You Become Like this Child* (San Francisco 1994).
174 *GL* VII, p. 539.

death that the glory has at its heart. Anxiety in the presence of the God who is a consuming fire (Deut. 4:24) is changed into reverent service of the love of God *'because* our God is a consuming fire' (Heb. 12:28).[175]

And the Lord of glory must have the last word in the definition of that reflected glory, which in a right and proper 'triumphalism' the Catholic theologian will accord to the Church.

The risen Lord too is once more a visible form, but one that has passed through the gulf of the abyss. And it is precisely from the risen Lord that the earthly visibility of the Church has her soul and her spirit, so that she has as it were a form that is already alien to the world that is passing away, a form that has its home elsewhere. . . . She is the response of glorification, and to this extent she is drawn into the glorious Word to which she responds, and into the splendour of the light without which she would not shine. What she reflects back in the night is the light of hope for the world.[176]

175 *GL* VII, pp. 539–540.
176 *GL* VII, p. 543.

Select Bibliography

A. General studies of Balthasar

J. GODENIR, *Jésus, l'Unique. Introduction à la théologie de Hans Urs von Balthasar* (Paris-Namur 1984).

E. GUERRIERO, *Hans Urs von Balthasar* (Milan 1991).

M. KEHL and W. LÖSER (eds.), *The Von Balthasar Reader* (E.t. New York 1982).

A. MODA, *Hans Urs von Balthasar. Un' espozione critica del suo pensiero* (Bari 1976)

B. MCGREGOR, O.P., and T. NORRIS (eds.), *The Beauty of Christ. An Introduction to the Theology of Hans Urs von Balthasar* (Edinburgh 1994).

E. T. OAKES, *The Pattern of Redemption. The Theology of Hans Urs von Balthasar* (New York 1994).

J. O'DONNELL, S.J., *Hans Urs von Balthasar* (London 1992).

J. SAWARD, *The Mysteries of March. Hans Urs von Balthasar on the Incarnation and Easter* (London 1990) .

D. L. SCHINDLER (ed.), *Hans Urs von Balthasar. His Life and Work* (San Francisco 1991).

A. SCOLA, *Hans Urs von Balthasar. Uno stile teologico* (Milan 1991); E.t. *Hans Urs von Balthasar. A Theological Style* (Edinburgh 1995).

B. Studies of Balthasar's theological aesthetics

M. ALBUS, *Die Wahrheit ist Liebe. Zur Unterscheidung des Christlichen nach Hans Urs von Balthasar* (Freiburg-Basel-Wien 1976).

H. DANET, *Gloire et croix de Jésus-Christ. L'analogie chez Hans Urs von Balthasar comme introduction à sa christologie* (Paris 1987).

L. DUPRÉ, 'Hans Urs von Balthasar's Theology of Aesthetic Form', *Theological Studies* 49, 2 (1988), pp. 299–318.

M. HARTMANN, *Aesthetik als ein Grundbegriff fundamentaler Theologie: eine Untersuchung zu Hans Urs von Balthasar* (St Ottilien 1985).

J. A. KAY, *Theological Aesthetics. The Role of Aesthetics in the Theological Method of Hans Urs von Balthasar* (Berne-Frankfurt 1975; = *European University Papers* XXIII, *Theology* 60).

M. LOCHBRUNNER, *Analogia caritatis. Darstellung und Deutung der Theologie Hans Urs von Balthasars* (Freiburg 1981).

G. MARCHESI, *La Cristologia di Hans Urs von Bakthasar. La figura di Gesù Cristo espressione visibile di Dio* (Rome 1977, = *Analecta Gregoriana*, 207, *Series Facultatis Theologiae*: B.66).

J. SCHMIDT, *Im Ausstrahl der Schönheit Gottes. Die Bedeutung der Analogie in 'Herrlichkeit' bei Hans Urs von Balthasar* (Münsterschwarzach 1982).

G. DE SCHRIJVER, *Le merveilleux accord de l'homme et Dieu. Etude de l'analogie de l'être chez Hans Urs von Balthasar* (Louvain 1983).

J. F. THURMANN, *Time in the Theological Aesthetics of Hans Urs von Balthasar* (Washington 1974).

R. VIGNOLA, *Hans Urs von Balthasar. Estetica e singolarita* (Milan 1982).

S.-M. WITTSCHIER, *Kreuz, Trinität, Analogie. Trinitarische Ontologie unter dem Leitbild des Kreuzes, dargestellt als ästhetische Theologie* (Würzburg 1987).

Index of Subjects

Index of Names

265